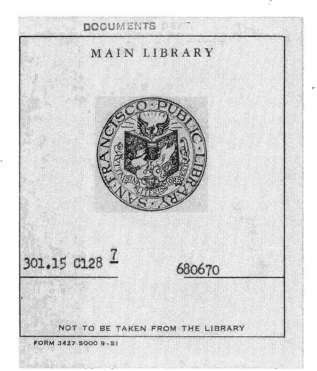

CALIFORNIA LEGISLATURE

Seventh Report of the Senate Fact-Finding Committee On Un-American Activities

1953

MEMBERS OF THE COMMITTEE

SENATOR NATHAN F. COOMBS   SENATOR CLYDE A. WATSON
SENATOR EARL D. DESMOND   SENATOR NELSON S. DILWORTH, *Vice Chairman*
SENATOR JOHN F. McCARTHY   SENATOR HUGH M. BURNS, *Chairman*

R. E. COMBS, *Chief Counsel*   MARY E. HOPE, *Executive Secretary*

Published by the
SENATE

LIEUTENANT GOVERNOR GOODWIN J. KNIGHT
President of the Senate

SENATOR HAROLD J. POWERS   JOSEPH A. BEEK
President pro Tempore   *Secretary*

LETTER OF TRANSMITTAL

SENATE CHAMBER, STATE CAPITOL
SACRAMENTO, June 8, 1953

Hon. Goodwin J. Knight
President of the Senate; and
Gentlemen of the Senate
Senate Chamber, Sacramento, California

MR. PRESIDENT AND GENTLEMEN OF THE SENATE: Pursuant to Senate Resolution No. 127, which appears at page 3944 of the Senate Journal for June 23, 1951, the Senate Fact-Finding Committee on Un-American Activities was created and the following members of the Senate were appointed to said committee by the Senate Committee on Rules:

Senator Hugh M. Burns
Senator Nelson S. Dilworth
Senator Clyde A. Watson
Senator Nathan F. Coombs
Senator Earl D. Desmond
Senator John F. McCarthy

The committee herewith submits a report of its investigation, findings and recommendations.

Respectfully submitted,

HUGH M. BURNS, *Chairman*
NELSON S. DILWORTH, *Vice Chairman*
NATHAN F. COOMBS
EARL D. DESMOND
JOHN F. MCCARTHY

TABLE OF CONTENTS

TABLE OF CONTENTS—Continued

TABLE OF CONTENTS—Continued

INTRODUCTION

In its 1951 report, this committee included a cumulative index which listed the names of all individuals, publications and organizations that had been mentioned in the reports previously issued by the committee in 1943, 1945, 1947, 1948 and 1949. Since the publication of that report the committee has received numerous requests to reprint all of the previous reports; but since this is a job which would be enormously expensive and practically impossible of accomplishment in less than six months of constant work, the committee has deemed it expedient to condense important excerpts from its previously published reports, all of which are now out of print, and to combine them in an appropriate place in the present volume.

During the early years of its operation the committee was confronted with the task of breaking through public apathy toward the real menace of Communism in this State. In order to accomplish that result the committee held numerous open hearings which were attended by considerable publicity. This technique of publicly exposing Communist front organizations and individual members of the Communist party apparatus was found to be an effective means of driving the Party to an underground position from which it was comparatively difficult to maintain effective contact with broad masses of the public. Ten years ago there were innumerable Communist-dominated organizations functioning in California. Now that most of them have been driven out of existence by constant exposure of their real nature and objectives, only a handful of active Communist fronts remain in business. These were mentioned in the committee's 1951 report and are: the Civil Rights Congress, the International Workers Order, the Committee for a Democratic Far Eastern Policy, the California Legislative Conference, the Arts, Sciences and Professions Council, the National Lawyers Guild, the American Russian Institute, the California Labor School, and a host of "peace" organizations that have sprung recently into existence to fit with the international Communist party line on the attainment of peace, Soviet style. These peace fronts will be dealt with in detail elsewhere in this report.

In 1952, the committee sponsored two meetings, one at the University of Southern California in Los Angeles, and the other at the University of San Francisco in the City of San Francisco. These meetings were attended by presidents of the colleges and universities of the State, and resulted in the establishment of an effective liaison between all of the institutions of higher learning and representatives of the Committee on Un-American Activities to the end that the problem of Communist infiltration on the faculties of our schools could be attacked at its source.

Shortly after the plan was put into operation the State Superintendent of Public Instruction, Dr. Roy E. Simpson, suggested to the committee that it be expanded to include the 11 state colleges, and thus California has become the first State in the Union where a solid and cooperative plan between the State Legislative Committee on Un-American Activities and the administrative heads of the State's colleges and universities has been put into effective operation.

This plan, which will be explained in more detail in the appropriate portion of this report, has thus far operated far better than was originally anticipated. One accurate measure of its success is found in the constant attacks from the Communist propaganda media, some of which have emanated from the State of New York, criticizing the plan as a "gigantic Gestapo in the educational institutions of the country," and against the maintenance of a large group of undercover informants who are supposed to keep the committee advised concerning subversive activities on the several campuses. An analysis of this Communist propaganda indicates that the committee was wise in not disclosing the exact machinery by which the plan functions. Consequently, the Communist functionaries have been thus far unable to ascertain the identities of the liaison men on the several campuses, and have been unable to keep abreast of the operation of the scheme on a state-wide basis. It is only necessary to state in this introduction that many undesirable faculty members who have long, documented records of affiliation with Communist-dominated organizations have been quietly eliminated from our educational institutions, and many more who have applied for teaching positions have been rejected on the ground that their affiliations and activities of a pro-Communist nature have indicated to various educational administrators that persons of that type should be denied teaching positions and that the vacancies should be filled by individuals who are academically as competent and about whose loyalty there is no question.

An indication of the far reaching ramifications of the Communist organization is to be found in that section of this current report which deals with the organization, history and activities of the Hindustan Gadar Party. This organization, which has for many years been active in California, was recently the subject of an intensive investigation launched for the purpose of ascertaining whether or not rumors that it was Communist-dominated were accurate, and to determine the extent of the membership and the nature of the organization's activities in this State. By the very nature of the subject it was found impossible to adequately investigate the organization and its activities without also going into the current Communist Party line concerning the attempted subversion of the new Indian government as a part of the master plan of the Cominform for the subjugation and Communizing of all of Asia. As will be seen, some of the most active agents in this undertaking were members of the California Gadar Party who were sent to the Soviet Union for training in the espionage school and thence to various parts of India for the purpose of subverting the government of that country and softening it up for the eventual Communist kill.

The present report, which was written by R. E. Combs, the committee's counsel, also undertakes to bring up to date the Communist operation in California, its organization, its personnel, its front organization activities, its underground techniques. As will be seen, the entire Communist approach has been radically altered within the past two years, which necessitates the altering of the committee's technique in endeavoring to keep abreast of the problem and ridding important divisions of the State Government from Communist agents who are insinuated into key positions.

In the section of this report dealing with Communist infiltration of the Los Angeles City Housing Project, it will be seen how the techniques that were described in the 1951 report were employed with considerable success by the Communist functionaries who directed the infiltration of the housing project in Los Angeles. Furthermore, that section of the report describes most graphically the interlocking nature of the Communist organization. It was discovered in the process of investigating the infiltration into the housing project that the United Public Workers of America, headed by Abram Flaxer, was a part and parcel of the Communist scheme, and constituted the base from which the infiltration of the housing project and the infiltration of the Los Angeles City School System was directed.

The committee has received requests for the publication in the current report of a bibliography of reliable books from which laymen can receive an accurate knowledge of the history of the Communist movement in the United States and reliable information concerning Communist activities in general. Unfortunately, many of the popular books in this field are written by persons who have either had too limited an experience or who are so eager to sensationalize the subject for financial gain that they take broad liberties with facts. Sinning at the opposite extreme are many books which are written by persons with documentable records of Communist front affiliations, and which are subtly slanted in a pro-Communist direction. Between these two extremes there is a middle ground comprising books of unquestioned accuracy written by people whose long years of experience in counter-subversive work eminently fits them as the authors of completely reliable material.

The committee also wishes to point out that it has held fewer public hearings during the past two years of its activity than ever before. This has been done for several reasons. Witnesses who were subpenaed to appear in public invariably seized the opportunity to use the committee rostrum as a medium from which to make long propaganda speeches. If the committee attempts to curtail this activity, the witness and the front organizations, which are Party controlled, immediately object that the witness' civil liberties are being stifled. Invariably, a witness concerning whom the committee has advance information of Communist activity will refuse to answer questions about his Communist Party affiliations on the ground that his answers might tend to incriminate him under the Fifth Amendment to the Federal Constitution.

The Communist Party will not permit a member to admit his affiliation because if he does so, court decisions provide he can then be questioned concerning other persons in his Communist Party unit, the identity of the individual to whom he pays dues, dates and places of Communist Party meetings which he attended, the identity of the individuals by whom he was recruited, and other questions concerning his affiliations and associations in the Party apparatus. This, obviously, opens too wide a door and the Communist Party therefore has a hard and fast rule which prohibits its members from ever admitting Communist Party membership unless they are already publicly known as Communists. On the other hand, the Party will not permit its members to make a categorical denial of Communist Party membership, because if the committee produces witnesses who can prove membership, then the individual in question can be prosecuted for perjury, which is a felony and carries a sentence in the state penitentiary upon conviction. All of the hostile witnesses examined in public hearings have demonstrated over and over again their eagerness to seize the opportunity to make long speeches for the benefit of the press and for the benefit of their comrades who invariably jam the meeting place.

At closed hearings where the press is not admitted and where the witness appears alone before the committee with his counsel, there are no long propaganda speeches for the simple reason that there is no audience. Consequently, the witness answers the questions, or refuses to answer them on constitutional grounds, the hearing proceeds smoothly, and the committee can therefore keep complete control of the situation, analyze the transcript of testimony and issue appropriate releases for the benefit of the press. To put the matter tersely, this technique allows the committee to hold an investigation and a dignified hearing instead of an exhibition. Every Communist is eager to discredit the activity of legislative committees investigating Communism by attempting to turn all of the public hearings into a cheap exhibition.

The Communist Party, not only in California, but elsewhere throughout the United States, is now almost entirely underground. A skeleton organization is left on the surface, not only for the purpose of carrying on propaganda activities and more or less open recruiting, but also for the purpose of diverting attention from the more important underground operations which are being stepped up day by day. It must be remembered, however, that every Communist Party member is an activist. There is no such thing as a dormant Communist Party member. Even in the underground organization there must be contacts and efforts to recruit new members into the Party apparatus. There must be efforts to propagandize, even from these undercover positions, and if one is thoroughly familiar with the underground organization and technique of operations, it is not too difficult to dig deep enough to expose the hidden Communist cell and take appropriate measures to render it ineffective.

Several years ago the old type of open hearing, with all of its sensational attributes, was a necessary expedient for the purpose of breaking through public apathy and convincing the people of this State that the Communist menace was a very real and a very grim one indeed. The exposure of atomic espionage agents, the expulsion of several large and critical unions from the CIO because they were Communist dominated, the Korean War, the exposure of the Institute of Pacific Relations as a cover for Communist espionage activities, the infiltration of the United Nations organization with Communist agents and sympathizers, the conviction of Alger Hiss and numerous other exposures by state and congressional committees, have all combined to convince even the most naive individual that the Communist menace is more critical today than ever before, and that it is absolutely necessary for a trained and efficient legislative committee to be maintained so that constant vigilance can be exercised against the infiltration of departments of the State, trade unions, schools and other organizations.

Contrary to popular opinion, the prime purpose of such an interim committee is the assembling of facts and not necessarily the recommendation of corrective legislation—although that, of course, is a vital and important function. It is equally obvious that one can no more legislate a Communist conspiracy out of existence than one can legislate against a form of insanity, or put an end to kidnaping by simply passing a law to the effect that kidnaping shall henceforth be illegal. In fact, the whole controversial field of anti-Communist legislation is fraught with subtle constitutional dangers which do not readily meet the eye. While it is essential that adequate legislation be enacted for the purpose of combatting the Communist menace, it is equally important that we approach the problem calmly, coolly and intelligently lest, in an over abundance of zeal to accomplish a laudable and patriotic effect, we destroy our democratic way of life in the very process of accomplishing that result.

In its recent investigations, the committee was able to procure a photostatic copy of a lecture delivered by a professor at the Lenin School in Moscow. This school, which we have heretofore described as the international training center for Communist espionage and sabotage agents, has been in existence since 1926. In the address delivered by one of the professors of that academy for traitors, we find a complete and detailed description of the underground organization and techniques to be employed by the Communist Parties of the world. The committee has carefully analyzed this document and compared it with information available concerning the underground activities of the Communist Party in California. So far we have found that the Lenin School blueprint has been followed to the letter. The contents of this document, of unquestioned authenticity, also provides full corroboration for the testimony of Paul Crouch, for 17 years an important figure of the Communist Party of the United States, and who testified before this committee in 1950 concerning the underground activities of the Communist Party in Alameda County, where he was in charge of all Party activities.

THE COMMUNIST MOVEMENT

Scattered throughout the six reports that have been published by this committee since its creation in 1941 are many references to the origin and development of international Communism. The committee is convinced that it should bring these fragmentary sections together in chronological sequence so that the layman may have a ready handbook, written in such a manner that it will be intelligible to the most uninformed reader, and which will present a concise history of the origin and development of the world Communist movement since its inception until the present time. While such an undertaking may, at first glance, appear to have no practical value, any expert on Communism readily appreciates the fact that unless one is familiar with the origin and development of the movement he can hardly be in a position to take effective measures to combat its effects and cannot possibly understand the activities of the Communist organization today. While there is a certain elasticity connected with the activities of the Communist movement, nevertheless every indoctrinated Marxist is a slave to the past. All Communists are completely and fanatically devoted to the theoretical concepts established by Karl Marx which he published in the Communist Manifesto in 1848; all of the disciples who have followed and preached his principles insist that modern Communism is squarely based on the concepts of Marx and that the slightest deviation therefrom must be considered serious heresy. In beginners' classes the embryonic Marxist must first be thoroughly drilled in Communist ideology as expressed by Karl Marx, and it is therefore completely impossible to adequately understand the movement without understanding these principles and something about the life of the man who conceived them.

In addition, unless one understands the development of the Communist movement in Russia and can follow the development of the Russian secret police, the international espionage system established shortly after the Communist revolution, the establishment of the Comintern as a high board of strategy for international revolution and the foundation and operation of such centers as the Lenin School as a training academy for espionage and sabotage agents, one cannot possibly appreciate the complete control over the Communist Parties of the world which is exercised from the Kremlin; nor can one adequately appreciate the implications in the disclosures made by former Communist espionage agents such as Whitaker Chambers, Elizabeth Bentley, Hede Massing, Nora Murray, and a host of others who have informed us in no uncertain language about the real threat of Soviet espionage in the United States.

The committee has never seen a concise and simply-expressed account of the origin and development of international Communism between the covers of a single volume. Most of the books deal with the history of the Russian Revolution, the life of Marx, the history of the Comintern, autobiographical accounts of personal experiences in the Communist Party or in its espionage apparatus—but so far as we are aware, there is no concise account that gives a chronological development of world Communism from its inception until the present time. For the purpose of filling that gap and making the material available to speakers and students, as well as to provide a background for the more detailed sections of this report, the committee deems it expedient to set forth such an account herewith.

KARL MARX

The life of Karl Marx is a story of contradictions. All of his male ancestors on both sides of the family had been rabbis for several generations, yet he proclaimed that, "religion is the opium of the people." His parents were well enough situated to give him an excellent college education, yet he advocated the abolition of all private property. He despised aristocrats as members of the privileged class, yet he married the daughter of a German baron. He detested those who lived as parasites on the side of society, yet he was content to pursue his researches while his impoverished family lived solely on the generosity of friends.

Marx was, indeed, the inventor of Communism. It was his own theory, developed step by step through years of persistent research and study. The ideas of this man have swept the world and have exerted profound changes in its social structure. There is hardly a person living today who has not felt, directly or indirectly, consciously or otherwise, the effects of Marxism—through Communist-inspired strikes which affect his economic welfare; through the agitation of racial minority groups; through an ever-mounting flood of Communist propaganda; through the subtle efforts of Communist Parties throughout the world to gnaw and nibble away at the countries in which they exist and thereby soften them up for the eventual Communist kill.

Now as never before has the American people, always slow to realize the seriousness of dangers from within, shown an increased interest in Communism as a world movement. Since it is manifestly impossible to understand the movement adequately without some knowledge of the man who originated it, we must turn to the life of Karl Marx.

He was born at Treves, Germany, in May, 1818. His father was the first of a long line to forsake the Jewish faith, which he did when Karl was six years old by dropping his given name of Hirschel and taking the name of Henrich when he became a Protestant.

As a school boy Marx was shy, retiring and serious. There is no record of boyhood companionship. The cold and diffident traits that later drove him into academic seclusion after each failure in the field of political action became more sharply etched in his personality as he grew older.

At the University of Bonn he began the study of law, his father's profession, but soon found the subject distasteful and turned his attention to history and philosophy. His keen and incisive mind and his retentive memory enabled him to make rapid progress, and it was while he was engaged in these studies that young Marx began to view with alarm the turbulent social conditions then existing in Germany. The remnants of feudalism had melted away before the growing era of industrial development. The discovery of steam power, the invention of new devices for the production of basic commodities, the rapid growth of transportation and communication had resulted in large-scale commercial activities by 1830. Under the feudal system men had banded themselves together under the protection of a powerful lord, and in return for his protection they tilled his soil, rendered him military allegiance and bound themselves and their descendants to him as vassals through succeeding generations. With the coming of the industrial revolution of 1750, many believed that this type of exploitation would vanish. Marx was forced to the belief that here was only a new form of servitude, industrial instead of agricultural; that the feudal lords of yesterday had become the industrial barons of his time. He saw more and more wealth being concentrated in the hands of the few at the expense of the many. Wealth, to Marx, meant power and greed and selfishness and the enslavement by a rich minority of the toiling majority by which that wealth was produced.

As he became more alarmed at this condition, Marx's studies now took a new turn. He commenced searching for some solution to the problem. It was plain to him that the unorganized, illiterate and impoverished masses could never emancipate themselves. On the contrary, they were, as he saw it, becoming more and more conditioned to their status. They functioned as cogs in a vast industrial machine; as commodities creating profits for the employers, the surplus value being used to build more and more employer power. There must be some definite program to follow, thought Marx; the masses must be organized, disciplined, provided with leadership.

Fired with enthusiasm, Marx realized that he had now found his mission in life: the emancipation of the working masses of the world. He turned at first to the writings of the great philosophers—Strauss, Bauer, Fuerbach, and finally to Hegel—then acknowledged as the master of them all. But the ideas of these men seemed impractical to Marx. They were spun of vague, utopian theories that found no place in his practical plans.

In 1842 he joined the staff of a newspaper in the Rhineland; a paper controlled by conservatives but actually run by young students who, like Marx, were seriously concerned with the social conditions of the time. Within a few months Marx became editor and his penetrating articles brought him considerable reputation. It was not, however, the sort of reputation the paper's owners appreciated. As they became more critical the articles became more liberal, until publication was suspended by government decree early in 1843.

Through his articles Marx had been brought in contact with prominent socialists throughout Europe, and he then realized that his own knowledge of the subject was far too limited. Paris was, at that time, the center of socialism, and there Marx determined to go to pursue his researches. While still a student at the university he had fallen in love with Fannie von Westphalen, the daughter of a German baron. The courtship was violently opposed by her family, for obvious reasons, but the couple was married shortly after Marx left the paper and the new bride went with her husband to Paris.

With a little money saved from the paper and with a little more earned through writing a few articles, Marx was able to live fairly well at first. He conferred with those who had been attracted by his writings and made amazingly rapid progress in the study of socialism. It was in Paris in 1844 that Marx met two men who were destined to play the most vital roles in his life—his closest friend and his bitterest enemy, Freidrich Engels and Michael Bakunin. Engels was the son of a wealthy German merchant. He was two years younger than Marx and had already gained considerable recognition as a revolutionary through his own articles. He and Marx were immediately attracted to each other, agreeing in their political ideas and planning to collaborate on a book, to be called *The Holy Family.*

Bakunin was a veteran Russian revolutionary, older than Marx, more experienced in practical affairs and whose basic ideas were quite different from those of Marx. Neither man was blessed with much tact, but Marx was vain, sensitive and arrogant, while Bakunin' was simply blunt and stubborn. Their discussions on subjects of mutual interest frequently ended in quarrels that were soon forgotten. The real antagonism developed several years later, and, as will be seen, was not only provoked by Marx, but he was by far the more venomous and unethical of the two throughout the struggle.

An analysis of his early writings reveals how Marx was slowly evolving the basic concepts that were later to be embodied in his most famous work, *The Communist Manifesto of 1848.* Thus he wrote of religion in 1843:

"Man makes religion; religion does not make man. Religion, indeed, is the self-consciousness and the self-feeling of the man who has either not yet found himself, or else, having found himself, has lost himself once more. But man is not an abstract being, squatting down somewhere in the world. Man is the world of men, the state, society. The state, this society, produced religion, produced a perverted world consciousness, because they are a perverted world. Religion is the generalized theory of this world, its encyclopedic compend, its logic in a popular form. * * * The fight against religion is, therefore, a direct campaign against the world whose spiritual aroma is religion.

"Religion is the sigh of the oppressed creatures, the feelings of a cheerless world, just as it is the spirit of unspirited conditions. It is the opium of the people.

"The people cannot be really happy until it has been deprived of illusory happiness by the abolition of religion. To demand that the people should shake itself free of illusion as to its own condition is the demand that it should abandon a condition which needs illusion."

In 1845 Marx's activities had aroused the attention of the Paris authorities, and he was forced to seek refuge in Brussels. Meanwhile Engels, somewhat disappointed at the reception accorded the dry and ponderous tome of 300 pages—most of which had been written by Marx—and published under the name *The Holy Family,* had busied himself by organizing a series of Communist meetings in England. Engels' name on the title page of the book had caused an upheaval in his family and he went to Brussels for another conference with Marx. After a brief visit to England where Marx studied the economic conditions of that country, the two returned to Brussels and resumed their labors.

By 1847 Marx had written another work called *The Poverty of Philosophy* in which he stated:

"The existence of an oppressed class is the vital condition of every society based upon class oppressions. Consequently, the liberation of the oppressed class necessarily involves the creation of a new society. If the oppressed class is to be able to liberate itself, it must have reached a stage at which the already acquired forces of production and the already extant social institutions can no longer continue to exist side by side. Of all the instruments of production, the greatest productive force is the revolutionary class itself. The organization of the revolutionary elements as a class presupposes the existence of all the forces of production within the womb of society.''

Incubus

Slowly, surely, the links were being forged. In each new piece of writing Marx expounded some of the fundamentals of his new philosophy—that religion was only a form of superstition; that there would be a class struggle between the bourgeoisie minority and the proletarian majority until all capitalist societies were crushed and swept from the face of the earth, all private property abolished, all class distinctions removed; that until these things were brought to pass all the wealth would inevitably be concentrated more and more in the hands of the few at the expense of the many, while the workers would sink proportionately lower into their economic servitude. As he plunged deeper into his work Marx exhibited increased irrascibility, and was utterly impatient with those who failed to grasp the theories that to him appeared so simple and fundamental. As his bad temper increased, so did his vanity, to the point that he could not bear to think of anyone else attaining a position of leadership in the revolutionary world. This morbid dread of rivalry became a passion with him and led him to openly insult many men who were leaders in various fields of revolutionary activity while Marx was still a school boy.

Brussels, under the pervasive influence of Marx and Engels, had become a center of revolutionary thought. The writings of Marx were far too deep and complicated for the masses, but the few radicals who mastered them were leaders who were unquestionably influenced by the audacity of the Marxian theories and the sweeping scope of the Marxian program to emancipate the toiling masses of the world. These were the men who first visited Marx at Paris, and who were bringing more and more visitors to see him at Brussels. All were attracted by his brilliant intellect; many were driven from him by his overbearing manner, his supreme conceit and his ill-concealed insults to their own intelligence. But these years from 1843 to 1848 were the years when Marx was most active in creating his new ideology—Communism. Into the fermenting mechanism of his brain were fed the thoughts of countless others—historians, sociologists, economists, anarchists, philosophers and revolutionary leaders of all countries—their ideas were examined, analyzed, accepted here, rejected there. Step by step, coldly, patiently, with passionate devotion and under great obstacles, Marx slowly perfected his theories, correlated them, wove them into proper sequence.

The Communist Manifesto

Meanwhile there had been rumblings of revolt among the masses. Organizations of working men sprang up in several countries, but withered away for want of a definite program and adequate leadership. Early in 1847 a group of exiles from Germany, France and England formed an association called ''The Federation of the Just,'' and solicited the support of Marx and Engels. The latter devoted considerable time to this movement in England and when its first congress was convened in London in November of that year, its name was changed to the Communist League. Marx attended the second congress the following month, and delivered a powerful address that resulted in the adoption of his ideas and the request that he and Engels incorporate them into a manifesto for the League. The first draft was written by Engels, but was rejected. Marx wrote most of the final document, which was printed early in 1848. In its Marx crystalized all his work. So profound has been the influence of this instrument, the Communist Manifesto, that it must be regarded for what it really is: the source of all Communist theory, the very soul of international Communism, containing the basic concepts that are burned deeply into the consciousness of every modern Communist, and which *must* be understood before one is equipped to understand modern Communist activities. From the following selected excerpts, the reader can readily understand the basic principles of this ideology; those principles remain the same today as they were in 1848, from the Communist viewpoint.

"The history of all hitherto existing society is the history of class struggles.

"Free men and slave, patrician and plebeian, lord and serf, guildmaster and journeyman, in a word, oppressor and oppressed, stood in constant opposition to one another, carried on an uninterrupted, now hidden, now open fight, a fight that ended each time either in a revolutionary reconstitution of society at large or in the common ruin of the contending classes.

"In the earlier epochs of history we find almost everywhere a complicated arrangement of society into various orders, a manifold gradation of social rank. In ancient Rome we have patricians, knights, plebeians, slaves; in the Middle Ages feudal lords, vassals, guild-masters, journeymen, apprentices, serfs; in almost all of these classes, again, subordinate gradations.

"The modern bourgeois [capitalist] society that has arisen from the ruins of feudal society has not done away with the class antagonisms. It has but established new classes, new conditions of oppression, new forms of struggle in place of the old.

"Our epoch, the epoch of the bourgeoisie, possesses, however, this distinctive feature: It has simplified the class antagonisms. Society as a whole is more and more splitting up into two great hostile camps, into two great classes directly facing each other—bourgeoisie and proletarian—[read: Capitalist and the Oppressed Masses.]

"Modern industry has established the world market, for which the discovery of America paved the way. This market has given an immense development to commerce, to navigation, to communication by land. This development has, in its turn, reacted on the extension of industry; and in proportion as industry, commerce, navigation and the railways extended, in the same proportion the bourgeoisie developed, increased its capital, and pushed into the background every class handed down from the Middle Ages.

"We see, therefore, how the modern bourgeoisie is itself the product of a long course of development, of a long series of revolutions in the modes of production and of exchange.

"Each step in the development of the bourgeoisie was accomplished by a corresponding political advance of that class. * * *

The executive of the modern state is but a committee for managing the common affairs of the whole bourgeoisie.

"The bourgeoisie has stripped of its halo every occupation hitherto honored and looked up to with reverent awe. It has converted the physician, the lawyer, the poet, the priest, the man of science into its paid wage laborers.

"The bourgeoisie has torn away from the family its sentimental veil, and has reduced the family relation to a mere money relation.

"The bourgeoisie cannot exist without constantly revolutionizing the instruments of production, and thereby the relations of production, and with them the whole relations of society. * * * Constant revolutionizing of production, uninterrupted disturbances of all social conditions, everlasting uncertainty and agitation distinguish the bourgeois epoch from all earlier ones.

"More and more the bourgeoisie keeps doing away with the scattered state of the population, of the means of production, and of property. It has agglomerated population, centralized the means of production, and has concentrated property into a few hands. The necessary consequence of this was political centralization. Independent, or loosely connected provinces, with separate interests, laws, governments and systems of taxation, became lumped together into one nation, with one government, one code of laws, one national class interest, one frontier and one customs tariff.

"* * * Bourgeois conditions of production, of exchange and of property, a society that has conjured up such a gigantic means of production and of exchange, is like the sorcerer who is no longer able to control the powers of the nether world whom he has called up by his spells.

"The weapons with which the bourgeoisie felled feudalism to the ground are now being turned against the bourgeoisie itself.

"But not only has the bourgeoisie forged the weapons that bring death to itself; it has also called into existence the men who are to wield those weapons—the modern working class—the proletarians.

"In proportion as the bourgeoisie, i.e., capital, is developed, in the same proportion is the proletariat, the modern working class, developed—a class of laborers, who live only so long as they find work, and who find work only so long as their labor increases capital. These laborers, who must sell themselves piecemeal, are a commodity, like every other article of commerce, and are consequently exposed to all of the vicissitudes of competition, to all the fluctuations of the market.

"Modern industry has converted the little workshop of the patriarchal masters into the great factory of the industrial capitalist. Masses of laborers, crowded into the factory, are organized like soldiers. As privates of the industrial army they are placed under the command of a perfect hierarchy of officers and sergeants. Not only are they slaves of the bourgeois class, and bourgeois state; they are daily and hourly enslaved by the machine, by the overlooker, and, above all, by the individual manufacturer himself. The more openly this despotism proclaims gain to be its end and aim, the more petty, the more hateful and the more embittering it is.

"The less the skill and exertion of strength implied in manual labor, in other words, the more modern industry develops, the more is the labor of men superseded by that of women. Differences of age and sex have no longer any distinctive social validity for the working class. All are increments of labor, more or less expensive to use, according to their age and sex.

"No sooner has the laborer received his wages in cash, for the moment escaping exploitation by the manufacturer, than he is set upon by the other portions of the bourgeoisie, the landlord, the shopkeeper, the pawnbroker, etc.

"The lower strata of the middle class—the small trades people, shopkeepers, the retired tradesmen generally, the handicraftsmen and the peasants—all these sink gradually into the proletariat, partly because their diminutive capital does not suffice for the scale on which modern industry is carried on, and is swamped in competition with the large capitalists, partly because their specialized skill is rendered worthless by new methods of production. Thus the proletariat is recruited from all classes of the population.

"The proletariat goes through various stages of development. With its birth begins its struggle with the bourgeoisie. At first the contest is carried on by individual laborers, then by the work people of the factory, then by the operatives of one trade in one locality, against the individual bourgeois who directly exploits them. They direct their attacks not against the bourgeois conditions of production, but against the instruments of production themselves; they destroy imported wares that compete with their labor; they smash machinery to pieces, they set factories ablaze, they seek to restore by force the vanished status of the workmen of the Middle Ages.

"At this stage the workers still form an incoherent mass scattered over the whole country, and broken up by their mutual competition. If anywhere they unite and form more compact bodies, this is not yet the consequence of their own active union, but of the union of the bourgeoisie, which class, in order to attain its own political ends is compelled to set the whole proletariat in motion, and is moreover still able to do so for a time. At this stage, therefore, the proletarians do not fight their enemies, but the enemies of their enemies, the remnants of absolute monarchy, the landowners, the nonindustrial bourgeoisie, the petty bourgeoisie. Thus the whole historical movement is concentrated in the hands of the bourgeoisie; every victory so obtained is a victory for the bourgeoisie.

"But with the development of industry the proletariat not only increases in number; it becomes concentrated in greater masses, its strength grows, and it feels that strength more. The various interests and conditions of life within the ranks of the proletariat are more and more equalized, in proportion as machinery obliterates all distinctions of labor and nearly everywhere reduces wages to the same low level. The growing competition among the bourgeois, and the resulting commercial crisis, makes the wages of the workers ever more fluctuating. The unceasing improvement of machinery, ever more rapidly developing, make their livelihood more and more precarious; the collisions between individual workmen and individual bourgeois take more and more the character of collisions between two classes. Thereupon the workers begin to form combinations [trade unions] against the bourgeoisie; they club together in order to keep up the rate of wages; they found permanent associations in order to make provisions beforehand for these occasional revolts. Here and there the contest breaks out into riots.

"Now and then the workers are victorious, but only for a time. The real fruit of their battle lies, not in the immediate result, but in the ever expanding union of the workers. This union is furthered by the improved means of communication which are created by modern industry, and which place the workers in different localities in contact with each other. It was just this contact that was needed to centralize the numerous local struggles, all of the same character, into one national struggle between classes. But every class struggle is a political struggle. And that union, to attain which the burghers of the Middle Ages with their miserable highways, required centuries, the modern proletarians, thanks to railways, achieve in a few years.

"This organization of the proletarians into a class and consequently into a political party, is continually being upset by competition between the workers themselves. But it ever arises up again, stronger, firmer, mightier. It compels legislative recognition of the particular interests of the workers by taking advantage of the divisions among the bourgeoisie itself.

"Finally, in times when the class struggle nears the decisive hour the process of dissolution going on within the ruling class, in fact within the whole range of old society, assumes such a violent, glaring character, that a small section of the ruling class cuts itself adrift and joins the revolutionary class, the class that holds the future in its hands. Just as, therefore, at an earlier period a section of nobility went over to the bourgeoisie, so now a portion of the bourgeoisie goes over to the proletariat, and in particular, a portion of the bourgeois ideologists who have raised themselves to the level of comprehending theoretically the historical movement as a whole.

"Of all the classes that stand face to face with the bourgeoisie today, the proletariat alone is a really revolutionary class. The other classes decay and finally disappear in the face of modern industry; the proletariat is its special and essential product.

"All the preceding classes that got the upper hand sought to fortify their already acquired status by subjecting society at large to their conditions of appropriation. For the proletarians cannot become masters of the productive forces of society except by abolishing their own previous mode of appropriation, and thereby also every other previous mode of appropriation. They have nothing of their own to secure and fortify; their mission is to destroy all previous securities for, and insurances of, individual property.

"All previous historical movements were movements of minorities, or in the interests of minorities. The proletarian movement is the self-conscious, independent movement of the immense majority, in the interest of the immense majority. The proletariat, the lowest stratum of our present society, cannot stir, cannot raise itself up, without the whole superincumbent strata of official society being sprung into the air.

"Though not in substance, yet in form, the struggle of the proletariat with the bourgeoisie is at first a national struggle. The proletariat of each country must, of course, at first settle matters with its own bourgeoisie.

"In depicting the most general phases of the development of the proletariat, we traced more or less the veiled civil war, raging within existing society, up to the point where that war breaks out into open revolution, and to where the violent overthrow of the bourgeoisie lays the foundation for the sway of the proletariat.

"The essential condition for the existence and sway of the bourgeois class, is in the formation and augmentation of capital; the condition of capital is wage labor. Wage labor rests exclusively on competition between the laborers. The advance of industry, whose involuntary promoter is the bourgeoisie, replaces the isolation of the laborers, due to competition, by their revolutionary association, due to association. The development of modern industry, therefore, cuts from under its feet the very foundation on which the bourgeoisie produces and appropriates products. What the bourgeoisie produces, above all, are its own grave-diggers. Its fall and the victory of the proletariat are equally inevitable.

"The immediate aim of the Communists is the same as that of all the other proletarian parties; formation of the proletarian into a class, overthrow of bourgeois supremacy, conquest of political power by the proletariat.

"The distinguishing feature of Communism is not the abolition of property generally, but the abolition of bourgeois property. But modern private bourgeois property is the final and most complete expression of the system of producing and appropriating products that is based on class antagonisms, on the exploitation of the many by the few.

"In this sense, the theory of Communists may be summed up in the single sentence: abolition of private property.

"In short, the Communists everywhere support every revolutionary movement against the existing social and political order of things.

"In all these movements they bring to the front, as the leading question in each case, the property question, no matter what its degree of development at the time.

"Finally, they labor everywhere for the union and agreement of the democratic parties of all the countries.

"The Communists disdain to conceal their views and aims. They openly declare that their ends can be attained only by the forcible overthrow of all existing social conditions. Let the ruling classes tremble in a Communist revolution. The proletarians have nothing to lose but their chains. They have a world to win.

"Working men of all countries, unite!"

Let us see precisely what Marx meant by all of this complicated language contained in the excerpts from the Communist Manifesto quoted above. Marx commenced the Manifesto by outlining the historical development of class antagonism between the capitalist minority—the bourgeoisie, and the "oppressed" majority—the proletariat. He then explains how the era of feudal society was replaced by the era of capitalism and how the new system must inevitably result in a steadily increasing concentration of wealth and power in the hands of the bourgeoisie or capitalists. He states that as the power grows so does the numerical strength of the working masses, and so does the spirit of rebellion against the exploiting class. Marx then lays down the master plan for world revolution. He insists that it must be a revolution by violence. He points out that at first the revolt will be unorganized and weak. Gradually it will gather power, until striking workers band together by industries, paralyze the industrial strength of their employers, smashing the implements of production, burning the factories in their struggle for freedom. Every strike, says Marx, is a means of intensifying the class struggle; of welding the workers more closely together. Eventually the masses will form their own political party, and gain through legislative pressure the means to carry forward the fight to higher levels of victory. During the final stages of the conflicts, he predicts, small segments of the ruling class will desert to the cause of the revolution—especially those ideologists, or teachers and students of social affairs, who have gained some understanding of the historical movement of Communism as a whole.

More than 100 years have passed since the Manifesto was promulgated. Lenin followed it meticulously in planning the strategy for the Russian Revolution of 1917. The first class struggles in that country were weak and transitory. As the workers banded together in unions, and as those unions were penetrated and propagandized, an epidemic of strikes spread like a raging fire from one factory to another, paralyzing the industrial strength of the nation. Transportation and communication were stopped; select segments of the ruling class did desert to the side of the revolution; the Czar's armed forces refused, in many instances, to fire upon the rioting workers. The revolution in Russia was conducted—and succeeded —by precisely following the pattern set forth in the Manifesto. Marx had also stated that the revolution must be international in scope. Two years after the 1917 revolution, therefore, the Third International, or Comintern, was formed at Moscow as a high board of strategy for world revolution. Communist Parties in all countries were established as sections of this International and were bound to it by the strongest disciplinary ties. We shall see how the same technique originated by Marx and described in the Manifesto, supplemented by the experiences of the Russian Revolution, has since been employed to gnaw away at the vitals of every democratic and capitalistic government, and how the class struggles in such countries have been carefully planned, coordinated and intensified—all in strict conformity with the basic precepts and mandates of the Manifesto.

The newly formed Communist League adopted this Manifesto. The principles contained therein were studied and restudied, understood by the leadership and completely misunderstood by the rank and file membership. Within a few weeks after the document appeared, revolution erupted in Paris and Marx was summoned there to give his counsel and leadership. This revolt was quite unexpected, and since it lacked adequate planning and preparation, died down within a few months, and Marx and Engels went to Germany where they considered conditions more favorable to their purposes. They started a newspaper at Cologne, seeking to fan the smoldering embers of unrest into flames through the column of the paper. The government, once again, was quick to act. Publication was stopped by an edict and threat of prosecution. Marx remained stubbornly at his desk, and with Engels and others was tried and acquitted and again sought to revive the paper. Once more, for the third time, an edict stopped publication in May, 1849. Marx, with his wife and three small children wandered about Germany until he was literally without funds, then went to Paris once more. Within 24 hours they were ordered to leave, and this time went to London where the fourth child was born a few weeks after their arrival.

In 1850, Marx and Engels started another journal and distributed it from Hamburg. It failed after six issues were printed. Marx had stated in the Manifesto that a German revolution was imminent and would spread throughout Europe. He and Engels were Germans by birth, familiar with the temperament of the country and with its economic condition. The world had first taken note of Marxian ideas through the columns of German newspapers in 1843, and it seemed fitting to both men that the revolution should be started in Germany. In March, 1850, Marx addressed the Communist League at London, and stated emphatically that in Europe a revolution by the proletariat was quickly developing. Remembering the prediction in the Manifesto about the imminence of a revolt in Germany, and fired with enthusiasm by the address, the delegates spread the news in their respective countries. In Paris, Brussels, London and Cologne preparations were made. When several months had passed and there were no signs of social upheaval, the enthusiasm slowly turned to doubt and then to suspicion that Marx was, after all, not infallible in such matters. But Marx had read the signs accurately. He could not have anticipated that gold would be discovered in California, an event that actually stemmed the rising tide of revolution by starting a counter-wave of prosperity throughout the economic world. Marx announced that the rebellion of the masses had been postponed, and his statement drove a wedge of dissidence through the heart of the league. Some of the delegates repudiated Marx and his high-flown theories. One of them challenged him to a duel. A majority, however, remained loyal, although their disappointments were ill concealed. By September, 1850, the internal strife had so weakened the organization that Marx attempted to save it by transferring the headquarters to Cologne, the scene of so much of his early work. Within six months after the change was effected, the leaders of the league were placed under arrest, and the weakened structure rapidly fell to pieces. Marx withdrew from the league, disillusioned and embittered.

Having perfected his political philosophies through years of intensive study, handicapped by poverty and persecution, Marx had confidently entered the field of political action through the Paris revolt, and attempted to solidify the forces of Communism through the medium of the Communist League. His peculiar personality repelled many from him even before his prediction of an impending uprising was proven wrong. After his withdrawal from the league he went into academic seclusion. supported, as usual, through the unfailing generosity of the faithful Engels. Between remittances, however, the Marx family was forced to exist in utmost poverty; there was not enough to eat, no clothes for the children—but Frau Marx was by this time accustomed to a life of squalor and her husband was far too absorbed in his work to pay attention to financial matters. It is quite probable, however, that some of the vicious statements in the Manifesto—the setting of the factories ablaze and the destruction of the machinery, the statement that it was impossible for a proletarian to enjoy his family in comfort, might have grown from a deep sense of bitterness, perhaps a sense of frustration in the realization that the author had himself been unable to support his family or even to give them the bare necessities of life.

Marx's writings now assumed a self-critical aspect, and were obviously designed to test the practicality of his theories. When the fortunes of Marx's family were at their lowest state, news came from America that Charles Dana wanted a series of articles on social conditions in Europe and was willing to accept them from Marx. The articles were printed in the *New York Tribune* from time to time at an agreed price of 2 pounds per article. Many of the first pieces, and virtually all of the last ones, were actually written by Engels. Few of them were deemed suitable for publication, however, and since Marx was paid only for those that appeared in the paper, his income from this source fell far short of his expectations. It is a tribute to his dogged perseverance and his utter devotion to the cause in which he believed so fanatically that he persisted in outlining the articles, and persuaded his loyal comrade, Engels, to keep the series flowing solely because he hoped to reach and convert new readers.

Poverty and Persecution

From the time of Marx's expulsion from the newspaper which first employed him in 1843, his life was one of poverty and persecution. Six children were born to Fannie Marx, and only four grew to maturity. The only boy had been his father's delight and had given promise of great intellectual attainment. Born in 1846, he died in his father's arms almost at the same time the last child was born in 1855. From 1850 until 1856, when Fannie Marx inherited a small sum from her mother's estate, poverty was the normal condition for the Marx family; sickness was always present, the children languishing for lack of proper nourishment and suffering because there was no money to spend for medical attention. During this period Marx plunged deeper into his work and exhibited fits of irritability and vanity that drove him even farther into the seclusion that he assumed after leaving the Communist League. It is one of the many contradictions in his nature that Marx— vain, blunt, irascible and domineering to adults, was unfailingly kind and gentle to children. On those infrequent occasions when he and Engels strolled through Hampstead Heath during the evenings, they loved to romp with the children who played there; riding them astride their shoulders, chuckling when their little hands were thrust into Marx's pockets in search of the candy he brought for them. Unable to endure the company of anyone he could not dominate, he was completely relaxed and natural with children. This, according to psychiatrists, may indicate a sense of inferiority—a lack of self-confidence. There was no occasion to impress children with his mental attainments or with the accuracy of his theories, so he unconsciously dropped the overbearing attitude, the impatience, the fits of rage, the caustic remarks that drove men from him. Even in his own home Marx frequently displayed quick bursts of roaring temper, but invariably received such a berating from Helene

Demuth—the servant who came with Fannie and had served her family since childhood—that Marx was always subdued and often apologetic. He also suffered considerably from stomach trouble during this period, which made him even more irritable than usual.

By 1862, Marx was again without funds—writing constantly, relying on Engels' remittances to keep his family from starvation.

It seemed at times that Marx was utterly devoid of all human feeling. When he learned of the death of Mary Burns, with whom Engels was deeply in love, he wrote his old friend as follows:

> "Dear Engels: The news of Mary's death has both astonished and dismayed me. She was extremely good natured, witty and much attached to you."

Having thus consoled his closest friend in the hour of his grief, Marx characteristically went into a long account of his own affairs winding up with a plea for more funds.

Engels replied:

> "You will find it natural enough that on this occasion my own trouble and your frosty attitude towards it have made it impossible for me to write to you sooner. All my friends, including acquaintances among the Phillistines, have on this occasion, which indeed touches me shrewdly, shown me more sympathy and friendship than I could have anticipated. To you it seemed a suitable moment for the display of the superiority of your frigid way of thinking. So be it!"

Marx was quick to apologize, was characteristically forgiven, and the remittances continued almost without interruption.

Yet another example of this peculiar attitude towards those closest to him was demonstrated when Marx heard of the death of LaSalle— always prominent in the field of radical socialism—and who had also sent money from time to time. He had assisted Marx in getting many of his articles published, tried to obtain his repatriation to Germany, and kept up his good-natured correspondence when Marx sent in return only a few vituperative letters. Concerning the death of LaSalle, Marx wrote:

> "It is hard to believe that so noisy, so stirring, so pushful a man should be as dead as a doornail, and have to hold his tongue altogether."

In 1862, an International Trade Exposition was held at London, in which the developments of the industrial world were displayed. Working-class delegates arrived from various countries, and were naturally contacted by representatives of the English trade union movement. It was decided to launch the nucleus of a Communist international association of working men, and the plan gained impetus from a revolt which occurred in Poland the following year. Marx once more decided to work actively for revolution in the political arena, and under his guidance delegates were sent to London and formed the International Workingmen's Association in 1864. The address which Marx delivered at the first meeting of the newly organized movement has been accorded a place second only to the Manifesto in Marxian literature. In the Manifesto Marx had set forth the theory for a world revolution of the proletariat;

in his address to the new international he instructed a group of individual revolutionists in the master plan for action. After reciting the reasons for the failure of the movement to date, Marx declared:

"* * * The emancipation of the working classes must be conquered by the working classes themselves; that the struggle for the emancipation of the working classes means, not a struggle for class privileges and monopolies, but for equal rights and duties and the abolition of all class rule. That the economical subjugation of the man of labor to the monopolizer of the means of labor, that is, the sources of life, lies at the bottom of servitude in all its forms, of all social misery, mental degradation and political dependence; that the economical emancipation of the working classes is therefore the great end to which every political movement ought to be subordinate as a means; that all efforts aiming at that concrete end have hitherto failed from the want of solidarity between the manifold divisions of labor in each country, and from the absence of a fraternal bond of union between the working classes of different countries. That the emancipation of labor is neither a local, nor a national, but a social problem embracing all countries in which modern society exists, and depending for its solution on the concurrence, practical and theoretical, of the most advanced countries."

Unfortunately for the newly launched movement, the various groups in the various countries did not usually see eye to eye, social problems in one country being quite different from those in another—although, according to Marx, the underlying causes were precisely the same. The inevitable result was a state of confusion among the rank and file membership, and a top-heavy and indecisive central organization at the headquarters in London. The movement needed discipline, control and clarification of purpose.

Following a conference of leaders in London in September, 1865, Marx was selected to direct the entire organization. It soon became evident, however, that although he was of inestimable value as the intellectual leader of world revolution, he was certainly no peace maker. His crabbed, irritable temperament hardly suited his new role, and internal dissension rapidly became worse instead of better. By the summer of 1865 he was again impoverished, unhappy, and on the verge of a nervous collapse. He once more sought solace in academic seclusion, and plunged into the writing of the first volume of *Capital.* When the organization held its congress in Geneva in September, 1867, he was too deeply absorbed in his work to even compose an agendum. The activities and propaganda of the new international had provoked the attention of the bourgeoisie, however, and several attempts were made to liquidate it. They merely served to focus more attention on it, however, and the effort proved more beneficial than detrimental.

Michael Bakunin

Michael Bakunin and Nicholas Bukharin, both Russian revolutionaries, are often confused. The former was a contemporary of Marx and the latter was a contemporary of Lenin, each playing an important part in the Marxist movement of his time.

Bakunin's life was one of constant harassment. In 1844, he had been condemned to death in Saxony. The Saxons surrendered him to the Austrians, where he was also sentenced to be executed. In 1851, the Austrians sent him back to Russia, where he was cast in prison and remained there until 1861. In that year he escaped to Siberia and eventually returned to Europe by way of Japan and the United States, arriving in England during the latter part of that year. It soon became apparent that Bakunin's ideas differed sharply from those of Marx, and it was therefore inevitable that their ideological hostilities should be developed into personal antagonism, at least on the part of Marx. When the Workers' Educational Society was formed, with the advice of Marx, its chief critic was Bakunin. After the forming of the International Workingmen's Association, Bakunin decided that this was the instrument through which the most effective work for world revolution could be carried forward; he joined the movement after complimenting Marx on his efforts to found it, and plunged into the new field of activity with great enthusiasm. Basically, however, the two men differed radically. Bakunin could never bring himself to agree with the Marxian doctrine that gave absolute power to the state. He considered this concept as infringing upon the individual rights and liberties of the workers, and wanted to bring about their emancipation from economic bondage and at the same time insure their personal liberties. Marx was extremely sensitive to this criticism, and while outwardly professing friendship toward Bakunin, worked to undermine his power and thereby remove him from the arena as a potential rival. On this Bakunin once wrote:

"As soon as he ordered a persecution, there is no limit to the baseness and infamy of his method. Himself a Jew, he has around him in London and in France, and above all in Germany, a number of petty, more or less able, intriguing, mobile speculative Jews (the sort of Jews you can find all over the place), commercial employees, bank clerks, men of letters, politicians, correspondents of newspapers of the most various shades of opinion, in a word, literary go-betweens, just as they are financial go-betweens, with one foot in the bank, the other in the socialist movement, while their rump is in German periodical literature. * * * These Jewish men of letters are adepts in the art of cowardly, odious and perfidious insinuations. They seldom make open accusations, but they insinuate, saying they 'have heard—it is said—it may not be true, but.' And then they hurl the most abominable calumnies in your face."

Marx had unleashed just such a campaign of subtle attack against Bakunin, and the stinging propaganda was proving effective. Its object always admired Marx for his intellectual powers, and was so fascinated with the first volume of *Capital* that he proceeded to translate it into Russian.

Another reason for the Marxian attack was a speech which Bakunin had delivered at Berne, wherein he made a blistering criticism of the basic theories which Marx had theretofore promulgated.

Through a committee, controlled by Marx, it was urged that Bakunin be expelled from the International on the ground that he had founded the Alliance of Social Revolutionaries and affiliated it with the International for the purpose of getting control of the latter organization. In this charge Marx was right. Bakunin wanted to work through the International, but clung to his basic beliefs that were completely opposed to those of Marx and therefore to those of the International itself. Not content merely to eliminate his rival from the field, Marx stooped to personal matters by accusing Bakunin of having misappropriated funds that had been given him for the translation of the first volume of *Capital* into Russian.

It was only natural that among the supporters of Bakunin in the International there was aroused bitter resentment—not so much because of the fact that he had been expelled—but more because of the tactics that were used to bring about his expulsion. In the process of casting out Bakunin the upheaval shook the International to its very roots. It was now more apparent than ever that in each country the revolutionary groups were commencing to function within the political structure of their respective governments, and that the problems were so different throughout the world that it was a practical impossibility to lay down any hard and fast set of rules at the headquarters in London and expect them to be uniformly followed by the revolutionary movements in other nations. Thus the International began to disintegrate and grew rapidly weak and impotent. At the last congress at Geneva in 1873, even Marx was forced to the conclusion that the organization had served its usefulness and could be held together no longer. As a final gesture of bitterness toward Bakunin, however, Marx directed the preparation and publication of a pamphlet, written by himself with the collaboration of Engels, and which was a turgid display of personal venom. Bakunin was now an old man. He replied to this last attack as follows:

"This new pamphlet is a formal denunciation, a gendarme denunciation directed against a society known by the name of *The Alliance.* Urged onward by furious hatred, Monsieur Marx has not been afraid to box his own ears, by undertaking to expose himself before the public in the role of a sneaky and calumniatory police agent. That is his own affair; and, since he likes the job, let him have it. * * * This has given me an intense loathing of public life. I have had enough of it, and, after devoting all my days to the struggle, I am weary. * * * Let other and younger persons put their hands to the work. For my own part, I no longer feel strong enough, and perhaps also I lack the necessary confidence to go on trying to roll the stone of Sisyphus uphill against the universally triumphant reaction. I therefore withdraw from the arena, and ask only one thing from my dear contemporaries—oblivion."

On July 1, 1876, he died, as he wished—in oblivion.

The Death of Marx

After the collapse of the International, Marx once more retired from the political field of action. The first volume of *Capital,* in effect a recapitulation of all of his previous writings, had little circulation. In 1868, Engels sold the mercantile business he had inherited from his father and moved to London to be near his old friend, to whom he had literally devoted both his life and his fortune. At the suggestion of Engels, Marx fixed a sum that would be adequate for his annual support, and that sum was regularly paid until Marx died in 1883.

Meanwhile, romance had developed in the Marx household. In August, 1866, Marx wrote to Engels:

"Since yesterday Lora is half pledged to Monsieur LaFargue, my creole medical student. She has been treating him much like the others, but the emotional excess is characteristic of creoles; a certain fear on her part that the young man (he is some 25 years old) would do himself a hurt, and so on, perhaps some predilection for him, cold as ever in Lora's case (he is a handsome, intelligent, and vigorously developed fellow), have led more or less to a compromise. The young man attached himself to me at the outset, but soon transferred the attraction from the old man to the daughter. Economically speaking, he is moderately well off, being the only child of a sometime planter."

After the marriage of Lora, Jenny, too, found a suitor in the person of Charles Longuet, a member of the general council of the ill-fated International from France. When Jenny left for Paris with her new husband in 1873, only Eleanor was left with her mother and the ever-faithful Helene Dumuth in the household. Marx then moved to Maitland Park Road, there to spend the remainder of his days. His health was shattered, few people ever came to see him, the turbulent current of social history churned and seethed along without him; he felt both ignored and isolated—which was indeed a fact. Even his new sons-in-law paid him little attention, which moved him to write testily to Engels in 1882:

"Longuet is the last Prodhounist and LaFargue is the last Bakuninist. To the devil with them both!"

Fannie Marx had died in December, 1881, a blow from which her husband never recovered. The sudden death of his daughter Jenny in 1883, sent Marx into a fatal decline. After the death of his wife he had moved from one health resort to another, but after 1883, he remained at home, unable to work and in constant pain. He died in a coma on March 14th of that year—forgotten and deserted by the new disciples of revolution; a lonely, broken man. There was only the faithful Engels who was with him at the end, and who delivered the oration over his grave.

Thus lived and died the man who, indeed, invented Communism. It was a product of his own mentality—an ideology that was to sweep into Russia and pave the way for the revolution in that country; that was to establish its roots throughout the nations of the world through the medium of the Third International, or Comintern, organized in Moscow two years after the Russian revolution.

It has been said that the thoughts of Karl Marx have exerted more influence on civilization than those of any other man who ever lived. It remains to be explained how his works were caught up in Russia during the latter part of World War I, gave impetus to the revolutionary movement in that country, and spread over the face of the world, mounting in intensity and seriousness until at the present time the globe is divided into two hostile ideologies—the Communist-dominated nations against the free world.

THE RUSSIAN REVOLUTION.

Marx and Engels had, for reasons already explained, concentrated most of their attention on Germany as the country where a serious revolution of the proletariat was most likely to occur. They had paid little attention to conditions in Russia, perhaps because of the long conflict between Marx and Bakunin, which served in a measure to alienate the Russian followers of the latter from Marx's circle. But Bakunin had translated the first volume—and by far the most important—of *Capital* into Russian, with the result that the theories of Marxism were being studied by little groups of revolutionaries in that country. In 1892, another Russian, Georgi Plekhanov, set about to translate all of Marx's works, and almost immediately they became popular with the leaders of the anti-Czarist forces.

The Russia of that period was an admirable proving ground for Marxism. Nicholas II was a weak and vacillating ruler. His imperial court was a thing of barbaric splendor, supported through exploitation of the peasantry and serfs. Here, indeed, was the concentration of wealth, the sharp class antagonism, the oppression of the many by the few—the precise conditions that would pave the way for revolution according to the precepts of the Manifesto. Marx had tried, through the ill-fated International, to organize the working masses of the world; he had predicted that a revolt would begin in Germany and sweep throughout Europe. The scene now shifted to Russia, but the action occurred long after Marx's death. Here was a new arena for action; here were the ideal conditions according to Marxian theory. It remained to be seen whether the vast unorganized proletariat of that country could be organized, trained in the basic theory of Marxism, provided with adequate leadership, and break the power of the bourgeoisie.

LENIN

Vladimir Illyich Ulianov—known to history as Nicolai Lenin, was born at Ulyanovsk in 1870, and had already studied Marxism thoroughly by the time he entered the University at Kazan—having participated actively in a Marxist discussion group in that city. By 1895 he had become the Marxist leader in St. Petersburg, where he formed an organization called The League for the Emancipation of the Working Class. This was actually the inception of a definite revolutionary movement in Russia based wholly on the Marxian concept—a movement destined to spread throughout that country and thence throughout the world. From 1895, Lenin devoted almost his entire time to the building of this revolutionary class and to creating the conditions for the seizure of power from the Czarist forces.

One of the things that prompted Lenin to his fanatic activity may be found in the fact that his brother, also a radical, was captured, tried, convicted and executed for treason against the Czar when his younger brother Lenin, was at an especially impressionable age. Such a terrible experience would, of course, have a lasting effect on anyone; on Lenin, a youth who had already absorbed some of his older brother's revolutionary ideas, the experience was burned deeply into his consciousness and naturally exerted a powerful influence on him thereafter.

Endowed with great intellectual capacity, possessed of boundless energy, always eager to champion the masses and fully as modest as Marx had been vain, Lenin quickly rose to a position of leadership. From the time he first gained recognition through his articles in various newspapers and magazines, his rise to prominence was steady in the radical circles, and he remained the supreme commander of the Russian revolutionary forces until his death in 1924.

There were, as will be seen, many internal quarrels, many dissident groups, but through each contest for power Lenin emerged stronger than before. It was Lenin who brought organization and discipline to the Russian proletariat; it was Lenin who planned the strategy of the Revolution of 1917; it was Lenin who guided the victorious proletariat through more than two years of civil war. Unequestionably Lenin, aside from Marx himself, who was the most influential Marxist.

With the consummate skill of a general he marshalled his forces, perfected his plans, assigned his lieutenants to their tasks. He selected Trotsky as his second in command, and he assigned to Stalin the role for which he was best suited—an organizer of strikes and riots. Throughout the formative stages of the revolution the two outstanding leaders were Lenin and Trotsky, who first met in 1902. Whereas Marx, Engels and Plekhanov had been political philosophers, Lenin was both a theoretician and a man of action. His intellectual powers were respected by Trotsky, and his practical side provoked the admiration and respect of Stalin, who first met him in 1905. Trotsky had spent his life in writing revolutionary articles; Stalin was then an unimportant revolutionist. Lenin, it would seem, possessed the virtues of both of his lieutenants and the weaknesses of neither.

Almost immediately after assuming command, Lenin set about training a group of professional revolutionaries who would devote the whole of their lives to the achievement of the ultimate goal: the overthrow of Czarism and the establishment of the dictatorship of the proletariat. He told these men:

> "When we have detachments of revolutionary workers, especially prepared by long training, no police in the world will be able to master them."

By constantly writing, speaking at mass meetings, organizing the workers and peasants and spreading the doctrines of revolt, Lenin and his Marxist forces developed from a handful of intellectuals into a small, well-disciplined army.

During this formative period, from 1900 to 1905, there was no Communist Party as such, but a series of organizations, functioning under various names but aiming at the same ultimate goal and founded on the Marxian idea. The most important of these groups was the Workers Social-Democratic Party, which was soon divided into two factions, the Bolsheviks, led by Lenin, and the Mensheviks, led by Plekhanov. The former advocated direct revolutionary action through violence, while the latter sought to obtain the same result through uniting with the liberal bourgeoisie elements and by the process of education and political action. It was basically a struggle between a left and right faction, radicals against conservatives.

While the fight for control was thus being waged, dissatisfaction was spreading among the workers. Strikes broke out in many key industries, ending with a general strike at St. Petersburg. By 1905, the Czar was persuaded to put an end to the insurrection once and for all, so he launched a savage and bloody attack against the workers that only drove them underground and provoked them to more determined action.

Thus began the Revolution of 1905—an uprising that was unexpected by the Marxist leaders. Undoubtedly they recalled the prophetic language of the Manifesto, heretofore quoted:

"At first the contest is carried on by individual laborers, then by the work people of a factory, then by the operatives of one trade in one locality, against the individual bourgeois who exploits them."

The demonstrations of 1904-1905 were spontaneous, starting with individual struggles among small groups of workmen, then spreading to the strikes in the oil fields of Baku and the Putilov Locomotive Works, and reaching a climax in a general strike and the temporary subjugation of the strikers by the Czar. On January 22, 1905, the real explosion was touched off when a delegation of workers was machine-gunned in the act of presenting a petition of rights to the Czar. The leaders of the liberal and conservative factions quickly forgot their differences and sought to bring a semblance of organization to the mob activity. This was no simple task, since by now a great number of strikes were occurring in all parts of the country. Through the unifying effect of the occurrence, however, Trotsky, who had been one of the leaders of the Menshevik element, agreed to work with Lenin in the common cause. In October, 1905, the Czar sanctioned the drafting of a new constitution and the trouble was temporarily over.

The Bolsheviks viewed the affair as a complete failure, but Plekhanov and his Menshevik following regarded it as the first victorious step along the long road to revolution.

Lenin, who had been in exile during the first stages of this uprising of 1905, supporting it by his writings and his advice, returned in October. He found the movement more closely bound together than before. Trotsky agreed to serve as Lenin's lieutenant, but had always maintained, and still maintained, that too much concentration of power in the hands of a few revolutionary leaders was as dangerous as too much concentration of wealth in the hands of a few of the bourgeoisie. He was fearful that with the growth of revolutionary discipline there would develop a clique of leaders who would be reluctant to relinquish their power once the revolution was won—and that the very purpose of the movement would therefore be defeated. According to excellent authority, in fact, Lenin stated on his deathbed that Trotsky had been eminently correct in this prediction.

The positions of the two prime leaders of the Marxists, Lenin and Trotsky, had been brought in bold relief by this abortive revolution of

1905. Stalin was still obscure. His first impression of Lenin was written after the two met in Finland in December, 1905:

> "I met Lenin for the first time in December, 1905, at the Bolshevik conference at Trammerfors, in Finland. I expected to see the mountain eagle of our party a great man, not only politically but physically, for I had formed for myself a picture of Lenin as a giant, a fine figure of a man. What was my disappointment when I saw the most ordinary individual, below middle height, distinguished from ordinary mortals by nothing, literally nothing. A great man is generally permitted to be late at meetings so that those present may be apprehensive at his nonarrival, and that so before the great man's appearance there may be cries of 'Hush—silence—he is coming.' This ceremony appears to me useful, for it creates respect. What was my disappointment to find that Lenin had arrived before the delegates, and was carrying on the most ordinary conversation with the most ordinary delegate, in a corner."

Analysis of Stalin's reactions, so expressed, provides an excellent index to his character. Always the realist, he expected a gigantic intellect to be housed in a gigantic body. Always alert for artifices to catch and hold attention, he was disappointed because Lenin had neglected to dramatize his entrance. He failed to realize that here was a sincere leader who cared little for personal power, was too busy to bother about his personal appearance, had come early because he felt himself a part of the conference and was not above discussing his problems with one of the less important delegates. Stalin looked for tricks and dissimulation, and was disappointed because he found none.

Early in 1906, the revolution began to wane and the old feuds over ideological matters were resumed. The aroused forces of the Czar drove the Marxists underground and there began an era of conspiratorial action, intrigue and plotting. It was during this era that the personality of the third member of this revolutionary trio manifested itself in Stalin's peculiar talents in such activities. As the movement was forced further and further underground, Stalin rose higher as he organized strike after strike, plot after plot, and directed the distribution of clandestine propaganda. In 1907 and 1908, he perfected his own support in the organizations through which his intrigues were executed. His work was wholly along these lines, and while Lenin was the acknowledged guiding genius of the revolution, and while Trotsky was busy with his writings and his speeches, Stalin was weaving his plots, gathering his small army of spies and *agents provocateur*, and playing one minor figure against another— undermining one man here, boosting another there. He never expressed one single revolutionary opinion in writing from 1907 to 1911.

It was natural for the leaders of the revolution in those days to assume names other than their own for purposes of protection—and in most instances these "Party names" clung. Thus Ulianov became Lenin; Lev Bronstein became Leon Trotsky; Josef Dzugashvili became Josef Stalin; Meer Wallach became Maxim Litvinov, and Scriabin became Molotov. One Party name usually sufficed, but Stalin had many aliases— due to his precarious underground activities he was constantly running afoul of the police and spent a good deal of his time either in prisons or escaping from them. To his intimates in the Party he was usually known as *Koba,* or Bear.

It is difficult to form an adequate estimate of any man who is or was prominent in the history of the Russian Revolution. Even in the case of Marx, in those accounts of his life which may be purchased at the many Communist book shops in·this country, there is no mention of the fact that he was supported by the generosity of Frederich Engels and other friends. On the contrary, the reader is led to believe through pointed inference that he earned a living from his literary works.

In the case of Stalin there are two fields of source material—those written by Party members and sympathizers, which eulogize him too lavishly, and those written by his enemies which sin in the other direction. There are too few objective biographies of the man. Those who fail to flatter him or who expose the slightest deficiency in his character are immediately charged with being Trotskyites and Fascists; those who acknowledge his powers and admit that he gained his objectives are charged with being Communists or Party sympathizers. There seems to be no middle ground. The fact is, that lovable traits are hard to find in Stalin's brooding, scheming personality. He is depicted to the Russian people patting little children on their curly heads, pausing for a few words with some withered crone while his entourage stand respectfully by—but such pictures were also shown of Hitler and Mussolini and other men with political ambitions. They mean nothing. Men are the sum total of their heritage and their experiences. It is not so hard to evaluate a man accurately if one takes the trouble to follow his life through the years.

In Stalin's case his early life is well-known. His role during the early years of the Russian Revolution is quite another matter. Stalin, or Josef Vissarionovich Dzugashvili, was born at Gori, Georgia, in 1879. His father was a peasant, much inclined to drunkenness, and his mother was a deeply religious peasant of meager education. As a boy he attended a religious school. Having thus obtained a primary education, he was enrolled in a seminary in Tiflis when he was 14 and remained there until he was 20. His studies were chiefly religious subjects, but there was probably a good deal of Marxism, as well, since the movement had been well grounded in Russia through the translations by Georgi Plekhanov of Marx's more important works. It is certain that Stalin, embittered by the life of poverty he had been forced to lead, had dipped into revolutionary matters, one of his biographers having stated that he led Marxist study groups even in the seminary. In any event, shortly after he left he was engaged in revolutionary activities. In 1903, he corresponded with Lenin. In 1905, he met with him in Finland, and a few months thereafter was active in the abortive revolution. From that point on his life was inseparably linked with the careers of Lenin and Trotsky.

It is of the utmost importance to bear in mind that Stalin, in 1905, was just one of thousands of minor figures in the Marxist ranks. He had not provoked attention either by writing or by action. While Marx, Engels, Bakunin, Plekhanov, Lenin, and Trotsky were all schooled in social philosophy and other fundamental subjects that impelled each to develop ideas of his own, and to understand thoroughly the concepts of Marxism, Stalin was still concerned with only a smattering in this field of knowledge. He was, then, compelled to start his revolutionary career under a considerable handicap, and naturally turned his attention to practical matters; first, in organization, then to the field of practical power politics, in which he was preeminently successful.

· From 1905 until 1907, he organized the workers in the Baku oil fields. He was sent to prison in 1908 and escaped in 1909. In 1910, he was again in prison, this time for five years. In 1911, ·he once more managed to escape, but in September was caught and was sent into exile for three years. By December, he had reappeared at St. Petersburg. Even while in prison Stalin continued his work by forming groups of Marxists. In 1912, he became a member of the Central Committee of the Social-Democratic Party, the party of Lenin and Trotsky. In 1913, he was again in exile.

Lenin, realizing that the basic split in the two factions of the Party was growing wider, had quietly gathered about himself a group of men who were amenable to discipline. The Menshevik clique was still strong. There was now no revolutionary activity to shunt aside the internal discord, and the old fight between the liberal Bolsheviks and the conservative Mensheviks was resumed. There was yet no Communist Party in Russia; it was to grow from the Bolshevik functionaries who rallied around Lenin as a sort of staff for the coming revolution. There were many subordinates as the great uprising of 1917 grew nearer, but there was always only one supreme commander, and he was Lenin.

Here was precisely the type of highly centralized authority that had been opposed by Bakunin and Trotsky. Bakunin had argued with Marx that too much power in the state meant too little freedom for the individual. Trotsky claimed that the power assumed by a few leaders of a revolution would not be easy to relinquish. Now there appeared still another factor. If there was to be only one general who towered head and shoulders above the others in his army, what would happen to that army if the general died? It was plain, even to the Bolsheviks themselves, that it was Lenin's intellect and capacity for organization which was the keystone that held the entire Bolshevik structure together. Trotsky, meanwhile, held himself aloof, hesitating to give either faction his full support lest the common purpose of the Party be lost in petty bickering.

In 1914, the revolutionary movement was once again approaching unity and strength, only to be interrupted by the first world war. After two years of fighting, the vacillating character of the Czar's government resulted in hopeless chaos at the front; a bewildering maze of conflicting orders, a lack of ammunition and supplies for the armed forces, and a scarcity of food for the civilian population had reached almost famine proportions.

The Revolution of 1917

In February, 1917, another epidemic of strikes commenced. The strikes became more and more general, here and there turning into riots. The time for a second attempt at revolution was rapidly growing near, and this time the leaders were able to take advantage of the bitterness against the government that had been engendered by the war. The abortive revolution of 1905 had been crushed because the armed forces remained obedient to their Czar. When the revolution of 1917 was launched, the armed forces were split between loyalty to the government and sympathy for the strikers. Now, as before, the revolution simply exploded from widespread discontent, but the work of penetrating and propagandizing the working classes had been carried to a much higher degree in the meantime. On February 23rd, there were 90,000 strikers; on the following day there were 180,000; on the 25th, 240,000. Street riots were flaring up in city after city, particularly in Petrograd. There was little opposition from the army, but the police battled furiously against the rioting workers. The 26th fell on a Sunday and the closing of the factories hindered the strikes to some extent. On the 27th and 28th, small detachments of the more disciplined troops were hurled into the breach and, as was the case in 1905, the spontaneous revolt was crushed by trained soldiers battling against an unorganized mob. Lenin was then out of the country, Stalin was in exile, and most of the other leaders were unable to direct the activities for one reason or another—largely because nobody had anticipated that open revolt would occur so soon.

It was plain to see that the masses were more affected by the general condition of the country than they were by any planned propaganda, although, of course, it played no inconsiderable role. The Russian peasants and workers had been conditioned to oppression and exploitation for centuries, but the war demonstrated to them as nothing else could that their ruler was a weakling, and their armies were demoralized. They were brought face to face with their own condition of servitude.

Lenin hurried back from Switzerland. Trotsky arrived from America in May. Stalin returned from his exile. The leadership was now at hand, and preparations were made for the all-out effort. Once again the petty differences between liberals and conservatives were swept aside. Lenin was acknowledged by both factions as their supreme commander. Trotsky instilled fresh zeal in the masses through his gift for dynamic expression. Stalin stood by, ready to carry out the plans of his superiors in the field. Lenin was always ready with sincere and lavish praise for Trotsky's work, the latter gradually came to regard himself as Lenin's disciple; a relationship that was to continue until Lenin's death in 1924. Stalin's part in these crucial times has been minimized by many writers, and the criticism has been inaccurate. It is true that he wrote little, but that was being well attended to by men far more capable than he. He spoke little, but that was not his forte. In all fairness it must be said that Stalin was as valuable an asset in his role of a lieutenant in the field as Trotsky was in his role of a lieutenant on the forum. And it was Lenin who had shrewdly assigned each to the place where he was best suited to work.

Riot succeeded riot, strike succeeded strike, the economic life of the country was completely paralyzed, and large detachments of the armed forces were going over to the side of the revolutionaries as Marx had predicted when he wrote the Manifesto in 1850. The provisional government that had been set up when Nicholas II abdicated literally fell to pieces by November, 1917. The military revolutionary committee simply took over the reins of government—almost without a struggle. It was Lenin who had decided precisely when the final blow should fall. During the night of November 7th, his organized and disciplined units slipped into their assigned places; others arrested the leaders of the provisional government and took over their duties. The Revolution was won.

The Central Committee of the Bolshevik group was the governing body charged with the operation of the new regime. In the very process of building his revolutionary machinery, Lenin proved that the fears of Bakunin, Plekhanov and Trotsky were not without foundation, for in creating his powerful revolutionary machine Lenin unconsciously played the role of a Dr. Frankenstein. It had been necessary to concentrate great power in his hands to stop internal dissention and weld the working masses together. Now that the Revolution had been won, it was necessary to retain and solidify that authority, to establish the new dictatorship of the proletariat on a firm foundation. Leadership was needed now as never before, and there was no leader but Lenin. As his power grew it became increasingly apparent that many of the theories of Marx —the classless society, the self-governing workers, the vesting of all power in the state—would simply have to wait until stability had been established in a nation torn by the ravages of war and centuries of oppression of the people.

Thus the Revolution of 1917 exploded prematurely so far as the Bolshevik leaders were concerned, most of whom weren't even in Russia at the time. They had worked unceasingly to spread the propaganda, evolve the plans and organize the leadership, but they had by no means reached the 170,000,000 people for whose benefit the entire enterprise was undertaken. Virtually all of the Russian people were as unfamiliar with Marx as they were with Lenin. They were hungry, illiterate, embittered and unorganized. The Revolution occurred simply because the enervated government of the Czar fell to pieces from internal dry rot, and when it began to disintegrate the Bolsheviks were prepared to help it go with their small, compact, disciplined minority. They simply took over, eager to establish their revolutionary government, build their Marxist utopia and spread the revolution to the other nations of the world. In studying the history of Marx and of leaders of the Russian Revolution and in familiarizing oneself with the Revolution, one begins to understand much more clearly the problems of international Communism and the aims and objectives that it seeks to attain. It is important to bear in mind that the strategy, the propaganda, the organizational policies and many of the other practices that were originated during the Revolution of 1917, are being carried out today by the Communist Party in the United States.

THE CIVIL WAR

After the Bolsheviks had actually seized the reins of power there was no mass exodus of the Czar's men, as might be expected in the case of a deposed regime. Many of the former leaders remained politically powerful and respected by the people. These deposed leaders formed the core of counter-revolution, and sought to weld together a force strong enough to crush the Bolsheviks and re-establish a regime of their own. Many of the Czar's generals still controlled bodies of armed troops; the industrialists still held the loyalty of many of their employees; landlords managed to rally many of their old tenants; officials still controlled many of their subordinates. There was no wave of public enthusiasm for the Bolsheviks—the masses were glad to get rid of a weak government, but knew little of the Lenin Revolutionaries.

As the conflict developed on many fronts during the first six months of 1918, and the Red forces battled the White in a civil war for power, the Allies sent forces into Russia for the purpose of protecting their interests against a German invasion, which they feared might be undertaken despite the treaty with a revolutionary regime which had been initiated by Trotsky. No matter which force won, the rich oil fields and grain regions of an unprotected Russia might prove tempting to the Germans. Germany surrendered in November, however, and thereafter the Russians fought fiercely in a civil war that lasted until 1920.

It was clearly apparent from the first that whichever side won the confidence and support of the masses would emerge the victor. The civil war was actually a continuation of the Revolution, because the Bolsheviks did not manage to secure control of the government or the country until 1920, and during all of that time the Revolution was continued. Lenin vested full military authority in Trotsky, who organized the Red Army, supervised all military operations and used an armored train as his headquarters as he went from one strategic point to another throughout the country.

On June 6, 1918, Stalin was sent to Tsarytsin for the purpose of obtaining much needed grain. He was ordered to get the necessary supplies and proceed to the Caucasus. On June 13th, he telegraphed to Lenin that the opposing forces were advancing toward the city, and that he would be forced to remain where he was. General Voroshilov was nearby, eventually routed the White enemy, and Stalin remained at Tsarytsin in complete charge. After nearly three months had passed things were getting steadily worse along the southern front, and both Trotsky and Lenin suspected that all was not well in Tsarytsin with Stalin and Voroshilov. There was a lack of cooperation between the military commanders, and a breakdown of morale. Trotsky's orders were delayed, lost, or simply disobeyed. Finally, Lenin ordered Stalin to Moscow, and sent an emissary to see that the order was promptly obeyed. Trotsky, then, went to the southern front, established harmony and returned to present his report to the Sixth Soviet Congress. He went into the matter of Tsarytsin thoroughly, although he refrained from mentioning Stalin by name—which was unnecessary, as everyone present knew the situation quite well. Stalin sat stolidly and said nothing. The fact of the matter was that even before leaving for Tsarytsin, Stalin had been long nurturing a smoldering jealousy of Trotsky. Content to play the role of organizing strikes and riots during the early stages of the Revolution, now that power had been secured, Trotsky had risen to dazzling revolutionary heights as the leader of the Red Army during the two years of the civil war, while Stalin had been virtually passed over and ignored. When he was sent to Tsarytsin to confer with Voroshilov he managed to persuade the latter to ignore the orders received from Trotsky, and thus the enmity between the two men broke into the open for the first time.

The strain of the civil war, or the continuing Revolution, whichever you please, was too much for Lenin's health. His first illness came in May, 1922, but he was almost recovered by the following October. A second stroke seized him in December, 1922. As he lay stricken during the early part of 1923, he realized something of the struggle for power that was beginning to develop between Trotsky and Stalin. The third stroke came on March 9, 1923, but he had commenced to convalesce by

October of that year. Lenin must have pondered much during his illness. At last the years of revolution were over and there now remained the gigantic task of building up the economic might of the country, of educating the masses and providing modern facilities.

His dreams had been realized, and his sacrifices, the loyalties of his old comrades, the carefully planned strategy had all come together to achieve success. Lenin must surely have foreseen the inevitable result of the incipient rivalry between Trotsky and Stalin—he must have realized that all of his work would go for nothing if selfish men were to sacrifice an entire people, the destiny of a nation, on the altar of personal ambition. Such melancholy reflections undoubtedly contributed to Lenin's death. He expected to recover fully and to take no chances with anyone and handle the matter personally. In November of 1923, he had left his bed and partially regained his old vigor. On January 21, 1924, he died of cerebral hemorrhage.

THE RISE OF STALIN

In 1922, Stalin had been elected General Secretary of the Communist Party. Theretofore this position was one of a mere chief clerk, but under Stalin it became a stepping stone to the securing of absolute personal power. Taking advantage of Lenin's illness and Trotsky's preoccupation with other matters, Stalin began his old trick of manipulating subordinate men around the political chessboard in order to solidify his own strength and weaken that of Trotsky and Lenin. In this connection it is important to know that a few years before Lenin's death, he dictated a message that was to be read to a Communist Party caucus, and which, had it come two or three years earlier, might have changed the entire history of the world.

During the spring of 1922, when Lenin was still seriously ill, he became aware of the mounting jealousy between Stalin and Trotsky for personal power, and convinced of the responsibility which Stalin bore for the entire controversy. He therefore dictated a memorandum which was to be presented to the forthcoming Communist Party Congress, to meet in December of that year. If the memorandum had ever been presented to the Congress and acted upon, or had been written a year or so earlier, it might have produced an effect that would have altered the course of world history, for this is what Lenin dictated:

"I think that the fundamental factor in the matter of stability—from this point of view—is such members of the Central Committee as Stalin and Trotsky. The relation between them constituted, in my opinion, a big half of the danger of that split, which might be avoided and the avoidance of which might be promoted, in my opinion, by raising the number of members of the Central Committee to 50 or 100.

"Comrade Stalin having become the General Secretary, has concentrated an enormous amount of power in his hands; and I am not sure that he always knows how to use that power with sufficient caution. On the other hand Comrade Trotsky, as was proved by his struggle against the Central Committee in connection with the People's Commissariat of Ways and Communications, is distinguished not only by his exceptional abilities, personally he is, to be sure, the most able man in the present Central Committee; but also by his too far-reaching self-confidence and a disposition to be too much attracted by the purely administrative side of affairs.

"These two qualities of the two most able leaders of the present Central Committee might, quite innocently, lead to a split; if our party does not take measures to prevent it, a split might arise unexpectedly."

A few days later Lenin added:

"Stalin is too rude, and this fault, entirely supportable between us Communists, is entirely unsupportable in the office of General Secretary. Therefore, I propose to the comrades that they find some way to remove Stalin from that position and appoint to it another man in all respects different from Stalin only in superiority— namely, more patient, *more loyal* (committee's italics), more polite and more attentive to comrades, less capricious. The circumstances may seem an insignificant trifle, but I think that from the point of view of preventing a split and from the point of view of the relation between Stalin and Trotsky, which I discussed above, it is not a trifle, or it is such a trifle as may require a decisive significance."

In this clear-cut declaration there is found additional ground for the conclusion that the rivalry between Stalin and Trotsky was purely personal—certainly not engendered at that time through any suspicion that Trotsky was guilty of the slightest counter-revolutionary activity. He was an obstacle in Stalin's path to power; a power that was mounting at an alarming pace, now aided immeasurably by the secret police whose chief had cooperated in the matter of assisting Stalin in ousting many of his political enemies.

If Lenin had regained sufficient strength to attend the Congress and if he had pressed his charges against Stalin, he undoubtedly would have left that assemblage with the political scalp of the ambitious General Secretary dangling from his belt; and in that case, the history of the Soviet Union might have been quite different. But Lenin's condition became worse instead of better, and the matter of Stalin's disposition was never brought to a head at the Congress. Trotsky, himself, has stated that papers signifying the intention to deal with Stalin were delivered by three of Lenin's secretaries on March 7, 1923. The confidential note, together with its supplement, was not presented at the Congress, however, and was made known only after Lenin's death.

There has been a considerable diversity of opinion concerning this note. If Lenin wrote it, and if he realized that he might not be able to attend the Congress personally, why, then, didn't he take every precaution to have it presented? Lenin thought too much of the Party, too much of the plans he had fought for, to take any risks that the split which he saw so clearly developing should be permitted to develop further. He had laid his plans. Why, then, did he not carry them through? According to Boris Souvarine, an acknowledged authority on the subject, Lenin left no specific instructions either with his wife or his secretaries, and they, therefore, simply did nothing. He had not handed the note to anyone else, and so it remained among his papers until after his death.

Trotsky hesitated to use the information because of Lenin's condition, and that hesitation was fatal to his cause. Stalin went calmly ahead with his plans, and formed an alliance with two men with whom he was to remove the last vestige of opposition to his rise to absolute power—a power far stronger than Lenin ever wished for himself or would have tolerated in others. These two men were, with Stalin, to form the second of the Communist Triumvirates. The first had been composed of Lenin, Trotsky and Stalin—named in the order of their importance. The second triumvirate was formed by Stalin, Kamenev and Zinoviev.

The Party Congress met on schedule, and was chiefly concerned with economic problems. Thereafter, Stalin moved all of Trotsky's most loyal supporters to widely separated posts throughout the country and concentrated his own power. By the middle of 1923, the Party machinery was controlled by the Central Committee and the Soviet secret police, and both of these organizations were controlled by Stalin. By October, the bureaucratic rift had become so wide that Party activity was stifled and there was a reaction among the workers that was manifest in sporadic strikes.

Trotsky sent a letter of criticism to the Central Committee protesting the centralization of authority and the employment of incompetent men merely because of their loyalty to the prevailing clique. The Central Committee replied by accusing Trotsky of seeking to establish a military and economic dictatorship for his own selfish purposes and drew attention to his earlier disagreements with Lenin. There had been considerable disagreement between Stalin and Lenin, too, and Trotsky dryly called attention to this fact in a second letter which was, of course, ignored.

Trotsky, who had suffered an illness that prevented his taking an active part in the mobilizing of his own political strength, realized that he must move rapidly in order to make up for his past inaction. Early in December, he dispatched a letter in which he sharply called attention to the new tactic of rule by force and terror through use of the secret police. The furor caused by this letter indicated to the bureaucrats that they must act before Trotsky had time to organize a formidable opposition. They decided upon the only effective course open to them—a vicious personal campaign of slander and abuse against Trotsky. Stalin fired the opening gun with an article in *Pravda* on December 15, 1923:

> "As is apparent from his letter, Comrade Trotsky counts himself as one of the Bolshevik old guard, declaring his readiness to share in the responsibilities arising from this fact, if charges of later heresies are brought against the old Bolsheviks. In expressing his willingness for self sacrifice, Comrade Trotsky undoubtedly displays nobility of sentiment. Agreed. But I must undertake the defense of Trotsky against himself, for reasons which will be readily understood; he cannot and should not hold himself responsible for any later heresies of the original group of old Bolsheviks. His offer of sacrifice is no doubt a very noble thing, but do the old Bolsheviks need it? I do not think so."

With these sarcastic remarks, the acknowledged leader of the bureaucrats gave the signal for a personal attack against Trotsky with no holds barred. The *Pravda* article naturally aroused widespread resentment among the masses. Trotsky was still convalescing and unable to do more than rely on his prestige, which was considerable. It was evident from the reaction to the article of December 15th that the time was not yet ripe for an all-out frontal attack against him, so the bureaucrats decided to conciliate the masses while they assiduously whittled away at Trotsky's underpinning from behind the scenes. More articles assured the people of willingness to cooperate with the popular leader, while the Stalin appointees in strategic places whispered rumors, insinuations and subtle propaganda designed to deify Stalin and undermine Trotsky.

By January, 1924, sufficient foundation had been established to enable Stalin to present to the political bureau a list of the six fundamental errors committed by Trotsky. They were: (1) differentiating between the Communist Party and the bureaucratic or machine element, thus driving a wedge in the Party harmony; (2) creating a basic antagonism between the younger Party members and the Bolsheviks; (3) publication of critical remarks concerning the current regime and calling for a new course of organization; (4) adopting an ambiguous position; (5) demanding freedom of organization within the Party and, (6) describing the anti-Communists as the most accurate analysts of the needs of the people.

In June, 1924, a Communist World Congress was held in Moscow under the direction of Zinoviev, and his agents diligently spread the anti-Trotsky propaganda among the Communist delegates from foreign countries. Thenceforth the tempo of the hate campaign was accelerated until its effect was felt in every country where a Communist organization had been planted. Throughout the Soviet Union anyone who expressed pro-Trotsky sentiments was immediately branded as a traitor, a counter-revolutionary and a Party outcast. Gradually the term "Trotskyite" came to carry all the evil significance of a political curse—and was freely applied to anyone who engaged in activities or expressed opinions displeasing to the new triumvirate—which actually meant Stalin.

Communists everywhere were instructed to hate Trotsky with all the venom at their command, and the power of the Kremlin over the far-flung foreign sections of the Party was demonstrated in a crusade of vilification that swept through the Communist world. Despite the vigor of the campaign, however, it was not a simple matter to change the opinions of the older leaders and the younger intellectuals; they obeyed through fear and habit—but many of them felt a revulsion of conscience in doing so. Thus it was that Stalin found it necessary, in fact unavoidable, to offset this allegiance by systematically distorting, denying, and ridiculing or ignoring Trotsky's military leadership, his devotion to the Revolution, his loyalty to Lenin and his incalculably valuable services during the civil war. His followers and his family were threatened and intimidated by the secret police, and running along with the historical distortions and inventions concerning Trotsky was a crusade of equal intensity to build up Stalin's prestige out of the same artificial materials.

In October, 1924, Trotsky published a two-volume work in which he said some uncomplimentary things about the triumvirate. This did little more than provoke a new tirade of abuse which churned through the columns of *Pravda* and erupted from the army of speakers who warned the people that Trotsky had at last revealed himself openly as the arch-enemy of Leninism and the hypocritical foe of the dead leader he once professed to revere. Once again Trotsky was manipulated into the position of opposing the existing regime, which was carrying on the Lenin tradition and consequently represented everything good, whereas, Trotsky, by the simple act of opposing the new government, represented everything evil. Some writers have contended that Trotsky was weak in failing to carry his fight directly to the people and thus launch an effective opposition before it was too late. It would appear, however, that with Stalin and his henchmen in control of the press, the radio, the schools, the secret police and an army of spies, that such an effort would have been utterly fruitless.

Thus the year 1924 witnessed profound changes in the Communist Party of the Soviet Union. Lenin died, and since he was the one man who had perfected the strategy for the Revolution of 1917, had welded the Party together through the sheer force of his ability, had subordinated his own interests to those of the people, and had, indeed, been the only general among a welter of lesser leaders, his loss plunged the Party into understandable chaos. The triumvirate had seized all power. Trotsky had been definitely eliminated as a possible successor to Lenin, the country was reeling under the incompetence of its new officials, and dissension was growing among the top-flight leadership.

As Stalin went ruthlessly ahead to absolute power, Zinoviev and Kamenev, the two junior members of the firm, had cause to wonder about their own future in the Party. They, therefore, launched a move of increased vituperation against Trotsky, and at the same time a *sub-rosa* move to depose Stalin from the office of General Secretary and make him Commissar of War. But their own offices were now swarming with Stalinite spies and their activities were easily discovered and crushed. Zinoviev tendered his resignation, which was rejected. Too late the two disgruntled members of the second triumvirate discovered with amazement and horror that while they were helping Stalin undermine the political power of Trotsky, he was doing precisely the same thing to them.

The tremendous concentration of power which yesterday had belonged to the triumvirate was now found vested firmly in the office of the General Secretary, Josef Stalin. He had employed the old technique in quietly scattering the supporters of Zinoviev and Kamenev throughout the country and replacing them with men of his own choice, thereby isolating his two co-conspirators.

Matters speedily came to a showdown when Kamenev, realizing the futility of trying to cope with Stalin's machine, arose in a Party Congress and threw down the gauntlet by stating:

> "We cannot consider normal, and think harmful to the Party, a situation in which the secretariat unites policy and organization, and, in fact, predetermines policy. I have become convinced that Comrade Stalin cannot play the part of coordinator of the Bolshevik general staff."

These words, uttered in 1925, threw the session into immediate uproar and confusion. The Stalin majority shouted their disapproval, and it only remained to deliver the political *coup de grace,* which Stalin proceeded to do as only he could, with the result that after the 1925 Congress his power was more firmly established than ever.

Eclipse of Trotsky

In 1927, Trotsky and Zinoviev were expelled from the Central Committee on charges of counter-revolutionary activities presented by the chief of Stalin's secret police. In November of the same year, it was proposed that both Zinoviev and Kamenev be expelled from the Communist Party. One must realize that these two men had come up through all of the vicissitudes of the Revolution. They were members of the Bolshevik old guard. They had fought shoulder to shoulder with Lenin, and were literally part and parcel of the revolutionary movement from its very inception; it was their very life. Now, through an abrupt decree, they were to be cast loose from all these things, isolated and set intellectually adrift—disgraced by the Party they helped create and the revolutionary movement they helped to win. Faced with this threat of expulsion, they weakened and broke. They confessed to a variety of imaginary charges and thereby became Stalin's tools forever. With their ''confessions'' tucked securely away in the secret archives, there was no need for further worry about these two former members of the second triumvirate; they might still prove useful.

In January, 1928, it was announced that Trotsky and a group of his followers had been ordered exiled from Moscow, but Zinoviev and Kamenev were not among them. On the contrary, they were quick to heap abuses on their former comrades, and were therefore permitted— at least for the time being—to retain their status as Party members in more or less good standing. So disgusted was Krupskaya, Lenin's widow, with this ruthlessness in purging the old Bolsheviks that she was prompted to declare, in effect, that if Lenin were then alive he would undoubtedly be languishing in some remote Stalinist prison as a political traitor to the regime.

Finally, Trotsky was ordered from Russia and went to Turkey under a secret police escort. There were four children in his family, two boys and two girls. His daughter, Nina, was suffering from tuberculosis, too ill to be moved from Moscow, so her father was compelled to leave her behind. A few months later she died for lack of medical attention. Several years later, his daughter, Zinaida, committed suicide when Stalin forbade her to enter the Soviet Union and see her husband and child. Sergei, one of the sons, was a serious scientific student who had taken no part in any political activity. He was arrested and whisked away to a secret police prison, and when his father refused to cease his journalistic attacks on Stalin in return for assurances that his son's life would be spared, the boy was never heard from again. Sedov Trotsky, the other son, was most active against the Stalin regime from a Paris headquarters, where he had gathered together a little group of followers. He died of a mysterious malady in a Paris hospital, the suspicion being that he was poisoned. Within a few weeks after his death, the headless body of his successor, August Klement, was found floating in the Seine.

Thus all of the Trotsky children were hounded to death. Only the father and his faithful wife, Nathalia, were left. The parents wandered from one country in Europe to another, and each time they were politely but firmly requested to leave. There had been more pressure from the Kremlin, and European nations were not anxious to offend the new Communist government. By 1937, Trotsky had tried in vain to find a place of permanent refuge in France, Holland, Italy, Spain and the

Scandinavian countries. When he wearily settled down in Turkey once more, his home and many of his records were burned.

Then came word that Diego Rivera, the Mexican artist, had persuaded the government of his country to offer a place of domicile and political refuge to the man who had been ordered away from the country he once helped to rule. Trotsky had seen his old comrades liquidated in the early purges, but did not realize that beginning in 1937 there was to come the bloodiest upheaval of all, in which the last vestiges of the Bolshevik old guard would disappear. In January, 1937, Trotsky and his wife sailed for Mexico, where he lived with Rivera for two years at his home in Mexico City. He then moved to the suburb of Coyoacan and established himself in a 20-room house surrounded by a high wall—prompted partly by the increasing petty quarrels with the temperamental Rivera, but more probably through apprehension of attack because of the new fury of the purges of 1937-1938.

Machine guns were placed at strategic points about the wall. A squad of Mexican soldiers was on guard 24 hours a day, and Trotsky was attended by four secretary-bodyguards. The premises occupied an entire block and were considered impregnable even against Stalin's resourceful secret police. Here Trotsky moved his large files of documents and notes and busied himself with taking up his facile pen in the anti-Stalin crusade to which he had dedicated his life.

Meanwhile, a mysterious international figure had arrived in Paris by the name of Jacques van den Drescht, who represented himself as being a wealthy Belgian radical with sympathies for the Trotsky faction and bitter hatred toward Stalin. He occupied himself with studies at the Sorbonne and gradually succeeded in insinuating himself in the pro-Trotsky organization. Through liberal contributions to the cause and constant participation in its activities, he managed to divert all suspicion. In 1938, Sylvia Angeloff, a New York social worker, came to Paris on a visit. Van den Drescht met her through some of his friends, having learned that she was intimately acquainted with Trotsky. In a short time she fell in love with this suave and sympathetic "Belgian," and he followed her to New York the following year.

As the courtship progressed, van den Drescht expressed his burning desire to meet the man for whom he professed such profound admiration, and late in 1939 the two arrived at Mexico City. Thus through the medium of the innocent Sylvia Angeloff, Trotsky was introduced to his assassin.

Van den Drescht was well-educated, an able actor, and soon wormed his way into Trotsky's confidence. He was a frequent visitor at the Coyoacan residence and was admitted without question. He played his part so well, indeed, and exhibited such eagerness to assume the anti-Stalin campaign, that his unsuspecting fiancee was content to return to New York while he remained in Mexico City to be near Trotsky and study under his guidance.

Early on the morning of May 24, 1940, the sleepy Mexican guards were awaiting their relief, and observed a group of men approaching the guardhouse clad in the uniform of Mexican soldiers. They opened the door of the guardhouse and were immediately faced with leveled guns and forced to submit to bonds and gags. The intruders then made their way to the main entrance and it has been said that they used van den

Drescht's name in gaining admittance. At any rate, they succeeded in entering the house, and riddled Trotsky's study and bedroom with machine-gun bullets. The guards on duty in the house returned the fire, but the intruders escaped, taking with them Robert Harte, one of Trotsky's secretaries. His body was found a month later.

Trotsky and his wife escaped with no more serious injuries than cuts from splintered glass that was shattered by the gunfire. An attempt was made to burn the house with incendiary bombs, but the blaze was quickly extinguished. Preparations were immediately made to render the premises attack-proof. The guards were redoubled. Automatic alarms and steel doors were installed, and added precautions were taken against the admission of strangers.

On August 20, 1940, Jacques van den Drescht, who had apparently returned to the United States when the trouble occurred, again appeared in Mexico City, this time traveling with a Canadian passport under the name of Frank Jacson. He proceeded shortly to Coyoacan and gained admittance to the Trotsky residence without difficulty. He and Trotsky went into the latter's study, as had been their custom. The visitor handed his victim a manuscript to inspect, and as Trotsky leaned over his desk to examine it, was struck on the head with the steel ax of an alpenstock, which van den Drescht had concealed under his overcoat. Trotsky did not immediately lose consciousness, but grappled with his assailant, who struggled to draw a revolver and finish the execution. The commotion attracted guards who quickly subdued the assassin and tried to assist Trotsky, but it was too late. He lingered for two days then died in a hospital in Mexico City.

Jacques van den Drescht was arrested and charged with the crime of murder. He was duly convicted and sentenced to life imprisonment, which was the maximum penalty under Mexican law. He steadfastly refused to give any explanation for his actions which made the slightest sense; refused to admit that he had been working with anyone else; refused to discuss his birth, his activities, or anything pertaining to the case. He only uttered one sentence that may have been—probably was—true. As he fought savagely with his captors while the bleeding Trotsky lay at his feet, and when he was being beaten into submission and was keyed up to a pitch where he could well have uttered an involuntary truth, he muttered: "They imprisoned my mother!" There has never been any explanation given for this statement, but it will bear analysis. If, as all who have investigated the case are agreed, the assassin was an agent of the Russian secret police, he undoubtedly had relatives in Russia. By holding his mother as a hostage, the secret police could guarantee that her son would carry out his assignment as Trotsky's executioner.

The murderer is confined in Mexico City in what would correspond to a small court—occupying a suite complete with bedroom, bathroom, and a machine shop where he pursues his hobby of woodwork. He is provided with plenty of tools, plenty of clothes, his food is brought to him from nearby restaurants, and some of his dressing gowns have been observed to bear the label "Brooks Brothers, New York." He is, however, amply guarded. It is the habit of the Soviet secret police to seal the lips of persons possessing such damning information in a very grim but effective manner. So far as is known, the prisoner has made no application for executive clemency and it may be that he prefers his not too onerous but restrained existence in prison to no existence at all.

The Moscow Purges

After Trotsky's exile to Turkey in 1928, Stalin had shrewdly played one dissident clique against another. He flattered some, threatened others, spied on all. As each new official rose to a position of power, he was liquidated; as each new top functionary of the secret police carried out Stalin's intrigues for these liquidations, he, too, was liquidated and thereby silenced. Trotsky was not the only obstacle in Stalin's path to power—he was the most important one because he was Lenin's heir-apparent, and by far the most capable man in the Communist heirarchy. His exile had removed him from direct contact with the people, but he still waged the battle with his pen.

During the latter part of 1929, Stalin moved to eliminate the influence of religion. Marx had provided the excuse by stating that religion was the opiate of the people, so the Soviet secret police raided the places of worship, destroyed the sacred books, the relics, the icons, took over the monasteries and the parochial schools and scattered the leaders of the church like leaves before the wind.

In 1930, the program of production by compulsion was stepped up to such a degree that despite the lessons of the purges, there was bitter resentment from the workers. Stalin countered by arresting hundreds of thousands who expressed the slightest opposition to this unprecedented move. Men were told where to go and what they were to do, and there they remained and there they worked at the assigned tasks until they were ordered elsewhere. The collective farms were hated as concentration camps, and in fact, there was no discernible difference. Not even under the Czars had there been such bondage. No one dared ask what had become of the Marxian theory of rule by the workers and of Lenin's fight to establish a dictatorship of the proletariat. Such inquiries were now deemed counter-revolutionary tactics to be dealt with by the dreaded secret police. Lenin had been completely sincere in his efforts to emancipate the people from the Czarist regime. In the chaos that followed the revolution, he had soon realized that the masses were too illiterate, too accustomed to years of servitude to govern themselves, and he, therefore, resorted to discipline as a practical necessity.

All opposition to the program of production through compulsion was thus swept aside. In 1931 and 1932, the program was further intensified. Hundreds of bureaus and sub-bureaus were created to administer the project, and since Stalin would permit no independent thought or action in his officials, they were all men of mediocre ability. By the end of 1932 there was widespread famine and suffering. As conditions rapidly became worse the country was flooded with weasel promises and false statistics. The people were told through the controlled press that they were accomplishing miracles of production. They were quite aware of the fact that they were, nevertheless, starving.

Another purge had been launched in 1934, 10 years after the death of Lenin, and was touched off by the assassination of one Sergei Kirov, who was typical of the thousands of fawning, servile Stalin sycophants.

After the fall of Zinoviev from favor, Kirov took over as President of the Leningrad Soviet, where he proved both obedient to Stalin and incapable as an administrator. He was, nevertheless, Stalin's prime favorite, and his murder on December 1, 1934, provoked a furious scourge of arrests and mass executions—not so much to avenge the death of Kirov, the individual, as to terrorize those who presumed to display opposition to the Stalin bureaucracy. In a series of purges, all stemming from this affair, Stalin continued to wreak his vengeance against the real or imagined enemies of his regime. Over and over the dead Kirov was verbally exhumed so more candidates for liquidation could be accused of his murder. Truly, it seemed that Kirov was of more value to his master dead than alive.

In 1935, the people were promised a new constitution, complete with such modern democratic equipment as freedom of speech, freedom of the press, freedom of religious worship, right of assemblage and—sanctity of the person. This constitution was adopted in 1936, but it provided that there could only be one political party, the Communist Party, which, at that time, comprised about 3,000,000 members out of a total population of some 170,000,000 people. Party members held all key governmental positions. They conducted the elections. They operated the press and the systems of communication and transportation. They operated the industrial machinery of the nation. They were banded together in a tightly knit, perfectly disciplined body which functioned through countless bureaus under the suspicious scrutiny of the ever-present secret police. At the head of both the Communist Party and the secret police stood Josef Stalin.

Under such a system the democratic freedoms set forth in the new constitution meant nothing. The sanctity of the person was, in fact, assured, but only on condition that the person concerned was extremely careful to express no criticism of the dictatorship, that he obey all orders from above, that he heed the advice of the Communist officials, and that he associate with the proper people. Otherwise, he would be deemed guilty of counter-revolutionary activities, would not be entitled to any sanctity of the person, and would suffer arrest, imprisonment, trial and execution, all at the hands of the secret police.

This, then, is the story for Stalin's struggle for power. He had succeeded in undermining Trotsky, and finally of driving him from Russia. He then went about removing the last remaining obstacles, first the church, then the dissident scattered groups, and then he gave the people a new constitution that purported to secure their democratic freedom, but which, in reality, only served to ensure the perpetual dictatorship of the Communist Party minority with Stalin in supreme control.

In the light of what has already been said, we are now able to discern in Stalin two salient characteristics: an unquenchable thirst for power and a deep sense of his own inferiority. The intellectual strength of Lenin and Trotsky had aroused his jealousy. He, too, wanted to be prominent, to be revered and honored and showered with adulation. His role throughout the revolution, even during the civil war, had been one of comparative mediocrity. Lenin and Trotsky were immensely popular in Russia and revered by Marxist circles in foreign countries. Stalin yearned for the same prominence. What he could never have obtained through his own ability, he took through force. By his actions he demonstrated that he would sacrifice his old comrades, the ideals of Lenin, or anything else that stood between him and his burning ambition for absolute personal power. Like all men of small caliber, he was compelled to rule through fear; to build a huge force of secret police and informers that would always be subservient to his slightest wish. With supreme disregard for fact, he changed the official records to suit himself, magnifying his own role in the revolution and minimizing the activities of everyone else. He was incapable of making history, so he rearranged it after it had been made by others. Incapable of competing on equal terms with men like Trotsky, Zinoviev, Kamenev, and Bukharin, he simply liquidated them. Fearful that the people would not support his dictatorial reign, he erected a vast and intricate bureaucracy and kept it in line through a secret police and periodic blood purges. He took advantage of every opportunity—even his own birthday—to advertise himself. Through the channels of information which he controlled, he systematically sought to create a myth about himself—his omniscience, his intellect, his benevolent leadership, his brilliant grasp of Marxist theory. These are not the actions of a truly great man, who has neither the need nor the time for such artificial stratagems. They are the actions of a little man and a ruthless man, who seeks to cover up his deficiencies and his fears.

Since the foregoing was written Stalin died on March 5, 1953. He had been in complete command of the Soviet Union and the international Communist movement for 28 years. Lenin had occupied a similar position and when he died there was a scramble for power with Stalin emerging the victor. After Stalin's death, will there be another such struggle between Malenkov, Beria and Molotov? Thousands of writers have turned out tons of newsprint on the subject, expressing a wide variety of conclusions.

No dictator has ever survived unless he controlled a system of secret police. The Roman Caesars had their Praetorian Guards, Hitler had his Gestapo, Mussolini had his Blackshirts, and Stalin had the Soviet secret police. Any student of Russian revolutionary history knows that Stalin used this instrument of terror to secure himself in power. He shrewdly scattered his own agents throughout its structure and received reports of the slightest criticism of his regime. Every party bureaucrat lived in a state of constant fear, a fear that Stalin deliberately created by his bloody purges that exterminated thousands of the most highly-placed government officials.

Lavrentri Beria is now the chief of the Soviet secret police. He is also in charge of all atomic research in the U. S. S. R., and we may be certain that no foreign espionage agents have access to any information concerning the status of Russia's atomic weapons.

Malenkov is, of course, perfectly aware of the technique Stalin used in ruling with the assistance of the secret police. He served as Stalin's personal secretary and then rose to the post of Secretary of the Russian Communist Party—Stalin's old job. Knowing these things, it was easy to predict that Malenkov would succeed Stalin, as he was obviously being groomed for that purpose.

But there are two other members of this triumvirate, Beria and Molotov. The latter was referred to by Lenin as the best file clerk in the Soviet Union. The British diplomatic corps refer to him as Aunt Molly. He is dour, modest, loyal and hard-working, but he lacks the drive, the colour and the strength of personality that are possessed in some degree by the other two.

Beria looks more like a school teacher or an accountant than chief of the dread secret police, but underneath this disarming facade he is a crafty, tough, ruthless and extremely efficient man. He, too, is well acquainted with the secret of Stalin's power. He must fully appreciate the fact that even his own life was in constant peril so long as Stalin lived—for, as we have seen, no one knew how many of Stalin's agents were sifted through the secret police system.

If Stalin picked Malenkov as his successor, we may assume that the latter also took over Stalin's elaborate system of informers and spies. But Stalin was the very personification of ruthlessness and implacable vengeance. His bull neck, coarse mustache, and pock-marked face; his thick, wiry hair and the force of his animal magnetism made him the symbol of quick and terrible punishment for all of his real or imaginary enemies. In addition he was literally deified through the Party's propaganda machinery until his statues and his pictures and his name were constantly before the Russian people in every city and hamlet, office and factory, school and university, railway station and airport from one end of the country to the other. One Party bureaucrat risked his life by declaring that if some cultural society wanted to erect a monument to the memory of Pushkin, the Russian literary genius, it would probably turn out to be a huge statue of Stalin holding a small volume of Pushkin's verses. There was more truth than poetry in this facetious remark.

Malenkov looks tough; but his roly-poly figure gives him the appearance of a chubby, petulant baby. Allegiance to Stalin is one thing. Allegiance to Malenkov may turn out to be something quite different. Gradually the pictures of Stalin will be replaced with those of his successor. Gradually Stalin will be criticized in *Pravda* and *Izvestia*—in fact, some timid criticism of Stalin's one-man regime has already appeared in these papers. Gradually, as Malenkov cautiously feels his way, the few old Bolsheviks whom Stalin allowed to escape the purges, will quietly vanish from the scene. Men like Molotov, Vyshinsky, Kaganovitch, Voroshilov, and Bulganin will be replaced by younger men who will be handpicked by Malenkov. To accomplish this purpose the new ruler needs time. He must step up the peace propaganda and lull the western democracies—especially the United States—into a false sense of security. He must hold the allegiance of the Balkan satellites and of the Chinese Communists. He must maintain a firm grip on the world Communist movement and the Soviet Union's gigantic espionage network. And to accomplish these objectives, Malenkov must have the cooperation of the Soviet secret police. This would seem to point up a conflict between Malenkov and Beria. It may not come for some time, but as matters now stand it appears inevitable.

Lenin sought to rule the Soviet Union and the world Communist movement with two others, Trotsky and Stalin. This was the first Troika, and the effort resulted in simply another Czar: Lenin. Stalin made a gesture toward ruling with the help of two others, Zinoviev and Kamenev. This was the second Troika, and the gesture simply resulted in a second red Czar: Stalin. Malenkov seeks to rule with the help of two others, Molotov and Beria. This is the third Troika.

With the death of Stalin and Malenkov established as his successor, the Soviet people could appropriately utter the traditional remark: The king is dead, long live the king! Foreign observers are now appropriately asking: How long?

THE COMINTERN—STAFF FOR
WORLD REVOLUTION

There were three so-called "Internationals," or associations. The first was the International Association of Workingmen, the Communist group organized by Marx and Engels in 1864, and which has already been mentioned in the section which deals with the life of Karl Marx. The second was the Socialist International, organized in 1889. The third is commonly known as the Third International or Comintern, and was formed under the leadership of Lenin in March, 1919. The followers of Karl Marx believed, as he did, that the effort to emancipate the working classes of the world must be an international undertaking. The very essence of Communism has always been international in character; a world movement for the "toiling peoples" of the whole earth. It gave promise of a new social order, and it was with these principles in mind that the Comintern was established. The following telegram was sent to Communist groups in various countries inviting them to send representatives:

"On January 24, 1919, eight Communist Parties and organizations headed by the Communist Party in Russia, addressed to all revolutionary proletarian organizations standing on the point of view of the proletarian dictatorship in the form of Soviet power, a platform for a new International, and urged them to take part in an international congress which was to adopt the title of The First Congress of the Communist International."

In August, 1920, a second congress was held in Moscow and the governing machinery of the new International, or Comintern, was set up. The theses and statutes adopted at this session included the following:

"The aim of the Communist International is to organize armed struggles for the overthrow of the international bourgeoisie and the establishment of an International Soviet Republics, a transition to the complete abolition of the capitalistic state. The Communist International considers the dictatorship of the proletariat an essential means for the liberation of humanity from the horrors of capitalism and regards the soviet form of government as the historic necessary form of this dictatorship. * * * The task of the Communist International is to emancipate the workers of the entire world."

Lenin had worked out 21 conditions on which the various Communist Parties in foreign countries might gain admission as sections of the Comintern, obviously designed to insure perpetual control of the entire movement by revolutionary Communist leaders. The conditions were as follows:

"1. All publications of every party must be controlled by the Comintern through its central committee.
2. All socialists who held positions in labor unions must be replaced by Communists.

3. Each member party must maintain a secret, underground organization in addition to that portion of the organization which normally conducts public and semipublic activities.
4. Each member party must strive to disorganize and weaken the armed forces of the country in which it exists.
5. Each member party must work to infiltrate and organize the peasants and underprivileged workers according to Marx's theory.
6. Each member must fight against patriots and pacifists in the labor movement.
7. Each member party must eliminate conservative elements from labor and socialist groups.
8. Each member party must assist in revolutionary activities in the colonies of the country in which it exists.
9. Each member party must establish reliable members to work within the structure of the trade union movement in order that non-Communist labor leaders may be replaced with party members.
10. All member parties must pledge exclusive allegiance to the Red Trade Union International.
11. The governing machinery of all member parties must be subordinated to their respective central committees.
12. Each member party must submit to iron discipline, and be bound by the absolute power of the central committee.
13. Each member party must submit to periodic purges of its personnel.
14. Each member party must support all of the Soviet Republics of the U.S.S.R.
15. Each member party must submit its activities to the executitve committee of the Comintern for approval.
16. The decisions of each member party may at any time be overruled by the executive committee of the Comintern.
17. Each member party must be officially known as a Communist Party.
18. Each member party must submit all of its important documents to the executive committee of the Comintern for approval.''

Conditions 19, 20 and 21 described the procedure by which the various member parties should subscribe to and adopt the foregoing requirements and conditions for admission to membership.

On paper the Comintern was to be governed by world congresses which would meet from time to time in the Soviet Union, and at which the delegates from the various sections would establish the program and elect members of the executive committee, which had absolute power in the intervals between the meetings of these congresses. Actually, there was always a majority of Russian Communists on the executive committee and always the elected leaders of the Comintern have been Russian Communists: Zinoviev, Bukharin, Manuilsky, and Dimitrov.

The Third Congress met from June 22 to July 12, 1921, and was chiefly concerned with the selection of leaders for the new organization.

The Fourth Congress met from November 5 to December 5, 1922, and was the last attended by Lenin. One of the more important basic theses adopted at this congress was:

"The Fourth World Congress reminds the proletariats of all countries that the proletarian revolution can never be completely victorious within one country, but that it must win the victory internationally, as the world revolution."

The Fifth Congress met from June 17 to July 2, 1924, and approved a new "United Front" theory, which simply meant that henceforth the various Communist parties would cease holding themselves aloof from all liberal non-Communist organizations, but should penetrate them, cooperate with them, subvert them, and seek to convert them to the Communist ideology or turn them to advantage for the Communist movement. A thesis adopted at this congress provided that member parties should:

"* * * Establish firmer contact with the masses in order to link up the Communist parties of the west with the trade unions."

During this era of the "United Front" the underlying theme was that the labor movements in all countries should be penetrated and eventually controlled from the top. Once this control was achieved—although it might require a long time—the mass strike could be used as a weapon to prevent the capitalists from resisting the constant demands of the workers. In this manner class antagonism could be intensified until all segments of the working mass were convinced that every capitalist was a class enemy and that such struggles were inevitable under the capitalist form of government, which should be abolished at once. Lenin was well aware of the fact that it would be impossible for a minority of Communists in countries like Great Britain, France and the United States to directly overthrow those governments by force. He had sowed the seed of dissatisfaction among the Russian workers and for years paved the way for revolution by fomenting a series of mass strikes that paralyzed the industrial life of Russia. He knew that if the employees of the shipyards, munition plants, railroads and other essential utilities; communication workers, agricultural laborers and others could all be caused to strike simultaneously, it would be a tremendous step forward for the revolutionary cause. It might be difficult to convert the armed forces of such nations to Communism, but soldiers have to eat. Armed forces must have the ammunition, shoes, uniforms, guns, blankets, medicines, communications facilities and transportation which must, in turn, be provided by workers. If Party members could be insinuated into top-control positions throughout the key labor organizations of the capitalist countries, they could determine the strike strategy—and there would be no need to propagandize the entire rank and file membership. That system was not original with Lenin, it was the invention of Karl Marx, as has already been seen, and it had been used with success in the Russian Revolution—it should likewise work in other countries. Accordingly, the delegates to the Fifth Congress of the Comintern were instructed to conduct:

"* * * Painstaking day to day work in a revolutionary manner among the masses, and especially in the trade unions, in the factories, among the unemployed, among agricultural laborers * * * ."

Thousands of copies of Lenin's book, *Left Wing Communism,* were circulated in the United States and other countries, with particular emphasis placed on his keynote advice:

"* * * To resort to all sorts of devices, maneuvers and illegal methods, evasion and subterfuge, in order to penetrate into the trade unions, to remain in them, and to carry on Communist work in them at all costs."

In line with this new mandate the American Communist Party issued pamphlets of its own, instructing its members to:

"Practice trickery, to employ cunning, and to resort to illegal methods—to sometimes even overlook and conceal the truth * * * in order to penetrate the trade unions."

The Sixth World Congress, July 18 to September 1, 1928, came at the height of the purge trials. The delegates must have been impressed with the manner in which discipline was maintained in the fatherland of Communism, bloody though the process was, and the meeting was important for the many new and inflexible credos that were promulgated. The introduction of the new program stated:

"Expressing the historical need for an international organization of revolutionary proletarians—the grave diggers of the capitalist order—the Communist International is the only international force that has for its program the dictatorship of the proletariat and Communism, and that openly comes out as the organizer of the International Proletariat Revolution."

From the program of the Communist International, published in 1936, comes the following frank statement:

"The conquest of power by the proletariat does not mean peacefully capturing the ready-made bourgeois state machinery by means of a parliamentary majority. * * * The violence of the bourgeoisie can be suppressed only by the stern violence of the proletariat. The conquest of power by the proletariat is the violent overthrow of bourgeoisie power, the destruction of the capitalist state apparatus (bourgeois armies, police, bureaucratic hierarchy, judiciary, parliament, etc.), and substituting in its place new organs of proletarian power, to serve primarily as instruments for the suppression of the exploiters."

The same publication deals with the subject of religion, and in these excerpts we find, years after the promulgation of the Communist Manifesto, a slavish following even of its language:

"One of the most important tasks of the cultural revolution affecting the wide masses is the task of systematically and unswervingly combating religion—the opium of the people. The proletarian government must withdraw all state support from church, which is the agency of the former ruling class; it must prevent all church interference in state-organized educational affairs, and ruthlessly suppress the counter-revolutionary activity of the ecclesiastical organizations. At the same time, the proletarian state * * * carries on anti-religious propaganda with all the means at its command and reconstructs the whole of its educational work on the basis of scientific materialism.''

Once more the necessity for obedience to the Kremlin was hammered home by the specific injunction on page 85 of the program:

"In order that revolutionary work and revolutionary action may be coordinated, and in order that these activities may be guided most successfully, the international proletariat must be found by international class discipline. * * *

"The international class discipline must find expression in the subordination of the commercial and local interests and in the strict fulfillment of all decisions passed by the leading bodies of the Communist International.''

The Communist themselves have made some revealing statements concerning the purposes and functions of the Comintern. For example:

"The proletarian vanguard of the United States can take just pride in the fact that it participated actively in the building of the Communist International, whose fifteenth anniversary falls in March of this year (1934). At the same time, the revolutionary vanguard of this country can derive deep satisfaction from the fact that it unfailingly received brotherly advice and guidance from the Communist International in the struggle for the revolutionization of the American working class. It was, from the outset, and continued to be so, a mutual collaboration of the revolutionary proletariat of all countries, organized in a world party, for the victory of the dictatorship of the proletariat, for the establishment of a World Soviet Republic.''

(*Milestones in the History of the Communist Party,* by Alex Bittleman, Workers Library Publishers, New York, 1937, page 71; see also *The Communist,* March, 1934.)

Stalin, himself, gave considerable impetus to the activities of the American Communists through the medium of the Comintern when he delivered a speech in May of 1939, provoked by an internal fight for control:

"I think, comrades, that the American Communist Party is one of those few Communist Parties in the world upon which history has laid tasks of a decisive character from the point of view of the world revolutionary movement. You all know very well the strength and power of American imperialism. Many now think that the general crisis of world capitalism will not affect America. That, of course, is not true. It is entirely untrue, comrades. The crisis of world capitalism is developing with increasing rapidity and cannot but affect American capitalism. The three million now unemployed in America are the first swallows indicating the ripening of the economic crisis in America. The sharpening antagonisms between American and England, the struggle for markets and raw materials, and, finally, the colossal growth of armaments—that is the second portent of the approaching crisis. I think the moment is not far off when a revolutionary crisis will develop in America. And when a revolutionary crisis develops in America, that will be the beginning of the end of world capitalism as a whole. It is essential that the American Communist Party should be capable of meeting that historical moment fully prepared, and of assuming the leadership of the impending class struggle in America. Every effort and every means must be employed in preparing for that, comrades. For that end the American Communist Party must be improved and Bolshevized. For that end we must work for the complete liquidation of factionalism and deviation in the Party. For that end we must work for the re-establishment of unity in the Communist Party of America. For that end we must work in order to forge real revolutionary cadres in the real revolutionary leadership of the proletariat, capable of leading the many millions of American working class toward the revolutionary class struggle. For that end all personal factors and factional considerations must be laid aside and the revolutionary education of the working class of America be placed above all.''

These remarks of Stalin's reveal many important things. They remove all doubt as to the international ambitions of the Russian Communists. They came when the United States was convulsed by economic depression. They re-emphasized the all-important formula of Marx and Lenin for revolutionary technique; penetration and indoctrination of the labor movement and the launching of strikes. In this speech, Stalin again demonstrated the trait which characterized his rise to power—to profess loyalty when an adversary is strong, thereby lulling him into a false sense of security, and all the while patiently plotting his downfall when that adversary is weak; all the while working subversively to accelerate that weakness. Thus has Stalin played the role of the leader of world revolution when capitalist powers are enervated and weakened, and the role of the Russian isolationist when they appeared powerful.

D. Z. Manuilsky, who once served as head of the Comintern, wrote on the same general subject in 1939:

"In the U. S. A. the antifascist movement swept aside demagogues of the type of Father Coughlin. A left wing, known as The Committee for Industrial Organization (CIO), emerged from the reactionary-led American Federation of Labor, leading the larger section of the labor movement in the adoption of the position of the class struggle. Taking advantage of an improvement in the economic situation, the working class organized a number of big strikes, which in the majority of the cases resulted in a victory for the workers. There were strikes of 1,000,000 textile workers, 400,000 miners and the workers in other branches of industry. Half a million students organized a demonstration strike against the impending war. The democratic movement grew and won an enormous victory at the presidential elections. On the wave of this movement, the Communist Party in the U. S. A. increased in size.''

(*The World Communist Movement,* by D. Manuilsky, Workers Library Publishers, New York, 1939, page 18.)

The foregoing was part of a speech delivered by the ex-chief of the Comintern to members of its executive committee on March 11, 1939. It should be noted that he also reported on the progress of Communist activities in Spain, Great Britain, Holland, Belgium, Mexico, Cuba, Chile, China, India, France, Germany, Japan and Italy. In describing how the subversive work in various countries must change in tempo and technique from time to time, with the varying internal conditions in each country, keeping elastic to take immediate advantage of the slightest opportunity, Manuilsky quoted Stalin as follows:

"* * * 'Revolution,' said Stalin, 'does not usually develop along a straight ascending line, as a continuous rise, but in zigzags, in advances and retreats, in ebb and flow, hardening the forces of the revolution in the course of development and preparing the way for its final victory.' "

The Seventh World Congress of the Comintern was held in Moscow July 25 to August 20, 1935. The principal address was delivered by Georgi Dimitrov, the squat Bulgarian revolutionary, whose funeral was recently celebrated with great pomp in Moscow as well as in his native country, and whose influence was felt the world over after he assumed command of the Comintern, and who, even after relinquishing active control of that body, was a powerful influence in welding together the Communist governments in Bulgaria, Rumania, Greece and other countries. It was this famous speech of Dimitrov's that ushered in the era of the Trojan Horse. He said:

"Comrades, you remember the ancient tale of the capture of Troy. Troy was inaccessible to armies attacking her, thanks to her impregnable wall. And the attacking army, after suffering many sacrifices, was unable to achieve victory until, with the aid of the famous Trojan Horse, it managed to penetrate into the very heart of the enemy's camp.

"He who fails to understand the necessity of applying such tactics * * * is a windbag * * * and not a revolutionary."

The first leader of the Comintern was appointed by Lenin. He was Gregory Zinoviev, heretofore mentioned, and who gave the organization its first direction. As has been seen, he joined with Stalin in the process of securing power after the death of Lenin and was, himself, executed. He was selected for two excellent reasons. First, Lenin trusted him. Secondly, he was a popular and capable organizer and a thorough student of Marxist history. When Zinoviev was liquidated by Stalin, his place was taken by D. Z. Manuilsky, whose book, *The World Communist Movement,* was widely read shortly following its publication in the United States in 1939, but which suddenly became a scarce item in Communist bookstores during and after the war when the Soviet Union was anxious to placate the United States for the purpose of milking us of all of the supplies and munitions she could obtain. Bukharin had served as titular head of the Comintern for two years, 1927 to 1929, but was not given the office of president.

With the convening of the Seventh World Congress in 1935, Manuilsky's place was not filled by a Russian Communist. The last of the purge trials had cast deep suspicion throughout the ranks of the Soviet hierarchy, so Dimitrov, the Bulgarian, assumed leadership. The Trojan Horse era of international Communism was explained by this tough, crafty veteran of the international underground. His statements have been quoted above, and simply mean that Communists everywhere were thenceforth to concentrate on infiltrating throughout the structure of capitalist governments, posing as liberal patriots, but concealing their true affiliations and objectives. Dimitrov headed the Comintern from 1935 until its ostensible liquidation in 1943.

The Comintern was governed almost exactly the same as the Soviet Union itself; that is, by the Russian Communist Party under the dictatorial authority of Josef Stalin. The congresses were always held in Moscow. Headquarters for the all-powerful executive committee was in Moscow. The Comintern building was situated just across the way from the Kremlin. The Comintern had its constitution, too, just as the Soviet Union did, and was full of the same sort of democratic language. Theoretically, the delegates to the various congresses exercised authority. Actually, they did as they were told.

In carrying out the theory of world revolution, the Comintern was of inestimable value. It served to bind the many Communist Parties of the world together in a well-organized, well-disciplined group. The policies made in Moscow and sent to the various Parties which constituted the member sections of the Comintern could thus be coordinated. In this manner it was possible to launch a world-wide propaganda crusade and erect the necessary front organizations with split-second timing, always geared to suit the exigences of the Soviet Union. It was possible to handle the delicate matters of "accumulating information" concerning matters of special interest in the great nations of the world to be transmitted back to the nerve center in Russia. In the chapter concerning the activities of the Party in the United States these matters will be discussed in detail.

THE COMINTERN GOES UNDERGROUND

There were two good reasons for the apparent dissolution of the Comintern in 1943. In the first place, the several Communist Parties had become so conditioned to accept orders blindly from their Soviet superiors that the matter of discipline could well be transferred to another agency. In the second place, Russia was at war, and many of the nations allied with her had suffered considerable irritation because of the activities of the Comintern and the Comintern agents who flocked to the foreign countries of the world for the purpose of laying down the Communist law and seeing that the edicts of the Comintern were put into effect without delay. The Russian Communists were anxious not to antagonize these countries, from which poured the materials of war that enabled the Red army to withstand the German blitzkrieg. In short, the Comintern had served its purpose, and simply was no longer needed. As we shall see, the "Trojan Horse" strategy of infiltration inaugurated by Dimitrov had worked amazingly well. The machinery for world revolution was simply shifted into another gear, and its operation thenceforth was more silent and effective. Those persons so naive as to believe that the disappearance of the Comintern was a signal that the Russian Communists had abandoned their aspiration for world revolution, have either made no careful study of the record or have been blinded by their prejudices. Russian Communists cannot possibly abandon that goal without abandoning the very essence of Marxism, and the post-war activities of the Communists throughout the world indicate a rededication to this basic Marxian objective; certainly no abandonment of it. If Stalin were to tell his people that there would be no further effort to attain a world dictatorship of the proletariat, it would be comparable to the Pope informing the members of his church that they should renounce religion.

According to Marxian strategy, 1943 was simply the time when the Comintern was to go underground. It was a characteristic piece of Russian double-dealing. When Igor Gouzenko, the code clerk in the Russian embassy in Ottawa, Canada, decided that what he saw in Canada could not possibly stand up to the propaganda he had received at home, and decided to make his sensational disclosures to the Canadian Northwest Mounted Police, he established, without any question of a doubt, that in 1945—two years after the Kremlin announced the dissolution of the Comintern—he, himself, sent messages addressed to the Intelligence Division of the Comintern, Moscow, Russia. As late as 1946, other evidence of the fact that the Comintern had merely gone underground was uncovered to completely corroborate the information disclosed by Gouzenko. Contrary to much popular opinion, the Comintern continued to function in the Soviet Union, across the street from the Kremlin, precisely as it had since its inception. The Cominform, with headquarters at Bucharest, is simply, as its name implies, an information medium through which propaganda material is disseminated to the various Communist Parties of the world. It is in no sense a substitute for the Comintern, whose agents continue to operate undercover for the purpose of carrying directives from the Kremlin to the member Communist Parties abroad, and for the purpose of coordinating political espionage activities on an extremely high level.

The various subdivisions of the Comintern have been discussed in the previous reports issued by this committee. In them it was pointed out that two of the most vital divisions were the Profintern, or Red Trade Union International, through which the infiltration of trade unions was carried out, and the MOPR, or International Red Aid, through which assistance is immediately mobilized for all Party members who run afoul of the law. For years the American division of International Red Aid was known as the International Labor Defense and its lawyers flew to the assistance of Communist espionage agents, activists and propagandists and made every effort to turn the courts of our land into a sounding board for Communist propaganda and to disrupt the orderly administration of justice. At the present time, the Communist organization which functions to achieve the same end is known as the Civil Rights Congress, and maintains its branches in virtually every large city in the United States. Its activities were thoroughly discussed in the committee's 1951 report, which is still in print, and there is consequently no necessity for repeating the material here.

For the purpose of laying a foundation for the discussion of Communist infiltration into the educational system of California, some attention should be paid to a third important subdivision of the Comintern, known as the Young Communist International. This organization, obviously, coordinated the indoctrination and recruiting of the youth of the world into the Communist movement, and for some inexplicable reason, most of the educators in the United States simply refuse to believe that there is any serious problem of Communist infiltration in our educational institutions. So long as there is no epidemic of infiltration, and exposure of hordes of Communist agents plying their nefarious trade on educational campuses, an alarming number of professional educators dismiss the entire problem with a shrug, while under their very noses a compact, small and completely disciplined group of Communist fanatics are indoctrinating students right and left at every opportunity.

Manifestly, the problem is not one of how many Communists there are on a given faculty, but how much damage one man can do in a strategic position. There was only one Alger Hiss in the State Department, but it has recently been disclosed that he passed on all of the personnel that was supplied to the United Nations from this country, and it is hardly credible that he would fill the positions with anti-Communists. One atomic scientist in the right place would be of more danger to the welfare of this country than a thousand Communist bricklayers who built the structure which housed the atom-smashing machinery. One dean of a liberal arts college in a great university could do more harm than a thousand teaching assistants, because he could open the gateway to an infiltration of Communist Party members—not many of them, but enough to accomplish the Party's objectives at that particular institution. All of these matters will be discussed in detail in the section dealing with educational infiltration by Communists.

It must be realized that each of these Comintern subdivisions, and certainly the Young Communist International, had its own complete staff and was organized on a bureaucratic basis so that the directives could be taken from the top of the triangle down to the broad masses at its base.

Anyone who takes the trouble to read the Sixth Report of this committee, which is thoroughly documented, cannot possibly have any doubt about this seriousness of the Communist attempt to capture the minds of our youth.

THE AMERICAN COMMUNIST PARTY

The history of Communism in the United States is in many respects similar to the development of the Party in Russia. In each country there was originally a Socialist movement, which was divided into a radical and a conservative element, and in each case the Communist Party grew from the radical element. In each country the theory was that leadership should be democratic, but it actually became more and more autocratic and disciplined until all control was finally vested in the apex of the organizational triangle instead of at the bottom—with the difference that the American Communists have always taken their orders from Russia.

The Socialists, and particularly the radical element, had been closely following developments abroad. They were aware of the split in the ranks of the Russian Social-Democratic Party, but were astonished when they received the electrifying news that the radical clique had managed to lead the Russian masses in a successful revolution. The American left-wing immediately urged the creation of a new organization armed with the discipline and the Marxist theory which had provided the driving power for the Russian Revolution. In this proposal they received the enthusiastic support of the Russian Bolsheviks.

Trotsky and Bukharin were, in 1918, regarded as international heroes by the Slavic members of the American Socialist Party, and it was largely through their influence and agitation that the American radical element came to feel that without Marxian leadership and discipline they could accomplish nothing. This, then, was the attitude in 1919 when the Comintern was formed. When the invitation was received in the United States to send delegates to assist in drafting the basic plans for a Communist International, or Comintern, the American radical element in the Socialist Party received the news with great enthusiasm, completely convinced that through the Comintern a medium would be established whereby all Communist organizations would profit by the experience of the Russian Bolsheviks and could work to emancipate the working classes of the world.

In 1919, all Communists—even the Russians, were convinced that the victory of 1917 was only an initial step, and that similar revolutions were imminent in the capitalistic nations. In Moscow the American delegates were treated as novices in the fine art of revolution and attended the meetings in a spirit of awe and reverence while such dazzling figures as Lenin, Trotsky, Zinoviev and Bukharin explained to them how the Comintern would operate, outlined the conditions which had been established as prerequisites for admittance to membership, and merely asked the assembled delegates to ratify the entire prearranged plan. There was unhesitating acceptance of Lenin's 21 conditions for membership, which bound every Communist Party in the world to function thenceforth as a tool of the Kremlin.

3—L-4294

Approval of the basic plans did not mean that the American Marxists obtained immediate admission to the newly-formed Comintern. There was yet too much internal struggle between the two American factions in the Socialist Party, and the Russians sought to first bring about an amalgamation of the bickering groups. In September, 1919, a convention was held at Chicago and from it emerged not one but two Communist organizations: The Communist Labor Party and the Communist Party. Each group sent delegates to the Comintern, and each agreed to be bound by the conditions for admission, but there was still no recognition from Moscow. Meanwhile two agents had arrived from Russia, Josef Pogany and Ludwig Martens, equipped with the authority of the Comintern and plenty of funds. Through their joint efforts a merger was finally effected in 1922 between the two dissident American groups, and the first front organization was also formed in that year, the American Friends of Soviet Russia. Through this first front, large sums of money were collected for the ostensible relief of starving Russians, but the money was actually used for the support of the new movement to establish firmly a Communist Party in the United States and to subvert the government of this country.

Earl Browder, William Z. Foster and the late Sidney Hillman had much to do with the development of Communism in America. There is no direct evidence that Mr. Hillman ever became a Communist and there is considerable evidence to the contrary. There is, of course, no doubt concerning the other two, who have been leaders of the movement since its inception and up to the time that Browder was expelled from the Party.

In 1921, Foster and Browder made a trip to Russia at the suggestion of the Red Trade Union International, or Profintern, which paid their expenses. The purpose of this visit was to perfect a scheme for the penetration and indoctrination of the American labor movement. Hillman was already in Moscow at the time on a mission of his own. The three men conferred with Lenin, who directed them to return to the United States and direct a campaign for industrial organization, the theory being that it would be far simpler to indoctrinate labor through industries than through individual craft unions. Foster had already started what he called the Trade Union Educational League, but it had become anemic through lack of funds and leadership. He returned from Russia an ardent Communist. Browder agreed to serve as his assistant, and Hillman pledged his cooperation. The crusade was financed with money from Moscow, Foster directed the work, always obedient to his Russian superiors, Browder edited a paper for the league, the *Labor Herald,* and Hillman assisted according to plan.

PROFINTERN ACTIVITIES IN AMERICA

By August, 1922, the American Communist Party had begun considerable activity. It advocated the merging of all unions in the several industries into a few huge industrial organizations; it advocated frequent and militant strikes; it agitated for immediate recognition of Russia by the United States and the abolition of the capitalist form of government. Foster's Communist affiliations were carefully concealed, by orders of the Russian bosses, and these proposals came from a new liberal, "non-Communist" organization as "liberal reforms." William Foster thus entered the Communist movement as a labor organizer and his activities have always been chiefly in that field. Browder ran the paper while Foster ran the practical matters, and therein lies the basic difference between the two men. Foster is militant, blunt and practical. Browder has always fancied himself as an intellectual Marxist, a writer, and the Party's leading propagandist. During the war he functioned in that capacity, trying to stifle any Party activity that might prove offensive to American industry, which was becoming quite popular abroad. Foster, meanwhile, busied himself as unobstrusively as possible, with his ceaseless campaign to infiltrate the ranks of American labor with Communist organizers and agents. When the hostilities ceased, Browder stepped down and Foster took command through a flimsy artifice which will be discussed later in detail as a classic example of international Communist duplicity.

Foster's identity as a member of the Communist Party was exposed in 1922, and he was forthwith expelled from the American Federation of Labor, but persisted in continuing his campaign for several years thereafter, although he changed the name of his organization to Trade Union Unity League. The basic trouble experienced by Foster was the fact that his Russian superiors had no adequate understanding of labor conditions in this Country. It was the same trouble that the Marxian International of 1864 had encountered—a central organization cannot lay down a hard and fast set of rules to be followed by revolutionary elements in foreign countries. There was too much diversity of conditions. The situation in one country and the comparable situation in another were often completely different and could not be governed by the same inflexible rule.

Prior to the Revolution of 1917, the Russian workers were eager for liberation. Their life under the Czar was, in fact, a life of poverty, illiteracy and serfdom. They could hardly fare any worse under a new form of government. The situation in America was quite different. Labor in this country was neither illiterate, impoverished or doomed to a life of serfdom. It was, in fact, lusty, courageous, and accustomed pretty much to having its own way. There were periodic economic depressions, as there were in other nations, but on the whole the lot of the American worker was not only good, it was getting better. There was no secret government police in the United States, no forced labor camps, no co-operative farms, certainly no lack of labor unionism. The Russians did not realize that before the toiling masses of America could be taught to rise in revolt they would first have to be convinced that they *were* an oppressed class. Mr. Foster soon discovered that his task was not an easy one. There were, of course, certain dissatisfied elements in most of the unions, but they were in the vast minority. With these minority cliques he did make sufficient headway to sow the seeds and lay the foundation for infiltration that was later accelerated.

By 1935, Foster's attempts to bring about industrial organization of American labor, according to Lenin's plan, had almost died. It was in 1935 that the Seventh World Congress of the Comintern was held, and Georgi Dimitrov took the rostrum to deliver his famous "Trojan Horse" speech which heralded both his own leadership of the Comintern and an era in which the Communists in all countries were instructed to gain through strategem and indirection what they had been unable to gain through a more frontal and frank attack.

During the latter part of 1935, John L. Lewis, who was definitely no Communist, unwittingly played into the hands of the Party by launching his own campaign for industrial organization. Within two years the CIO trebled its membership. Organization progressed at such a dizzy rate that the astonished Mr. Lewis found himself running short of organizers. He didn't have long to wait, however. Trained Communist organizers flocked under his banner in droves, fanning out through his entire organizational structure and firmly entrenching themselves in key positions throughout the most strategic unions. The rank and file membership was no more sympathetic toward Communism than was Mr. Lewis. But they were assuredly apathetic toward it, and so was he.

Communism can never succeed in any country where labor holds itself aloof from the blandishments and false promises of Communist organizers. Marx's theme, as expressed in the Manifesto, acknowledged that the revolution must be gained through penetration and indoctrination of the working masses. That concept was followed by Lenin and his Bolsheviks in preparing the way for the Russian Revolution of 1917. All Communist literature heavily emphasizes this basic premise. In 1939, a Soviet commission under the personal direction of Stalin prepared a work called *An Official History of the Communist Party in the Soviet Union,* in which the precise strategy for revolution is set forth step by step in meticulous detail. This book was printed in many languages and 12,000,000 copies of the first edition were distributed throughout the world to the various Communist Parties to be studied as a textbook for revolution. Within five months after the first batch was received in the United States more than 80,000 copies had been sold. In the September, 1939, issue of *The Communist,* monthly ideological publication of the American Communist Party, Earl Browder said:

> "This is no ordinary book to be skimmed through and then laid aside on a bookshelf. It is a scientific textbook to be studied and mastered, not for mechanical quotation of extracts but to understand the essence of the theory of Marxism-Leninism so that it can be *applied* to the most varied and difficult problems and situations, so that this theory can be enriched with the new experiences of the revolutionary working class movement also of our own country."

Over and over again this text emphasizes that the Party in any capitalist country must commence its revolutionary work by a long and tedious process of penetrating and ultimately gaining control of the working masses. Over and over again the Communist press in this country has stated that the American Communists constitute, "the vanguard of the working class," and the Party has always worked to regiment and indoctrinate the labor movement so it would wield a potent influence at the polls and replace those patriotic and independent statesmen who refuse to carry the Party line with liberal politicians who would be more tractable. This textbook, in describing how labor was regimented as a prelude to the Russian Revolution, states:

> "The Bolshevik Party during this period set an example in all forms and manifestations of class struggle of the proletariat. It built up illegal organizations. It issued illegal pamphlets. It carried

on secret revolutionary work among the leadership of the various legally existing organizations of the working class. The Party strove to win over the trade unions and to gain influence in people's houses, even in universities, clubs and sick benefit societies.

"* * * The revolutionary movement of the workers steadily developed, spreading to town after town, region after region. In the beginning of 1914 the workers' strikes, far from subsiding, acquired a new momentum, they became more and more stubborn and embraced even larger numbers of workers."

(*History of the Communist Party of the Soviet Union* (B), International Publishers, Inc., 1939.)

This statement agreed precisely with one that Stalin made in 1926, when he wrote:

"Confidence of the working class in the Party is not attained at one stroke, and not through the medium of force directed at the working class, but by the Party's prolonged work among the masses, by a correct Party policy, by the ability of the Party to convince the masses through their own experiences of the correctness of its policy, and by the ability of the Party to gain the support of the working class to follow its lead."

(*Problems of Leninism,* by Josef Stalin, pages 44-51.)

Earl Browder followed these theories to the letter by instructing the American Communists as follows:

"Trade unions are the primary organizations of the working class. It is in the unions that the workers learn the first lessons of organization and of struggle, without which there can be no development of revolutionary consciousness. Consequently, Communists have always emphasized that one of their central tasks is to work within the trade unions. We cannot win the majority of the working class to our program unless we base all of our large-scale, united working front upon united activities among the unions.

"The trade unions are schools in which the workers learn the elementary lessons of the class struggle, and through them they grow into more conscious and more effective fighters against capitalism."

(*What Is Communism* by Earl Browder, pages 109-110.)

These were the principles which caused the Russian leaders to instruct William Foster, Earl Browder and Sidney Hillman to bring about the industrial organization of labor when they made their pilgrimage to Moscow in 1921. The effort failed, although Foster persisted in his determination to accomplish the goal for almost fifteen years. The golden opportunity was found when John L. Lewis started the CIO. From 1935 until 1941 he was the idol of the Party; he was praised in the Communist press and flattered by his fellow-traveling subordinates.

Meanwhile, Sidney Hillman had fallen from favor. He had committed the unpardonable sin of resisting the attempts of the Communists to take over his Amalgamated Clothing Workers Union and was, therefore, subjected to vicious attacks by Communist writers whose arsenal of insulting adjectives is a constant source of amazement to the layman.

Hillman was also an ardent supporter of President Roosevelt before Russia was invaded by the German forces under Hitler in June of 1941. From August, 1939, until June 22, 1941, the American Communists hated Roosevelt because he was advocating preparedness. That was the period of the Hitler-Stalin nonaggression pact. When Hitler invaded Russia on June 22, 1941, the Soviet Union desperately needed American help; this resulted in overnight approval of Roosevelt's preparedness program.

Here are some·excerpts from the Party's monthly ideological and propaganda publication, *The Communist*. On page 201 of the March, 1940, issue is this flattering statement about Mr. Lewis:

> "* * * In short, the coalition position formulated by President Lewis has in it the elements of transition for the American working class to a higher stage of political activity."

And as part of the same article, on page 203, is found this sarcastic comment about Mr. Hillman: ·

> "* * * Consider, for example, one of the recent expressions of President Hillman of the Amalgamated Clothing Workers, publishing a statement of the ACWA political policy in the February issue of *Advance,* that is, after Roosevelt's Congress message and war budget. President Hillman manages to muster sufficient courage (or is it something else?) to tell the workers that

>> '* * * There is no man in public life in whom we can so fully and safely confide, and for the balance of the journey.'

> "Confide, mind you. Giving yourselves away. In trusting your fate passively and unconditionally to one of the most militant spokesmen of Wall Street imperialism. And 'for the balance of the journey.' "

In 1940, Lewis was still valuable to the Communists, so they continued to flatter him. The following excerpt is taken from page 388 of the May, 1940, issue of *The Communist:*

> "These practical objectives arise from the most intimate and burning needs of the masses of the people. They are the immediate needs of the American working class and its allies—the toiling farmers, the youth, the Negro people and the aged. They are the needs of the great gathering coalition for which John L. Lewis spoke so eloquently to the miners of northern West Virginia on April 1."

By 1941, however, the Communists were in control of the national structure of the CIO and Mr. Lewis had been squeezed dry of his usefulness, so the Party press characteristically began to pepper him with acid adjectives. In the October, 1943; issue of *The Communist,* this blast was fired:

> "The A. F. of L. Council's failure to accept John L. Lewis' application for reaffiliation of the United Mine Workers, however, was a service to labor, and it came as a blow in the face to that defeatist, Lewis, insolent and autocratic, who hoped to use the A. F. of L. Council as an instrument against the war and to split the workers away from President Roosevelt."

In the same magazine for January, 1944, page 64, the Party was still taking pot shots at Mr. Lewis, as follows:

"* * * Guided by this consistence, the Communists have been able to exert a positive influence on such vital issues as * * * the no-strike pledge made by labor and the struggle to defeat and isolate the defeatist and insurrectionist elements led by John L. Lewis inside labor's ranks."

CIO INFILTRATION

Having gained control of the national structure of the CIO, the Communists set about to mold it into a potent political machine. The Communist propagandist, who, in the March, 1940, issue of *The Communist* said that Lewis' coalition idea contained the elements to bring the working class to a higher stage of political activity apparently knew whereof he wrote. In the person of Sidney Hillman, who had been praised when he returned from Moscow and booed when he came out for Roosevelt in the 1939-1941 period, was discovered the ideal man to head the political organization of the CIO; Hillman was a non-Communist, who had, nevertheless, straddled the line on more than one occasion. He was well acquainted with such Party functionaries as Foster and Browder; he had even conferred with Lenin. His wife, Bessie Abramowitz, had contributed $3,000 to the Jewish-Communist paper, *The Freheit;* he had served as a trustee of the Garland Fund with William Foster; he was pro-Communist during the era of the trade union leagues, anti-Communist when his clothing workers' union was covetously eyed by the Party, cooperative in agreeing to head the CIO Political Action Committee in 1943.

As the Communists infiltrated the CIO, they paid particular attention to certain key unions. In the field of communication and transportation, in agricultural unions, maritime unions, among scientists and technicians, state, county and municipal employees, in government offices and in such media for propaganda as the radio and motion picture industries they consolidated their strength.

The National Executive Board of the CIO which created the Political Action Committee in 1943, consisted of 49 members, at least 18 of whom had records of active collaboration with the Communist program. This minority actually controlled the CIO during that period, because they voted according to the number of members in their respective unions. The 18 were: Lewis Alan Berne, President of the International Federation of Architects, Engineers, Chemists and Technicians; Donald Henderson, President of the United Cannery, Agricultural, Packing and Allied Workers of America; Joseph P. Selly, President of the American Communications Association; Julius Emspak, Secretary-Treasurer of the United Electrical, Radio and Machine Workers of America; Grant W. Oakes, President of the United Farm Equipment and Metal Workers of America; Eleanor Nelson, Secretary-Treasurer of the United Federal Workers of America; Joseph F. Jurich, President of the International Fishermen and Allied Workers of America; Ben Gold, President of the International Fur and Leather Workers of America; Morris Muster, President of the United Furniture Workers of America; Harry Renton Bridges, President of the International Longshoremens and Warehousemens Union; Ferdinand C. Smith, Secretary of the National Maritime

Union of America; Lewis Merrill, President of the United Office and Professional Workers of America; Abram Flaxer, President of the State, County and Municipal Workers of America; Michael J. Quill, President of the United Transport Workers of America; Joseph Curran, President of the National Maritime Union of America; Reid Robinson, President of the United Mine, Mill and Smelter Workers of America; E. F. Burke, Secretary of the Marine Cooks and Stewards Association of the Pacific Coast, and Frank R. McGrath, President of the United Shoe Workers of America.

In justice to Mr. Morris Muster, it must be added that after trying vainly to get along with the comrades in his union, he resigned because of the complete domination of his organization by Communists, according to an article which appeared in the *Los Angeles Times* on July 1, 1946. And much the same situation applied to Joseph Curran, who, after having cooperated with the Communist element of his organization for some time, has since devoted most of his efforts to cleaning the Communists out of his organization, an undertaking in which he has had considerable success.

THE COMMUNIST "FRACTION" TECHNIQUE

Penetration of the unions of America was greatly facilitated through the use of a strategem commonly known as the *Communist Fraction.* It was employed as follows: at a secret meeting of the Party in a given locality it was decided that there should be a certain resolution enacted at the next meeting of the union. Passage of the resolution would be used as an entering wedge for Communist infiltration and to further the Communist international party line. Three Party members whose Communist affiliations had been carefully concealed from the union are instructed to attend the meeting and present the resolution. The procedure is followed to the letter and it is almost always successful because the tiny Communist fraction in the larger non-Communist group is organized and the rest of the membership is not.

On the evening of the meeting, the three go to the union hall separately and take widely separated seats. Member A proposes the adoption of the resolution; member B immediately takes the floor in opposition, stating that the proposal is entirely too radical, that it sounds suspiciously Communist-inspired and is wholly unsuited to a patriotic American labor organization. Member C follows with some cogent argument in support of the resolution, thereby dividing the membership into factions. When the discussion has reached the proper stage and before too much opposition has been allowed to develop, member B rises once more and proclaims that while he did oppose the measure originally, he has listened to the arguments pro and con with great attention and now understands the real purpose of the proposal much better and that since he is, after all, a man of moral honesty, he wants to be the first to second the motion for the adoption of the resolution. Usually there are many more than three undercover Communists in the fraction, which, of course, makes its operation that much easier. These men distribute themselves strategically on the floor of the meeting room in what is known in Communist vernacular as the "Diamond Pattern." Each man is thoroughly trained in the rules of parliamentary procedure, knows exactly what role he is to play, the entire operation is carefully timed, planned, rehearsed in advance, and is almost always successful.

A few trade unions have employed trained teachers to explain to the rank and file membership exactly how these Communist tactics are worked and how they may be detected and exposed. The results have been astounding. In many instances the entrenched Party members are swept from office overnight and replaced with men who are fully as capable and thoroughly American. When the average trade union member is convinced that he has been duped and led around by the nose by a small clique of Communists, he becomes angry and starts to clean house. He then assumes command of his own union. Apparently that is what has happened to both the National Maritime Union and the United Furniture Workers of America.

When the activities of the Communist-controlled CIO unions became too arrogant and open even for the parent organization to tolerate any longer, each was investigated, reports were made to a national CIO convention, and the Communist-controlled union organizations were expelled from the parent group. Nevertheless, they continued to operate much as before and constitute a critical menace to the welfare of this country that has been endured far too long.

BLANKET INFILTRATION

The Communists have succeeded in the space of 33 years in blanketing the nation with their members. They have established their own school systems, their own newspapers, their own magazines, their own disciplinary machinery. They have penetrated to the very heart and core of our industrial system through their infiltration of key labor unions. They have created thousands of front organizations through which they recruit sincere liberals and collect vast sums of money. They have penetrated the educational institutions of the nation and converted both students and faculty members. The Communists in America, as even in the Soviet Union, are a minority. But it must be admitted that they work much harder to undermine our government than the average citizen does to preserve it. The amazing achievements made by the American Communists is not, however, mainly due to their own activities. It is chiefly because they have met with virtually no opposition during those 33 years.

It has been explained in a preceding section how Zinoviev and Kamenev broke and confessed to a variety of imaginary crimes against the government when they were first threatened with outright expulsion from the Communist Party of the Soviet Union. Members of the Party in America dread expulsion for much the same reason. A new Communist soon discovers that his life is undergoing a profound change. His new acquaintances are all members of the same vast international conspiracy, bound together by the same subversive ties, subject to the same inflexible discipline. He reads little but Communist literature and propaganda. His entire time is occupied in endless meetings, forums, lectures and conventions. As he is drawn ever deeper into the Party he draws farther away from his former friends and contacts and is taught to regard them as capitalists and therefore class enemies. He has become a comrade in a tightly-knit local organization that keeps track of his every activity and almost his every thought. If he becomes thoroughly indoctrinated, there is little cause for worry. If he becomes restive under the discipline, if he indicates the slightest disillusionment, he is made to realize that too much knowledge may become a dangerous possession. If he is expelled from membership he will be hated by his former Communist comrades and shunned by his former non-Communist friends. In addition to a life of ostracism he will be subjected to a campaign of vilification and abuse that will hound him wherever he goes. His employers will receive anonymous tips that they are harboring a Communist spy, and his neighbors will hear whispered rumors that he is untruthful, dishonest, incapable, perverted and psychopathic. By this technique he is undermined and isolated so that if he should ever wish to reveal any of the secrets of the underground organization he will be readily discredited. This technique, incredible to the average American, is no myth. The same story has been told too often by too many ex-Communists in widely separated parts of the country to be lightly tossed aside.

WHAT IS PARTY LINE?

The term "Party line" means the policy being followed by the Communist movement at any particular time. It is invariably controlled from Russia and consequently is geared to suit the purposes of that government. The abrupt changes in the policy of the Communists in this country has provided complete proof of the subservience to the dictates of the Soviet Union, as Mr. Foster frankly admitted under oath in 1931.

During the period from 1933 to 1939, Adolph Hitler waged a relentless ideological war against Communism. From the Communist presses throughout the world came a torrent of derogatory statements concerning Hitler and his ambitions for world conquest; about his Fascist methods and his militaristic attitude. All of this was, of course, echoed and supplemented by the American Communist propaganda machinery.

On August 23, 1939, the nonaggression pact was concluded between Communist Russia and Nazi Germany. Overnight the international Party line changed. The attitude of dictators is difficult to understand. Nazi Foreign Minister von Ribbentrop had declared on February 7, 1939:

"We will never come to an understanding with Bolshevist Russia."

About a week after this unexpected pact had been signed, Molotov confidently told the Russian people:

"* * * The conclusion of a pact of nonaggression between the U. S. S. R. and Germany is of tremendous positive value, *eliminating the danger of war between Germany and the Soviet Union.* (Committee's italics.)

"As you see, Stalin hit the nail on the head when he exposed the machinations of the western European politicians, who were trying to set Germany and the Soviet Union at loggerheads. It must be confessed that there were some shortsighted in our own country who, carried away by oversimplified antifascist propaganda, forgot about this provocative work of our enemies. Mindful of this, Stalin even then suggested the possibility of other, unhostile, good-neighborly relations between Germany and the U. S. R. It can now be seen that on the whole Germany correctly understood the statements of

Stalin and drew practical conclusions from them. The conclusion of the Soviet-German Nonaggression Pact shows that Stalin's historic prevision has been brilliantly confirmed."

On October 31, 1939, Molotov declared to the Supreme Soviet:

"The relations between Germany and the other western European bourgeois states have in the past two decades been determined primarily by Germany's efforts to break the fetters of the Versaille Treaty, whose authors were Great Britain and France with the active collaboration of the United States. This, in the long run, led to the present war in Europe. * * * The relations between the Soviet Union and Germany have been based on a different foundation, which involved no interest whatever in perpetuating the post-Versaille system. *We have always held that a strong Germany is an indispensable condition for a durable peace in Europe.*" (Committee's italics.)

Thus the signal for a change of the international Party line was given from the Kremlin, and Communist Parties throughout the world ceased hating Hitler on August 23, 1939, and became his ardent admirers the following day. In America, Roosevelt overnight became a warmonger. As the friendship between Russia and Germany became closer, the attitude was reflected in the United States in a wave of strikes in important defense industries. The preparedness speeches of President Roosevelt were ridiculed, his conscription program vigorously opposed, and an embargo was demanded against a shipment of goods to belligerent nations. A new front organization, The American Peace Mobilization, appeared and spread its isolationist propaganda and the slogan of the Communist Party was "the Yanks are not coming." The CIO was easily drawn into the campaign. V. J. Jerome, Communist leader of the cultural front, proclaimed in 1940:

"Since the warmongering campaign opened, innumerable trade unions and other mass organizations have adopted resolutions against this country's involvement. A. F. of L. and CIO, state labor bodies and city councils, national unions and locals, the unemployed, church bodies and the vital youth movement are saying, with the National Convention of the CIO: Labor wants no war or any part of it.

"* * * The voice of militant labor rings forth in ever-swelling volume in the slogan first sounded by the Maritime Federation of the Pacific: 'the Yanks are not coming!' The Communist Party of the United States declares: '* * * We Communists will continue the broadest collaboration with all elements in the labor movement to advance the struggle for working class unity by educating, rallying, and unifying the workers against capitalist reaction and exploitation to keep America out of the imperialistic war."

(*Social Democracy and the War,* Workers Library Publishers, Inc., 1940, pages 45-46.)

This program continued just so long as the Soviet Union and Germany maintained friendly relations. Molotov's statement about a strong Germany insuring European peace, and Stalin's historic prevision were forgotten, however, when, on June 22, 1941, Hitler's Panzer Divisions crashed simultaneously and without warning over the nonaggression pact and the borders of the Soviet Union. Now it was time to hate Hitler once more. In its analysis of this abrupt change in the Party line, the California Legislature's Committee on Un-American Activities had this to say:

"Your committee here wishes to point out that on June 22, 1941, it was Russia and not the United States that was invaded by Germany. The news of this event, however, was attended with repercussions in the United States and in California that were immediate and profound. A strange and significant quiet prevailed over America's labor front. Overnight the imperialist war of June 21, 1941, was changed by some strange, international magic, into a people's war which involved the Soviet Union. The American Communists would now take all the Yanks they could get. American Communists were now declaring that 'Now * * * this is our war,' as did Rose Segure and other California Communists and fellow travelers. Foreign Commissar Molotov now ordained that it would be all right for America to lift the embargo on arms to belligerents; particularly to the Soviet Union and Britain.

"Your committee wishes to emphasize the significant lesson to be learned from this period of Communist disparity. Americans everywhere should concern themselves seriously with the changes that came to California and the United States; changes which effected the release of defense industries from the strangle-hold of Communist dominated unions, the sudden change in propagandizing in our State educational institutions.

"It should be carefully noted by all students of these matters that these changes were caused, not by anything happening in or to the United States. Again they turned on the need and foreign policy of a foreign government thousands of miles away. Your committee wishes to emphasize the fact that there exists in the State of California an organized group of subversive individuals completely dominated by that foreign power which has sufficient influence in our American labor movement to launch a strike epidemic in our defense or war industries when the purpose suits the foreign power, and to turn it off again like water from a tap when the foreign policy of the dominating foreign power commands. While the needs of the foreign power dominating these groups in California and in the United States may correspond presently with our own needs, it may well be, in the future, that the needs of the dominating force exerted on these American subversives may be detrimental in the extreme to our own needs and purposes. Your committee believes that it is high time for the people of this State thoroughly and completely to understand and realize that the members of the Communist Party are organized into an iron disciplined group and controlled unquestionably by a foreign power, Soviet Russia. These people should be regarded for what they actually are—agents of a foreign power, and should not be in any way looked upon as superpatriots and saviours of the working class of America and California, as they would like us to believe."

(1943 Report, Joint Fact-Finding Committee on Un-American Activities in California. California State Printing Office, pages 51-52.)

PARTY LINE SUBSTITUTION—FOSTER FOR BROWDER

We now come to the strangest Party line change of them all, the expulsion of Earl Browder from the American Communist Party and the election of William Z. Foster in his place. This unprecedented occurrence has caused widespread misunderstanding and bewilderment. Some have said that there were just too many abrupt changes in the Party line and it caused a general upheaval in the Party. That is simply absurd. Communists are too well disciplined. Others believe the story the Communists tried to have them believe, and that is the story which deserves scrutiny here.

Earl Browder had been the leader of the American Communist Party for 14 years. During that time he wrote many books and many articles. He edited the official party newspaper, the *Daily Worker,* and came to be regarded as the infallible Marxist. Earl Browder was born in Wichita, Kansas, on May 20, 1891. His father was a Socialist and the son joined the Socialist Party after his parents had moved the family to Missouri. There he worked for a while with William Foster in the labor movement, and was in prison during the first World War because he refused to register for the draft on the ground that he was a conscientious objector. After his release from Leavenworth Penitentiary in 1920, he plunged immediately into the Communist movement, and, as we have seen, went to Russia with Foster as a delegate to the Profintern Congress in 1921. Browder married a Russian Party functionary, was sent to China on international Communist matters, and in 1930 became the head of the Party in the United States, a position he held for almost 15 consecutive years.

In November, 1943, President Roosevelt, Prime Minister Churchill and Premier Stalin opened their conferences at Teheran. Browder closely followed these proceedings and in them saw a new course of cooperation opened between the Communists and the capitalists—at least for the duration of the war. In his book, *Teheran—Our Path in Peace and War,* he made some remarkable statements. On page 71 of the first edition, which appeared in pamphlet form, he said:

"Since we Marxists, who are convinced socialists, are accepting for a long period the necessity to cooperate and make capitalism work in America for the benefit of our people and the world, it would be rather stupid for us to gag at the necessity to listen respectfully to its pet-name, 'free enterprise.' Therefore, we declare in advance our understanding that the democratic-progressive camps to which we adhere will adopt the defense of 'free enterprise,' that we understand this term as a synonym for capitalism as it exists today in our country, and that we will not oppose it nor put forth any counter-slogans."

And on page 74 he acknowledged that the American system was not only successful from the standpoint of production, but that there was a great need for that production during the critical period of the war. He put it thus:

"There can be no effective national unity in America to secure and unfold the program of Teheran that does not include the capitalists able to fight for and win at least a certain minimum of participation on the part of their whole group."

In making any accurate analysis of Browder's proposal that the American Communists declare a truce in their historical battle to wipe out capitalism according to the precepts of Marx and all his followers, one must bear in mind that the orders always came from Moscow. One of the 21 conditions of membership in the Comintern, laid down by Lenin himself, and heretofore quoted, was that all such matters must be approved by the Soviet Union. No one in this country knew that any better than Earl Browder. Nevertheless, he certainly followed either one of two courses: He either acted independently and on his own initiative—which he had never done before—or he acted according to secret instructions that would operate for the best interests of the Soviet Union to which he owed his first allegiance. Browder had been to the Soviet Union many times and was quite familiar with the purge trials, the international discipline, and the fundamental fact that no leader of a Communist Party would ever presume to adopt any new and vital policy without approval of the Kremlin. If Browder acted independently, he gained nothing for himself and risked the implacable vengeance of the Soviet secret police. If he acted pursuant to orders he would be bringing about a situation that would be of vast benefit to the Soviet Union. His policy would switch the entire Communist movement in the United States from its fight against capitalism to active cooperation with it—which meant that there would be no interruption in the flow of materials to the nations fighting together against the common enemy. For the duration of the war, at least, there would be no strikes by Communist-dominated unions, there would be no activity by the Communists that would antagonize American industry, there would be no political activity and no propaganda activity by the American Communists at all.

The Comintern, as has been seen, was ostensibly dissolved a few months before the Teheran conference. In January, 1945, the delegates to the National Party Convention at New York unanimously voted to liquidate the Communist Party of the United States and to function thenceforth under the name of the Communist Political Association. Then, carrying out Browder's proposal to the fullest extent, the Young Communist League became known as American Youth for Democracy and the monthly magazine changed its name from *The Communist* to *Political Affairs.*

A careful examination of the issues of *Izvestia* and *Pravda,* and other sources of propaganda originating in the Soviet Union during this period, reveals that there was no criticism of this change of American policy, and that the Kremlin was quite content that Browder put his startling and "hastily-conceived" plan into operation.

There was only one dissenting voice, and that was not a very strong one; it came, by a strange coincidence, from William Z. Foster, the man who was later to succed Browder as leader of the Communist Party of the United States a year later. The other comrades hailed the new policy or Party line as a stroke of Marxian genius. From January, 1945, until May, 1946, not one soul discovered that Browder had committed a serious blunder. Of all the students of Marxism throughout the Nation, not one single Communist criticized the new program—and even Foster accepted the change quietly. It was not until Germany capitulated and the threat to the Soviet Union was removed, that anyone at all criticized

Browder for having been a traitor to the Marxian cause of world revolution.

Outside of Russia, the most powerful Communist Party in the world was in France, with approximately 1,000,000 members. Jacques Duclos, its secretary and leader, had been a member of the all-powerful Executive Committee of the Comintern. He made a trip to Moscow in the spring of 1945, and when he returned he wrote an article which appeared in the French Communist press in April of that year. In this article Comrade Duclos literally tore Browderism to shreds, criticized the American Communists for having been so easily misled, and told them to quickly return to the militant path of Marxist rectitude.

Before news of the Duclos letter reached this country Browder celebrated his fifty-fourth birthday. On that occasion he was showered with the customary letters and telegrams of congratulation, hailing his "great Marxist leadership." Five days later the Duclos letter was published in the New York *Daily Worker,* and the very same comrades who had praised Browder now turned on him in a savage mass attack.

Then came the National Convention of the Communist Party, held in July, 1945. At this meeting there was much berating of Browder, confessions of individual stupidity on the part of the comrades, and no little praise for Jacques Duclos who had yanked the American Communists back into line—but not until after the Germans surrendered and not until after he had paid a visit to the Soviet Union. For almost a year and a half not even Duclos had said one word about Browder's blunder. Only one man had said anything about it at all, and that was Foster, who was to take Browder's place. And his voice was extremely weak; in fact, scarcely audible.

In the June, 1940, issue of *The Communist,* page 525, Comrade John Williamson said:

"The change of name from party to association is a means of facilitating and strengthening unity, understanding an activity of the broad democratic current in American political life."

But in *Political Affairs,* September, 1945, he wrote:

"We recognize that the change of name from Communist Party to Communist Political Association was basically incorrect."

On June 18, 1945, the high Communist officials met in New York to reconstitute the Party. The statements that were made on that occasion are well worth rereading. Said Comrade Morris Childs:

"Comrade Browder and we who supported him found justification in the pretentious conception that we are aiding something new to Marxism. * * * Let me be concrete. Taking Teheran as a departure, we completely revised Marxism-Leninism. I underline *completely* because we departed from the very basic concept of Marxism."

Said Comrade Gilbert Green:

"My own share of responsibility I consider particularly great. I did not follow blindly—I was firmly convinced that the main line was correct."

Said Comrade Roy Hudson:

"In the light of developments it would seem to me that these are views which Browder held all the time, and we swallowed them hook, line and sinker until we began to do some serious thinking as a result of the Duclos article. * * * I feel very deeply the responsibility that I share with the other board members for the mistakes made."

Said Comrade Elizabeth Gurley Flynn:

"If Comrade Browder had earlier made it clear how far his think- · ing went and that this was such a long-term perspective, I don't think any of us would have accepted it."

Said Comrade Doxey Wilkerson:

"* * * Our pre-Duclos analysis and over-all policy represented a disastrously illusory distortion of Marxism."

Said Comrade Samuel Donchin:

"I do not in my own conscience absolve myself from individual responsibility for the revisionist line."

Said Comrade Carl Winter:

"I feel deeply my responsibility as a national committee member and as a delegate from California to the national convention which dissolved the Party and formed the CPA, for my part in the course we adopted there. I feel responsible to the members who elected me as a delegate to the convention."

Said Comrade V. J. Jerome:

"In evaluating my work in the course of recent years I have come to the conclusion that I have failed to exercise sufficient vigilance and to do my share in struggling against the permeation of the bourgeois ideology into the ranks of the working class and its vanguard."

On February 13, 1946, Browder was expelled from the American Communist Party. He had persisted stubbornly in his contention that he had been correct in his views during the war, and he now refused to change them. For some reason this man, who had never exhibited the slightest aggressive characteristic, now evidenced no fear whatever of expulsion from the movement he had led for 15 years. Unlike the defendants before the Russian tribunals during the purge trials of 1937 and 1938, he would not even confess his sins.

The resolution of expulsion read as follows:

"The national committee has considered and approved the recommendation of the national board, and the demand from the ranks of our Party organization that Earl Browder be expelled from the Communist Party for gross violation of Party discipline and decisions, for active opposition to the political line and leadership of our Party, for developing factional activity and for betraying the principles of Marxism-Leninism and deserting to the side of the class enemy—American monopoly capital."

Browder apparently accepted his expulsion philosophically, and with his brother started a business advisory service in New York City. Then came the one event that threw more light on the situation than even the fact that his grave deviation remained undiscovered all during the war, when it was operating with great success for the Soviet Union, and was abruptly discovered after the war when it was no longer useful to that country, and it was time once again to take advantage of the postwar condition by turning on the militant anti-American propaganda and resorting to the old underground subversive activities.

Earl Browder went to Russia. He was received and entertained by no less a personage than Foreign Commissar Vyachaslav Molotov. He conferred at length with his old comrade and collaborator in China, Solomon Losovsky, and when he was ready to return to the United States on June 20, 1946, he came as sole agent for the sale of Soviet literature in this Country. When he reached England he was held incommunicado by the authorities. When his plane landed in America he merely stated that he had not seen Stalin. It is obvious to anyone who has read the newspapers for the past several years that traitors to Marxism do not voluntarily go to the Soviet Union. And if they do go they usually remain permanently.

Foster had no sooner assumed the office so recently vacated by his old comrade and collaborator for 26 years than he issued a characteristic statement:

"To eliminate Browder's opportunism and to build a strong dike against its future recurrence, the Party must radically improve the social composition of its membership and of its leadership. We must enlist more and more workers from the basic industries. We must, above all, recruit trade unionists and war veterans and bring them into our leadership. The winning of such members will be facilitated by the Party's present change of line."

Foster is still the nominal head of the Communist Party of the United States. During the past several years the entire Party structure has gone deeper and deeper underground, relying more upon perfection of its facilities for espionage than on any mass open activity.

The Party will always maintain a skeleton organization which will operate more or less openly. This serves to continue the printing of the two main Communist publications in the United States, the *Daily Worker* of New York, and the *Daily People's World* in California, as well as the monthly publication which carries the changes of the local Party line and ideological matters, and which is still printed under the name of *Political Affairs*. It will permit the continued operation of the various Communist bookstores in California and elsewhere throughout the United States, as media through which the Communist propaganda originating in foreign countries can be distributed to American Party members and thereby keep them abreast of the international Party line. It serves to maintain a small but vociferous group of Communist agitators, who are considered completely expendable by the Party and who regard themselves as martyrs to the cause. The noise emitted by this aboveground group of extreme fanatics is far out of proportion to their numbers, but they are zealous workers and are always ready to march in the picket lines, to vilify the police and courts of the county, to form delegations to call in protest upon state, county and municipal executives; to organize marches on the State Capitol when the Legislature is in session; who serve by their clamor to attract attention to themselves and divert it from the more subversive and underground operation of the hidden portion of the Party apparatus; to act as leaders in the few Communist front organizations that still operate along the Pacific Coast.

In the 1951 report, this committee explained in detail the nature of the physical organization of the Communist Party of the United States, and recited in detail the testimony of Paul Crouch, who was the head of the Communist Party in Alameda County at a time when lectures were being delivered there to Communist leaders preparatory to perfecting the underground organization of the Party.

NEED FOR UNDERSTANDING COMMUNISM

It is hoped that the readers of this report will realize that it is extremely difficult to cope adequately with an international conspiracy unless one thoroughly understands its origin, development and inherent characteristics. Members of labor unions can hardly be expected to cope with the problem of Communist infiltration unless they understand the techniques used by the Party in accomplishing that result. If they are thoroughly aware of the Communist fraction techniques and the diamond pattern, as explained elsewhere in this section of the report, they are prepared to handle the situation without much difficulty. The committee knows this to be a fact, because through the conduct of seminars and schools of instruction, it has disseminated accurate information concerning these matters and the results have been gratifying in the extreme. By the same token, educational administrators who are sincerely opposed to Communism, could hardly be expected to cope adequately with the problem unless they are first made familiar with the devious and subtle techniques by which that infiltration is effected and carried on in such a manner as to elude detection and exposure.

It is always difficult to fight something you cannot see. The world Communist movement is, by its very nature, secret and conspiratorial, and it has never been more so than at the present time. Its open activities are not particularly alarming unless viewed over the years; consequently, the average citizen who sees nothing of the underground operation and who knows nothing about the principles of Marxism, nothing about the Revolution of 1917 or the struggle for power between Stalin and Trotsky, nothing about the long range objectives of the International Communist movement, nothing about the history of the American Communist infiltration of the labor unions in this country, is naturally prone to pay little attention to the real seriousness of the problem. He is also apt to be influenced by protests of "witch hunting" and "red baiting" that pour constantly from the Communist propaganda machinery whenever an official body presumes to criticize or investigate the activities of the Party through the legal processes of the country.

PUBLIC APATHY DECREASING

The committee has found that public apathy toward the Communist problem as a whole has pretty well disappeared; the average American is vigorously opposed to Communism, but he knows virtually nothing about how Communism originated, how it operates, and how best to combat its influences. It is gratifying to this committee that since the publication of its first report in 1943, there has been a steadily increasing demand for subsequent reports, until they are now all out of print with the exception of a few remaining copies of the report which was published in 1951. A survey of the larger bookstores in California discloses an enormously increased demand for books dealing with Communism; before service clubs, fraternal organizations, trade unions, and at conventions and other meetings of all descriptions there is a great demand for speeches by people who are recognized as experts in the field of counter-subversive activity. All of this is enormously encouraging, particularly when the committee contrasts this attitude with the complete public apathy that was exhibited when it commenced its activities in 1940.

It has frequently been stated, but the fact will bear repeating, that there are more Communists in the State of California than in any other state of the union with the single exception of New York. With the opening of hostilities in Korea, the Pacific Coast and particularly California, assumed a position of great strategic importance from a defense standpoint. The Communist reaction to this condition has been manifest. From other parts of the United States key members of the Communist apparatus have entered California for conferences with Communist leaders. A day-by-day analysis of the Communist propaganda publications from foreign countries and a comparison of their contents with the Party line as echoed by the Communist Party of California, indicates the close cooperation that exists between the Party here and Communists in foreign countries. Many American Communists have come to California for brief conferences and then gone into Mexico, and several individuals who were formerly active in the motion picture industry have gone to Mexico and applied for Mexican citizenship—all of them have long records of Communist affiliation and activity in this State.

Thus the problem of keeping accurately informed about the various phases of Communist activity in California is a fluid and elastic matter. It is absolutely essential to understand the constantly-changing aspects of the international Communist Party line in order to anticipate the effects of that international line among the Communists of California. At the present time, for example, the great international Communist propaganda subject is peace at any price. This information was disclosed several months ago by an analysis of the publications from England, India, the Iron Curtain countries, Red China and the Soviet Union obtained from the Communist bookstores in this state. Immediately thereafter, the sentiments were echoed in the *Daily People's World,* and Communist-front organizations clamoring for peace sprang up all over California.

A year ago the monthly ideological publication of the American Communist Party carried an article to the effect that it would be necessary to start increased agitation among the agricultural workers along the Pacific Coast. Within two weeks after the appearance of that publication in the Communist bookstores of California, scores of underground Communist activists were observed working among migratory agricultural laborers in the Sacramento, San Joaquin and Santa Clara Valleys, endeavoring to recruit new Party members and to incite strikes and riots.

By thus keeping abreast of Communist activity as it develops and manifests itself, the information can be disseminated to the proper authorities and the effects of the activity effectively combatted. It is, of course, necessary to keep at hand accurate and documented information concerning the whereabouts and activities of individuals who for years have been known as Communist leaders. The instant one of them moves from one part of the state to another, his arrival is almost invariably attended by a burst of activity in the field of Communist operation in which he is known as a specialist. For example, the committee is aware of the fact that Steve Nelson operated in California as an espionage agent. It is also aware of the fact that Bernadette Doyle, once a candidate for State Superintendent of Public Instruction, had served as his secretary. Consequently, Miss Doyle is disclosed as an extremely highly placed Communist Party member who is sufficiently indoctrinated and trusted by the national Party apparatus that she can serve as secretary to an espionage agent of international stature. If Philip M. Connelly, recently convicted under the Smith Act, leaves Los Angeles for a visit in San Jose or Stockton, it might reasonably be anticipated that he is going for the purpose of trade union organization, especially in the journalistic or propaganda fields. Thus, by familiarity with the leadership of the Communist Party organization in this State, and a knowledge of the specialized work performed by the various leaders of the movement, it is quite possible to keep abreast of the activities of the Party here whether those activities are carried out by the open Communist organization or the underground.

As will be seen in a succeeding section of this portion of the report, the mere fact that a large section of the Communist apparatus is functioning from an underground position does not at all mean that it has surrounded itself with impenetrable secrecy. The individuals who are now functioning as underground members of the Party were once members of the above-ground organization, their records are available, and they have merely been removed from front organization activities, work on the Party newspaper, in Party bookstores, the California Labor School, and from any other places where their activities would be relatively unconcealed. There is, however, no such thing as an *inactive* Communist Party member. Therefore, each of the underground Communists is assigned to carry on duties in conformity with his particular aptitude, and if one is aware of what that aptitude is, his activities can be followed without too much difficulty.

Since the publication of the 1951 report, there has been no organizational change in the structure of the underground section of the Communist Party. None of its units comprise more than five members, and most of them comprise only three. This precaution, as has already been pointed out, was taken for the purpose of preventing the infiltration of counter-espionage agents, and to protect the Party against disclosures made by such of its members who might be disillusioned and inclined to disclose their knowledge to official agencies. Since the Smith Act convictions, there is virtually no activity around the head office of the Communist Party of California at 942 Market Street, San Francisco; the Party leadership having moved its offices to more remotely located quarters, from where they carry on the work of directing Party activities much as before, but with a different group of leaders.

It should be added that most of the Party activities in California are carried on in the southern part of the State. This is because most of the State's population is concentrated in that region, because there are more members of racial minority groups in Southern California, and because there is far better opportunity for mass infiltration and indoctrination of trade unions in basic defense industries. Leadership of the Communist Party in California has, however, always been located in San Francisco. As was pointed out in the 1951 report, when the Communist Party of the United States divided this country into 20 Communistic districts years ago, California, Arizona and Nevada comprised District 13, with headquarters in San Francisco, and the Party has been run from that locality ever since.

LOS ANGELES CITY HOUSING AUTHORITY

Early in September, 1952, the Los Angeles City Housing Authority was engaged in a condemnation proceeding in the Superior Court of Los Angeles County, the defendants being Mosier M. Meyer and others. One of the witnesses for the Housing Authority was Mr. Frank Wilkinson, its information officer, who was asked to take the witness stand and testify as an expert on behalf of the Authority. In the process of cross-examining the witness concerning his qualifications, opposing counsel asked him about the organizations to which he had been affiliated, and when Wilkinson showed some hesitancy in giving a full and complete reply, pressed him to the point that he eventually refused to answer the question on the advice of his attorney, Mr. Robert W. Kenny.

The attorneys for the defendants in the case immediately charged that Mr. Wilkinson was a secret member of the Communist Party of Los Angeles County and had been affiliated with the Communist Party there during the entire time that he was employed by the Housing Authority in a responsible position. In the light of his continued refusal to answer questions concerning his organizational affiliations, Mr. Wilkinson was suspended by the Housing Authority pending a further and more thorough investigation of his background.

On September 5, 1952, Senator Hugh M. Burns, Committee Chairman, received a letter from Howard L. Holtzendorff, Executive Director of the Housing Authority, which read as follows:

"Dear Senator Burns: This will confirm our long distance telephone conversation of Wednesday, September 3, 1952, wherein this agency officially requested that your honorable committee investigate the public charges recently made concerning the alleged affiliation of Mr. Frank Wilkinson, an employee of the Housing Authority, with the Communist Party.

"I am now enclosing a copy of a letter of even date to the Honorable Edmund G. Brown, Attorney General, wherein an official request was made of that office for an investigation of the same charges as they relate to a possible violation of the Oath of Allegiance which this employee executed pursuant to Chapter 8, Division 4, Title 1 of the Government Code of the State of California. It is our understanding that your committee will cooperate with the Office of the Attorney General and the Office of the Los Angeles County District Attorney in their investigation of this aspect of the matter.

"In making this request, it is our understanding that your committee will not only make a full and complete investigation of the charges against Mr. Wilkinson, but of any and all other employees of the Housing Authority whose loyalty has been questioned on affiliation with any alleged subversive organization charged.

"This agency, of course, will give you, and the members of your committee, our complete cooperation and will take such disciplinary action as may deemed appropriate in the light of any evidence that may be developed.

"Please accept our thanks for your assistance in this matter.

"Very truly yours

"HOWARD L. HOLTZENDORFF
"Executive Director"

Subsequently, the California Attorney General communicated by telephone with the committee, stated that he had discussed the matter with Mr. Ernest Roll, District Attorney of Los Angeles County, and that the two offices requested the California Senate Committee on Un-American Activities to conduct an investigation and hearing pursuant to Mr. Holtzendorff's letter. It should be added that throughout the entire investigation, at the time that the hearings were held in Los Angeles in September and October of 1952, and since that time, the committee has enjoyed the full and cordial cooperation of both the district attorney's office in Los Angeles and the office of Hon. Pat Brown, State Attorney General.

A cursory investigation of the situation at the Housing Authority soon indicated to the committee that in order to do a thorough job it should investigate the records of all employees, and particularly those who were closely associated with Mr. Wilkinson.

Following the preliminary investigation, subpenas were issued and the following persons were examined under oath: Mr. George A. Beavers, Vice Chairman of the Board of Commissioners of the Housing Authority; Howard L. Holtzendorff, Executive Director of the Housing Authority; Jess N. Swanson, head of the Housing Authority's Personnel Department; Sidney Green, Sarah Fefferman, Allan Carson, Fay Covner, Adina Williamson, Jessie L. Terry, H. L. Sunshine, Dorothy Foster, Ruth Johnson, Elizabeth Smith, Frank B. Wilkinson, Jean Wilkinson, Eleanor Raymond, Patrick Burns, Pauline Schindler, Jack Naiditch, and Frances Eisenburg. Since some of the witnesses were friendly and cooperative, while others were extremely hostile and uncooperative, and since the committee found that the entire subject of public housing in Los Angeles County was embroiled in a vigorous political turmoil, it was decided to hold most of the hearings in executive session in order that the witnesses would testify more readily, and because the committee did not wish to become involved in any way in the political controversy concerning the housing program. As the committee saw it, the job was to investigate the personnel of the Housing Authority, publicly expose any Communist Party members and to counsel with the Housing Authority to the end that infiltration of the personnel by Communists or Communist sympathizers would be made much more difficult. Some of the opponents of public housing objected because the committee held a part of its session behind closed doors. To these critics Senator Burns issued the following statement:

"Such hearings afford protection to witnesses who cooperate with the committee and who would be reluctant to testify freely in an open session; they afford no opportunity and provide no audience for hostile witnesses to make propaganda speeches for the benefit of press and public, thereby turning the initial phase of an investigation into a cheap exhibition; it affords the committee an opportunity to carefully evaluate the testimony and to investigate newly developed leads without having the entire procedure prematurely tried in the press; it permits the committee to keep the entire investigative procedure within proper limits instead of having persons demand the right to make long statements at public expense for the sole purpose of exploiting their own political or personal views which are wholly extraneous to a thorough, objective and dignified investigation.''

At the time of the first hearing, which was commenced in open session at 10.30 a.m. on September 26, 1952, Mr. Beavers, on behalf of the Board of Housing Commissioners, read the following statement into the record:

''Mr. Chairman and Members of the Committee: In the absence of the Chairman of the Housing Authority, Mr. Nicolai Giulii, from the city, the Commissioners of the Housing Authority of the City of Los Angeles have authorized me to make the following statement for the record on behalf of the Housing Commission.

''The authority sincerely appreciates the cooperation of your committee in granting our official request of September 3, 1952, to investigate the public charges recently made concerning the alleged affiliation of Mr. Frank Wilkinson, an employee of the Housing Authority, with the Communist Party. We also appreciate your further consent to make a full and complete investigation of any and all personnel of the authority whose loyalty and/or organizational affiliations have been questioned.

''At the time our request was made we not only pledged our full cooperation in such an investigation, but also agreed to promptly take such administrative action as would be deemed appropriate in the light of any evidence that might be adduced before your committee. This is still our position.

''The Commissioners of the Housing Authority of the City of Los Angeles, a quasi-public agency of the State of California, have long been aware of their duties and responsibilities in the field of government security and employee loyalty and have, since 1942, required either a sworn loyalty oath or statement of all its employees as a condition of employment. Attached to this statement are various loyalty oaths and/or statements taken from the official files of the authority.

''And I want to especially call the attention of the members of the committee to this fact, that we have included with the statement evidence of our continued action regarding the matter.

''The commission, from the beginning, has not only firmly believed in the old adage, 'Eternal vigilance is the price of liberty,' but has on every occasion supported that belief by prompt and vigorous action. Attached to this statement is a memorandum dated September 21, 1951, transmitting a copy of the commission's decision wherein the authority summarily dismissed the petition of the United Public Workers for collective bargaining recognition because the loyalty of that organization was publicly in question.

''In addition, the records of the Federal Bureau of Investigation, as well as all other law enforcement agencies, will show that the

Housing Authority has, from the beginning, fully cooperated with all matters including subversive activities.

"In view of the fact that all 450 employees of the Housing Authority have, without exception, executed the Oath of Allegience required by Chapter 8, Division 4, Title 1 of the Government Code of the State of California and have also executed similar sworn statements in their applications for employment, the commission believes that the overwhelming majority of all its employees are good, loyal American citizens. On the other hand, if there are any disloyal employees within the authority we want to know about it.

"While the commission is not unmindful of the constitutional privileges of its employees, it is the commission's view that all employees have a duty to answer any and all proper questions propounded by any court of law or legally constituted investigating committees. While employees have a constitutional right to refuse to answer questions which they feel would tend to incriminate them, they do not have a constitutional right to continue in the employment of the Housing Authority. It is the position of the commission that under existing circumstances the voluntary exercising of such constitutional privilege is inconsistent with the employees' duty to both the public and the authority. In taking this position the commission is not unmindful of our duty to exercise due care and deliberation to assure fair and just treatment for all employees.

"Gentlemen of the committee, you can be assured that it is the unanimous feeling of the commission that there is no place in the authority for any disloyal person or for anyone who raises doubt of his loyalty by refusing to answer proper questions. The commission, therefore, will promptly separate from service of the authority any employee who has been proven to be disloyal or who refuses to answer any and all proper questions of your committee."

TESTIMONY OF HOWARD HOLTZENDORFF

Mr. Howard Holtzendorff, Executive Director of the Housing Authority since February, 1941, testified that he was the chief administrative officer in charge of supervision of all operations and personnel. In the operation of approximately 11,000 dwelling units of various types, 3,400 of which were operated by the authority, and the balance of which were being run by the authority for the State or Federal Government. Mr. Holtzendorff estimated that there were between 35 and 40 thousand persons occupying the Housing Authority facilities, and that approximately 60 percent of that residential population was comprised of the following racial minority groups: Mexican-American, Negro, Chinese, Japanese, and Filipino, the location of their residence in the authority coinciding with the neighborhood residential patterns of the City of Los Angeles.

Questioned concerning the matter of Communist infiltration of the Housing Authority personnel, Mr. Holtzendorff testified as follows:

"Q. (By Mr. Combs): Have you from time to time during the period of your employment as Executive Director of the authority, received any information concerning Communist activities or infiltration of your employees or your residents in the housing units?

"A. Yes, sir.

"Q. Over how long a period of time?

"A. Oh, I assume they were received—I assume we have received information of some type or other since I have been here.

"Q. You were here during the testimony of Mr. Beavers, were you not?

"A. Yes, sir.

"Q. Now, when you got information of that kind did you report the information to the commission?

"A. I reported it if I felt that it was anything but the rankest hearsay or rumor or gossip. Most of it would fall into that category. The only matters I reported to the commission were matters that I felt were of a serious nature and that they should be advised about.

"Q. And was there any particular effort on the part of the authority to establish any screening or any investigation of any kind touching on the eligibility of prospective employees as far as their subversive affiliations might be concerned?

"A. Yes, sir.

"Q. Will you explain that?

"A. Yes. The primary consideration which I recommended to the commission soon after I came here was the installation of an oath, the actual oath which is in evidence here I believe is Exhibit 1 as a part of Mr. Beavers' statement, a sworn oath which followed the language of the loyalty oath which is required, or which was then required of all federal employees at that time. And then after that as the Federal Government changed their policy as to whether it was an oath or a part of their application for employment, the Housing Authority likewise changed.

"And so attached to Exhibit 1 now in evidence you will find the various oaths and applications for employment which were installed, and where the employee was required to state in essence that he is not now and never has been a member of any organization which advocated the overthrow by force or violence of the Government of the United States or of the State of California, and we have required that oath of our employees and made it a condition of employment.

"Then in addition to that the personnel department, and a large part of it has come from the head of that department, has been instructed by me from the beginning to very carefully review all references. You will note in our application forms, which I will again refer to as a part of Exhibit 1, a place for references so that we had a dual check insofar as it was possible and which followed primarily the federal procedure, which I brought with me. I came to the authority from the Federal Government where I was Regional Counsel in San Francisco for the 11 western states, and being familiar with the federal procedure I installed that procedure here and also the oath change and the application change that followed the form of the federal until 1950. In 1950, when the State Government first faced up to the problem and passed the Levering Act all the employees took that oath, but nevertheless we continued after that, and still do require that oath as a condition of employment, and if an employee violates that it is an immediate reason for dismissal.''

''Q. Mr. Holtzendorff, have you ever had anybody refuse to sign that oath?

''A. No, sir.

''Q. Everybody signed it?

''A. Yes, sir.

''Q. Now, you heard Mr. Beavers' opinion concerning the establishment of implementation for your oath awhile ago. What are your views on that proposal?

''A. Well, I think it is something that unfortunately has not been made available to public agencies in the State of California before, for the reason that my problem as an administrator has been that I have not had access to a procedure whereby employees could be screened in advance in such matters as would not appear from injurious statements on a application for employment, and I think that the committee is to be congratulated upon for the first time offering at least the public agencies, and I assume you will do the same thing for private agencies if the Legislature permits you to implement your philosophies to that extent—I think it may be the only hope of legal agencies in this State being able to obtain correct and adequate information instead of having to rely upon hearsay, scuttlebut, rumor and gossip; and I certainly, as an administrator of this agency, would strongly recommend to the Housing Authority that they accept or ask the assistance of your committee to install a similar procedure for the Housing Authority of the City of Los Angeles; and further than that, as a member of the California League of Housing Authorities, of which there are 54 in the State of California, to recommend that the league itself in turn ask the cooperation of your committee so that all the housing authorities in California will have the benfit of such services. I think it is an excellent idea.

''Q. Mr. Holtzendorff, now getting down to the specific case of Mr. Frank Wilkinson; Mr. Frank B. Wilkinson of course was personally known to you, was he not?

''A. Yes, sir.

''Q. His personnel record shows that he was first employed by the authority in the summer of 1942 and that at that time he came to you from an organization known as the Citizens Housing Council of Los Angeles, of which he had been executive secretary. Did he work continuously for the authority since the time of his employment, original employment?

''A. The file will show. My recollection is that the answer is yes.

''Q. Yes, the file so shows. What position did he occupy at the time of his separation?

''A. He was the Director of the Office of Information for the authority. That includes research and information.

''Q. That position, of course, as the Director of Information would, at least I assume, have given Mr. Wilkinson access to all the files, records and documents of the authority, would it not?

''A. No, sir.

''Q. What records would he have access to?

"A. He would have access to only the general research and information documents. He definitely did not have access, and no one else does, to the personnel files or the finance files. The financial files are under the jurisdiction of the Controller, all our financial books and records, and all the personnel files are under the supervision of the Personnel Department, and no one else has access to them except the heads of these departments or myself or the commission.

"Q. Then the one that would have access to the personnel files would be the director, who is Mr. Swanson.

"A. Mr. Swanson is the Director of the Office of Information and he has several departments under him, one of which is the Personnel Department. The Personnel Department is headed up by Mr. Swanson, but Mr. Wilkinson is active in that as well as other departments.

"Q. And what were Mr. Wilkinson's duties and responsibilities?

"A. It was Mr. Wilkinson's duty and responsibility to represent the authority in speaking engagements and conducting tours on request by various groups to see the slums or housing projects, and to generally supply information to organizations or individuals who sought such information from the Housing Authority; and in addition to that his other main duty was to do necessary research on statistics going out having to do with the degree of continuance or noncontinuance of slum conditions in the City of Los Angeles.

"Q. From what basic material would he conduct that type of research?

"A. That type of research, as far as slum conditions were concerned, was conducted from two primary documents, one a real property inventory in 1938 wherein as part of a WPA project, Works Project Administration project, they set up a survey of all substandard housing in Los Angeles. It is a very voluminous document of four or five volumes. That was the first time a real property inventory of the City of Los Angeles had ever been made.

"That was the original document. The document he has worked on subsequently is the Decennial Census of the Federal Government, 1940-1950, and any special studies made by the Bureau of the Census for the Housing Authority on special contract.

"Q. As another part of his duties would he have access to all the residential units operated by the authority?

"A. No, sir. No one has access to all the residential units operated by the authority other than myself.

"Q. How about the managers of each separate unit and the administrative staff that was working under the managers of those units?

"A. As the head of the Office of Information, for example, if we had a complaint or wanted information on a family or someone living in a specific project, then he had authority to go to the manager and get that information and give it to the people who had made inquiry. He would have access in that way to the manager or assistant manager of the particular project.

"Q. That is what I was getting at. In other words, in his particular type of activity one of his functions, I take it, would be to maintain a contact with the various administrative heads of the authority?

"A. Only as relates to his field of public information and research. If he had a question about finances he would have to go to the Controller for his information. If he had a question about our park program, he would have to go to the Park Director for figures and estimates, etc. So he would have access as part of his job to get the material from the proper source."

Having thus determined when Mr. Wilkinson was employed by the Housing Authority and the character of his duties there, it was felt necessary to ascertain when Holtzendorff had any suspicions concerning Wilkinson's affiliation. The testimony in that regard was as follows:

"Q. (By Mr. Combs) : Now, Mr. Holtzendorff, prior to the refusal of Mr. Wilkinson to answer questions, had you any prior intimation of his hesitancy in revealing his organizational connections?

"A. No, sir.

"Q. Had you prior to that time regarded him as a trustworthy, reliable and loyal employee?

"A. Yes, sir.

"Q. And you had no reason to view him in any other light?

"A. None whatsoever.

"Q. Immediately following his refusal to testify under the circumstances that I have described, and which are, of course, set forth verbatim in the copies of the testimony, what, if anything did you do about him?

"A. I suspended Mr. Wilkinson immediately.

"Q. Did you talk to him first?

"A. Yes, sir.

"Q. Did you ask him whether or not he was a member of any subversive organization?

"A. No, sir.

"Q. You did not?

"A. No.

"Q. You merely notified him that he was suspended?

"A. No, I asked him why he didn't answer the questions?

"Q. And what did he say?

"A. He said he wouldn't answer the questions because in his opinion it would be a violation of his personal rights concerning his business or political affiliations.

"Q. Where did that conversation occur?

"A. The conversation took place in the secretary's office of Superior Court Department 55.

"Q. Was anyone else present?

"A. No.

"Q. Did you have any subsequent conversation with him—personally, I mean?

"A. Yes, sir.

"Q. When and where did that occur?

"A. If my memory serves me, it was on September 5th in my office.

"Q. Did you at that time and place discuss with him the matter of his possible affiliation with subversive organizations or organization?

"A. Yes, sir.

"Q. Was anyone else present?

"A. No, sir.

"Q. Will you repeat the substance of the conversation to the best of your recollection?

"A. I again inquired why he would not answer what I considered to be a proper question, and in substance he reiterated a similar position.

"Q. And that was the substance of the conversation?

"A. That was the substance of the conversation, yes, sir.

"Q. You haven't personally discussed anything with him since?

"A. Not since that date, no, sir."

A subpena had been issued for Mr. Wilkinson, but after it had been drawn and before it could be served on him, he entered a hospital for the purpose of having an operation performed on his knee, and the officer served the subpena in the hospital. It was then agreed between the committee and Mr. Robert S. Morris, Jr., an associate in the law office of Robert W. Kenny, that Mr. Wilkinson would be called to testify at a later date after he had recovered from the effects of the operation. He was examined, as will be seen, on October 28, 1952.

CLOSED HEARINGS

The committee wishes to emphasize at this point a situation that it has frequently mentioned before, and which cannot be repeated too often. In the process of conducting its work, the committee frequently finds it necessary to subpena persons who are perfectly loyal and cooperative and concerning whom there is not the slightest question of Communist affiliation or any subversive connection or suspicion of any kind whatsoever. In all such cases the committee has taken great pains to make it crystal clear that merely because a person is served with a subpena should give rise to no presumption that the individual was the subject of an investigation. This condition was particularly applicable to the two hearings held in Los Angeles regarding the Housing Authority— and was the main reason why the witnesses were examined during closed sessions of the committee, although in all cases even the most hostile witnesses were permitted to consult with their attorneys at all stages of the proceedings.

Prior to the hearings, representatives of the committee had interrogated many persons, some of whom were employees of the Housing Authority, and others who had formerly been employed there, and still other individuals who had no connection with the Authority at all but who did have pertinent information regarding the Communist infiltration and the names and activities of individuals who were believed to be members of the Communist Party itself.

Sidney Green

The first witness to be called on the morning of September 26, 1952, was Mr. Sidney Green, 4558 Vantage Avenue, North Hollywood, accompanied by his attorney, Daniel G. Marshall, 1151 South Broadway, Los Angeles. In view of the intense interest evidenced by residents of Los Angeles in these hearings, the committee deems it appropriate to quote liberally from the transcript, and at this point wishes to point out that regardless of the fact that a committee may hold executive hearings at which the press is not represented, nevertheless, the printed transcript is on file in the State Capitol at Sacramento or the committee offices at Fresno and can be read from cover to cover by any interested citizen at any time. Some individuals apparently were of the false opinion that such hearings are shrouded in mystery, assume the character of star chamber sessions, and that no one is permitted access to the transcript. In every hearing that the committee has ever conducted, and in all hearings that it will conduct in the future, every word that is uttered is taken down in shorthand by a court reporter, the testimony thereafter transcribed and sworn to by the reporter as a true and correct transcription of his shorthand, or stenotype notes; all of the exhibits, whether documentary or otherwise, are filed with the committee, and the transcript itself, being a full and complete record of everything that transpires at the hearings, whether open or closed, is filed at the State Capitol at Sacramento. In the belief that no useful purpose can be gained by printing the entire testimony of the witnesses in a report of this nature, the committee quotes liberally from the testimony and for further detailed information refers interested persons to the official transcript.

Mr. Green testified that he was born in New York City, received his primary education there, and attended New York City College, a parochial school, and Columbia University. Late in 1935, he came to California, and from September, 1939, until January, 1941, was employed by the State Relief Administration in this State. The first indication that Mr. Green would be an uncooperative witness was made when he was being interrogated about his employment by the Relief Administration in Southern California, as follows:

"Q. (By Mr. Combs): Who was your immediate superior when you first were employed by the SRA?

"A. I'm sorry, sir, I haven't the vaguest recollection of the name.

"Q. Who was in charge of the office in which you were employed?

"A. That I remember as a lady——

"Q. Wouldn't it possibly be on your application sheet there?

"A. Oh, I'm sorry. I didn't think of that. No, it is not on this sheet but I think——

"Q. Isn't there a space on the questionnaire provided for your immediate supervisor?

"A. Well, the entry made on this blank is that—the entry I made was 'Varied.' Now I'm trying, however—I am remembering the lady's last name. It was something very close to Bergerman. It was either Bergerman or something that sounded exactly like that.

"Q. Did you ever know a man by the name of Richard Sasuly?

"Mr. Marshall: Let me have that last question, Mr. Reporter. (Record read to witness' attorney.)

"The Witness: I am afraid I have to decline to answer that question on the ground that I would be compelled to give testimony which might in some way incriminate me.

"Mr. Combs: Well, may I point this out, Mr. Green and Counsel, as I told you in the beginning these questions are limited to his own personal background, and I think the name of Richard Sasuly appears in the document, doesn't it?

"Mr. Marshall: I will hand you the document, Mr. Combs.

"Mr. Combs: Yes, it does, and I presume that is in your own handwriting, isn't it, Mr. Green?

"The Witness: I wish to claim the privilege of the Fifth Amendment on this document.

"Q. (By Mr. Combs): On the document in its entirety?

"A. Yes, sir.

"Q. Now will you repeat the grounds on which you refuse to testify concerning that document?

"A. It is an attempt to compel me to give testimony which may tend to incriminate me——

"Q. Just a moment, Mr. Green, before you read from a document, of course, we would like to have some foundation laid for it. Did you prepare that document yourself?

"A. I claim the Fifth Amendment on that question, sir.

"Q. Concerning the document to which you now refer?

"A. Yes.

"Mr. Marshall: The one he has in his hand?

"Mr. Combs: The one he has in his hand as distinguished from the one contained in his personnel file.

"The Witness: I claim the Fifth Amendment.

"Q. (By Mr. Combs): You refuse to answer the question on the ground that your answer may tend to incriminate you.

"A. Yes, sir.

"Q. Well, and you do that on the advice of counsel?

"A. Yes."

The document referred to as being shown to the witness by the committee's counsel was his own personnel record, executed in his own handwriting, signed by him, and containing his application for a position with the Los Angeles Housing Authority. The name, Richard Sasuly, which appeared thereon, was listed as a reference given by Mr. Green, the witness, and he even refused to identify his own signature on the application form.

Mr. Green also refused to answer questions concerning his presence as an observer at the Warner Bros. studio strike at Burbank, California in 1945, again claiming that his answers might tend to submit him to prosecution for an offense.

The witness readily answered questions concerning his employment, however, stating that he was a management supervisor, made $743 per month and commenced his work with the Housing Authority in 1941, working as a junior interviewer, whose duties included the inspection of the dwellings of persons applying for public housing, the rating of those dwellings according to their condition of substandardness, and reviewing applications of all persons and reporting on them to the authority.

There then followed a line of questions and answers that are set forth herewith in full:

"Q. (By Mr. Combs): Is it not a fact that in 1946 you were a member of the Hollywood Independent Citizens Committee of the Arts, Sciences and Professions?

"A. I decline to answer that question upon the ground that it is attempt to compel me to give testimony which may tend to incriminate me.

"Q. Is it not a fact that in 1947 you were regularly on the mailing list of the Hollywood Writers Mobilization, at which time your address was Aliso Village Housing Committee, 1401 East First Street, Los Angeles, California, which of course is this address?

"A. I decline to answer upon the ground it is an attempt to compel me to give testimony which may tend to incriminate me.

"Q. Mr. Green, did you ever own a Chevrolet sedan automobile?

"A. Yes.

"Q. A 1939 Chevrolet sedan, wasn't it?

"A. To the best of my recollection.

"Q. And you owned such a car in June of 1948?

"A. Well, now, I don't recall. If I would be permitted to think just a second I can trace back on the trade-ins and so on.

"Q. I will give you the exact date. Is it not a fact that you were the registered owner of a 1939 Chevrolet sedan on June 12, 1948?

"A. I'm sorry, I don't remember.

"Q. Do you remember that you drove that automobile yourself on the evening of June 12, 1948, to the residence of Mrs. Julian Sieroty, whose address at that time was 1002 North Rexford Drive, Beverly Hills, California, at which time and place you attended a meeting?

"Mr. Marshall: Will you excuse me until I get a book that I left outside, just a moment?

"Mr. Combs: Yes.

"Mr. Marshall: Will you read the question now, please?

" (Question read by reporter.)

"The Witness: I decline to answer the question upon the ground that it is an attempt to compel me to give testimony that may tend to incriminate me.

"Q. (By Mr. Combs): Is it not a fact that on June 4, 1950, you attended an organizing convention of the Union of California Veterans at the Embassy Auditorium on Grand Avenue in the City of Los Angeles?

"A. Would you be kind enough to repeat the name of that outfit?

"Q. All right, the Union of California Veterans.

"A. The same answer.

"Q. You refuse to answer on the ground that your answer might tend to incriminate you?

"A. Yes, sir.

"Q. Mr. Green, were you acquainted with Frank Wilkinson when he was employed by the Los Angeles City Housing Authority?

"A. I decline to answer that question upon the following grounds: it is an attempt to compel me to give testimony which may tend to incriminate me, contrary to the Fifth Amendment of the Bill of Rights, and Article 1, Section 13 of the State of California.

"Q. Is it not a fact, Mr. Green, that you were recruited into the Communist Party as a member by Frank Wilkinson in the year 1945, and that your membership in the Communist Party has continued since that date, and that you are still a member of the Communist Party of Los Angeles County?

"A. I decline to answer that question upon the following grounds: it is an attempt to compel me to give testimony which may tend to incriminate me contrary to the Fifth Amendment of the Bill of Rights and Article 1, Section 13 of the Constitution of this State.

"Mr. Combs: That is all."

Fay Kovner

Miss Fay Kovner was called as a witness because when she had been employed by the housing authority she worked with Mr. Sidney Green and under his direct supervision. Miss Kovner, apparently apprehensive of the danger in answering questions that would tend to expose her to possible prosecution for the commission of a crime, was extremely cautious, as the following excerpts from her testimony will show:

"Q. (By Senator Burns) : You may be seated, and will you give us your full name and address, please.

"The Witness, Fay Kovner: With respect to giving my address, I refuse to answer the question upon the following grounds: it is an attempt to compel me to give testimony which may tend to incriminate me, contrary to the Fifth Amendment of the Constitution of the United States, and Article 1, Section 13 of the Constitution of this State, the privileges of which I hereby claim.

"Senator Burns: You mean that telling us your address will incriminate you?

"The Witness: The same answer.

"Q. (By Mr. Combs): May I ask you this question, are you married?

"A. I claim the same as I did previously.

"Q. As to your marital status?

"A. Yes.

"Q. Isn't it true that your husband's name is Muks?

"A. I refuse to answer the question upon the following grounds: it is an attempt to compel me to give testimony which may tend to incriminate me, contrary to the Fifth Amendment of the Bill of Rights, and Article 1, Section 13 of the Constitution of this State, the privileges of which I hereby claim."

The witness then stated that she was born in the City of New York, attended high school there and came to California in 1946; she stated that she was first assigned by the Housing Authority to work as a clerk-stenographer at Basilone Homes under the supervision of Sidney Green and that she resigned to get married on November 30, 1950. When questioned in detail about her associates and her activities, the witness invariably invoked the Fifth Amendment to the Constitution of the United States and refused to answer the question on the ground that in doing so she might subject herself to a criminal prosecution.

"Q. (By Mr. Combs): Do you have a brother named Julius Kovner?

"A. I refuse to answer the question——

"Q. And that his wife's name is Jeannette?

"A. I refuse for the same reason.

"Q. And that at the time you were living at 4253 Fulton Avenue, Sherman Oaks, you were living in their home?

"A. I refuse to answer the question upon the following grounds——

"Q. Did you ever hear of an organization called American Youth for Democracy?

"A. Yes, I did.

"Q. Did you ever belong to it?

"A. I refuse to answer the question upon the following grounds——

"Q. And is it not a fact that your affiliation with American Youth for Democracy, which was a continuation of the Young Communist League, lasted from 1943 through 1948?

"A. I refuse to answer on the same grounds.

"Q. While you were employed by the Los Angeles Housing Authority is it not a fact that you were at that time a member of the Communist Party of the County of Los Angeles?

"A. I refuse to answer the question upon the following grounds——

"Q. And is it not a fact and within your own personal knowledge that during the time that you were living with your brother, Julius, and his wife, Jeannette, at 4253 Fulton Avenue, Sherman Oaks, California, that your brother, Julius, was chairman of the North Hollywood Section of the Communist Party of Los Angeles County?

"A. I refuse to answer the question upon the following grounds——

"Q. During the time of your employment by the Housing Authority of Los Angeles were you acquainted with Mr. Frank Wilkinson?

"A. I know Mr. Wilkinson as a fellow employee.

"Q. Did you ever go to his home?

"A. I refuse to answer that on the ground that it is an attempt to compel me to give testimony which may tend to incriminate me——

"Q. When did your acquaintance with Mr. Wilkinson originate?

"A. I am not exactly sure when.

"Q. Well, what I am getting at, of course, is before you were employed by the authority or afterwards.

"A. Oh, no.

"Q. Afterwards?

"A. Yes.

"Q. Did you know him socially as well as professionally?

"A. I refuse to answer that on the same grounds.

"Q. During the period of your employment with the Housing Authority were you acquainted with Sidney Green?

"A. Yes.

"Q. And did you ever visit in his home?

"A. I refuse to answer on the same grounds.

"Q. During the period of time of your employment with the Housing Authority did you know Oliver Haskell?

"A. Yes.

"Q. Did you ever know him socially?

"A. I refuse to answer on the same grounds.

"Q. Did you know Irma Sapiro during that period of time?
"A. No.
"Q. You did not?
"A. No.
"Q. Did you ever know her at all?
"A. I refuse to answer on the same grounds.
"Q. During that period of time did you know Adina Williamson?
"A. I decline on the same grounds.
"Q. During the same period of time did you know H. L. Sunshine?
"A. Yes.
"Q. Socially?
"A. No, I decline on the same grounds.
"Q. Sarah Fefferman?
"A. I knew her.
"Q. Socially?
"A. I refuse to answer on the same grounds.
"Q. Dorothy Foster?
"A. I knew her.
"Q. Socially?
"A. I refuse to answer on the same grounds.
"Q. Did you know her professionally?
"A. Professionally, yes.
"Q. Elizabeth Smith, did you know her professionally?
"A. No, I did not.
"Q. Did you know her at all?
"A. I met her this morning for the first time.
"Q. Have you ever been a member of the Communist Party?
"A. I refuse to answer on the grounds stated before, self-incrimination.
"Mr. Combs: The witness may be excused?
"Senator Burns: Yes, the witness may be excused."

Adina Williamson

Adina Williamson testified that she resided at 1152 East Adams Boulevard in Los Angeles and during the course of her testimony consulted from time to time with her attorney, Mr. Leo Branton, Jr., 1111 East Vernon Avenue in Los Angeles. Miss Williamson stated that she was born in St. Louis, Missouri, had resided in California for about 12 years and was employed by the Los Angeles City Housing Authority since April of 1942, formerly having been manager of Imperial Courts Project, and having been promoted from one job to another until, at the time of her appearance before the committee, she was making about $403 per month.

All of this testimony Miss Williamson gave without the slightest hesitation until she was asked the following question:

"Q. (By Mr. Combs): Now, Miss Williamson, you knew Frank Wilkinson, did you not?
"A. Yes.
"Q. Did you ever know that he was a Communist Party member?
"A. Well, I will have to declare my rights on Article 1, Section 9 of the California Constitution, the First Amendment to the United

States Constitution, and Article 1, Section 13 of the California Constitution, and the Fifth Amendment to the United States Constitution. I decline to answer this question for fear of incrimination on the grounds stated.

"Q. Now, Miss Williamson, is it not a fact that you were recruited into the Communist Party by Mr. Wilkinson, and at the time that you joined the Communist Party you expressed apprehension lest Mrs. Terry find out that you were a member of the Party?

"A. I will have to decline to answer the question on the grounds stated——

"Q. When did you last see Mr. Wilkinson?

"A. I don't even remember.

"Q. Can you approximate it—about how long ago?

"A. I really don't know.

"Q. Let me ask you this question: have you ever been in his home?

"A. I must decline to answer that question on the grounds before stated.

"Q. All right. Are you now a member of the Communist Party?

"A. I must decline to answer that question on the grounds before stated.

"Mr. Combs: That is all."

Elizabeth L. Smith

Elizabeth L. Smith appeared without an attorney and testified that she resided at 2001 South Gaffey Street in San Pedro and that she was born in South Dakota and had come to California in the spring of 1938. Miss Smith testified openly, frankly and readily up to the point which will be indicated by excerpts from her testimony, telling the committee that she had previously been employed in Seattle, went to San Francisco in 1938 and there secured a position as secretary to the Executive Director of Labor's Nonpartisan League, a man named Mr. J. Vernon Burke, and that she had, in December, 1939, obtained a position with the California State Relief Administration under the direct supervision of Mr. Leigh Atherton. In her capacity as an employee for the State Relief Administration, Mrs. Smith testified that she had been membership secretary for a union known as the State, County and Municipal Workers of America, concerning which there will be considerable reference elsewhere in this portion of the report.

"Q. Now, our information is, Mrs. Smith, that one time some time ago you became a member of the Communist Party but that your membership was terminated by you and that you no longer have any connection with it. Is that true?

"A. I wouldn't answer that question. * * * I mean, I feel that people if they want to belong to the Communist Party, that is their business. They have to stand up for what they want to believe in. I am a Democrat and I stand up for what I believe in, and I believe in their rights.

"Q. I think you don't want to answer the question in such a way that it will involve anyone else and endanger anyone else?

"A. That is correct.

"Q. Isn't that the main reason for your hesitancy?

"A. That is the main reason for my hesitancy.

"Q. (By Senator Watson) : Well, who are you most loyal to, your country or your friends?

"A. Well, the people I know have not been named disloyal, as I have known them, and some of them I have worked with.

"Q. (By Mr. Combs) : I can't go any further without disclosing to you the things that I shouldn't reveal in advance in connection with the questions, Mrs. Smith. I'm sorry. I can't do that. I can only go this far. I have told you already that my information is that you are no longer a member of the Party.

"The Witness: That is correct."

After a considerable discussion concerning the rights of witnesses in general and the rights of this witness in particular, the question was put again and answered as follows:

"A. I refuse to answer that on the basis that it may incriminate me.

"Q. Is it not a fact that you at one time were a member of the Communist Party?

"A. I refuse to answer that question on the same ground."

H. L. Sunshine

Mr. H. L. Sunshine, who appeared without counsel, testified that he resided at 29 Laverne Avenue in Long Beach, and after having attended Denver University in Colorado, came to California and after working in San Diego from 1935 to 1940, and for about a year in Washington, D. C., returned to California and accepted a position with the Los Angeles City Housing Authority in October of 1945.

When questioned concerning his association with Communists, Sunshine replied as follows:

"I despise the Party and it is a dirty lie. I mean whoever made that statement is a filthy liar, because I have no use for it. It is trying to undermine our government, and I love my country more than to belong to anything like that.

"Q. (By Mr. Combs) : Were you ever solicited by Frank Wilkinson to become a Communist Party member?

"A. Well, I don't know if you would say I got solicited or not. * * * We were living over at Channel Heights at the time, and I was manager at Banning Homes and I had an assistant manager there by the name of Carole Andre and Carole had been voiced around as being Red, but frankly I didn't pay much attention to it because I know a lot of people are said—even though, they are fascists or something, and especially around the housing authority, you know, a group of people there. But one night—once in awhile at our house, maybe a mechanic would come over or somebody with a problem after I got home, about the project—I think all the managers have the same thing. So one night she called up, I think we were just eating, and said she would like to drop by, she had something very important to tell us, and she said she had Mr. Wilkinson with her and I said, 'O. K., as soon as we finish eating,' and so they came over I think about a half hour later.

"Q. Where were you living then?

"A. Up at Channel Heights. That is a housing development right near Banning. We moved out there so we could be close to my work and so they came up and they seemed very mysterious to us. I don't know, it kind of amazed us because in working with Carole Andre and knowing her every day this was an entirely different type of attitude on her part than what I had known.

"Q. Well, was it a different attitude on the part of Frank Wilkinson than what you had known?

"A. Well, his was quite reserved, like a hush-hush deal it seemed to me.

"Q. Was anyone else present beside you and your wife and Carole Andre and Frank Wilkinson?

"A. No, I don't know if our children were still up or not.

"Q. No other adults?

"A. No, sir. It is too bad too, because it helped us make our minds up, but I guess they don't work that way, I mean, the way things work out to me now I think I can almost say he is a Party member. Well, anyway, they came out and they said, 'We would like to talk to you and Janice'—that is my wife's name—'if she would like to hear it.' And then they started in and they started to discuss the Communist Party. I can't give you the exact wording; it has been about four or five years ago.

"Q. Well, just give us your best recollection.

"A. Then they started discussing the Party and I think they had some introductory statement or something up to that time and my wife was amazed and I was too, because I said, 'Gee, Frank, what the heck goes on here?' 'Well,' he said, 'Hi,' he said, 'You know Carole and I have for a long time thought that you know how to handle people. You have been promoted you know to this job and you have handled a tough situation down at Aliso Village several times where the people were going to do this and that and the other and we know that you have a good head on you.'

"Q. Mr. Sunshine, what type of residents did you have in Aliso Village as distinguished from the other units?

"A. Well, I don't know if there was any difference, some of them I think were hotter.

"Q. What do you mean by hotter?

"A. Well, they always plagued the authority, they always seemed to get silly stuff there and wanted to plague us with it.

"Q. You had a little more trouble there?

"A. Yes.

"Q. In the service and the like?

"A. Any sort of meetings. I know when I first came here I think I was really baptized with fire the first month I was here. They called a mass meeting for about—I don't know, there was about six or seven items there that they wanted the Housing Authority to do and they told me they didn't want me at the meeting.

"Q. Didn't Sidney Burke live there for awhile?

"A. No, sir, I don't think so.

"Senator Dilworth: Does the Housing Authority give you any authority to deal with that sort of thing?

"The Witness: Yes, it does, I've done so many times.

"Q. (By Mr. Combs) : You were in charge of that entire unit?

"A. I was in charge of Aliso Village. We had a lot out at Roger Young Village a couple of years ago when it seemed like a bunch of Communists might take over there and we got together with another group and got them out. They wanted to hold meetings and I told them no meetings.

"Q. That was after your conversation with Carole Andre and Frank Wilkinson?

"A. Yes.

"Q. All right. Will you get back to your meeting now.

"A. And they started explaining the virtues, I guess you would call it according to what their thinking is, of the Communist Party you see, and the thing was that they never came out directly and asked me to join nor did they come out directly and say that they were members.

"Q. Did you have the feeling they were feeling you out as to your attitude?

"A. That is what my wife and I thought—that they were feeling me out as to my attitude. I didn't think the good things were good enough for me and I believed in the American system of doing business, and so on, and we had quite an argument because it was really a shock to me. And it finally ended up by me saying, 'Frank, you be on your way and I don't want you to ever mention that to me again because next time you do I'll make it rough for you,' and I guess they were there about a half hour or so and left.

"Q. Was there any doubt in your mind whatsoever after that experience with both of them, Carole Andre and Frank Wilkinson, were pro-Communist?

"A. No, sir.

"Q. No doubt whatsoever?

"A. No.

"Q. That was made very clear, wasn't it?

"A. No, in my heart I thought they were definitely pro-Communist.

"Q. And did you feel and do you feel now that it was their purpose to see whether or not your attitude would be favorable or unfavorable, and if favorable they would try to recruit you into the Party?

"A. I think so, yes.

"Q. Was that your wife's opinion also?

"A. Yes. That is why she was so disturbed and wanted us to go to some law authority and spill our hearts.

"Q. Which you have never done before?

"A. No, sir, but I am sure glad to be here today, although I hate the publicity.

"Q. That is one reason we are holding this session as a closed session.

"A. And it is kind of rough on the wife and kids.

"Q. We will try to take care of that in every way we can.

"A. It will certainly be wonderful if I can get a clean bill of health and I certainly hope I do.

"Q. What was the attitude of Frank Wilkinson and Carole Andre to you after that time as contrasted to their attitude prior to this meeting?

"A. It was chilly and I know Frank put a lot of digs in against me in the authority and he and I never hit it off after that. We do business, we are on the job and I mean that is about all I could think of that happened.

"Q. Who played the dominant role at the time of your conferences between Frank Wilkinson and Carole Andre?

"A. Well, it seemed like one would start and the other one would take over. I think Carole Andre was more persuasive than Frank Wilkinson. I think maybe she took a little more prominent role in it.

"Q. Did the conference disclose anything to you about the extent of Communist infiltration in the authority?

"A. No. The only thing I thought was if they are trying to recruit people into the Communist Party I wasn't the only one they hit. I mean that was my feeling. They were feeling people out and if it seemed like they would go along with that kind of junk then they took them in and I think that is what the deal was.

"Q. Mr. Sunshine, were you ever asked to participate in any other Communist organization or front?

"A. Not that I know of.

"Q. Civil Rights Congress?

"A. No.

"Q. Artists, Sciences and Professions Council?

"A. No, sir.

"Q. International Labor Defense?

"A. No, sir.

"Q. American Youth for Democracy?

"A. No, sir, I never participated in that. They had one in some of our projects and we finally got them out.

"Q. American Youth for Democarcy?

"A. I think that is what it was.

"Q. Do you know what that organization was?

"A. Well, I think it is Communist now, isn't it, or something?

"Q. Well, it doesn't exist any more. It was originally the Young Communist League.

"A. I understand, but I wasn't a member of that.

"Q. I understand, but there was a Young Communist League.

"A. Yes, they were in several of our projects.

"Q. Were they eliminated?

"A. Yes.

"Q. Did you participate in eliminating them?

"A. Yes.

"Q. To what extent?

"A. Well, they would want to have—at first I didn't know what they were to tell you the truth, so it was just like any other group. But later on when we found out about it, we just didn't allow them to have meetings in the Housing Authority on the basis it was a controversial group as far as we were concerned.

"Q. Mr. Sunshine, are you able to give us an approximation of how long it was after you came here from San Diego in 1945, that this meeting at your home with Carole Andre and Frank Wilkinson occurred?

"A. Yes, sir, it was about—I am trying to think when I was living up there at that project, I think it was about 1947.

"Q. About 1947?

"A. About two years, a year and a half or two years, maybe not quite that long. I think—maybe a little over a year or a little less than two years. It was between one and two years I think."

The witness was then interrogated at some length concerning his information about other members of the Housing Authority personnel and his testimony in that regard is worth repeating.

"Q. (By Mr. Combs) : Do you have any other information concerning Communists in the authority?

"A. Gosh, I think if I did I think it would be very vivid in my mind because this really burned a hole in it.

"Q. Do you know Sidney Green?

"A. Yes.

"Q. How long have you known him?

"A. I knew Sidney Green—well, here is when I first met Sidney Green. You see, he was at Aliso Village as interim manager. A fellow by the name of Roger Johnson was before him when I was in San Diego and they called me for the job. I took an examination and they gave me a wire asking me if I would accept and I said I would. He was manager at that time, I think, for about three months or so.

"Q. Did you ever have any suspicion about his Communist affiliation?

"A. Well, I might have, yes.

"Q. Well, did you?

"A. I would say, yes. I mean that is all I can say because of his close affiliation with Frank Wilkinson.

"Q. And Carole Andre?

"A. I don't know if it was as close with Carole Andre or not. I knew it was close to Frank Wilkinson. Yes, I did have suspicions.

"Q. You suspected Sidney Green?

"A. Yes, I did.

"Q. You don't know anything about what he testified to here, do you?

"A. I have heard.

"Q. Did it verify your suspicions?

"A. Yes."

When questioned about his personal affiliations with the Communist organization itself, Mr. Sunshine's replies were refreshingly different from those given by the witnesses whose testimony has been quoted above.

"Q. (By Mr. Combs) : All right, I will put these categorical questions to you.

"A. Surely.

"Q. Have you ever been a member of the Communist Party?

"A. No, sir, I never have.

"Q. Or the Communist Political Association?

"A. No, sir.

"Q. Or the Young Communist League?
"A. No, sir.
"Q. American Youth for Democracy?
"A. No, sir.
"Q. Or the Labor Youth League?
"A. No, sir.
"Q. Or any other Communist organization or Communist Front to your knowledge?
"A. Not to the best of my ability, not that I know of, no, sir.
"Mr. Combs: I think that is all.
"The Witness: Unless something popped up there that I wouldn't know it I would surely get out of it in a heck of a hurry.
"Senator Burns: Thank you, Mr. Sunshine, and you are excused.
"The Witness: Thank you, very much and I am sure glad I had an opportunity to tell you what I know because it has stuck in my craw for the last four or five years and I never had an opportunity before, maybe I should have had the brains to go to somebody about it.
"Senator Burns: Thank you, very much, you have been very helpful."

Jack Naiditch

Mr. Jack Naiditch, who appeared before the committee at its hearing held on October 28, 1952, testified that he resided at 6215 Goodland Avenue in North Hollywood, and that he had been regularly employed by the Los Angeles City Housing Authority as a painter for a period of 10 years. Prior to that time he was a resident of the State of New York, having been born in New York City, and had lived in California ever since he first came to this State in 1922. Mr. Naiditch was not accompanied by an attorney and after having testified freely concerning the place of his birth and his occupation, was questioned as follows:

"Q. (By Mr. Combs): Did you once live at 1122 North Guage Avenue in Los Angeles?
"A. Yes.
"Q. Was that in April, 1936?
"A. About that.
"Q. Did you register as a Communist in that year?
"A. I am not saying.
"Q. You mean you refuse to answer the question?
"A. I refuse to talk, yes. From my experience, what I have observed and what I have heard and my convictions, I have nothing to do with committees whatsoever."

From that point on the witness was uncooperative and hostile. He refused to tell the committee about his associations, his acquaintance with other employees of the housing authority and flatly refused to answer any further questions whatever and was therefore released from the subpena.

Frank Wilkinson

Mr. Frank Wilkinson had recovered from the effects of his operation by October 28, 1952, and at 10.30 a.m. on that day appeared as a witness before the committee accompanied by his attorneys, Robert W. Kenny,

Robert S. Morris and Mr. Daniel G. Marshall. During his examination on preliminary matters, Mr. Wilkinson testified that he was born at Charlevoix, Michigan, on August 16, 1914; moved from that state to Arizona and came to California in 1925. The witness stated that he had attended Beverly Vista Grammar School and Beverly Hills High School and in 1932 enrolled as an undergraduate student at the University of California in Los Angeles, where he majored in economics and political science with a minor in economics and sociology. He received his bachelor of arts degree in 1936, and thereafter took a trip through Europe with a fraternity brother, the trip having been financed, so far as the witness was concerned, by his father as a graduation present. Counsel for the committee had before him the personnel record of Mr. Wilkinson, obtained from the Los Angeles Housing Authority files, and read to the witness the following statement therefrom:

> "Immediately following graduation from the University of California in Los Angeles, I set out with a fellow student from the university to travel throughout the major cities of the United States, all of Northern Africa, the Near East and all European countries, with the exception of Latvia, Lithuania, Bulgaria and Yugoslavia."
>
> "A. That is correct.
> "Q. Is that accurate?
> "A. That is accurate."

In 1939, the witness testified, he returned to the University of California at Los Angeles and did graduate work in the field of political science and psychology, and after having devoted a single semester to this graduate work, obtained a position with the State Relief Administration from September 1, 1939, to March, 1940. At this point the examination began to develop the witness' associations and contacts with other individuals, and he began to invoke his constitutional immunity against incriminating himself by answering such questions, and his attorney, Mr. Robert Kenny, stipulated with the committee that to avoid a long and repititious statement as to the grounds on which the witness might refuse to answer succeeding questions, it would be presumed that the refusal would be based on the constitutional provision against incrimination together with other technical objections, all of which appeared in the reporter's transcript of the witness' testimony and which need not be repeated.

Wilkinson then testified that from March, 1940, to September, 1941, he acted as executive secretary for an organization known as the Los Angeles Citizens Housing Council; then from September, 1941, to about April 15, 1942, he was employed by the Federal Work Relief Program as director of a university research project, which involved the University of Southern California, the University of California at Los Angeles, the California Institute of Technology, Santa Barbara State College and the Scripts Institute of Oceanography, Wilkinson's work in this field being wholly supervisorial and consisting mainly of the securing of adequate personnel for the purpose of handling the research work at the various institutions.

From this point, since the witness was questioned concerning his organizational affiliations, and, for the most part, refused to answer the question. The transcript is quoted in full:

"Q. (By Mr. Combs): Now, Mr. Wilkinson, while you were an undergraduate student at U. C. L. A., were you acquainted with a man by the name of Gilbert Harrison?

"A. Yes.

"Q. Did you belong to any student organization with him while you were an undergraduate?

"A. Just a minute. Yes.

"Q. Did you and Gilbert Harrison belong to an organization at U. C. L. A. known as the American Student Union?

"A. I will decline to answer the question, Mr. Combs, on the basis of the grounds we have previously agreed upon.

"Q. And is it not a fact that you and Gilbert Harrison were members of the American Student Union and that you made a report to the American Student Union on the twenty-fifth day of April, 1936?

"A. I decline to answer the question on the grounds previously given.

"Q. Is it not a fact, Mr. Wilkinson, that on the seventh day of May, 1943, you attended a class of the Workers' School conducted by the Communist Party of Los Angeles at the First Unitarian Church, 2938 West Eighth Street in Los Angeles?

"A. Mr. Combs, I will decline to answer the question on the grounds previously stated.

"Q. Mr. Wilkinson, in connection with your lectures concerning your European trip, did you ever speak at a place known as the Downtown Forum at 215¾ South Spring Street in Los Angeles?

"A. I'm sorry, I must decline to answer the question on the grounds previously stated.

"Q. And is it not a fact that you did give a speech there concerning your European travels in November of 1945?

"A. I will decline to answer on the grounds previously stated.

"Q. Are you familiar with an organization known as The Congress of American Women?

"A. I'm sorry, I must decline to answer the question on the grounds previously stated.

"Q. And is it not a fact that you, in a speech that you gave at the Friday Morning Club in Los Angeles on the twenty-sixth day of October, 1946, publicly endorsed the organizational conference of the Congress of American Women?

"A. The same question, I believe, because of the reference to this organization and the same answer.

"Q. Is it not a fact that while you were residing at 360 Oakhurst Drive in Beverly Hills——

"A. It was 300 South Oakhurst Drive.

"Q. 300, excuse me, that is right (continuing) in 1939, that you also received as a subscriber a publication known as *The Daily People's World?*

"A. I decline to answer upon the grounds previously stated.

"Q. And is it not a fact that while you were a resident at 2019 Rodney Drive you received as a subscriber *The Daily People's World* at that address?

"A. The same general question, the same answer.

"Q. And then in 1942, while you were a resident at 2351 Edgewater Terrace, that you received *The Daily People's World* at that address as a subscriber?

"A. The same general question, the same answer.

"Q. And is it not a fact that from 1943 until 1949, you were a regular financial contributor to an organization known as American Youth for Democracy?

"A. I decline to answer on the grounds previously given.

"Q. And is it not a fact that on August 28, 1943, you attended a public social function——

"A. What is that date again?

"Q. August 28, 1943?

"A. All right.

"Q. A social function, the purpose of which was to raise money for *The Daily People's World,* the function being held at 2400 Hidalgo Street in Los Angeles?

"A. The same general question and the same answer.

"Q. Are you familiar with an organization known as the National Negro Congress?

"A. I refuse to answer on the basis of the grounds previously stated.

"Q. And is it not a fact that you spoke for the National Negro Congress in the City of Los Angeles on September 19, 1946, according to the issue of *The Daily People's World* of that date?

"A. The same general question and I refuse to answer the question on the grounds previously stated.

"Q. And is it not a fact that on September 23, 1946, you spoke at a meeting of the National Negro Congress at 4016 South Central Avenue on the same platform with the following speakers: Robert Pate, Philip M. Connelly, Revels Cayton and William Bidner, at which time all of those individuals were personally known to you as members of the Communist Party of Los Angeles County?

"A. I refuse to answer on the basis of the grounds previously stated.

"Q. Now, Mr. Wilkinson, you mentioned previously in your testimony that your interest in public housing antedated your employment by the Los Angeles City Housing Authority, did you not?

"A. What do you mean antedated?

"Q. Well, preceded.

"A. That is correct.

"Q. The time that you were employed by the Housing Authority?

"A. That is correct.

"Q. In connection with that interest, did you know of an organization known as the Association of Veteran Home Buyers?

"A. Yes, I know that organization.

"Q. Were you affiliated with it in any way?

"A. What do you mean by affiliated?

"Q. A member of it.

"A. I really don't recall if I was a member of it. I attended some of their meetings officially for the Housing Authority. They asked several representatives of various city agencies to be there. Their's was a problem involving veterans' homes that were never completed or were completed with faulty construction and they were trying to get their grievance settled, it ultimately was settled, but they invited us to be there.

"Q. The question was simply whether you were a member and you stated you didn't remember whether you were or not.

"A. I don't recall whether they had members or not, I honestly don't recall.

"Q. And you did speak before the organization on one or more occasions, did you not?

"A. I believe I did.

"Q. According to *The Daily People's World* of February 10, 1947, page one, column one, you did address the organization and that is the Association of Veteran Home Buyers on February 10, 1947, do you have any independent recollection of that occasion?

"A. I recall primarily one meeting that was held in the City Library or in the City Recreation Building in Santa Monica. There may have been other meetings, but that is one where I do recall being present and I may have spoken at that time.

"Q. Mr. Wilkinson, in connection with your interest in housing, either before or after your employment with the Los Angeles City Housing Authority, did you come in contact with or know a man by the name of Harper Poulson?

"A. We would like to know more about Harper Poulson, Mr. Combs.

"Q. Well, Harper Poulson was one of the originators, according to my information, Mr. Wilkinson, of an organization known as the Committee on One Thousand Home Buyers. Does that refresh your recollection any?

"Mr. Marshall: Is Harper Poulson the person whom you have listed as a subversive person or a member of a subversive organization, Mr. Combs?

"Mr. Combs: Frankly, I'm not positive, but I will say that we had Mr. Poulson before the committee several years ago and interrogated him concerning the organization of which I speak. Whether or not we listed the organization as subversive I very much doubt, but I wouldn't be prepared to say specifically. But I can refresh the witness' recollection and will do so further. I think this may refresh his recollection.

"The committee's information is, Mr. Wilkinson, that on February 7, 1947, you were the principal speaker at a meeting of the One Thousand Home Buyers, which was also known later as the Veteran Home Buyers Association, in the Los Angeles High School Auditorium and the other speakers, in addition to yourself, on that occasion were: Harper W. Poulson, Byron V. Citron and Sam Houston Allen. Does that refresh your recollection?

"The Witness: On the basis of your additional identifications there, Mr. Combs, and your own answer as to whether he has been listed by you as a member of a group which you call subversive, I will decline to answer on the grounds previously stated.

"Q. Is it not a fact that on February 28, 1947, Mr Wilkinson, you participated in an affair which was termed in *The Daily People's*

World of February 28, 1947, page 1, column 1, as a 'joint housing rally by the Negro and Allied Veterans of America?'

"Mr. Marshall: Is that a listed group?

"Mr. Combs: No, it is not.

"Mr. Marshall: Do you have the names of any persons identified with it?

"Mr. Combs: Yes, I have.

"Mr. Marshall: Would you give us those names?

"Mr. Combs: Karen Morley, Frances Williams and Lloyd Gough.

"The Witness: Then on the basis of your further identification, Mr. Combs, I am sorry, but I will have to decline to answer that one on the grounds previously stated.

"Q. Mr. Wilkinson, of course you are acquainted with Mr. Howard Holtzendorff, are you not?

"A. Yes, very, very well.

"Q. Did Mr. Holtzendorff ever ask you whether or not you were a member of the Communist Party?

"A. I'm sorry, but I must decline to answer the question on the grounds previously stated.

"Q. Is it not a fact that in 1947 Mr. Holtzendorff in his office asked you whether or not you were a member of the Communist Party and you assured him you were not?

"A. The same general type of question, same answer.

"Q. On the grounds previously stated?

"A. On the grounds previously stated.

"Q. In 1948, were you familiar with an organization known as the California Legislative Conference?

"A. I decline to answer the question on the basis of the grounds previously stated.

"Q. Is it not a fact that on the 28th of April, 1948, you attended the meeting sponsored by the California Legislative Conference at the Alexandria Hotel in the City of Los Angeles and there gave a speech, the documentation for that being contained in *The Daily People's World* of April 29, 1948, page 3, column 2?

"A. The same general question and I refuse to answer the question on the grounds previously stated.

"Q. Is it not a fact that on the fourteenth of August, 1948, you were a speaker at a meeting of the Los Angeles Chapter of the Congress of American Women held at the Alexandria Hotel and that other speakers of that time and place were Pearl Fagelson, Virginia Brodin, Frances Williams, whose name has heretofore been mentioned, and William B. Esterman, an attorney.

"A. I am refusing to answer that question on the basis of the grounds previously given.

"Q. Are you familiar with an organization and were you familiar with it in 1950, known as the California Labor School?

"A. I decline to answer the question on the grounds previously stated.

"Q. Are you acquainted with Beatrice and Stanley Johnson, 10763 Valley Heart Drive, North Hollywood?

"Mr. Marshall: Are either of the persons you just named listed by this committee or any other committee as subversive persons?

"Mr. Combs: Not to my knowledge.

"Mr. Marshall: Or as having been members of any listed organization or having held meetings at which listed persons were present?

"Mr. Combs: I'll get to that. The question is, whether he knew them. Whether or not they are listed I don't know. They are not to my knowledge.

"The Witness: I know a Mrs. Beatrice Johnson.

"Mr. Combs: Yes.

"The Witness: And I believe I have met—I believe that I have met, and I underline the word believe, Mr. Johnson.

"Q. Did you ever visit in their home at 10763 Valley Heart Drive?

"A. I have gone there frequently to go swimming, they have a swimming pool.

"Q. Did you go there on November 2, 1950 to attend a joint meeting of the California Labor School and the Independent Progressive Party?

"A. That question I decline to answer on the basis of the grounds previously stated.

"Q. Were you familiar with a man by the name of Oliver Haskell, who was formerly employed by the housing authority?

"Mr. Marshall: Mr. Combs, is Oliver Haskell a person whom you have listed as subversive?

"Mr. Combs: Not to my knowledge, counsel.

"Mr. Marshall: Is he a person for whom this committee has issued a subpena?

"Mr. Combs: No, he is not. The committee issued no subpena for Oliver Haskell.

"Mr. Marshall: We have a recollection of having read in the newspapers that the committee had issued a subpena for a person named Oliver Haskell, but that is not so?

"Mr. Combs: That is not the fact.

"Mr. Marshall: He is a perfectly innocent and innocuous person so far as this committee is concerned; is that it?

"Mr. Combs: Well, no, I won't go that far. I don't think he is even in California. My understanding is that for some time he has been in Michigan or some place, he is a former employee of the authority.

"The Witness: I think I had better decline to answer the question, Mr. Combs, on the basis of the grounds previously stated.

"Q. (By Mr. Combs): Were you acquainted with a former employee of the housing authority by the name of Drayton Bryant?

"Mr. Marshall: Is the gentleman whom you have just named a person listed by this committee——

"Mr. Combs: Not to my knowledge.

"Mr. Marshall continuing: ——as a member of any listed organization?

"Mr. Combs: Not to my knowledge, counsel. You understand I am speaking only from recollection.

"Mr. Marshall: Yes. Is he supposed to be a man of good reputation?

"Mr. Combs: I have never met him, I have never seen him. As far as I know, he is, I don't know.

"The Witness: I do know Drayton Bryant.

"Q. Presently?

"A. He doesn't live in Los Angeles presently. I did know him, put it that way.

"Q. While you were both employed by the housing authority?

"A. He was employed here at the housing authority for a number of years.

"Q. Now, I am going to name several people together, Mr. Wilkinson, and ask you if you knew any or all of them at the time that they were all employed by the housing authority. Fay Kovner, Sidney Green, Carole Andre, Adina Williamson and Irma Sapiro?

"A. To my recollection, Mr. Combs, these are all people whom you have called before or have tried to call before your committee——

"Q. That is correct.

"A. (Continuing)——in this current investigation revolving around me somewhat and I feel very clearly therefore that I must invoke the grounds previously stated. Otherwise I might become a witness of some sort against myself.

"Q. Were you ever acquainted with a man by the name of Samuel Berland.

"A. On the advice of counsel I must decline to answer that question.

"Q. Regarding Samuel Berland?

"A. That is correct, on the basis of the grounds previously stated.

"Q. Now, Mr. Wilkinson, is it not a fact that you know Oliver Haskell as a member of the same Communist unit with which you were affiliated and that on one occasion shortly before he left the housing authority, you and Mr. Haskell had a violent disagreement concerning the role that the Communist Party was to play through that unit in the housing authority, as a result of which you threatened to have disciplinary proceedings instituted against Mr. Haskell?

"A. The same general question involving Mr. Haskell and the same answer on the same grounds as previously stated.

"Q. Did you ever hear of an organization known as the Altgeld Club No. 1?

"A. Of what?

"Q. Of the Communist Party of Los Angeles County.

"A. I decline to answer that on the basis of the grounds previously stated.

"Q. Is it not a fact that at one time you were educational director of that club?

"A. I decline to answer the question on the basis of the grounds previously stated.

"Q. And is it not a fact within the purview of your own knowledge that the Altgeld Club No. 1 was composed of social workers, some of whom were employed with you at the same time by the Los Angeles Housing Authority?

"A. I decline to answer on the basis of the grounds previously stated.

"Q. And is it not true that other members of the Altgeld Club No. 1, in addition to yourself, included Carole Andre, Sidney Green and Samuel Berland?

"A. I decline to answer on the basis of the ground previously stated.

"Q. And that meetings of the Altgeld Club No. 1 were held in your home, in the home of Carole Andre and in the home of Sidney Green and at the home of Samuel Berland, whom I will now further identify as the international representative of the local lodge or chapter of the United Public Workers of America.

"A. I decline to answer on the basis of the grounds previously stated.

"Q. Is it not a fact that you attended a meeting of the Altgeld Club No. 1 about October, 1950, in the home of Carole Andre at which, among other persons, Samuel Berland and William Taylor were present, at which time and place you were instructed that your contribution to the Communist Party thenceforth would be $32 a month?

"A. I decline to answer on the grounds previously stated.

"Q. And that at the time and place a discussion occurred between you and Samuel Berland and William Taylor concerning the strategy of the Communist fraction in the Los Angeles Housing Authority?

"A. I decline to answer the question on the basis of the grounds previously stated. There is no shorter way of putting that, is there?

"Q. Is it not a fact that in February, 1952, you were notified by the Communist Party of Los Angeles County that thenceforth you would be regarded as a member-at-large for the purpose of protecting you from exposure as a secret member of the Communist Party?

"A. I decline to answer the question on the basis of the grounds previously stated.

"Q. And are you now, or were you ever acquainted with a woman in San Francisco by the name of Sylvia Steingart?

"A. I decline to answer, Mr. Combs, on the basis of the grounds previously stated.

"Q. Mr. Wilkinson, can you recall where you were on October 17th of this year?

"A. Can you help me along a little bit there?

"Q. Well, I can help you this much, yes. Do you recall attending a meeting at 607 Southwestern Avenue at the hour of 7.30 on the evening of October 17, 1952?

"A. Who sponsored that meeting?

"Q. The Arts, Sciences and Professions Council.

"A. I am sorry, but I must decline to answer the question on the basis of the grounds previously stated.

"Q. At which time and place the following people were present: Richard Jambol, Robert Alexander, Frank Wilkinson, yourself, Mike Myers, Dr. P. Price Cobbs, Jane Downs, and Garrett Eckbow?

"A. Is that a question?

"Q. Yes.

"A. I decline to answer the question on the basis of the grounds previously stated.

"Q. Do you know any of the persons whose name I have read, in addition to Robert Alexander?

"A. In the context with which this is asked, Mr. Combs, I regret that I must decline to answer on the basis of the grounds previously stated.

"Q. Now, for the purpose of the record, Mr. Wilkinson, I show you a ticket issued under the auspices of the Los Angeles Negro Labor Council, 4118 South Central Avenue, and ask you whether or not such a ticket was purchased by you at any time?

"A. I decline to answer the question, Mr. Combs, on the basis of the grounds previously stated.

"Q. Now, Mr. Wilkinson, were you acquainted with another employee of the Los Angeles City Housing Authority by the name of Hyman Sunshine.

"A. I want to answer this one in my own way.

"Q. Well, just answer, if you will, whether or not you knew him and then I will ask you another question. The question was whether you were acquainted with him at the time he was employed?

"A. Well, I was acquainted, Mr. Combs, with a Mr. Hyman Sunshine, but——

"Q. All right.

"A. May I go a little further?

"Q. You may in just a moment, but I want to fix this foundation in the record first, if you don't mind.

"A. All right.

"Q. When did your acquaintance with him begin as well as you remember?

"A. I didn't get to finish my answer, you stopped me, Mr. Combs, before I could finish it because I was going to decline to answer the question.

"Q. Oh, you were going to decline to answer the question?

"A. Yes, you got me a little too early there.

"Q. All right, go ahead.

"A. My question was, I did—whatever I said—know of a Mr. Hyman Sunshine here at the housing project, but that inasmuch as he has been called here as a witness before your committee in an investigation apparently revolving around me, I feel that I must decline to answer the question on the basis of the grounds previously stated.

"Q. Is it, or is it not a fact that shortly after Mr. Sunshine came from San Diego to Los Angeles and accepted a position with the Los Angeles City Housing Authority that you and Carole Andre called at his residence and asked him to join the Communist Party?

"A. I will decline to answer the question on the grounds previously stated and on the basis of the newspaper reports that I have had of his testimony here, I feel that I should refuse to answer on the additional grounds that *the Mr. Sunshine that I used to know is so changed as to degrade my character to identify him on any basis;* but my main reason for declining to answer is on the general grounds previously stated. (Committee's italics.)

"Q. Are you acquainted with Dr. P. Price Cobbs?

"A. I decline to answer on the basis of the grounds previously stated.

"Q. Are you now a member of the Communist Party, Mr. Wilkinson?

"A. I decline to answer on the basis of the grounds previously stated.

"Mr. Combs: That is all."

Jean Benson Wilkinson

The next witness was Mr. Wilkinson's wife, Jean, who was also represented by the same attorneys who had acted as counsel for her husband. After stating that her name was Jean Benson Wilkinson and that she resided at 2019 Rodney Drive in Los Angeles, she was asked whether or not she was the wife of Frank Wilkinson, who had preceded her on the stand, and she replied as follows:

"Answer: I refuse to testify in this particular hearing because it is obviously an investigation into my own husband's political activities. So therefore, I must refuse on the grounds of Section 1881 of the Code of Civil Procedure. You gentlemen, no doubt, some of you anyway, are married. You know it is a very difficult position to be in.

"Q. Mrs. Wilkinson, my questions are not concerning your husband's activities, but your own activities. I will ask no question concerning your husband's activities.

"A. But this is a housing investigation and it involves by husband and his political activities. Anything I could say would be——

"Mr. Combs: Well, that is for the committee to find out, Mrs. Wilkinson. My questions to you, you can either answer or not, depending on the advice of your counsel, of course; but I want to make it clear that my questions to you will in no way affect your husband's activities.

"Senator Burns: May I further clarify this situation and while the committee is primarily investigating activities in the Housing Authority of Los Angeles, the committee in any meeting at any time could broaden the scope of its inquiry should it see fit to do so. So, therefore, the scope of the inquiry is not necessarily limited to the activities of the various people connected with public housing in Los Angeles and it is perfectly proper and it is perfectly within their rights to do so.

"The Witness: That may be true, but I overheard one of the reporters on the phone there talking about the fact, after they had just talked to you people, that this was a housing inquiry and it would be very obvious to the public certainly and it is obvious to you people that anything I would say, whether it is about my own activities or about Frank's, would be damaging to him and I am not going to do that."

It was then stipulated that the witness would refuse to answer any questions on the ground that conversations between husband and wife were confidential and therefore not the proper subject of inquiry before the committee, the counsel even going so far as to caution her against admitting that she was born in California, whereupon the witness said:

"I will have to take it back then, I am not used to this sort of thing."

Then came a series of questions specifically dealing with the affiliations of the witness herself, all of which she refused to answer for the reasons previously stated. The questions were as follows:

"Q. Mrs. Wilkinson, is it not a fact that in 1941 you joined the Communist Party of Los Angeles County?

"A. The same answer on the same grounds.

"Senator Burns: May it be stipulated in the event that the witness refuses to answer questions that she is refusing to answer because of the conversations between husband and wife being confidential. Is that the reason?

"Mr. Kenny: Because of Section 1881 of the Code of Civil Procedure and the right to protect——

"Senator Burns: Is that satisfactory?

"Mr. Combs: Yes, it isn't satisfactory, but it is clear.

"Senator Burns: And in reply you will state that you refuse to answer the question on the grounds previously stated.

"The Witness: All right, I refuse to answer the question on the grounds previously stated.

"Q. (By Mr. Combs): And is it not a fact that you are now and for several years last past have been a member of the Los Angeles Federation of Teachers, Local 430?

"A. I refuse to answer the question on the grounds previously stated.

"Senator Burns: The chair will rule that the reasons given for refusal to answer are not sufficient and in each and every instance the witness is requested to give a reply to the question.

"Q. (By Mr. Combs): Are you acquainted with a woman by the name of Frances Eisenberg?

"A. I refuse to answer the question upon the grounds previously stated.

"Q. And is it not a fact that you and Frances Eisenberg both taught at the same time at the Canoga Park High School in Los Angeles County?

"A. I refuse to answer the question on the grounds previously stated.

"Q. And that you are now employed as a teacher in the East Los Angeles Girls Vocational High School?

"A. I refuse to answer the question on the grounds previously stated.

"Senator Dilworth: Well, now, Mr. Chairman, it seems to me that her conversations with her husband have nothing to do with her employment in the high school.

"Senator Burns: That is the ruling of the chair and the witness in each instance is requested to reply to the question.

"Q. (By Mr. Combs): Are you acquainted with Alvin Averbuck?

"A. I refuse to answer the question on the grounds heretofore stated.

"Q. Are you acquainted with Evelyn Averbuck, his wife?

"A. I refuse to answer the question on the grounds previously stated.

"Q. Is it not a fact within the scope of your own personal knowledge, Mrs. Wilkinson, that Alvin Averbuck is the organizational secretary of the Communist Party of Los Angeles County?

"A. I refuse to answer the question on the grounds previously stated."

The witness was then interrogated about her affiliation with the League for Industrial Democracy and her present membership in the same Communist Party club as her husband, to wit, the Altgeld Club No. 1 of the Communist Party of the County of Los Angeles, and also whether or not she was presently a member of the Communist Party, all of which questions she refused to answer and was thereupon excused from further attendance before the committee.

Patrick Burns

Mr. Patrick Burns was subpened by the committee, appeared without a counsel and stated, in response to preliminary questions concerning his occupation and residence, that he was employed by his father who was a realtor and land developer in the City of Los Angeles and that the witness had served in the United States Navy, having received his honorable discharge in April of 1946 and having been working with his father since that time. The committee had received information to the effect that Mr. Burns had attended certain classes at which Frank Wilkinson had lectured and desired to obtain his information in that connection. The following excerpts from his testimony are presented, not only for the purpose of developing this particular subject, but also to show the difference in attitude exhibited by Mr. Burns and Mr. Sunshine and certain other witnesses whose testimony will be quoted later as distinguished from those represented by counsel, who advised them continuously not to answer certain questions on the ground that their answers might tend to incriminate them.

"Q. (By Mr. Combs) : Now, Mr. Burns, did you have occasion to take a course at the University of Southern California through the medium of which you met a man by the name of Frank Wilkinson?

"A. Yes, I did.

"Q. When did you start taking the course?

"A. That was the fall semester of 1949-1950. The beginning of the class was September, 1949.

"Q. What was the nature of the class?

"A. Well, the class was called Economics 550A, it was sponsored by the Sloan Foundation.

"Q. Sloan Foundation?

"A. Yes, it was called a Housing Seminar and from what I understand, the Sloan Foundation has the course at different universities around the country and they discuss different topics each semester, a topic a semester, and this happened to be housing.

"Q. Who was in charge of the course?

"A. Dr. Robert B. Pettingill.

"Q. And what was his status at the University of Southern California at that time, if you know?

"A. He was in the Economics Department there.

"Q. Was he a full professor?

"A. I do not know. His title in this course was the Director.

"Q. He was, however, a regular member of the faculty at the university, was he?

"A. As far as I know, I wouldn't want to say definitely.

"Q. At any rate he was there in that capacity during the period that you took the course?

"A. Yes.

"Q. And he was actually in charge of the course, was he?

"A. Yes.

"Q. Well, now, would it be a part of his duty, or do you know, to bring speakers to address the students from time to time?

"A. Yes.

"Q. Did he ever bring Frank Wilkinson in there for that purpose?

"A. Yes.

"Q. And did he address the students?

"A. On two occasions he made formal addresses.

"Q. How many students comprised the class?

"A. Twenty-two.

"Q. Ranging in age limits between what figures?

"A. Oh, I would say between 25 and 40.

"Q. And do you have some documents in your possession that relate to the course you took and the people who appeared there?

"A. Yes.

"Q. Would you kindly examine them and refresh your memory as to the date on which Mr. Wilkinson appeared and lectured to the students.

"A. I have a program here of the class and its speakers. Here it is—here is one of them. This is October 13, 1949, Mr. Wilkinson spoke. Now, I don't have the date of his other speech engagement because he took the place of somebody else who couldn't speak at that time and I don't recall whose place he took.

"Senator Burns: Will you repeat the date again?

"The Witness: Yes. October 13, 1949.

"Q. (By Mr. Combs): Now, were there any other people from the housing authority who appeared and lectured at that class besides Mr. Wilkinson?

"A. Yes, they appeared but didn't lecture.

"Q. Who?

"A. Miss Carole Andre, who was the assistant manager of Basilone Homes.

"Q. Which is or was, at that time at least, a part of the Los Angeles Housing Authority?

"A. Yes.

"Q. All right, anyone else?

"A. Well, there was Ulysses Gregg.

"Q. Was he a Negro?

"A. Yes, he was and he was manager of one of the Negro housing projects, I do not know which one.

"Q. Was there anyone else?

"A. There was—well, Robert Alexander, who is an architect and has been identified with the housing authority but he was not connected with the housing authority.

"Q. Was not employed by the housing authority directly but who was connected with the housing authority?

"A. Yes.

"Q. That would be under contract, or do you know?

"A. The writing of architectural contracts?

"Q. Yes.

"A. Yes, I suppose he would be.

"Q. He lectured there?

"A. Yes, they all gave reports.

"Q. Anyone else from the housing authority who spoke?

"A. No, I can't say that there ever was, no, sir.

"Q. Well, I want to describe to you at this point a well known technique used by the Communist Party in educational institutions on the college and university level in particular and to a lesser degree in high schools, and ask you whether or not you observed that technique used in the class that you have just described. This was presented in the last report of this committee, in the 1951 report so that the subject matter can be corroborated and documented. And the technique is this:

"That at the university and college classes if there was any attempt to recruit members of the class to Communism or Marxism, that attempt is not ordinarily made at the classroom but at off-campus meetings at the residence of a faculty member or some person who has been brought into the class from the outside, and there off the campus away from the jurisdiction of the administrative authorities in the university, the actual recruiting attempt is made. Did you or did you not observe any such technique in connection with the class at the University of Southern California which you mentioned?

"A. Yes, Dr. Pettingill had meetings at his home, and they were evening meetings where movies were shown and local people that were connected with housing were invited to speak.

"Q. Did Frank Wilkinson or Carole Andre participate in any of those meetings?

"A. I did not attend any of the meetings at Mr. Pettingill's home. However, I know that Mr. Wilkinson and Miss Andre were there on one occasion because we returned from a tour of the slum area which Mr. Wilkinson had taken us on to Mr. Pettingill's house and they went in. I wasn't able to go, I had a previous engagement.

"Q. But you know that Frank Wilkinson and Miss Carole Andre both went into Mr. Pettingill's home?

"A. Yes.

"Q. Which is off campus, is it?

"A. Yes, it is on LaSalle Street.

"Q. Now, were you able to detect any evidence of an effort on the part of Frank Wilkinson or Carole Andre or either of them to deliver slanted or propaganda talks to the members of the class in which you participated.

"A. Well, their talks were naturally slanted because they were employed by the housing authority and filled with enthusiasm in that connection. And of course that was—their point of view was towards that.·

"Q. Well, you would naturally expect any employee of the housing authority, I suppose, to be pro-housing.

"A. Yes.

"Q. The committee is not interested in whether any individual is for or against housing basically, but what I was getting at was whether there was any Marxism or Communism in any slanting of the remarks of Mr. Wilkinson or Miss Andre in to.the class?

"A. There were occasions when Mr. Wilkinson used people as examples of what he considered practically treason. I was going through my notes of one talk he made and he said that Eugene Conser, who was at that time—I can't exactly tell, perhaps you know, sir?

"Senator Dilworth: His position?

"The Witness: Yes.

"Senator Dilworth: Executive Secretary of the California Real Estate Association.

"The Witness: Executive Secretary of the California Real Estate Association, that is right; and he said he had been against temporary housing and had—let's see. These were just very informal sketchy notes I took out of my notebook, he said he had obstructed public housing and slum clearance and slowed down the war effort in this regard which was treasonous in his opinion.

"Q. (By Mr. Combs): Well, he painted him as virtually a traitor because he opposed slum clearance?

"A. Yes. On another occasion concerning my father, which was in one of the first sessions of the class, he might not have known who I was, he rather misquoted him and said he advocated depressions because he had stated one time in a speech that racial housing was at its what you might say normality during a depression, because you had a high amount of density in low rents. He had taken the words and jumbled them and said that Mr. Burns advocated depression in order to cure the housing ills.

"Q. Did Frank Wilkinson and Carole Andre usually come to these classes together?

"A. I can't say that, sir.

"Q. Do you have with you, Mr. Burns, a list of the persons who attended the class?

"A. Yes I do, sir.

"Q. May we have that for an exhibit?

"A. Yes, you may.

"Q. Do you have a list of the textbooks or supplementary textbooks that were recommended to you by the person who directed that class?

"A. Yes, I have that, the textbooks were all to be found here at the housing authority in the housing authority library.

"Q. You mean at this place?

"A. Yes, sir.

"Q. All right, now do you have a summary of the class itself, an outline of the curriculum?

"A. Yes, I have the procedural notes which include the informal evenings. This is what I was looking for awhile ago.

"Q. That is what you showed me earlier, isn't it?

"A. Yes.

"Mr. Combs: Mr. Chairman, I would like to introduce the class list at the Housing Seminar at U. S. C. as Burns Exhibit No. 1.

"Senator Burns: It will be so admitted.

"Mr. Combs: The list of books at the Housing Authority of the City of Los Angeles, 1401 East First Street I will introduce as Burns Exhibit No. 2; the procedural notes of the Economics 550A, Public Policy Toward Housing, fall semester, 1949, as Burns Exhibit No. 3; and in connection with the description of the technique used by the Communist Party on university campuses which has been identified by the witness, I wish to read from paragraph 5, which is as follows:

" 'Informal evenings at home of the director, 4238 LaSalle Avenue, wives and husbands invited. October 1, 7.30—10 motion pictures of European trip. November 26, informal talk by some local expert in the housing field.'

"Q. (By Mr. Combs) : And it was at 4238 LaSalle Avenue, identified here as the home of the director, Mr. Burns, that you have observed Carole Andre and Frank Wilkinson going in with some of the students of the class after you returned from a tour?

"A. Yes.

"Q. Who conducted that tour?

"A. Mr. Wilkinson conducted the tour.

"Q. Was a bus provided for your transportation?

"A. Yes, it was.

"Q. And who provided the bus?

"A. Mr. Wilkinson did.

"Q. Mr. Wilkinson did?

"A. Yes.

"Q. Did he lecture to you as he stopped from place to place going through the unit?

"A. Yes, he lectured throughout the tour, took us through the slums, the worst buildings he could find in downtown Los Angeles and also out in the valley, in the Pacoima region around there. We came by here on our trip through town, stopped here at the village building. We came in and looked around and he showed us the building and we refreshed ourselves and went on out through the valley and back to Dr. Pettingill's home in the evening.

"Q. Mr. Wilkinson at that time was an official representative of the housing authority staff, was he not?

"A. Yes.

"Q. And so was Carole Andre?

"A. Yes."

The witness submitted other documentary evidence to the committee and his examination concluded as follows:

"Q. (By Mr. Combs): Now, you are not represented by counsel, are you?

"A. No, I am not.

"Q. And you were subpened by me, weren't you?

"A. Yes, I was.

"Q. And you and I had never met before you were subpened?

"A. No, we had not.

"Q. Didn't know one another at all?

"A. No.

"Q. And had had no prior conference?

"A. No.

"Q. In view of that I am going to ask you a specific question now. Are you or have you ever been a member of the Communist Party?

"A. No.

"Q. Do you have any hesitation in answering that question frankly?

"A. Absolutely none.

"Q. You don't feel that your constitutional rights are being invaded?

"A. No.

"Q. Or your right of privacy invaded?

"A. No, I don't.

"Q. And you appear here before the committee as a cooperative and friendly witness?

"A. A free agent, I am perfectly happy to do anything that I can.

"Q. Do you have any feeling of antipathy against a committee of the Legislature of the State of California which is mandated to investigate subversive activities, which endeavors to carry out its mandate by asking whether an individual is a member of the Communist Party?

"A. No, I don't.

"Q. Do you regard that as a part of the committee's duty?

"A. Yes, I regard it as a part of their duty to cover all those matters.

"Mr. Combs: For my part I think it is very refreshing to have a witness who has that attitude in view of the many witnesses that we have had who refused to answer questions on the grounds of invasion of privacy and possible self incrimination.

"Senator Watson: It is refreshing to have a witness here who doesn't have an attorney to tell him not to answer."

It should be emphasized at this point that Dr. Pettingill, referred to in the testimony of this witness, has not been employed on the faculty or in any other capacity at the University of Southern California for several years. A photostatic copy of a catalog issued by the People's Educational Center, heretofore identified as a Communist-dominated school, listed Dr. Robert B. Pettingill as a lecturer at that institution during the summer of 1944; and it should also be pointed out that the People's Educational Center has been officially listed by the Attorney General of the United States as a Communist institution.

LETTERS FOR WILKINSON

It should be observed that when Mr. Wilkinson refused to testify concerning his organizational affiliations in the superior court action, he was immediately suspended from his position at the housing authority by Mr. Howard Holtzendorff, its executive director. From that time until shortly after he appeared before the committee in October, 1952, he was technically an employee of the housing authority but notice of his suspension had been published in most all of the daily newspapers in the City of Los Angeles. Immediately after this information appeared in the press, the office of the housing authority was flooded with letters asking that Mr. Wilkinson be reinstated forthwith.

All of these letters were turned over to the committee, and a check was made to ascertain whether or not individuals of the same political persuasion joined together in a planned and concerted campaign to pressure the Executive Director of the Housing Authority into restoring Mr. Wilkinson to his status as a full-time employee. On many previous occasions, under similar circumstances, the committee has received evidence that almost overnight the Communist propaganda machine has unleashed a torrent of letters, postcards, mimeographed statements and telegrams for the purpose of mobilizing pressure in behalf of its members, or for the purpose of putting over a project in which it is particularly interested. It was, therefore, no surprise to the members of the committee to find that an overwhelming majority of the individuals who thus showered Mr. Holtzendorff in protest against Wilkinson's suspension were persons long familiar to the committee and who had long and persistent records of continual affiliation with one Communist front organization after another.

In the interest of time, the committee subpened only three of the individuals who wrote these letters and the committee's reasons for selecting these particular witnesses will become readily apparent when excerpts from their testimony are hereafter set forth. In the interest of time, the committee did not deem it necessary to subpena all of the persons who wrote letters, but for the purpose of establishing the pattern the following information is considered pertinent:

The writer of letter No. 1, dated September 3, 1952, had acted as an officer of the People's Educational Center, heretofore mentioned in connection with Dr. Pettingill; the writer of letter No. 2, dated August 28, 1952, was a registered member of the Communist Party; writer of letter No. 3, dated September 1, 1952, had intervened in behalf of Communists who were convicted of contempt before the Congressional Committee on Un-American Activities; the writer of letter No. 4, dated September 6, 1952, had also intervened in behalf of the same defendants who were convicted of contempt of the congressional committee and was the signer of at least four other letters of a similar nature; the writer of letter No. 5, dated August 28, 1952, was listed on an official booklet of the People's Educational Center as an instructor during the summer term of 1946, was featured as a lecturer at the California Labor School in San Francisco, also designated by the United State Department of Justice as a Communist organization, was identified with the Civil Rights Congress, also listed as a Communist-dominated organization by the United States Department of Justice, had signed other letters of a similar character on behalf of individuals convicted of contempt before congressional committees and listed as having been affiliated with several organizations officially designated as Communist Fronts; the writer of letter No. 5, dated September 2, 1952, was listed as having attended meetings of the People's Forum, mentioned in connection with the testimony of Frank Wilkinson, and is a subscriber to the Communist newspaper in California; the writer of letter No. 6, dated September 1, 1952, was listed as affiliated with two Communist-dominated organizations; the writer of letter No. 7, dated August 2, 1952, was listed on the official booklet of the People's Educational Center, heretofore mentioned, as a guest instructor during the winter term of 1944 and the spring term of 1945; the writer of letter No. 8, dated September 1, 1952, was listed as having participated in many enterprises to raise funds for the Communist newspaper in California, as a sponsor for American Youth For Democracy, heretofore mentioned in the testimony of several of the witnesses who appeared before the committee in the two hearings which are the subject of this portion of the report, was a sponsor for the Joint Anti-Fascist Refugee Committee, designated by the Department of Justice as Communist-controlled, and has been listed as a member or sponsor for at least 10 Communist Front organizations; the writer of letter No. 9, dated September 1, 1952, was discharged from a position of employment by reason of the fact that the individual refused to submit to a loyalty check concerning the organizations to which he was affiliated; the signer of letter No. 10, dated August 31, 1952, was listed as affiliated with two Communist Front organizations and the writer of letter No. 11, dated August 21, 1952, is listed as a director of one of the Communist Front organizations, designated as such by the United States Department of Justice.

Eleanor Raymond

Eleanor Raymond, subpenaed before the committee as a witness, testified that she resided at 8103 Blackburn Avenue, Los Angeles, but refused to give her business address on the ground that her answer might tend to incriminate her. So persistent was this witness in her refusal to answer all questions, indeed, that an analysis of the complete reporter's transcript in connection with her appearance will not disclose the purpose of the committee in calling her. She refused to state whether or not she was executive secretary and director of an organization known as the California Legislative Conference, refused to state whether or not she was registered with either House of the California State Legislature as a representative of the California Legislative Conference, refused to state whether or not she was a member of the Communist Party or the Communist Political Association, and refused to tell the committee whether she was acquainted with Mr. Harper Poulson, Frank Wilkinson, Samuel Berland, international representative of the United Public Workers of America, or Harold Orr, President of Local 430 of the Los Angeles Federation of Teachers. She was thereupon excused from further attendance before the committee.

Pauline Schindler

Pauline Schindler, who, like the witness who preceded her, Eleanor Raymond, had written one of the letters to Director Holtzendorff in behalf of Frank Wilkinson, was not accompanied by an attorney, but was advised from time to time by a man who identified himself as her friend, and whose name was D. A. Gordon. Mrs. Schindler, after stating that she resided at 835 North Kings Road in Hollywood, availed herself of what she considered to be the protection of the Fifth Amendment to the Federal Constitution and refused to tell the committee whether or not she was affiliated with the Arts, Sciences and Professions Council; whether or not she was a subscriber to the Communst newspaper; stated that she did not remember whether or not she had registered as a Communist in 1936; refused to tell the committee whether or not she was acquainted with John Howard Lawson; and deviated to some extent from the pattern of answers established by other witnesses when Senator Burns advised her as follows:

"Senator Burns: Mrs. Schindler, everything you say in here is part of the record and I think you should be informed to that extent. Now, we asked you to come in here and give us the benefit of your knowledge, and it naturally must go into the record.

"The Witness: Very well. Then it will be assumed that I am a member of the Communist Party. You may or may not be quite wrong in that position, but I am telling you quite frankly my reason for refusing is not fear of anything but merely a principle.

"Senator Dilworth: We make no assumptions in here.

"Senator Burns: What makes you think that no one has any right to ask you whether you are a Democrat or a Republican? The law compels a statement to that effect when you register. Any duly constituted body has a right to require it as a matter of record. Now, let's go a step further. This committee has been mandated in the Legislature for a long period of years to investigate the Communist Party, among other subversives, and by that act and by that law it is given the legal right to inquire into whether or not you are a member of the Communist Party. Now, that is our viewpoint."

Mrs. Schindler did testify, specifically and categorically, that she wrote the letter in behalf of Mr. Wilkinson entirely on her own volition and without being solicited by anyone. But she, nevertheless, refused to answer any and all questions concerning her own registration as a Communist, her subscription to the Communist newspaper and her affiliation with Communist Front organizations and her association with individuals concerning whom she was questioned. She was thereupon excused.

Frances Eisenberg

The last witness to be heard by the committee was Mrs. Frances Eisenberg. Mrs. Eisenberg had previously appeared before the committee at a hearing held in 1947. At that time she admitted that she was a member of the Board of Directors of the People's Educational Center, officially designated as a Communist organization as heretofore explained, and that she was a member of the Los Angeles Federation of Teachers, Local No. 430.

Mrs. Eisenberg was accompanied by her attorney, Mr. William B. Esterman, 6425 Hollywood Boulevard. She testified that she resided at 5114½ Clinton Street in Los Angeles for about 12 years, taught at the Canoga Park High School for about 15 years, having left there in 1950, and was at present an instructor at the Fairfax High School in Los Angeles.

When questioned concerning her possible acquaintance with Jean Wilkinson, the wife of Frank Wilkinson, Mrs. Eisenberg refused to answer the question on the ground that such an answer would be giving testimony against herself under the Fifth Amendment to the Constitution of the United States and the Constitution of the State of California. And in the interest of time, it was thereafter stipulated between Mr. Esterman and counsel for the committee that any subsequent refusals to answer questions would be deemed based upon all of the amendments to the Constitution of the United States and the State of California, including, of course, the provision against self-incrimination.

When asked about her affiliation with the Los Angeles Federation of Teachers, the witness stated that she was an officer of the organization, proud to be affiliated with it, and that her membership had continued over a period of approximately 10 years under the presidency of Mr. Harold Orr, and that she was the editor for the official publication of the union, *The Los Angeles Teacher.*

Mrs. Eisenberg's response to questions concerning her participation in the activities of the People's Educational Center, the facts concerning her connection with American Youth for Democracy, the Arts, Sciences and Professions Council and the Communist Party of Los Angeles County were all answered in exactly the same way—by her refusal to answer the question on constitutional grounds, including self-incrimination. She was thereupon excused.

Other witnesses questioned by the committee were Sarah Fefferman, Allan Carson, Jessie L. Terry, Dorothy Foster and Ruth Johnson. Mr. Carson, an attorney, had never been a regular employee of the housing authority, but was associated with a law firm that did legal work for the authority from time to time. Mr. Carson proved to be an uncooperative witness and relied upon his constitutional rights against self-incrimination when interrogated about his Communist Party affiliations and other organizational connections. As to Miss Fefferman, Mrs. Terry, Miss Foster and Miss Johnson, the committee wishes to make it abundantly clear that it found no evidence of subversive affiliation on the part of any of them and found them to be cooperative, helpful witnesses throughout the course of the testimony of each of them.

Mr. H. L. Sunshine, whose testimony was fully set forth above, was also a helpful, cooperative witness, answered the questions frankly and willingly, and the committee has no evidence of any Communist or subversive connection so far as he is concerned.

From the time the committee was asked to conduct its investigation and hearings by Mr. Holtzendorff, he and all of the administrative employees of the housing authority cooperated with the committee to the fullest extent, making available all records and documents that were requested, providing facilities for the conduct of the two hearings, and giving the committee every possible cooperation. There was not the slightest indication of any effort on the part of the housing authority or any of its employees, other than those who appeared under subpena and whose testimony speaks for itself, to offer the slightest hindrance to the committee during the entire process of the investigation and hearings. In conformity with the position of the housing commission as expressed by Mr. George Beavers, its vice-president, all witnesses who refused to answer the questions of the committee concerning their affiliations and activities were immediately discharged. These persons were: Frank Wilkinson, Sidney Green, Adina Williamson, Elizabeth Smith and Jack Naiditch. Fay Kovner was no longer employed by the authority and Sarah Fefferman, H. L. Sunshine, Jessie Terry, Dorothy Foster and Ruth Johnson are still employed by it, so far as the committee knows.

For the sake of completeness, it should be added that the name of Miss Nita Blackwell had been mentioned in connection with the investigations and hearing. Miss Blackwell had been a former employee of the housing authority, but the committee did not issue a subpena for her. It should be made clear that the committee has no evidence of any subversive affiliation so far as Miss Blackwell is concerned, and has already given her a letter to that effect.

CONCLUSIONS

In evaluating the evidence obtained during the investigation and hearings concerning the Los Angeles City Housing Authority, one is necessarily struck by the willingness of some of the witnesses to testify frankly and honestly about everything except their Communist affiliations, acquaintances and activities. Invariably such witnesses were accompanied by lawyers who have appeared again and again at these hearings to caution their clients against answering any question about Communism, and repeatedly urge them to invoke the Fifth Amendment to the Constitution of the United States and refuse to answer on the ground that the question, if answered truthfully, might subject the witness to a criminal prosecution.

The committee has learned that in all such cases the Communist Party has laid down a hard and fast directive to its membership. By the terms of this directive Communist Party members are not permitted to acknowledge their Communist affiliations, as many of them would prefer, because they would then invite a long series of probing questions about meetings, dues and other details the Party could not afford to disclose. On the other hand, these witnesses are not permitted to deny Party membership because the committee might thereupon produce undercover agents or former Communist Party members to prove the witness is a liar and thus lay the basis for a perjury conviction—which is a felony. Faced with this dilemma, the witness is told to invoke the constitutional privilege against self-incrimination whenever he is asked about his Communist connections.

The committee has invariably found that in all cases where a witness appears with one of the lawyers who habitually handles such matters for the Communist Party, that the witness may be expected to invoke the fifth amendment and refuse to answer questions about his Communist actions and affiliations—and the committee invariably possesses an extensive dossier showing that the witness has been active in a long array of Communist front organizations, has subscribed .to various Communist propaganda media, has associated with known Communists, and has generally aided and abetted the Communist Party line and the Communist cause.

The Fifth Amendment

The committee, on the other hand, is continuously amazed at the sharp line of demarcation drawn between witnesses of this character and the other type of witness concerning whom there is no such dossier. This type of witness is subpened, not because of any suspicion of subversive activity, but because the committee desires to obtain the benefit of his testimony under oath. If he is accompanied by an attorney, which is rare, such lawyers are invariably found to have no long record of affiliation with Communist causes, and neither the attorney nor the client exhibit animosity toward the committee and when asked whether or not he is a member of the Communist Party, the witness, without being cautioned by his counsel, frankly and simply answers the question by saying, "No."

Senator Pat McCarran, Chairman of the United States Senate Subcommittee on Internal Security, that has accomplished such valuable and objective work, recently said something about the witnesses who thus hide their affiliations behind the Fifth Amendment to the Constitution. He declared:

"If a man comes here and he is asked 'are you a horse thief?' And he is not a horse thief all he has to do is say, 'No, I am not.' If he comes here and he is asked if he is a Communist and he is not a Communist, all he has to do is say, 'No, I am not.'

"But when he resorts to the Fifth Amendment and says, 'It might incriminate me if I answer,' his attitude and his conduct must be judged by his answer."

(Foreword to U. S. Senate Subcommittee on Internal Security Hearing, October 8, 1952, page 4.)

The international commission of jurists who advised Secretary Trygve Lie concerning his duty to discharge from the United Nations' employ any Americans who refuse to testify before congressional committees, said:

"We now come to the second question to be considered in this section of our opinion, namely, what should be the attitude of the secretary-general toward an officer who pleads some constitutional privilege against answering questions on the ground that such answers might incriminate him with regard to activities involving disloyalty to the United States. As we have said above, in our opinion membership of the staff of the United Nations does not and should not deprive the officer concerned of the constitutional or other legal rights guaranteed to him by the law of his host country, whether his own country or not. Nor should these rights be in any way limited, abridged, or qualified by reason of his membership on the staff of the United Nations.

"The matter arises with particular force in the United States of America, where one of the constitutional rights that may be invoked is a right guaranteed to every American citizen or resident in the United States of America by the Fifth Amendment to the Constitution of the United States; although it is possible, in our opinion, that similar questions might arise in other countries.

"The Fifth Amendment to the United States Constitution provides that no person 'shall be compelled in any criminal case to be a witness against himself.' This protection may not only be invoked in the actual course of a criminal trial but also in other proceedings which may be precursory of criminal proceedings. For example, this protection may be and has been invoked before the special grand jury referred to above and also before the above-mentioned Subcommittee of the Judiciary Committee of the United States Senate. It is commonly referred to as 'privilege against self-incrimination' —a phrase we have ourselves used above.

"In our opinion a person who invokes this privilege can only lawfully do so in circumstances where the privilege exists. If in reliance upon this privilege a person refuses to answer a question, he is only justified in doing so if he believes or is advised that in answering he would become a witness against himself. In other words, there can be no justification for claiming the privilege unless the person claiming the privilege believes or is advised that his answer would be evidence against himself of the commission of some criminal offense. *It follows from this, in our opinion, that a person claiming this privilege cannot thereafter be heard to say that his answer, if it had been given, would not have been self-incriminatory.* (Committee's italics.) He is in the dilemma that either his answer *would* have been self-incriminatory, or if not he has invoked his constitutional privilege without just cause. As, in our opinion, he cannot be heard to allege the latter, he must by claiming privilege be held to have admitted the former. Moreover, the exercise of this privilege creates so strong a suspicion of guilt that the fact of its exercise must be withheld from a jury in a criminal trial.

"It is clear also that, in addition to arousing a suspicion of guilt, the plea of privilege may well affect conditions of employment. The privilege is an absolute right and it is legal in the United States to assert it, but it does not follow that a witness claiming this privilege, whether he be a national of the United States or otherwise, suffers no ill consequences by the mere fact of his asserting the privilege.

"Indeed, in the United States much legislation has been passed restricting federal, state, or municipal employment in cases of persons connected with organizations declared subversive and machinery established to ascertain whether such connection exists. We refer (interalia) to 5 United States Code, Section 118(j), Executive Order 9835, 12 Federal Regulations 1935, the Feinberg Law (SEC. 3022 of the Education Code), the New York City Charter, Section 903, and the case of *Adler* v. *Board of Education* (342 U.S. 485).

"There can be no doubt that in the United States of America it is not contrary to the Constitution for legislative or other consequences affecting employment to follow from the exercise by an employee of some constitutional right or privilege.

"It appears to us, therefore, that in cases where this privilege is invoked in the United States, the secretary-general must take notice of the fact and be prepared to take the appropriate action."

(Opinion, pages 24-26.)

Thus this trio of distinguished jurists, the best Mr. Trygve Lie could find, commented concerning witnesses who avail themselves of the immunity against self-incrimination.

This committee has always regarded such witnesses with suspicion. In its 1951 report we discussed the same problems and arrived at virtually the same conclusions as the three eminent jurists whose opinion is cited above.

As we see it, only an idiot or an enthusiastic pro-Communist could regard anyone who immediately flees behind the Fifth Amendment when questioned about Communist matters, who is invariably represented by fellow-traveling or Communist lawyers and whose dossier reflects a steady pattern of Communist activity over a period of years, without having his suspicions aroused concerning the pro-Communist proclivities of the individual.

And to this committee it is a disgusting spectacle to see persons employed by state, county and municipal governments, as teachers or members of university faculties at the expense of the taxpayer, arrogantly refuse to state to a legislative committee whether or not they are Communists. This committee, as a result of almost 14 years' experience, has learned that when it possesses a stack of original documents, such as catalogs of Communist schools, brochures of Communist fronts, stacks of Communist papers and reports of Communist activities—all of which repeatedly mention a certain person; and when such a person is subpenaed and appears at a hearing accompanied by a lawyer with a similar record; and when the witness repeatedly invokes the Fifth Amendment as a refuge when questioned about his Communist affiliations, although perfectly willing to answer all other questions—that the committee can draw no other conclusion except that the Communist record of the individual as reflected by the committee's files and the pattern of interrogation is entirely accurate.

Precisely this situation was true in the cases of Frank Wilkinson, Sidney Green, Elizabeth Smith, Adina Williamson and Jack Naiditch. The committee confronted each of them with an alleged record of Communist affiliations and activities, and in each case the witness was advised by counsel to refuse to answer questions on grounds of self incrimination. Elizabeth Smith was the only such witness not represented by counsel, but, as is quite evident from the transcript of her testimony, she came before the committee confident that her San Francisco affiliations and activities had been well concealed. When questioned concerning these matters her attitude, theretofore frank, friendly and cooperative, switched abruptly to one of ill-concealed hostility, and she, too, invoked the Fifth Amendment.

The committee issued subpenas for Jean Benson Wilkinson, Frances Eisenberg and Samuel Berland to establish a link between the Communist Party of Los Angeles County, the Los Angeles Federation of Teachers, the United Public Workers of America and the Los Angeles City School System.

Mrs. Wilkinson was represented by the same attorneys who appeared for her husband, and Mrs. Eisenberg was accompanied by William B. Esterman, whose name has been cited on seven occasions by this committee and several times by the Senate Committee on Education. Both women are employed as teachers in the Los Angeles City Schools, and both are connected with the Los Angeles Federation of Teachers, Local 430, which, in turn, is a subsidiary of the United Public Workers of America, which is represented in Southern California by Mr. Samuel Berland.

Basing its conclusions on the information with which Frank Wilkinson, his wife, Jean, Frances Eisenberg, Sidney Green, Adina Williamson, Elizabeth Smith and Jack Naiditch were each confronted, and the refusal of each to answer questions concerning their Communist affiliations and activities, the committee finds that each of them was a member of the Communist Party of Los Angeles County, and associated together for the purpose of maintaining and expanding Communist units in the Los Angeles City Housing Authority and in the Los Angeles City School System. The committee further has concluded, based on the evidence hereinbefore set forth, that this plan of infiltration is aided and abetted by the Los Angeles Federation of Teachers, Local 430, and the United Public Workers, Local 246, with which it is affiliated. Each organization was found to be Communist dominated by the parent labor organizations, the A. F of L. and the C. I. O. respectively, and expelled for that reason. It should be noted, in passing, that Mr. William Esterman is also attorney for the United Public Workers of America. He has been identified by witnesses before the House Committee on Un-American Activities as a Communist. His client, Mrs. Eisenberg, is the editor of the publication of the Los Angeles Federation of Teachers, and was a director of the Communist school in Los Angeles which was operated under the name of People's Educational Center.

Genealogy of Two Fronts

The collaboration between the United Public Workers, Local 246, and the Los Angeles Federation of Teachers, Local 430, is characteristic of pressure tactics employed by all Communist front groups. These two organizations in Los Angeles County have joined in spearheading the Communist Party's ceaseless effort to insinuate its members into the school system, the Housing Authority and into other positions of enormous strategic importance. The Los Angeles Federation of Teachers, Local 430, has been headed by Harold Orr for several years. He has received 13 citations in the various reports issued by this committee, and several citations in the reports issued by the Senate Committee on Education.

The United Public Workers of America, headed nationally by Abram Flaxer, and in Southern California by Samuel Berland, was for several years under the jurisdiction of Harry S. Jung, who committed suicide in May of 1950.

In April, 1948, Jung and Orr appeared before the Los Angeles City Board of Education to protest against alleged racial discrimination being practiced by Mrs. Nell Haas, a primary school principal. The familiar pressure tactics of the organizations represented by Messrs. Jung and Orr and their followers are fully described in the Sixth Report of the California Senate Committee on Education, published in 1949. That committee conducted a hearing in December, 1948, at which Jung, Orr and members of the Los Angeles City Board of Education were questioned.

Both Jung and Orr, under the practiced guidance of Mr. Esterman, refused to answer any questions concerning Communist connections. Thus when Mr. Jung was questioned about his connection with American Youth for Democracy, listed by the Attorney General of the United States as a Communist organization, he dodged the question until confronted with documentation in a Communist newspaper which he did not choose to refute.

"Q. (By Mr. Combs): You were also a sponsor for American Youth for Democracy, were you not?

"A. Are you telling me this?

"Q. Yes, I am. It appeared in the *People's World* on the 7th of December, 1945, page 3, column 5. Did that organization, to your knowledge, interest itself in protesting the loyalty check—to your knowledge?

"A. What was the name of the organization?

"Q. American Youth for Democracy.

"A. I don't recall whether they did or not.

"Q. You were a sponsor, were you not, for American Youth for Democracy?

"A. You just told me I was.

"Q. I am asking you now; were you?

"A. Well, I don't recall, except that you told me. I am sure that if the *People's World* published that, that I was."

Mr. Orr, at this 1948 hearing, refused to answer questions concerning his collaboration with Jung in organizing the pressure attack against Mrs. Haas and the school board. He also declined to explain the organizational structure of the Los Angeles Federation of Teachers and to discuss Mrs. Eisenberg's connection with it.

Just as the letters suddenly poured in on Mr. Holtzendorff beseeching him not to suspend Frank Wilkinson, so was the board of education flooded with protests in 1947 and 1948 against their loyalty program for teachers and beseeching them to fire Mrs. Nell Haas. Just as a majority of those who interceded for Wilkinson had records of Communist front affiliations, so did those who wrote to the school board in 1948. And just as the infiltration of the Housing Authority and the Los Angeles City School System has been spearheaded by the United Public Workers and its subsidiary, the Los Angeles Federation of Teachers, so did these two organizations combine to discredit Mrs. Nell Haas and the school board's loyalty program in 1948—an effort which came to a miserable failure because of the firm attitude adopted by the board of education and the exposure of these two organizations by state committees.

United Public Workers of America

Communist-controlled organizations usually change their names from time to time in an effort to conceal their true character and to mask their real objectives. Thus the Young Communist League became American Youth for Democracy and is now operating under a new name, the Labor Youth League. Just as a criminal adopts aliases to cover his illegal activities, so the Communist fronts and the Communist-dominated unions adopt new names for much the same reason; and Party members are given Party aliases or Party names as a security measure against exposure.

Following this pattern the United Public Workers of America has been known by several names or aliases, and is worth discussing in considerable detail at this point because it has become one of the most vital unions in the Stalinist solar system. Its members, as the name of the organization implies, are employed by federal and state governments, and by counties and cities throughout the United States. These members of a Communist-controlled union work as switchboard operators, clerks, stenographers, secretaries, janitors, maintenance men, teachers, social workers, and in a wide variety of government positions. About 500 work for the Treasury Department's Bureau of Engraving, others for the Post Office Department, some for the Immigration Service, and others have been employed in the Army's super-secret Aberdeen Proving Ground where the latest weapons are tested.

The United Public Workers was actually started in 1936 when the A. F. of L. expelled several of its lodges because of their radical activities. These expelled lodges joined together, affiliated with the C. I. O., and called themselves the United Federal Workers of America. In 1937, another radical union of public workers switched from the A. F. of L. to the C. I. O. and called itself the State, County and Municipal Workers of America. These two C. I. O. unions, the United Federal Workers and SCMWA, functioned independently until they merged in 1946 and became known as the United Public Workers of America with a total membership of about 50,000. In 1950, the United Public Workers of America were subjected to a searching and vigorous investigation by the C. I. O. top command, was found to be Communist-dominated and for that reason was expelled. Since 1950, it has continued to operate as an independent union.

Bearing in mind that this organization, the United Public Workers of America, was formed by the merging of the SCMWA and the United Federal Workers of America, these two parent organizations will bear some scrutiny at this point. Since 1937, the SCMWA had been headed by Abram Flaxer. He was born in Lithuania in September, 1904, came to the United States in 1911, and became a citizen in 1917. He attended New York City College and soon after graduating from that institution launched into trade union work. Flaxer helped form the SCMWA, was its first national president, and when that organization merged with the United Federal Workers to form the United Public Workers of America, Flaxer became national president of the new organization, a position which he still holds.

Scores of witnesses have positively identified Flaxer as a Communist Party member, and when questioned concerning that matter under oath he has invariably refused to deny the charge, following the time-worn expedient of invoking the Fifth Amendment. At the time he joined the Communist Party he was attending Columbia University summer school in 1936, and was given the Party alias of "John Brant" by which he was commonly known in Communist circles.

Flaxer's first wife was Vivien White Sobeleski. In 1951, she testified concerning her ex-husband's Communist membership and activities before the United States Senate Subcommittee on Internal Security. She described a familiar bit of Communist deception that has been foisted on the American public for years, as follows:

"Q. (By Mr. Morris) : Mrs. Sobeleski, did Mr. Flaxer, to your knowledge, ever publicly admit his Communist Party membership?

"A. No, he never did, feeling that it would hamper his work and interfere with the recruiting in the union. And it was also Party policy that he not appear as a Party member.

"Q. What is your appraisal of the reason for the Party policy that he not appear as a Party member?

"A. The Party always felt it benefitted by having people prominent in public life, not Party members, agree with the Communist Party line, so it could not be labelled as a Communist Party position."

(Transcript, July, 1951, page 17.)

Frank Wilkinson followed this tactic to the letter. While associating with such prominent non-Communists as Monseigneur Thomas O'Dwyer and Supervisor John Anson Ford, he posed as a non-Communist whose real sympathies ran peculiarly parallel to those of the Communist Party line. By following this sort of expedient and carefully concealing his Party affiliations, Wilkinson was able to enlist the prestige and sympathies of many highly placed people, some of whom are well known for their outspoken Americanism and their vigorous opposition to all things Communist. This technique of practiced hypocracy, so repugnant to the average person, is not distasteful to the average Communist.

Communists are convinced that they are laboring for the benefit of downtrodden humanity, and that the end amply justifies any means they must take in order to achieve it; this sort of self-administered moral anesthesia enables them to spend a good portion of their time in undercover Communist activities which are surrounded with elaborate precautions against exposure, and the rest of their time concealing these things from their non-Communist contacts. In the case of Mr. Wilkinson, the evidence before the committee indicates that he was the head of the Communist unit in the Los Angeles City Housing Authority, but received his orders and Party assignments from a superior in his Party unit.

Wilkinson's Communist affiliations apparently began when he was a student at U. C. L. A. and continued thereafter until he moved progressively from one Communist unit to another. As his Party contacts broadened, he came into contact with Los Angeles functionaries who saw in him an idealist who could be extremely useful as a contact with influential non-Communist persons in Southern California and also as an active recruiter in the housing authority. It will be noted that Wilkinson endeavored to make it most clear to the committee that he *had* known a person by the name of H. L. Sunshine, but that the man he knew by that name was quite a different person from the individual who testified before the committee and who had stated positively that he detested Communism and that Frank Wilkinson had endeavored to recruit him into the Party. It should be added that Mr. Sunshine is not the only person in the housing authority who was a target for recruitment into the Communist Party by Frank Wilkinson.

It will be noted that Wilkinson had once been employed by the State Relief Administration, as had several of the other witnesses who appeared before the committee and refused to answer questions concerning their Communist affiliations. Virtually all of these people had been members of the State, County and Municipal Workers of America (SCMWA), which deserves a little consideration at this point on account of its activities in California since 1937.

State, County, and Municipal Workers of America

The first real Committe on Un-American Activities in California was created by Gordon Garland when he was Speaker of the Assembly. Mr. Garland, at the Special Session in 1940, created this committee for the specific purpose of investigating Communist infiltration in the State Relief Administration. The committee was mandated to subpena witnesses, hold hearings, and submit a report of its findings and conclusions to the 1941 Regular Session of the State Legislature. This report, now out of print but reissued at the insistence of Assemblyman Bernard Brady of San Francisco, indicates what the 1940 committee found concerning the State, County and Municipal Workers of America. It said:

"Your committee has been amazed at the extent of Communist infiltration into the State Relief Administration. Under the cloak of this branch of State Government, Communists have found their way into widely separated areas of the State. In these areas they are engaged in carrying out a well-planned scheme to undermine State Government. Some of the strategy employed by them is quite apparent. It follows very closely the pattern laid down by the founders of the Communist Party and it parallels to a great degree the strategy of the Communist Party in Russia—with allowances made for the differences and the problems faced by the Party because of the differences in the two nations.

"Communists in the State Relief Administration have used as a smoke screen for their activities a CIO union called the State, County and Municipal Workers of America. Such use of legal organizations is an old tactic of the Communist Party. By hiding behind what appears to be a labor organization, and by using as 'Fronts' non-Communists led into such an organization, they are able to screen their activities. The Communists then endeavor to make it appear that attacks on them are attacks on a labor union.

"Your committee knows that the leadership of this SRA group (SCMWA) is communistic. In order to deny this fact, when questioned before the committee, these leaders would have to perjure themselves. For this reason they devised the strategy of hiring attorneys, in every case either Communists or known sympathizers, who in purporting to represent the best interests of all members of the so-called union, made it clear to all of them that they should not answer questions relative to Communism. This meant that Communists and non-Communists alike, who were members of the so-called union, would refuse to answer questions relative to Communism. This saved the Communists from the necessity of being the only ones forced to refuse to answer in order to escape exposure or possible prosecution for perjury. Non-Communists were thus used as a screen.

"The records show that your committee constantly advised members of this Communist-controlled organization that if they were not Communists they should answer the questions frankly and not be dupes for Communist hoodlums. But the typical Communist discipline was already so well inculcated into the minds of the members of this organization, that only a few had the courage to defy their leaders by stating to the committee that they were not Communists, and that they did not believe in Communism. Those who did testify were dismissed from the union for so doing. In contrast to the attitude to the disciplined members of this so-called union were all of the other witnesses who came before the committee, in every case without attorneys, and in every case with the willingness to answer questions put by the committee relative to Communism."

Thus it will be seen in 1940, 13 years ago, the State, County and Municipal Workers of America was adopting the tactics which have since become so threadbare and familiar to the citizens of this State. The report of the 1940 committee continued:

"Use of legal organizations such as the SCMWA to cover up illegal, or what the Communists call 'Underground' activities, is a fundamental tactic of the Stalinists. This tactic is especially useful during periods when the attention of the people is directed toward the subversive character of their activities. This is the situation in America now and, as one would expect, the Communist Party is going 'underground.' In other words, fearing that it will soon be made illegal, it is preparing to combine illegal underground activity with work through controlled legal organizations like the SCMWA."

One of the witnesses who appeared before the U. S. Senate Subcommittee on Internal Security in December, 1951, was Mr. Henry W. Wenning, himself a former Communist, and who was active in the State, County and Municipal Workers of America with the national president, Mr. Flaxer. Mr. Wenning said:

"At the inception of the union the Communists in the union controlled it completely. As the union grew in size and as new locals were established away from the eastern seaboard, a lot of local unions and local leaders and influences were brought into the union that were not Communists, but despite that, I would say the Communist control of the union remained virtually complete. In almost every area, organizers and other key people were in the majority of cases either Party members or people who were considered to be very close to the Party." (Transcript of Hearing, December, 1951, page 66.)

United Federal Workers of America

In 1936, the American Federation of Labor expelled an organization whose members were employed by the Federal Government. This organization, known as the American Federation of Government Employees, thereafter affiliated with the CIO under the name of United Federal Workers of America, and from the time of its inception in 1937, was headed by Eleanor Nelson, who for several years continued as the president of the organization.

She has been identified, as has Mr. Flaxer, by many witnesses as a member of the Communist Party. In addition, she has participated in a long variety of Communist-controlled activities, and has been associated with an impressive array of Communist Party fronts, as follows:

I. National Council of American-Soviet Friendship

Other persons who were connected with this Communist-front organization with Eleanor Nelson were: Ruth Appleman, Rose Schneiderman, Zlatko Balokovic, Charles Chaplin, Lillian Hellman, Paul Robeson, Professor Henry E. Sigerist, A. F. Whitney, Professor Max Yergan, J. F. Jurich, Frederic March, Hugh Ernst, Professor Robert S. Lynd, Professor Kirtley F. Mather, Reverend Edward L. Parsons, Frank Tuttle, Abram Flaxer, Earl Robinson, Louis Adamic, Norman Corwin, Lion Feuchtwanger, Mary Van Kleek, Maxwell Anderson.

II. Friday

Other individuals connected with this Communist-dominated publication, in addition to Eleanor Nelson, were: Rockwell Kent, Richard Wright, Professor Max Yergan, Harry Bridges, George Seldes, Professor Walter Rautenstrauch, Professor Franz Boas, Paul Robeson, Ell Winter, Anna Louise Strong, Professor Robert Morss Lovett, Hugh De Lacy, Vito Marcantonio.

III. Joint Anti-Fascist Refugee Committee

Persons, in addition to Eleanor Nelson, who were connected with this Communist front organization were: Zlatko Balokovic, Max Bedacht, Paul de Kruif, Professor Henry Pratt Fairchild, Abram Flaxer, William Groper, Lillian Hellman, Ring Lardner, Jr., John Howard Lawson, Professor Emil Lengyel, Vito Marcantonio, Carey McWilliams, Arthur Upham Pope, Professor Walter Rautenstrauch, Earl Robinson, George Seldes, Herman Shumlin, Gale Sondergaard, Johannes Steel, Donald Ogden Stewart; Professor Dirk J. Struick, Dalton Trumbo, Max Yergan, Ben Gold, Donald Henderson, J. F. Jurich, Joseph P. Selly, Ferdinand C. Smith, Professor Edward K. Barsky, Reverend Stephen H. Fritchman, Muriel Draper, Paul Robeson.

IV. Washington Committee for Aid to China

Other persons connected with this Communist Front organization, in addition to Eleanor Nelson, were: Frederick Vanderbilt Field, Paul Robeson, Madeline Jaffe, Helen Silvermaster, Owen J. Lattimore.

Thus the two organizations that combined to form the United Public Workers of America were each headed by Communist Party members; they were, in fact, important parts of the Communist apparatus in this country for the purpose of infiltrating governmental offices with persons sworn to subvert and disrupt our way of life by every undercover method at their command. When the Los Angeles Federation of Teachers was expelled from the American Federation of Labor because it was found to be Communist dominated, it immediately was taken under the wing of the United Public Workers of America where it has been nestling every since.

What is the situation, then, as it now exists in California with regard to the United Public Workers of America? We have seen from the foregoing complicated genealogy, that the United Public Workers of America is actually an amalgamation of several union organizations that were thrown out of their parent organizations because they were found to be Communist dominated: (1) the United Federal Workers of America, (2) State, County and Municipal Workers of America, (3) the Los Angeles Federation of Teachers. All of these are merged in the United Public Workers of America, which itself was expelled from the CIO in 1950 because it was found to be Communist dominated. Through the medium of this union, fanatic Communists are sent from one end of the State of California to the other, burrowing their way into governmental positions and infesting our school system with Communist teachers. In this committee's opinion it is high time that this organization be recognized for what it is: simply an integral part of the Communist Party apparatus, headed by Communist members and run for the benefit of Communism. This being true, any subdivision of the State Government or any political subdivision of the State does business with this kind of an organization at its own peril.

In conclusion, it should be pointed out that five Communists out of a total of 450 employees in the Los Angeles City Housing Authority is obviously not a very heavy incidence of infiltration. The fact remains, however, as we have pointed out many times before, one Communist in the proper place can cause as much damage as a thousand. The housing authority is a natural target for Communist infiltration because the people who are forced to live in public housing units are more apt to be socially maladjusted and dissatisfied and therefore more susceptible to the blandishments of clever Communist recruiting specialists than the average person who has a home of his own. Furthermore, the element of congestion and the high incidence of racial minority groups combine to make the field even more fertile. This committee, by no stretch of the imagination, is to be construed as inferring that there is a high incidence of Communism in the residential personnel of the housing authority of Los Angeles City or any other place, but it is quite apparent that the Communist Party of Los Angeles County sent its agents into the employ of the housing authority for the purpose of capitalizing on the opportunity for recruiting among the other employees and the residential personnel throughout the entire project.

The committee also wishes to emphasize the fact that it has screened *every* employee of the housing authority, together with all of the administrative personnel and the five commissioners, and has, for that purpose, had access to other sources of compiled information in addition to its own. So far as the committee has been able to determine, the Los Angeles City Housing Authority is now free of Communist Party members. Mr. Holtzendorff and his staff, Mayor Bowron, the Los Angeles Police Department and other municipal agencies, gave the committee every possible cooperation during both the investigations and the hearings, and in following up the last hearing with a system whereby adequate preparations may be taken to prevent infiltration of the Authority in the future. Both the Office of State Attorney General and the District Attorney of Los Angeles County also cooperated with the committee to the fullest degree at all stages of the investigations and hearings.

COMMUNISM AND EDUCATION

On March 24, 1952, the Senate Committee on Un-American Activities collaborated with President Robert Gordon Sproul of the University of California and Fred Fagg, Jr., President of the University of Southern California in extending an invitation to all of the major colleges and universities in the southern part of the State to attend a meeting which was held at the University of Southern California in Los Angeles. Those who attended, in addition to representatives of the committee, were: Presidents Robert Gordon Sproul, University of California; Lee A. Du-Bridge, California Institute of Technology; George S. Benson, Claremont and Scripts Colleges; Arthur G. Coons, Occidental College; George H. Armacost, Redlands University; Father William C. Gianera, Loyola University, Dean of Arts and Sciences; Dr. F. Raymond Iredell, Pomona College Faculty Dean; Kenneth Richardson, Whittier College, Dean of Admissions; and A. S. Raubenheimer, University of Southern California, Educational Vice President, who represented President Fagg of the University of Southern California, who was unable to participate on account of illness.

At the conclusion of this meeting, all present agreed that the various institutions that were represented should collaborate with the committee in a cooperative, long-range preventive plan to eliminate Communist Party members from the faculties of California institutions of higher learning and to take steps to prevent the infiltration of faculties by Communist Party members, or those whose documentable record of Communist activities were so formidable as to raise a serious question concerning their ability to engage in objective teaching.

On June 23, 1952, a similar meeting was held at the University of San Francisco, as a result of which the Northern California educational institutions joined in the plan. They were: The University of California, the University of San Francisco, Stanford University, St. Mary's College, Mills College, Santa Clara University and the College of the Pacific. Shortly thereafter Dr. Roy E. Simpson, State Superintendent of Public Instruction, arranged with the Senate Committee to have the 11 state colleges participate in the plan.

The committee considers this cooperative enterprise between its staff and the colleges and universities in California a step of transcendent importance. By establishing constant liaison with the participating institutions, the information that has been collected by this committee over a period of almost 14 years of continuous activity is made available to individuals who have been specially trained to evaluate it properly with due regard to the safeguarding of civil liberties and academic freedom, as those terms are understood in their true senses. Such a plan virtually eliminates the necessity of the long series of public hearings, which are not only expensive and attended by considerable sensational publicity, but which are inevitably attended, also, by an atmosphere of excitement and tension which makes the work of the committee much more difficult once the smoke of battle has cleared away.

Thus far the plan has been attended by much more success than any of its participants had anticipated. More than 100 individuals have been eliminated from various campuses in California, and in each case this has been accomplished without fanfare or publicity and the institutions have been able, with the assistance of this committee, to handle the matters themselves. Of course, as has been explained to each participating institution, if the committee finds positive evidence that a Communist Party member or Marxian activist is buried deep in the heart of a university faculty, and if the institution by which he is employed neglects or refuses to take adequate steps to eliminate him, then the committee will exercise its power of subpena and conduct a hearing at which the individuals concerned can be questioned under oath.

In addition to weeding out the Communist Party members from university faculties, it is even more important to prevent their places from being filled by individuals whose records are just as bad if not worse. To that end the committee is making its documented information available to the colleges and the universities so that in cases where an applicant applies for a teaching position or a nonacademic job the university administration will at least have the opportunity to scrutinize such documentary materials concerning his Communist affiliations before it has placed the individual on its pay roll.

Another great advantage inherent in a plan of this character lies in the fact that the Communist Party apparatus is deprived of its opportunity to whip up hysterical front organizations, accuse the university and the committee of the shop-worn propaganda devices of undermining civil liberties, destroying academic freedom, witch-hunting, red-baiting, thought-control and maintaining a gigantic campus gestapo system; it prevents the Party from capitalizing on such matters for the purpose of enlisting moral and financial support from the fellow-traveling groups and raising the customary furor for its own hypocritical purposes.

California is the first State in the Union where a legislative committee on un-American activities and all of the major colleges and universities in the State have joined together to present a solid academic front against Communist infiltration of the institutions of higher learning. Obviously, it is possible to accomplish far more by such a cooperative plan than it is for a legislative committee to be faced with the constant necessity of investigating the situation independently on each of the campuses.

It is intended to implement this plan by holding seminars on the techniques of Communist infiltration and activity on campuses, together with information concerning the current Party front organizations that operate in the vicinity of educational institutions; such lectures to be given by former members of the Communist Party, each of whom was a specialist in this particular type of work. In addition, liaison has been established between the individuals at each of the larger institutions who are charged with the business of keeping abreast of activities on the campus in this particular field, and the constant exchange of information between them, and between the committee and the various institutions is now working smoothly and effectively.

The chairman of this committee pointed out in press releases at the time the plan was perfected, that the committee did not wish to imply that there was any sudden epidemic of Communist infiltration on the campuses of the educational institutions in this State. Such is simply not the case. It would be equally as foolish to state that there were no Communists on any of the faculties of any of the participating institutions, and that therefore such a plan was not needed. Some of the smaller institutions have, indeed, a negligible problem. Some of the larger institutions have a serious problem, but the problem consists more in the strategic positions occupied by the handful of the known subversives who are still on university pay rolls, rather than any danger because of a large number of such persons in any one university. Obviously, a Communist scientist doing research work on a secret weapon is far more dangerous than a Communist janitor or a Communist clerk in a dean's office. The committee is well aware of the fact that none of the participating institutions deliberately encourage the employment of Communists; there was, however, considerable apathy in many of the universities, a total lack of any definite plan to combat Communist infiltration, and an unfortunate lack of information concerning Communist techniques and practices in general.

It wasn't long before the Communist Party began to spread news of this project in California. In June, 1952, an issue of *Teachers' Bulletin,* published by the Communist-dominated New York Teachers local of the United Public Workers of America announced:

"In California, the State Senate *Un-American Committee* (Committee's italics), with the blessing of University of California President Robert G. Sproul, is creating a gigantic campus spy plan to function on 10 colleges and universities of the State. The plan calls for the appointment of contact men on each campus to report directly to the un-American committee on 'all levels' of alleged Communist activities on the part of students, faculty and administration."

This account, full of characteristic mis-statements, has been repeated in other terms from time to time by various Communist propaganda publications. To begin with, there is no spy plan. Each of the participating institutions handles its own individual problems with the assistance of the committee; there is no system of contact men who report to the committee on all levels of alleged Communist activities on the part of students, faculty and administration; there are 28 participating institutions instead of the 10, as stated in the *Teachers' Bulletin.*

COMMUNIST PLAN FOR EDUCATIONAL INFILTRATION

In its 1951 report, the committee devoted 161 pages to a discussion of Communist infiltration of schools in California. One portion of this section was devoted to a discussion in detail of Communist recruiting techniques as practiced by Party members on the faculties who were especially trained in this important field. Excerpts were taken from official Communist documents showing that there was a coordinated plan for educational infiltration in the United States which has been under way since 1920. The committee discussed at length the various student Communist organizations, commencing with the Young Communist League, the National Students League, the American Youth Congress, the American Student Union, American Youth for Democracy and the

Labor Youth League. Since the 1951 report was written, the committee has obtained additional information of even greater importance which shows the meticulous care with which the Communist Party in this Country selects members from the educational profession, trains them, and assigns them to carry out Party work in the various institutions at which they are employed.

William Z. Foster is now the titular head of the Communist Party of the United States. He and Earl Browder were charter members of the Communist Party, and when Browder was expelled from his position of control and read out of the Party, Foster took his place. In 1938 William Z. Foster went to the Soviet Union where he attended several sessions of the Comintern in Moscow. At these sessions, held in the Comintern Building near the Kremlin, were assembled the Communist Party leaders of the world: Browder and Foster from the United States, Palmiro Togliatti from Italy, Klement Gottwald from Czechoslovakia, Wilhelm Pieck from Germany, Chou En-lai from China, and other Comintern delegates from Argentina, Chile, Brazil, Peru, Cuba and Uruguay, as well as minor figures from Hungary, Macedonia, Spain and Indo-China. D. Z. Manuilsky and Georgi Dimitrov, two veteran Comintern leaders, led the discussions which revolved around the recruitment of fellow travelers from professional circles to carry out the work of the Party. Immediately after attending these sessions, Foster returned to the United States and wrote an article in the September, 1938, issue of *The Communist,* entitled "The Communist Party and the Professionals."

Fortunately, we are provided with the substance of the discussions which took place at the Comintern meeting of 1938 by referring to an account by Eudocio Ravines, a former Comintern agent, which he published on pages 265-268 of his book, *The Yenan Way,* Charles Scribner Sons, New York, 1951. He says:

"Then Dimitrov began to discuss the tactics and type of work that lay before us. Our program must be to gain ends through our friends, sympathizers and allies, while keeping ourselves in the background: 'As Soviet power grows there will be a greater aversion to Communist Parties everywhere. So we must practice the techniques of withdrawal. Never appear in the foreground; let our friends do the work. We must always remember that one sympathizer is generally worth more than a dozen militant Communists. A university professor, who without being a party member lends himself to the interests of the Soviet Union, is worth more than a hundred men with party cards. A writer of reputation, or a retired general, are worth more than 500 poor devils who don't know any better than to get themselves beaten up by the police. Every man has his value, his merit. The writer, who, without being a party member, defends the Soviet Union, the union leader who is outside our ranks but defends Soviet international policy, is worth more than a thousand party members.'

" 'Those who are not party members or marked as Communists enjoy greater freedom of action. This dissimulated activity which awakes no resistance is much more effective than a frontal attack by the Communists. The Communist Party of the whole world must learn the lesson of the Spanish War, where the efficacy of the fifth column was proved. Our friends must confuse the adversary for us, carry out our main directives, mobilize in favor of our campaigns people who do not think as we do, and whom we could never reach. In this tactic we must use everyone who comes near us; and the number grows every day'.''

'' 'The time has come, Comrades,' said Manuilsky, 'when we must cultivate carefully all outstanding personalities—soldiers, painters with a reputation, writers and union leaders, musicians and sculptors of some renown, outstanding sports heroes and actors of stage and screen. In Mexico we have Lombardo Toledano and his friends; they are not party members, but much more valuable for that very reason, and they render us greater service than the whole of organized Mexican Communism. In Hollywood we have people who work admirably for the Soviet Union. Browder knows that. In Brazil there is a group of writers and painters who are invaluable to us without a party card. And in Cuba, Juan Marinello is working out a more efficient policy than the whole Communist Party'.''

In conformity with this high-level decision, and the instructions then and there exported to the Communist leaders of the world, the practice of issuing any formal evidence of Communist affiliation to highly placed professional members was discontinued. Thenceforth, the college professor who was issued a formal party card or book became a rarity, and party members who were working on a policy-making level in the government were never issued cards and were never permitted to have any contact with known Communist Party members. As the committee has heretofore stated, the Communist Party in America has not issued any Communist Party membership cards, or books since late in 1947, and documentable evidence of membership, unless it antedates the winter of 1947, is simply not available. The more highly placed the Communist may be, the less likelihood there is that he would ever have any documentable affiliation with even a front organization, to say nothing of ever having been issued a Communist membership card or book.

When Foster returned to the United States after this significant meeting of Comintern representatives and delegates in the Soviet Union, he wrote the article for the September issue of *The Communist,* referred to above, that is of the utmost significance to all professional people, and particularly to educators. The article, which commences on page 805, reads, in part, as follows:

" * * * In late years, and particularly during our big recruiting campaign, an appreciable number of professionals—doctors, dentists, lawyers, engineers, teachers, scientists, writers, musicians, artists, actors, etc.—have joined our party."

"The entry of numerous professionals into the party is a testimonial to our party's growing influence among the broadest masses. At the same time, it presents to the party new problems and tasks which we must become conscious of and take the necessary steps to solve before we can fully utilize our Communist professionals."

"Considering, therefore, the question of the relationship of the party toward its professionals from the double angle of (1) developing their full revolutionary possibilities and (2) avoiding the danger of reformist individuals and tendencies among them, our party tasks group themselves roughly under three general heads:

"(1) Elective Recruiting. In drawing professionals into the party, care should be exercised to select only those individuals who show by practical work that they definitely understand the party line, are prepared to put it into effect, *and especially display a thorough readiness to accept party discipline* (committee's italics). It is not enough that professionals should support our general struggle for democracy and peace; they must also accept the socialist principles of our party. There must be selective recruiting far more than in the case of miners, longshoremen, railroad workers, etc. General party units which proceed on the basis of 'mass recruitment of lawyers,' or of 'drawing doctors into the party on a large scale,' have a wrong policy."

Let us consider Foster's three principles, one by one. When he speaks of selective recruiting, what, exactly, does he mean? The foregoing paragraph, couched in the obscure language so beloved by Party leaders, when reduced to its simplest terms, carries a grim portent. Foster declares that since the professional class can provide valuable leadership to the Party, extreme care must be exercised to recruit only those individuals who are willing to serve most actively. The Party will not tolerate professional people who are inactive or dormant, or who are not capable of being completely subservient to the most rigid Party discipline. Foster is here laying down the ground rules for the development of an elite corps of Communist leaders from the professional class; an elite corps of Party activists who must be willing to carry out specific directives from above, to fight constantly in furthering the cause of international Communism. These are not idle words, they come from the highest Communist functionary in the United States, the leader of the Party at the present time, and immediately after he had returned from the Moscow Comitern meeting with the international directives fresh in his mind.

Thus from the highest authority we are told that the Party has no use for inactive campus Communists. Even in 1938—15 years ago—great stress was being placed on the absolute necessity of recruiting only those professionals whose whole time would be dedicated to Communist activity. Foster then moved on to discuss his second principle.

"(2) Intensive Education. There must be special attention paid to the Marxian education of professionals entering our Party. This should have the definite goal of thoroughly Communizing their outlook and reorienting their previous intellectual training, so that its full value may be utilized in a revolutionary sense by our Party and the masses."

This paragraph is clear enough. Once the future activist is selected, his previous mode of thinking must be "reoriented." He must go through a brain-washing process until he is, as Foster puts it, "Communized." It is diabolically effective, and produces a new sort of person who is convinced that the end justifies the means; that he is perfectly justified in lying, subverting, committing perjury; and thenceforth he endeavors to present a pleasant and innocuous false front to his friends, at the same time concealing his real affiliations and covert activities. Foster then proceeds to set up point 3—which he expands in considerable detail, explaining the duties of the Communized professional.

"(3) Systematic Mass Work. It is necessary also that care be exercised to draw the professionals into mass work in an organized way, both in their respective callings and in the general mass struggle. Let me expand this point in some detail under a separate heading."

For our purposes, we are most concerned with subdivision D of Foster's succeeding explanation.

"(d). Communist professionals also have the very important task of advancing, and even revolutionizing the techniques and theories of their respective professions. They must take up the intellectual cudgels against the reactionaries on all fronts. Thus, our teachers must write new school textbooks and rewrite history from the Marxian viewpoint, our scientists must organize more effectively the battle of the materialists against the idealists in every branch of science, our doctors must introduce new methods into medicine (the American Medical Association is not only reactionary politically, but also medically), our lawyers must challenge musty capitalist legal conceptions and rewrite our legal history, our writers must bring forth the class struggle themes in literature and in the theater, etc."

This was the signal, then, for the Communist Party of the United States to carefully recruit its future leaders from the professional fields, to Communize them and turn them loose to Communize others. In obedience to the above directive, Marxian poison was pumped into books, movies, plays and radio programs. School texts *were* rewritten; classroom instruction swerved into intellectual free-wheeling as a new and abundant elite corps of carefully selected, reoriented, Communized professors and other intellectuals were activated and brought under Party discipline.

When Foster called for class-struggle themes in literature his directive was aimed in the general direction of such writers as Howard Fast, George Seldes, Albert Maltz, John Howard Lawson, Carey McWilliams, Langston Hughes, V. J. Jerome, Howard Selsam, Michael Gold, and others; when he called for more class-struggle propaganda in motion pictures, he found a solid phalanx in Dalton Trumbo, Lester Cole, Ring Lardner, Jr., Herbert Biberman, Alvah Bessie, and others; when he called on the doctors, he could enlist the aid of such individuals as Murray Abowitz, Thomas Addis, Jack Agins, and others; when he called for a resurgence of campus activity he could turn to Howard David Langford, Joseph Butterworth, Ralph Gundlach, Herbert Phillips, Morris U. Schappes, Holland Roberts, Frank Weymouth, Dirk J. Struick, Bernhard J. Stern, Haakon Chevalier, Frank Oppenheimer, Franz Boas, Robert S. Lynd, and others. And when D. Z. Manuilsky was addressing the Comintern conference, above mentioned, and stated that the Party should cultivate such outstanding personalities as soldiers, painters, writers and union leaders, he could well have referred to such persons in the United States as the late General Evans Carlson, Rockwell Kent, Professor Langford, and Abram Flaxer. The records of all of these individuals have thoroughly been documented in the files of virtually every official investigating agency in the field. From many former Communist Party members, all functioning at one time on a policy-making level in the Party apparatus, comes complete corroboration of Foster's declaration that every professional Communist, including teachers, must be carefully selected, carefully trained, and above all must be willing to accept and carry out Party discipline. Thus Louis F. Budenz, formerly a member of the National Committee of the Communist Party of the United States, discusses the matter in his latest book, *The Cry Is Peace*, Henry Regnery Company, Chicago, 1952.

Budenz calls attention to an article in the February, 1951, issue of *Political Affairs*, monthly ideological publication of the Communist Party of the United States, setting forth the proceedings of the 15th National Convention of the Party. Red professors were ordered to concentrate on:

"No militarization of the schools and classrooms. Defend academic freedom. Defend student deferments."

Said Budenz:

"We get a good glimpse of what 'no militarization of the schools and classrooms' means when we read further: 'Ways can be found to give voice to the public indignation at the war hysteria and chauvinism being injected into the schools and the communities, especially in the guise of atom bomb drills and civilian defense mobilization.' It is quite obvious in this and other statements what the Reds are after: to leave our civilian defense completely unprepared and our school children at the mercy of any invaders. That is in line with the instructions to emphasize that 'the draft and universal military service and training proposals are highly unwelcome,' and to accentuate among college students that they should not cut short their studies for military service. Such propaganda is not based on true opposition to war, but is simply a part of the Soviet offensive against the United States, the purpose of which is to make our youth both spiritually and intellectually unprepared for American defense."

"These professors, of whom we have only begun to call the roll, affect not only the students of the immediate moment but the community members and leaders of tomorrow.

"The Communists and those who work with them have long been interested in the lower schools and have concentrated much effort in that area. The banner-bearer in this field has been the New York Teachers Union, which has consistently followed the Party line and has been excluded from both the American Federation of Labor and the Congress of Industrial Organizations on the grounds of Communist control.

"As early as 1940, the *Daily Worker* recorded the achievements of those teachers who were working with the Reds in primary and secondary schools. A special article by David Gordon, party name for a teacher in the New York public school system, states: 'Teacher-student activity has gone beyond their occupational organizations. Teacher and student are to be found in such organizations as the American League for Peace and Democracy, American Youth Congress, in the progressive political life of the Nation. America will never forget the great student peace strikes and demonstrations conducted in our schools in the past several years. Nor will they ever forget the help the teachers gave.' The piece ended with directives to 'faculty and students to prevent Wall Street's ardent war hopes from being foisted on the American people,' in order that efforts be renewed for 'unity' of teacher and pupil in seeking this end.

"Such instructions were emphasized again today at the 15th National Convention of the Communist Party, and as an example it cites 'the gallant fight of the New York Teachers Union.' Hand in hand with this goes the penetration of parent-teacher associations. On this the 15th convention said: 'There is mounting indignation and protest on the part of parent-teacher associations against militarizing the public schools and terrorizing the minds of children with atom bomb 'defense drills.' In the Communist meaning of words, this is a strict directive to assure that this 'indignation' is fostered and forwarded.

"Aware of what investigations, particularly initiated by parents, would divulge concerning the Red conspiracy in the schools and colleges, the Communists have raised their old cry of 'academic freedom.' They urge, at this same convention, 'a struggle against Nazi-like control of the mind.' In the official proceedings we read denunciations of the 'Fascist black list and censorship campaign,' coupled with this exhortation: 'An outstanding example of resistance to Fascization of the college campus has been the struggle against the "loyalty oaths" in California'."

"* * * Every Communist educator and Red sympathizer in education is an active agent of the conspiracy, whose orders it is his duty to obey. In his own field, he is just as dangerous as the Communist espionage agent.

"The Communist educators, like all members of the fifth column, cannot merely hold certain opinions, they must act."

TESTIMONY OF BELLA V. DODD

In September and October, 1952, the United States Senate Subcommittee on Internal Security held hearings on educational infiltration by the Communist Party of the United States. One of the most important witnesses to appear before the subcommittee on that occasion was Bella V. Dodd. Her name has been familiar to counter-espionage agents for years. She became a devout Marxian in 1932 and received her Communist Party card in 1943. She served as a member of the National Committee of the Communist Party of the United States from 1944 to 1948, and left the Party in 1949. During her active membership she served on the usual committees, commissions, and fronts; she was also legislative representative of the New York State District Communist Party and was a member of the New York State Communist Party Committee.

Mrs. Dodd, being a teacher by profession, specialized in educational work for the Party. In 1932, she was an instructor in political science and economics at Hunter College having graduated from that institution as a Doctor of Jurisprudence in 1925. Mrs. Dodd went to Europe soon after leaving Hunter College, studied at the University of Berlin, and visited in France, Italy, Czechoslovakia, Poland, Austria and Hungary. While in Europe she became obsessed with a firm resolution to prevent the rise of Fascism in America as she saw it rising in Europe—and was convinced that this purpose could best be accomplished through Communism.

After returning to Hunter College she plunged deep into what she then believed to be anti-Fascist work. Actually, of course, she was simply working for Communism. This activity continued from 1932 to 1935, at which time a deep split developed in the New York Teachers Union, then affiliated with the A. F. of L., between the Communists and their opponents. Several hundred teachers were let out of the union and established themselves as a Teachers Guild, leaving about 1,500 members in the teachers union. After this split, Mrs. Dodd became legislative representative for the union, a position she held while a Communist Party member from 1936 to 1944. In explaining her activities to the committee, she said:

"* * * I soon got to know the majority of the people in the top leadership of the teachers union as Communists, or, at least, influenced by the Communist leadership in that city."

During the next three years following Mrs. Dodd's election as legislative representative, the membership of the teachers union had reached 11,000 and, of course, it was completely Communist-dominated because two-thirds of its executive board and all of its key officers were Communist Party members.

Like the caucuses of the Party fraction in the Marine Cooks and Stewards Union, explained in detail in a report heretofore issued by this committee, the Party fraction in the New York Teachers Union always met in advance of the regular union meetings to plan floor strategy, make individual assignments and correlate activity. In the event of disagreement at these caucuses, which was rare, a high functionary from the Party headquarters would appear and arbitrarily settle the matter.

"The Communist Party," said Mrs. Dodd, "was interested in seeing to it that the union, which was an A. F. of L. union, would carry out the line of the Party on political questions. Now, you couldn't take all political questions into the union because you had to present those questions then to the membership, and the membership might revolt against having too many political questions. But insofar as possible, they were going to bring as many political questions into the union as they possibly could."

When asked by the committee counsel, Mr. Arens, if the teachers union was used as a medium through which to recruit new members, Mrs. Dodd gave a reply that should be of enormous significance to all college administrators. She said:

"It is the function of every Communist group to recruit other members into the Communist Party."

Discussing the Party's attitude toward educational policy in general, Mrs. Dodd said:

"You take, for instance, the whole question of the theory of education, whether it should be progressive education or whether it should be the more formal education. The Communist Party as a whole adopted a line of being for progressive education. That would be carried on through the steering committee into the union.''

This Communist-controlled union flourished, said Mrs. Dodd, until it was exposed by an investigating committee appointed by the New York State Legislature. She was then asked:

"Did you, as a matter of fact, find that the investigation carried on by the New York State Legislature at that time did weaken the Communist force in the teaching field?"

And Mrs. Dodd replied:

"It most certainly did.''

She also stated that many innocent teachers in the union were totally unaware of the secret caucuses and the concealed Communist control.

"One of the real problems,'' she continued, "is that not only the members of the union didn't know, but a large number of the teachers who became Communists really didn't know what it was all about. I, myself, so long as I functioned on the trade-union level in the teachers union, why, my heavens, I was one of the staunchest of the Communists and would have called your committee a committee to smash the schools. It wasn't until I entered the Communist Party as a functionary in the Communist Party that I saw it was a full, true, cynical conspiracy and something which is so thoroughly evil that I would like to spend the rest of my days to tell the teachers who are entrapped in this thing how to get out.''

Until she became a functionary, Mrs. Dodd explained, she was convinced that the Communist Party was simply an organization dedicated to fighting against Fascism and for the interest of the working class.

"I didn't realize,'' said she, "until I got in that this is just nothing more than a masquerade, that these things are just used to capture many people and that actually they are not really interested in these various questions.''

"Teachers,'' Mrs. Dodd declared, "have always been a very important part of the Communist apparatus. As a teachers union member I was a delegate to the Central Trades and Labor Council, and I was a delegate to the State Federation of Labor. I was put in contact with Communist members of other unions who were to cooperate with me on the floor of the Central Trades and Labor Council. We would caucus. We would decide what should be stressed; what we would approve of; whom we would vote for, and whom we wouldn't vote for. So that we attempted to carry out the Party line in the labor field. We functioned on whatever levels the Communist Party uses teachers for, to get dues, to get finances. They are a stable group with an income and they are generous and conscientious. Secondly, they use them for personnel. Teachers are well equipped, I mean they are trained thinkers and if you can convince them that they should go out and fight for the cause, you can get them to go out and become section organizers, district organizers.''

Mrs. Dodd cited as an example, how she and other Communists in the teaching profession were mobilized to attack Senator Coudert of the New York Legislature, whose investigating committee proved so effective in exposing Communist teachers in 1940 and 1941. Said she:

"* * * The fight of the Rapp-Coudert committee was to expose Communist teachers. The Communist Party just couldn't permit a person of that kind, who had taken such a toll, to remain in public life."

She continued to explain how a lawyer—secretly a member of the Party—provided smear information about Senator Coudert which could be used to undermine him politically.

Mrs. Dodd estimated that in 1944 there were approximately 1,500 teachers in the United States who were members of the Communist Party —formal members. Applying the FBI theory, this would put the figure at approximately 15,000 under Party discipline. She added:

"* * * One thing I think people in America have to learn is that if you have one Communist on the campus, or one Communist in an organization, that person is dedicated to building a unit. And a unit consists of a minimum of three people. There are two ways of functioning. One, a Communist who is an idealist tries to take the Party line into his various organizations, whatever clubs he belongs to, and tries to find others who are sympathetic with him, or he finds where the sore spots are on the campus. If he finds that some people are being abused, discriminated against, some people are unhappy, he fastens himself onto them and pretty soon he's got them functioning with him. First they will function, not as Party people, but just as a committee or a group. Then later on, what you do is, you say to people, 'if we had a union we might get higher wages.'

"But then you point out that to really insure high wages, you can't get it until the Socialist system has been established, or until Communism has been victorious. In other words, you teach people that all they can get are little crumbs here and there, but ultimately they will have to join the Communist movement in order to make the real change.

"You choose an issue which you would bring up. Supposing you are a member of the faculty and you choose the issue, let's say, of increasing wages; you got up and made a definite proposal to let the wages be increased by 10 percent. And then you found out who spoke up with you, who seemed to be interested in the program. If you found two or three or four or five people, then you attached yourself to those two or three or four or five people, and you began to work on them day after day after day. You socialized with them, you made it your business to socialize with them. You made it your business to take them to lunch. And then you weeded out those who were not possible and those who were possible.

"As soon as you had three people who were committed with you, who felt that the Communist movement was a good movement, that that was the only way to change existing conditions, you established yourself as a unit. That unit then became attached to the district or the section or the city which had a Communist movement and the district organizer was always very sensitive to what was happening on the campuses.

"Your units might be a minimum of three and they were generally from three to about seven or eight. But I have seen units as high as 25, in the days when the Communist Party became lax. And then in the period when the Communist Party abolished all cells and established what we called street units—those were the days when they were emphasizing the importance of a democratic approach, and they established great big political clubs, and they used to try to convince people that within a large political club you had nothing to fear; nobody was going to know you. You weren't known by any name; you were just known by your first name or nickname. You used a thing of that kind. Only one person knew you, your organizer. It was to him that you paid your dues and reported on individual problems. But that was only a very short period.

"One of the things you have to understand is that the Communist Party tried to give to their members a certain degree of education along the Marxist-Lenin line and to provide for them a certain amount of initiative on their own part. So that the Communist Party said to you, 'we must build the American league against war and Fascism.' A little unit of three would take that directive into whatever mass organizations there were on the campus. If I were a member of the teachers in the English department, I would take it to the teachers in the English department. If I were a member of the political sciences, I would take it there. Wherever there were meetings, you saw that those meetings were covered with someone who brought the directive in there. You might see to it that one of the unit members would be a writer on one of the magazines or newspapers. You always tried to get someone on the newspaper or magazines of the college so that the columns of the newspaper might be open to you for expressing your opinion.

"The teachers unions were used a great deal to formulate public opinion in America. The teachers were active in the parents' organizations; they were active with the students; they were active in their own professional cultural organizations, and in the American Federation of Teachers we had our conventions. So that anything the Communist Party wanted to be popularized, they would see to it that you had a copy of the resolution, which you then modified to meet your own individual needs.

"Some organizations could stand a strong resolution, a total support of the thing; some organizations could go only one step. At any rate, the individual group modified the resolution to suit its own needs. But, at any rate, everyone was moving forward on that particular subject. But whether it was collective security, whether it was pro-war, whether it was against war, whether it was against the Dies Committee, whether it was against some congressional legislation, their resolutions would be introduced, and simultaneously you would have a large number of resolutions popularized in the newspapers, delegations going to the various men in public office, telephones, telegrams.

"* * * The American Federation of Teachers conventions were held once a year. And what would happen is that the Communist delegates going there would know in advance, they would be told by their own section organizers, or their own district leaders of the Communist Party, that they would meet so-and-so at the convention. The Central District of the Party here in New York always met with the steering committee of the convention in advance, to there decide what was to be accomplished at that convention. Then when we got to the convention we would meet with someone from the Communist Party in some hotel room. There would be a representative of the various districts of the United States, California, Michigan, the South, West, East. We would have representatives. We would get a line setting. That is, there would be some discussion as to what the perspectives of this convention were; how to accomplish it; whom to win over; what caucuses to build and what caucuses not to build.

"For instance, in addition to the Communist Party caucus, we would also have a 'united front' caucus. The 'united front' was always an alliance with someone who didn't go all the way with the group; those who didn't believe with you in everything you believed in, but who would go along. As I said once before, no one formed a 'united front' with the Communists without being weakened, because Communists form a united front when they are going to get strength from you and not when they are going to get weakened."

In discussing the matter of how one or two Communists in a large institution could effectively launch broad Communist units and exert an enormous amount of influence out of all proportion to their minority strength, Mrs. Dodd explained:

"The Communist influence is important only when strategically placed, and no Communist is ever satisfied with remaining in a position of inferiority. He seeks a strategic position. If you had Communists in these schools of education, that is a very strategic position because not only are they affecting the philosophy of education, but they are also teaching other teachers, who, in turn, are teaching the pupils. If you have one Communist teacher in a school of education and he teaches, let's say, three hundred teachers, who then go out all over the United States—that is a strategic position."

Concerning Communist hypocrisy, Mrs. Dodd had this to say:

"When I went into the apparatus at 12th Street as legislative representative, I thought that my job was to fight for good housing, milk, problems, the question of schools, and so on. I found that within the Communist Party there wasn't even a file on any of these social problems; that there wasn't any cumulative wisdom on these things; that almost any program which you could pluck from the air which was popular at the moment was the thing you supported; they weren't interested in carrying through on any of these problems; that these problems were only important as long as there was a group of dissatisfied people to whom this issue was important. But as soon as that issue died down, then they were no longer interested in that issue.''

On academic freedom Mrs. Dodd said:

''The Communists will use academic freedom as a cloak or a shield to protect themselves in the spread of any idea they are determined to spread. I think that academic freedom has to be the right for the professor or the teacher to search for the truth; but, by heavens, he must then find the truth and label it truth, and let the students and other teachers know what that truth is. You just can't ask for academic freedom in general and under that shield just promote anything that you want. That is not academic freedom. I have never known the Communists to go and fight for academic freedom for people whom they didn't agree with, and I think that is the test of it.''

On Party techniques used to influence a non-Communist educational administrator who was so highly placed that his strategic position would be of immense importance to the Party, Mrs. Dodd said:

''* * * But we had placed there in his office, as a secretary, a young lady who made sure that he saw the right reports and didn't see the wrong reports. In other words, when he came into the office at 3.00 o'clock in the afternoon, after teaching all day, he couldn't then be presented with a well-balanced diet of everything that had come in. This young lady, his secretary, would push certain letters under his nose and he would sign certain letters, and there were others there that she didn't want him to see. They would be hidden. She distorted it. That is one very prominent method whereby the Communist Party controls an organization; that is, to place a secretary at the disposal of a man who it not too alert on this question. And that person then either passes out copies of letters or information, reports, to the Party, or helps to control the person whom she is supposed to be serving.''

Explaining the grip Communism exerts on teachers, Mrs. Dodd explained:

''Communism is not just a belief in economics or in politics or in foreign affairs; it is not just the support of the Soviet Union. Communism is a whole philosophy of life. It permeates everything that you do. It permeates your family life, your relationship with your friends, your business relationships, the professional relationships. It has to do with your own thinking of what the importance of man is. Therefore, if you build up a philosophy of life and you were living by it and you lived by it for a certain number of years and then you make a break, you have to take every phase of your life, every strand of your body, practically, and every thought that you have and you have to re-examine and reformulate it into a pattern which is understandable. Now, many people break with the Communist Party— because the Communist Party has a tremendous turnover; and people come in and go out—but do not find any new philosophy to substitute for it. Therefore, they live as vacuums, and many of them disintegrate. I mean, just become morose people, or people who are just lost to a decent living. During the period of breaking away you are beset by all kinds of fears. You are beset by fears of unpleasant publicity; you are beset by physical fears; you are beset by emotional fears; you are beset by the fact that the old world that you lived in, the friends that you had, are cutting away from you, or have already cut away from you, and you are left alone. And there is nothing more devastating than leaving a man or a woman alone after having been surrounded or completely fenced in. During that period you have to sink or swim; you have to find some method of rationalizing this thing that has happened to you, or of finding some explanation for it.''

Regarding the sincere motives with which many teachers join the Communist Party, Mrs. Dodd said:

''* * * Many of these teachers joined the Communist Party without knowing what they were joining. They joined because they thought it meant freedom of speech, because they thought it meant a fight against discrimination, or a fight for better teaching conditions, or a fight for better conditions for the children. Most of the motives by which they joined were good motives. I realize now, as I never did before, that what they got into is something which is contrary to any of the principles that they hold, that it is nothing but a cloak which is used for the purpose of really destroying some of these values. Unfortunately, many of the teachers are not convinced of that. I, myself, might never have been convinced if I hadn't been on the inside of the Communist Party, if I hadn't worked with the apparatus. I trust and hope that the boards of education, both in this city and elsewhere, will do everything they possibly can to enable these teachers to disentangle themselves, give them an opportunity to disentangle themselves without either subjecting them to publicity, which is unpleasant, or to reprisals within their chosen profession. I think they should be given a decent opportunity to disentangle themselves, and if they don't, then it seems to me that further action should be taken.''

At the time Mrs. Dodd appeared and testified before the Senate subcommittee, the Board of Education in the City of New York was engaged in weeding out Communists from its pay rolls. The fight had been going on since 1951, and with the enactment of the Feinberg Law, recently upheld as constitutional by the United States Supreme Court, the board of education went about its task with renewed vigor. This activity, as might be expected, evoked blasts of propaganda and counter-action from the teachers union with which Mrs. Dodd had for several years been affiliated as legislative representative. As she said, the organization had been expelled both from the A. F. of L. and the CIO because of Communist domination, and it thereupon affiliated with the United Public Workers of America, which, itself, had been expelled from the CIO for precisely the same reason.

The California committee, faced with a similar problem, has made an analysis of some of the material issued by the *Teachers' Bulletin* of the Communist-controlled teachers union of New York. Thus on September 20, 1952, the union stated that the matter of discharging Communist teachers from the employ of the New York City Board of Education really turned on whether or not the individuals could be shown to have *taught* something of a propaganda or conspiratorial nature. Of course, the purpose of this diversionary tactic was to put the school board to the test of catching every suspect teacher in the very act of spreading obvious Communist propaganda in the classroom—whereupon it would attack the school board for having set up a spy system. In the issue of the union's publication for the same month, a cartoon was carried on page 1. It depicted a carnival sideshow, conducted by the United States Senate Subcommittee on Internal Security. The banner across the tent proclaimed "Star Attraction! The Incredible Singing Bird! Budenz" but his name is crossed out, and in its place is written: "Bella V. Dodd." On page 3 is a typical Communist smear article against Mrs. Dodd. She is accused of having joined the "enemies of public education," collaborating with "enemies of democracy," and castigated for having joined a church after leaving the Communist Party. The article concludes: "She should be recognized and fought for what she is—not only an enemy of democratic public education, but as a threat to what remains of intellectual freedom in the colleges and universities."

In the New York *Teacher News,* published by the same union, in the winter of 1952, is a statement by Rose Russell, who succeeded Mrs. Dodd as legislative representative, in which she attempts to dismiss the seriousness of Communist infiltration with a characteristic shrug. In connection with her remarks, however, a representative of the New York City Board of Education is also quoted, and his remarks seem worthy of repeating here. He said:

"It seems to me that the gravamen of all these cases is simply the refusal of a teacher to answer a question which the superintendent or his designee has put to him; a refusal which, according to the superintendent, has thwarted an inquiry into the question of whether or not such a teacher is or has been a member of the Communist Party. The object of it is not to demonstrate membership or past membership. The object is to demonstrate an active insubordination in supporting such an inquiry.

"Suppose there were in existence some sort of nefarious group of concededly evil purpose—imagine anything you will, but something that all people will agree is a profound evil. Suppose that the superintendent of schools received information to the effect that a teacher was or had been a member of this group, but he did not have sufficient evidence to establish the fact of active membership and active participation. Would you consider it improper for him to summons such a teacher and say, 'Are you a member of this group or have you ever been a member of such a group which has this evil purpose?' And would such a teacher be justified in refusing to answer such a question, however brilliant a record in the classroom the teacher might have?"

COMMUNIST PROPAGANDA IN TEXTBOOKS

During the 1947 Session of the California State Legislature, Assembly Bill No. 973 was introduced for the purpose of securing funds to buy free textbooks for elementary schools. The textbooks included a series of 30 supplementary texts intended for youth in the seventh and eighth grades, called *Building America*. Immediately the Senate Committee on Un-American Activities and the Senate Committee on Education raised objections, with the result that Mr. Combs, counsel for the first committee, was loaned to the Senate Committee on Education for the purpose of making an analysis of these books. At the 1948 Regular Session of the Legislature, the Senate Investigating Committee on Education issued its third report, all of which, running to 120 pages, dealt with the *Building America* series of supplementary texts. Some of the general language contained in that report is applicable to Communist propaganda in textbooks generally, and is, for that reason, reiterated here:

"It is much more difficult to detect Communist propaganda in a motion picture, in written form, or over the air, than it is to spot a Communist. Most party members have records of association with other known members and fellow-travelers. They subscribe to party publications, affiliate with known front organizations, and the pattern of their activities over a period of years is available to official investigating bodies. This type of information can be accumulated, correlated and documented until it is overwhelming in its implications concerning a given individual. In addition, the reports from trusted informants who joined the Communist Party and its front organizations for counter-espionage purposes are most helpful by way of corroboration.

"Communist propaganda is necessarily subtle. The Party is not so stupid as to openly or obviously urge the unlawful destruction of our Government, so it concentrates on the indirect approach. In labor unions, the Communists ostensibly strive for higher wages and better conditions, while actually they further the class struggle by setting the workers against the bosses. In racial minority groups, they ostensibly strive for tolerance and work against discrimination, while actually they foment strife by setting class against class. On the stage and screen and over the air, the technique has been particularly subtle and usually consists in portraying the employer as a corpulent exploiter, while the working class hero is underfed, underpaid and 'progressive.' News commentaries by left-wing broadcasters follow the current party line—urging us to fight any measure for military preparedness, to bring all of the troops home from overseas, to sabotage the Marshall Plan, share our atomic bomb secrets and abolish all agencies that presume to investigate Communists.

"It is quite conceivable that a Communist may write material that contains no propaganda, although such a thing is extremely unlikely. It is also conceivable that a non-Communist may unwittingly write Communist propaganda, but that is even more unlikely. If there is a covey of writers who have been affiliated with a long series of front organizations and they unite in providing basic materials for a series of supplementary texts for use in the seventh and eighth grades in our public school system, then obviously such books should be viewed with suspicion."

The *Building America Series* was rejected by the State of California, and rejected with the cooperation of such educational administrators as Dr. Roy E. Simpson, the State Superintendent of Public Instruction. In the process of documenting the records of the authors of the *Building America Series,* and in showing their activities and associates, the Third Report of the Senate Investigating Committee on Education presented 44 authors whose affiliations represented a total of 113 Communist-dominated front organizations. Among the individuals so listed in connection with the *Building America Series* analysis, were: Louis Adamic, Sherwood Anderson, Stuart Chase, Edward Corsi, Edwin Embree, Dorothy Canfield Fisher, Hallie Flanagan, Professor Willystine Goodsell, Owen Lattimore, Professor Helen M. Lynd, Professor Robert S. Lynd, Professor Kenneth Macgowan, Professor Kirtley F. Mather, Carey McWilliams, Rose Nelson, Professor H. A. Overstreet, Professor Paul Radin, Professor Holland D. Roberts, Professor Eugene Staley, Professor Bernhard J. Stern, Professor Carl W. Wittke. These names are mentioned because they will recur elsewhere in this section of the report dealing with textbooks. The full documentation of their records is set forth in the Third Report of the Senate Investigating Committee on Education.

It was found that the *Building America Series* studiously underplayed the good things about our American way of life, and placed heavy emphasis on all of its defects. This technique of carefully avoiding overt Marxian propaganda, but at the same time placing undue emphasis on slums, discrimination, economic royalism, unfair labor practices, crooked politicians, organized crime and vice, moral decadence and a great many other elements that comprise the seedy side of life in any country, lends to this type of text a distinctly Marxian propaganda flavor. Undeniably, our form of government is fraught with some defects, but the Party line text writer is in the habit of turning a political and social microscope upon them and magnifying them out of all proportion. When an examination of the front affiliations of such an author reveals that he has been active in a whole array of Communist-dominated groups, and has pursued his activity over a period of several years, the reasons for his gloomy and pessimistic treatment of our system of government becomes quite clear.

EDUCATION AND SOCIAL CONFLICT

In 1936, the Kappa Delta Pi Research Publication No. 3, written by Professor Howard David Langford, Ph.D., was issued under the name *Education and Social Conflict.* This was the third book published under the auspices of the educational fraternity, the other two having been *The Measurement of Teaching Efficiency,* by William H. Laucelot, Arvil S. Barr and Associates, and the other one having been issued under the name of *Education and Social Dividends,* by Will French. The third publication was selected as a prize winner by a trio from Kappa Delta Pi's Laureate Chapter, comprising Dean Henry Holmes of the Graduate School of Education of Harvard University, Professor W. W. Charters of Ohio State University, and Dr. Dorothy Canfield Fisher, whose name was listed in connection with the analysis of the *Building America Series* mentioned above.

In the foreword to this third publication of the Kappa Delta Pi fraternity, it is stated that:

"This volume, therefore, is presented as a lucid interpretation of the Marxian theory of an economic state, and a no less clear description of how proponents of this theory would employ educators and teachers in fashioning an American society patterned after the model of Soviet Russia. As an ardent proponent of the theory he expounds, the author alone is responsible for the views he presents. Neither the society nor its editor is involved beyond making it possible for supporters of American education to know what radical theorists are trying to achieve through the conversion of the American school as a huge agency of radical social reconstruction.

"Everyone interested in social development should know where the Red signals are located.

"It is the author's conviction that educators and teachers must participate in social reconstruction by defying those in control at the present status quo. Educational theory must be dynamic and propel itself into action (violent, if necessary) against all individuals and groups who exploit the 'workers.' And among the workers the author includes all professional men and women and, therefore, educators and teachers. Not until the schools become centers of propaganda for the Marxian golden age, it would seem, will the emergence of society into justice and peace be accelerated. First of all there must be a mental revolution, an orientation to a wholly new conception of society, classless and devoid of all profit motives; following this mental revolution will come militant action, if necessary, against capitalism and its system of exploitation."

This book, virtually unknown to the layman, and not very well known to professional educators, contains much language which is strangely reminiscent of the remarks made by William Z. Foster when he returned from the Comintern meeting in the Soviet Union and laid down the directives for the recruitment, communizing and activating of professional educators. The material contained in this volume is of the most profound significance and of vital importance in connection with the whole aspect of educational infiltration by Communists. It is necessary to note carefully that the society which sponsors this book did not agree or disagree with the frank advocacy of teaching and advocating Communism in our schools. The fact remains that this piece of propaganda was financed by the society—and apparently not balanced by a work that adopted the opposite point of view. The record of Dorothy Canfield Fisher, one of the members of the trio that selected this item for publication, will be fully set forth hereinafter, although the author of this report has no information concerning the degree of influence exerted by this well-known fellow-traveler in persuading her associates to make it possible for Dr. Langford to express his propaganda views in print.

In his preface Langford, obviously referring to the Communists of America, says:

"The education discussed here is not alone the education of the schools and colleges, nor of those potential informal agencies, the press, the radio and the talking picture. It includes all these in a more comprehensive program. It is the education—in action and in theory—of the masters and builders of the society of the future—millions of obscure but struggling individuals, moved less by any thought of a coming golden age than by their own wants. Their education must not only reveal the issues of the conflict which now shakes the foundation of the state: it must help this overwhelming majority—as yet only half-conscious of their collective strength, subject to powerful miseducative influences—to resolve the issues of that conflict in their own favor.

"This, the supreme task of forward-looking educators, offers them today the greatest opportunity in history. A necessary part of this task is criticism of existing institutions, practices and theories. Such criticism plays an essential part in shaping action. Criticism which claims to be impartial, 'objective,' too often condones a state of affairs in which the few, in the pursuit of their special interests, can render futile the efforts of many."

In writing his acknowledgments the author, Dr. Langford, makes low obeisances to Miss Marion Y. Ostrander, "on whose suggestion the project was first undertaken," Hubert Harkbeck, V. J. Jerome, David Ramsey, Dr. William H. Kilpatrick, Manley H. Harper, Marius Hansome, Warren G. Findley, Caroline Whitney, J. Herbert Bowman, P. Bernard Nordman, Harold F. Clark, John K. Norton, Grace Hutchins, Margaret Morris, Paul R. Mort, Ralph B. Spence.

Dr. Langford hauls off in his first chapter and gets right down to business. He contends that three scientific discoveries caused three basic educational problems. These scientific discoveries are the evolution of the physical universe through the interplay of natural forces, the evolution of organic life through the biologic struggle for existence, and the evolution of human societies through the struggle of the classes for possession of the means of life and culture.

The corollary educational problems, according to Dr. Langford, are "the problem of transmitting the expanding stock of information about the world we live in, the problem of securing the rounded development of the supposedly self-directing individual, and the problem of enlisting the impoverished and exploited workers of the world in organizing struggle for control of the means of satisfying their material and cultural needs."

Note, and note well, how this master-propagandist immediately discards everything not suited to his purpose and comes up blandly with the ammunition he wants.

"The first and second educational tasks are compatible with capitalism in its expanding phase. * * * This third educational task is incompatible with the present interests of capitalism."

Langford completely ignores the matter of equipping students to live a rich, abundant life, to make their own way in a free world, to rise as high in the economic scale as their natural endowments will permit—and having tossed them aside he embraces the class struggle concept and closes his first chapter by stating flatly that: "The social conflict with its third problem of education, is inescapable."

In chapter 2, the author writes: "The present condition under which the social conflict is being carried on makes it possible for a small but continuing minority to keep millions of individuals impoverished by their own immense and increasing private advantage. The supreme business of education is to end such frustration and poverty." Again on pages 13-14, he says:

"* * * Large numbers of people, through not fault of their own, find themselves confronted with effective barriers to the achievement of these goals—barriers in the form of unemployment or insufficient wages or economic security.

"The third problem of education is the problem of removing these barriers and creating a social system devised primarily to insure fuller, richer life for all. It is a problem not simply of instruction, in school or out, but of social transformation."

Having confidently put his own question, answered it in the affirmative and asserted that the teacher shouldn't teach but propagandize for a new and revolutionary social order, the author, who can assuredly not be accused of modesty, presumes to set himself and his radical clique up in place of parents for the purpose of teaching the children of America a new way of life. He now continues to expand his blueprint for the social order he seeks to achieve.

On page 22, Langford says that:

"* * * transformation of the social order is the central educational program," adding that, "the task of reconstructing the environment is accepted as central in the recent Chicago school survey and in the plan adopted in June, 1931, as the basis for the reconstruction of the city and region of Moscow."

In this connection he compares a Chicago school industrial project in the coal business with the industrialization of Moscow and its environs. The Moscow plan—cited approvingly as an example to be followed in America, could hardly fail. "Why," asks Langford, "were the Moscow planners able to proceed at once with the orderly execution of their plan as approved in 1931, and to gain approval for a vast extension of it?" He then answers his own question.

"This cannot be attributed to chance or the mere docility of the Russian character. It cannot be attributed to superior material or technical resources. The authors of the plan say it was because the forces opposed to this kind of planning had been decisively curbed in the Soviet Union."

"Before the transfer of power," Langford continued, "which made the Moscow plan possible, the Russian school officials and the Russian ruling classes generally did not consciously foster fundamental social change but strove to prevent it. The same opposition to change is as evident in the schools in planning programs in New York and Chicago as under the openly reactionary Czarist regime. Those who stand to benefit by change are under the same necessity for devising effective means of overcoming that opposition both outside and inside the schools."

In other words, Langford and his kind are going to brain-wash the children whether they or their parents like it or not.

On page 55, Langford says:

"* * * Recalling now the question raised at the end of chapter 1 as to whether conditions in the United States are comparable to those in Russia before the revolution, we recognize many differences but one of basic similarity—the struggle between the classes. Decisive resolution of this conflict in favor of the workers becomes as unmistakable an educational demand upon educational procedure in the United States today as in prerevolutionary Russia."

In chapter 4, the role of the university is discussed in relation to the class struggle.

"Universities have been called strategic factories of ideologies. They provide the theoretical weapons of the class war. Like the purveyors of guns and ammunition they sell their wares to both sides according to demand.

"The opposing sides of the class conflict call for two types of educational theory which are as divergent in their bearing on practice as the clashing interests of the two classes themselves. The purposes of the one type of theory is to reveal the issues of the class conflict with unmistakable clarity and to point the way to a solution favorable to the workers. The purpose of the other type of theory is to minimize the importance of the class conflict, to confuse and blunt its issues, to encourage false hopes for a better social order by advocating measures which help to perpetuate the present one.

"The best type of reasoning—the revolutionary type—we shall call dialectical reasoning; the second type—the status quo or utopian type—we shall call idealistic reasoning.

"To think of things (such as physical objects, people, ideas) dialectically is to think of them in their inter connections, their cause-and-effect relations, their historical development. To think of things idealistically is to think of them in isolation from each other, as though they were independent of their context and had abiding values and powers of their own apart from it.

"Theory which is intended to be progressive but which fails to recognize the essential antagonism between the classes or seeks to reconcile their opposing interests lends itself to the obstructive purposes of the present ruling class.

"The indicated procedure—conditions being what they are—is to strengthen and unify the forces of the masses to the point where they become strong enough to turn the balance in their own favor. It will then be possible to establish a system of production relations devised to meet the material and cultural needs of the vast majority rather than to accumulate profits for the few.

"If this procedure is followed educators and others interested in promoting the growth of individuals must be prepared to 'promote some forms of association and community life and work against others.' (Citing Kilpatrick's *The Educational Frontier*, page 291.) They must be prepared to support groups working for equitable distribution of material and cultural advantages in opposition to the highly-organized, highly-sensitive interests of business. This means a further sharpening of the social conflict.

"The conflict between 'individuals, groups and classes,' referred to in *The Educational Frontier* is not merely a figure of speech used by these university professors in drawing their word picture. It is an objective conflict—a conflict not confined to the thinking of these men, but actually taking place in our society, whether they wish it or not, whether or not they recognize its existence. It is an instance of the dialectical process traced by Hegel, Marx and Engels, Lenin, Bukharin, and others in nature and in society and in all intellectual activity."

"The characteristic leadership of the proletarian movement does not depend upon the personal ability or arbitrary power of any individual. It is a collective leadership, composed of the most class-conscious, most militant, and best informed section of the working class, organized into a compact body by strict discipline. Those who fail to recognize this function of the Communist Party, to which its character is due, as a function essential to the proletarian movement, tend to regard the Party simply as a ruthless minority, imposing a harsh regime on the majority for its own benefit. To hold this view is to remain under an impossible handicap in trying to understand the Soviet regime. Without the support of the masses the Communist Party would be helpless.

"The teachers are interested in the schools as a market for their labor power. They stand in the same relation to the school as the factory worker to the factory, the marine worker to the shipping industry, the farmer to his farm. Their interest in the schools is the basic interest of all workers and most parents in their personal share of the productive process—the interest of wage earners."

Then, on pages 144-45, Langford takes a jaundiced view of educational administrators. They are, says he, willing tools of the capitalist class enemy. At this point he takes up a matter of transcendent importance —the ways and means whereby the Communist elite can accomplish their thought-control. He explains:

"Working class [read: Communist] parents and teachers must work with all groups interested in reopening the schools and extending school services regardless of the motives of such groups. They must recognize the struggle as part of the fight against Fascism. But they must work at the same time for the qualitative transformation of the schools which most educational officials, both lay and professional, do not have in mind, do not want, and will strenuously oppose.

"The school need not be expected to work as a unit for fundamental change in the social system which it is meant to sustain. Neither can it be expected to work as a unit for a corresponding transformation in its own program. Such change must come as a result of organized collective effort on the part of those elements involved in the educational enterprise who see the need for change and are willing to work for it—militant groups of rank-and-file teachers, of parents and older pupils, of college and graduate students, and of trade union members.

"The planning of these groups, if it is to be effective, cannot be based on mere humanitarian sentiment. It must rest squarely on the solid foundation of the self-interest of the various groups concerned—self-interest enlightened in a new way, depending not on *laissez faire* individualism but on mutual aid—the enlightened self-interest of the workers and their allies in the struggle for socialism.

"Militancy needed in the classroom and on the campus. It is in this connection that the fight for freedom of speech finds its true significance for the workers. Not a few educational leaders who profess to stand for freedom of speech entertain a too narrow classroom conception of it. Reisner, for example, warns teachers that:

" '* * * The American people will not continue to tolerate teaching destructive to established institutions. It is not to be expected that the freedom granted to teachers in a democracy should extend to the point where they are allowed to propagandize for the destruction of that form of social organization'."

But Langford, with his cold, materialist viewpoint toward such matters, says:

"If freedom of speech means anything significant for the workers it needs freedom to seek the truth no matter where it may be found, and to act freely on the best conclusions of free discussion, no matter how disturbing such action may be to the existing order.

"Teachers who align themselves with the workers must be militant not only outside the school, and in their professional organizations, but in the classroom and on the campus. They must interpret academic freedom to mean the right to teach the best they know, whatever the subject taught, and whatever the age level of their student.

"In this era of declining capitalism their emphasis must be upon the contradictions of the present order, on the sharpening of class lines inside the school and out, on the building of militant organizations of teachers, students, and parents in every school and in every community, and on stimulating the growth of proletarian struggle and of proletarian culture within and about the very institutions designed for the cultivation of middle-class democracy.

"Teachers in every field of knowledge, on all grade levels, in the degree that they achieve the working class alignment will recognize and undertake as a major task a thoroughgoing reorientation of their subject matter. This will include both the pointing out of social applications of the subject and, in the case of most subjects, of much of the theory underlying it. It means making the subject at once an instrument for advancing the dialectical transformation of our capitalist society and for building and participating in the proletarian society, both before and after the transfer of power."

Those readers who have followed with some care the material set forth in this section of the report will note the peculiar similarity in the language contained in the text under discussion and the language employed by William Z. Foster when he came back from the Comintern meeting in the Soviet Union and published his significant article in the September, 1938, issue of the Communist monthly magazine. As

will be seen later, the author of this text, Dr. Langford, wrote it with
the active collaboration and advice of high ranking members of the
Communist Party of the United States who were sitting in meetings
with Foster on a day-to-day basis. Both Foster and Langford discussed
the necessity of rewriting textbooks, reorienting the thinking of students,
reaching out to influence parents, following Party discipline, of culti-
vating professional activists to carry the Party work outside the classroom and off the campuses into broader fields of contact where they
can select suitable soil for the planting of Marxian seeds in the production of additional crops of recruits to be Communized and activated.

Handbook for Communist Teachers

The next section in Dr. Langford's book must, of necessity, be given
almost in its entirety, because it takes the various fields of instruction
in universities and explains precisely how the Communist teacher must
twist and "reorient" each course to fit it into the pattern of Communist
propaganda. This is undoubtedly one of the most important parts of the
book—and apparently was written with considerable care and perhaps
advice from other sources. It must be constantly borne in mind that this
book is the official attitude of the Communist Party of the United States
toward education—perhaps the author didn't mean to say so, but he
nevertheless made that point crystal clear. By a very careful analysis
of these courses, and the Marxian twist recommended for each—adding
such independent data as the subverting of the department of speech at
various California educational institutions—a pattern may very easily
be established. We have seen fit to quote liberally from this particular
book because, while it does not make particularly exciting reading, it is
nevertheless of such profound significance and its precepts have been
followed so explicitly that it virtually forms a handbook whereby educational administrators may arm themselves to detect Communist practices
in their several institutions. Dr. Langford continues:

> "*Literature and Language Study.*   How the process works in the
> study of the native literature and language—indeed of all subjects,
> both in school and out—is illustrated in a paragraph from the report
> of the first Soviet Writers Congress:

> > 'The proletarian revolution does not merely destroy the capi-
> > talist system. Out of the bricks which have been created during
> > the entire period of man's cultural development it builds a new
> > edifice of human culture. In contrast to the peasantry, the prole-
> > tariat—the driving force of the proletarian revolution—begins in
> > part to take possession of the old culture even under the capitalist
> > system; in the person of its vanguard, it takes over the best ele-
> > ments of this old culture, creating with their help its picture of
> > the future world and attaining comprehension of its historical
> > tasks. Literature already begins to play a considerable part in the
> > development of the proletariat, while the latter is still a force
> > fighting against capitalism. And just as inevitably, the proletariat
> > must take possession of all of the achievements of the old culture,
> > after it has come to power, as it must take possession of all the
> > riches left it as a heritage of capitalism. But it does not passively
> > accept the heritage of the past. It makes a careful selection of this

inheritance. It creates the very elements of the new culture, and during the long process of revolution, while remodeling itself, it creates a new literature too.'

"This passage indicates the possible role of the teacher of literature, and the collective role of groups of such teachers, in interpreting the literary products of the past and of the present in terms of the workers' needs. Their field of study is by no means limited to works deliberately and completely favorable to the workers: it is potentially as wide as the literature of the whole world. But the particular poem or novel or drama is no longer thought of as an expression of universal thought and emotion. It is studied against the background of the historical period and of the class which produced it, and its meaning for the contemporary student is clarified accordingly. Such analysis is of the utmost importance today, when the conflict between the classes is reflected in the current literature in the most confused and contradictory fashion, not infrequently combining a growing awareness of the ills of society with the ideology of Fascism—its defeatism, its national or racial chauvinism, and its elevation of the egocentric individual above the mass.

"History. History, when studied in the same dialectical manner, ceases to be merely a medium for the glorification of national heroes or of a national tradition—democratic or otherwise—or a catalog of disconnected events and characters to be assimilated for examination purposes. It becomes in a new sense a science of human societies, and especially of the forms assumed by the class conflict in successive historical epochs, including our own. History so taught enables the workers, both children and grownups, to be not merely interested spectators of the course of events, but decisive participators in shaping events.

"Geography. Geography, inseparably connected with history, reminds the writer of a series of illustrated wall maps, showing the rich and varied products of the world—animal, vegetable, and mineral—and the means devised by man for increasing and disseminating this natural wealth. Its producers are sometimes sketched in, picturesquely attired in their native costumes. Such maps rarely show the worn faces, the bodies prematurely old, the grinding poverty of these millions of men, women, and children—peasants laboriously planting their rice in China or harvesting their rye in Poland, Cubans living on next to nothing amid endless fields of sugarcane for American tables and American pockets, Alabama share-croppers, Pennsylvania miners, New Jersey fruit and vegetable pickers, makers of cheap garments in New York sweat shops. These, the real makers of human geography, supply the informed teacher with an inexhaustible source of data for the *reinterpretation* of present course-of-study and textbook material. (Committee's italics.)

"Projects. Such data can be used to transform many a project, even in the elementary school. The study of physical and mechanical processes—as in the mining of coal, the production or distribution of milk, the building and navigation of ships, becomes primarily the study of labor-consumer relations.

"For class-conscious pupils projects of this type become a basis for militant action in support of workers demanding union recognition or consumers protesting excessive charges for living necessities or services.

"Under socialism such projects become media of articulation with the factory, the mine and the farm. Nursery school children, watering their plants in the school garden, can feel themselves a part of the five year plan.

"*Natural Sciences and Mathematics.* Science teaching on all levels, from the point of view of teacher and student, is too largely descriptive—concerned with merely describing the world—and only incidentally effective—concerned with transforming it. Technological change is apparently held to be the prerogative of the business or industrial executive. The workers need to know not simply the classifications of plants and animals but their social significance, their role in human life, past and present, and in the building of socialism. They need to know not simply the design and operation of the dynamo, the airplane, and the radio tube as separate pieces of mechanism, but the role of electrification in transforming factory production and the economy of the home, and the role of the instruments of communication and transportation in uniting the workers in each country and throughout the world. They need to know mathematics not simply as a subject to study in school but as an ever-present and essential part of production in all its technical processes and social planning.

"Few militant teachers can hope to set up special experimental schools for the promulgation of the proletarian program. *But they can make every subject they teach and all their contacts with the children and the parents contribute in no small measure to its emergence, wherever they do their teaching.* (Committee's italics.) Such activities of militant teachers within the schools and among the working-class parents and sympathizers cannot insure the development of the workers movement, much less its successful outcome. But such activities, if supported by effective organization, will help stimulate the movement and may materially assist it; and may provide an important and necessary basis for the reorientation of the teachers themselves.

"*Shop work and technical training under capitalism.* A feature of the school program not as yet referred to, namely, shop work, requires special attention here for two reasons. It presents an especially good illustration of the inadequacy of the school program under capitalism, and it indicates the line along which the schools must be reorganized.

"Shop work in our present schools is largely isolated from production. Not only does work in the factory remain mainly a routine job, inspired by the collective purpose of building the socialized economy. Shop work and technical training generally as carried on in the schools is too much concerned with the use of small tools, making for merely individual proficiency in specific trades. It is too little concerned with socialized activities in connection with larger units of production, which cannot be brought into the schools, which the young people must find in the factories and on the collective farms. It is too little concerned with polytechnical training, which puts the worker in possession of techniques applicable to many lines of work.

"Polytechnical training in the socialized economy. The development of modern industry resulted first in extreme division of labor. But with the progress of mechanization and socialization attention is redirected to generalized techniques. In the proletarian state it is intended that the technician should not only be a specialist in one particular field but must know his industry as a whole; he must see the significance of the various parts; he must be able to organize not only his own work but the work of the whole industry.

" 'The mere performance of a partial social function shall be superseded by an individual with an all-round development, one for whom various social functions are alternate modes of activity.' (Quoted from Karl Marx.)

"That is why the schools in the Soviet Union (including those on the university level) have been brought into close connection with industry and agriculture, and why extended periods of participation in industry are made a part of every course leading to a degree.

"Extra curricula activities and extra school education. Possible expansion of extra curricula activities. Mention of this proposed link between the students and the unemployed graduates indicates the kind of procedure required for the vitalizing of the so-called extra curricula activities. These activities represent a real advance from the monotonous and often barren routine of classroom instruction. Yet under capitalism they remain too largely an affair of the school, unrelated to the broader social issues faced by young workers. The school or college play can be a medium merely for practice in the techniques of dramatic production or for the self-expression of the individual members of the cast, or for the amusement of the players and their audience. With skillful work by an alert sponsor and interested members of the student body it can become a medium of social education. The school newspaper or magazine can provide journalistic experience for the members of its own staff, or be a purveyor of purely school news, or it can be an instrument of student opinion and student action on questions of the most vital interest to students on and off the campus. The opportunity offered here is especially challanging in view of the attitudes of many advisers (often reflecting reactionary administrative policies) and of the present leadership of student press conferences.

"The program of extra curricula activities developed along these broader lines extends beyond the school. On the senior high school and college levels it may include the National Student League and the Student League for Industrial Democracy (these two are now combined in the National Student Union) and the American League Against War and Fascism, as well as certain organizations of working-class children and youths, covering all age levels, which in the socialized economy become powerful agencies along with the schools in the education of the young workers and the building of socialism.

"Such organizations supply vital contacts with the world beyond the school—contacts for which our present school program does not provide, and which the official educational leadership seeks to curtail and discredit. In addition to these contacts there are the highly important connections with the trade unions and professional organizations, which provide the essential basis for a placement program under the control of the workers.

"*Education not to be identified with the school.* Over emphasis by educational theorists upon the function of the school has encouraged teachers and laymen to look upon education as though it were identical with the school. Under our profits economy the press, the radio, and the talking pictures are probably far more potent educational media than the school, and, like the school is officially conducted, they operate in the interests of capitalism. In the proletarian states these agencies are recognized to be as much a part of the apparatus of education as are the schools, and they are controlled accordingly in the interest of the workers.

"The individualistic tradition which has taught educators to regard the school as the American road to culture has taught them to underrate the potency of these other agencies in undoing the work of the schools.

"*The press a part of the apparatus of capitalist control.* Of all the wholesale threats to the younger generation in America that of war is perhaps supreme. The potency of the jingo press in fomenting war and the deadly effectiveness of the newspaper in regimenting public opinion when war arrives have been amply demonstrated.

"Official educational leaders, much as they may profess to abhor war, have been singularly reluctant to formulate realistic measures against the war makers, or even to consider such measures. This is due in part to the direct influence of business upon the schools and in part to the psychology created under capitalism as the ideological counterpart of this influence. This individualistic, supposedly objective, psychology keeps the attention of educational workers safely riveted upon the child's learning difficulties or personality traits while those whose interests, whether direct or indirect, prompt them to seek or tolerate war go calmly about their business of preparing to make mincemeat out of millions of these bodies and brains.

"The value of every possible aid in the fight against war should be recognized. But war cannot be stopped through planning to teach peace through official school programs, or even through a boycott of the alarmist press. Both the school program as officially conducted and the press are a part of the apparatus of capitalist control.

"*Possible role of teachers in counteracting miseducative influences.* The workers and their children can be put on their guard against the ideology of the war makers, and shown why wars come about, and why they are inevitable under capitalism. They can be stimulated and prepared to resist preparation for war, through mass action, as part of the proletarian movement to wrest from the capitalists their control of the schools and of the agencies of communication as well as of the means of production.

"Teachers prepared to take part in the fight against war along with the students and workers outside the schools can carry this fight much farther and can make it much more effective than school officials, however pacifically inclined, can possibly do in the absence of organized pressure by the teachers. They can do much to hinder complaint or reactionary officials from making the school an agency for the propagandists of super-patriotism and imperialism.

"*Anti-working-class influence of the commercial talking picture.* The prevailing individualistic psychology which hampers the workers in their fight against war also operates to minimize and obscure the anti-proletarian influence of the capitalist-controlled cinema. One specialist in the study of children, for example, apparently accepts the current motion pictures as being on the whole a constructive influence in the lives of the children, that is, under parental guidance, and presumably looking toward the development of critical discrimination in the child. The hope is implied that the child will eventually learn to distinguish good pictures from bad ones, to give his patronage to the good and withdraw it from the bad.''

Langford then points out that this may be very well for the sheltered, balanced, contented product of a bourgeoisie home, but not so good for the juvenile proletarians. Then comes the typical Langford solution to the whole problem: shoot the owners of the motion-picture industry and let the Langfords take over. He doesn't say this in so many words, of course, but note:

"*Control of agencies of communication vital to the success of the workers' program.* The children of the workers in the cooperative apartments, while they are exceptionally class-conscious, are subject to the influence of these movies. Pictures are a part of the very air they breathe. When a blatantly anti-working-class picture appears the families in the cooperatives may boycott the offending picture theater. But so long as workers have no control over the production of the pictures they are at a tremendous disadvantage in the face of subtle touches of propaganda which appear in so many pictures—propaganda to which even the most experienced proletarian critics are not always immune.

"Hence, the special need for achieving unchallenged control by the workers not only of the motion pictures but of the press and radio, which operate in a similar way. The object of this control is not merely to put an end to mass propaganda detrimental to the interest of the workers. It is to turn these means of communication into instruments for the promotion of the proletarian program.

"The expert in administration is not inherently a member or a supporter of the ruling class any more than is a teacher. The contrary is shown even within our capitalist system in the large number of principals and not a few superintendents, especially in smaller communities, whose meager salaries and continual insecurity lead them to identify themselves with the teachers, with whom they properly belong. It is in the larger school system, in which they are more sharply divided from the rank and file by wide differences in salary and by full-time administrative functions, that their true status as workers tends to become obscure.

"Under the socialized economy the expert in administration, far from going into eclipse, finds the field of his usefulness vastly expended. Like the American consulting engineer in the Soviet

Union quoted by Ella Winter, he ceases to be merely 'consultant to a corporation' (his local board) and becomes 'consultant to a nation.' (Quoting Ella Winter's *Red Virtue: Human Relationships in the New Russia,* page 76.)

"The difference between the two situations is to be sought in a system of social control. Under capitalism a school administrator becomes the dictator of the local school program—in other words, the tool of the capitalist class in the regimentation of the worker. In the socialized economy he becomes the expert adviser of the workers in building a world designed to satisfy their needs.

"*Essential features of effective organization for teachers.* Educational workers have their own special task in this connection, a task the successful accomplishment of which will depend upon their ability to develop a suitable type of professional organization. An organization which is to be an effective instrument for the performance of this task must meet the following requirements: (1) It must represent the broad masses of the educational workers, both employed and unemployed, in all fields and subject departments and on all levels of educational activity. (2) It must be responsive to the militant and growing rank and file membership. (3) It must be articulated with the trade unions and with militant organizations of students and parents. (4) It must be built up in every educational institution and every teachers' organization. (5) Its growth must be stimulated and guided by a militant, especially class-conscious, and politically developed nucleus willing to accept responsibility for organizing the great body of teachers." (Note: Here Langford agrees with Foster in calling for precisely the same sort of elite corps of professionals to be recruited to Communism, reoriented and sent into the field for active work subject to the complete disciplinary control of the Communist apparatus which they serve. The language is somewhat involved and sprinkled with typical Marxian phrases, but the grim meaning is all too clear as expressed both by Foster and Langford.)

"*Specific organizational needs.* Small groups of informal classroom teachers (as few as two or three) should take it upon themselves to organize their colleagues in the school or district into a teachers' council, building up its program around issues such as teachers' salaries, working conditions and social insurance, freedom of teaching and of social action, and the fight against war and Fascism." (Note: Here Langford is expressing in 1936 precisely the same matters announced by Foster in 1938, and explained by Bella V. Dodd in her testimony before the United States Senate Subcommittee on Internal Security only a year ago. It will be remembered that Mrs. Dodd explained how campus units of Communist teachers were never less than three, and sometimes as many as 25, and that their immediate duty was to recruit other teachers and launch other units, constantly expanding and extending the Communist control and insinuating the most reliable members into positions of strategic importance. It should by now become obvious to the reader that when Langford refers to "informed" teachers, he is referring to those teachers who agree with his views, i.e., the Communist teachers; when he refers to "progressive" teachers, he means precisely the same thing; when he is speaking of "masses of educated workers" he is referring to those members of the proletariat who are Communists. This sort of language has always been used by the American Communist Party for the simple reason that the entire Party structure is based on the Soviet prototype, and the Soviet language employed by Communist leaders is couched in the same obscure and involved phraseology. It makes dull reading, but this sort of material must be quoted verbatim in order to thoroughly understand its real import—and the import of this material is of the most vital significance.)

"The teachers' councils in each city or extended rural area (the township or county) should be organized into a teachers' union, so as to promote common understanding and effective mass action on all issues affecting the welfare and social usefulness of the teachers throughout the area. Where a teachers' union already exists it should be built up and brought under rank-and-file control. *All such unions should become locals of the American Federation of Teachers, in which the educational workers should give special attention as a stategic nation-wide instrument for furthering their purposes.*

"Nuclei of militant teachers should also stimulate thinking and appropriate action in other professional organizations of educators, local, state, and national, so as to promote the dialectical re-interpretation of the subject matter in all educational fields as well as a growing sense of solidarity among educational workers and among all members of the working class.

"All groups of educational workers should give special attention to the problem of defending their members from the attempt that will frequently be made to discharge or penalize them for union membership, or for participation in anti-war activities, or to curtail their freedom of teaching. The collective power of the teachers throughout the region or the nation can become a formidable protection against arbitrary measures by reactionary school or university officials as well as against political moves contrary to the interests of the teachers and other workers.

"But the program of the teachers' organizations must also include *positive* measures looking to the development of the proletarian program as outlined in preceding pages.

"*The classroom teacher and the official leaders.* The rank-and-file educational workers in developing their program may be supported by the official leaders in considerable numbers. They must be prepared to welcome support wherever it is offered, doing their best to help the individuals concerned to achieve a consistent working-class alignment. They will have to rely from time to time on technical assistance from experts who are far from accepting their general program. But in all their dealings with the present officials, whether it is whole-hearted participance, or as sympathizers or occasional technical advisers, the teachers must never forget that their group as a whole and not the administrators in their official capacity must decide the program of action. The moment even the most progressive of these officials begins to advocate policy detrimental to the interests of the rank-and-file teachers and of the working class, the teachers must be prepared to detect these policies and to overrule the pronouncements of the officials or brush them aside.

"One of the surest indications of the sincerity of these sympathizers or adherents to the workers' cause will be their willingness to fall in line with the judgments of the group without standing on their official dignity. They will sometimes have important contributions to make by virtue of the positions they occupy: but regardless of such positions they will vote as individual members of the group. Their value to the group will depend upon the insight they bring to it, and not upon the official authority they exercise over it.

"The proletarian school program is controlled by the organized groups of educational workers along with the representatives of all other bodies of workers in the community.

"Two tasks are of great importance in connection with the development of the teachers' professional organizations, namely: that of bringing the facilities for the professional preparation of educational workers into line with the proletariat program and that of transforming the program of educational research.

"*Professional education of teachers. Some limitations of the present teacher-training program.* The institutions which educate teachers—whether teachers' colleges or universities—are especially strategic for the proletarian movement. The typical programs of these institutions as conducted under capitalism fail (from the worker's point of view) to establish a fundamental unity among the subjects of instruction, and they fail to make the student teacher aware of his position as a potential member of a vocational group within the working class. Both limitations are effects of the control which governs these institutions as part of the machinery of capitalism.

"These rigid lines of demarcation which still exist between the subjects of study in many teachers' colleges and other institutions of higher learning, should not be attributed simply to the compartmentalized thinking of the teachers of these subjects. It would probably be more accurate to say that the compartmentalized thinking of these educators is largely due to the institutional machinery in which they work. In accordance with the pattern of machine production under capitalism they may perform their specific tasks with little responsible sense of the program as a whole.

"Despite the influence of the 'progressives' in modifying curricula in many schools throughout the country, the compartmentalized machinery still operates in a large proportion of the training institutions. This is probably due in part to the continued demand from many school authorities for teachers trained along the traditional lines, and in part to the vested interests which have grown up around the various subject departments within the training institutions themselves.

"The mere merging of subject departments into four or five broad divisions, or even their reorganization in an approach to the project curriculum on the college level, does not guarantee a program in keeping with the needs of the workers. Regrouping too easily tends to become mere correlation. The type of procedure based upon the project method or upon the guidance program centers too much in the individual or in the small group in the school. The main center of reference in the workers' program of the education of teachers, just as in their school program generally, is neither in the subject as such nor in the individual, but in the productive processes which sustain the workers' community and make possible its material and cultural development.

"In the developed workers' program extended participation in industry is required of every teacher in training. All subjects are taught with a background of experience with technological processes and organization and the political participation inseparable from these in the workers' state.

"The general deficiency in political education of so many teachers under our capitalist economy cannot be made good simply through the study of social theory; the lack can be reduced by promoting collective action of teachers on issues affecting their welfare and that of the working class as a whole.

"It is especially important that such action should be promoted among faculty members in the training institutions—who are bound to exert considerable influence over the teachers-in-training and among the students themselves. The value of such action can be greatly increased by linking it up from the first with the activities of professional organizations of teachers within the labor movement."

(NOTE: At this point it should be pointed out to the reader that Mrs. Dodd's testimony last year before the Subcommittee on Internal Security stressed the conception that from the Communist viewpoint one of the most strategic positions that could possibly be occupied by Communist teachers was to insinuate them into positions of influence in the teachers' colleges, so that they could "exert considerable influence over the teachers-in-training," as Dr. Langford expressed it in 1936.)

"All faculty members and students about to graduate should be drawn into active participation in the teachers' councils and the teachers' unions. This is important as a means of protecting and bettering the conditions of individual teachers and promoting their solidarity and *as a means for establishing a necessary basis for control of the professional programs by the workers.*

"*Importance of a thorough grounding on the theory of the workers' movement.* Political education obtained by the students and instructors in training institutions must not be based on mere idealistic enthusiasm or sentiment. It must be accompanied and guided by thorough going study of the workers' movement, not from the pens of commentators and interpreters but from the original sources.

"Little official encouragement is likely to be accorded in most institutions either to militant action or to serious discussion of the basis of revolutionary theory. The official emphasis is on individual proficiency rather than upon effective techniques of social action, and upon minimizing or discrediting the proletarian movement rather than advancing it. To shape the outlook and activities of the teachers in this way is to make them agents—witting or unwitting—of the drive toward fascism. It remains for a growing body of teachers and students in the training institutions to develop organized resistance to this influence, and to make these institutions contribute as far as possible under capitalism to the building of the proletarian educational program.

"*Educational research: limitations on educational research under capitalism.* Class-conscious research workers in the field of education have especially important work to do. Our educational research suffers from the same limitations as the educational program generally. The primary concern of the class that rules our society has been to exploit the labor and the buying power of the masses, not to promote their growth and culture as human beings. The efforts of the scientists and technicians in the service of this class have not been limited to applying the principles of physics and mathematics to the improvement of technological processes in industry. These experts have attempted to apply the same principles to education and the social processes. Capitalism has succeeded in building skyscrapers and in carrying on immense power and transportation projects, but not in creating a world designed to insure abundant life for the masses.

"The prevailing emphasis in educational research has been upon the first and second problems of education, its treatment of the third problem has been in the main mechanical and superficial.

"All positive advances in knowledge are to be respected, yet the vast body of data accumulated in the educational field with so much effort to get at the facts assumes the indefinite continuance of our capitalistic society—a society which is giving every evidence of unreliability and impermanence.

"The conditions of our present period demand a new emphasis in educational research. The great problem in the field of reading, for example, is not that of selecting suitable material for children to read or of refining the technique of teaching them how to read. It is that of helping the masses—partly through frankly propagandist literature—to free themselves from the mere struggle for existence. When that is made possible through the establishment of the proletarian state it becomes the problem of keeping up with an enormously extended market for reading matter among the workers, of reinterpreting the literature of the past in the terms of the workers' needs, and of stimulating and guiding the growth of a new literature, born of a new historical epoch, a new civilization. The most pressing problem of personality adjustment is not that of perfecting techniques for measuring the abilities of individual children, or of improving procedures for rehabilitating a few of the more obviously maladjusted individuals. It is the problem of sharpening and clarifying the class-consciousness of all workers in their struggle for emancipation from the exploitation and maladjustment inevitable under capitalism.

"In the sphere of research, as in the schools, the solution of the first and the second problems of education is bound up with the solution of the third problem. For the workers this means more than the reorganization of local units of school administration or tax reform. It means frank exposure of the contradictions and injustices in present day society, and uncompromising exposition of their implications of social action.

"Studies of this kind help the research student clarify his own position and add to the body of data which can be brought about in support of the proletarian program.

"*Present restrictions should be fought collectively by class-conscious research workers.* Whenever possible research workers and faculty members áligned with the working class should organize their forces for mutual guidance and support in carrying on their studies. This is especially necessary in view of the effort made in not a few graduate departments and departmental seminars to limit or suppress freedom of investigation, whether in the name of scientific impartiality or through the imposition of predetermined official patterns of research procedure. Such restrictions have reduced too many promising studies to mere clerical compilations, and under the pretext of keeping them objective have kept them sublimely innocuous. These restrictions should be fought by class-conscious research workers with the same vigor as they would bring to bear in fighting salary cuts.

"*The program outlined in these pages for the schools and the teacher-training institutions calls for the re-writing not only of most of our educational theory but of the psychology, the sociology, and the economics upon which it is based, and of nearly all our textbooks in most subjects of instruction.* (Committee's italics.) It offers a challenge to the research expert, to the candidate for the doctor's degree and to every teacher.

"The territory in which many of the more pertinent facts of educational research are to be found, far from being neutral ground, is the embattled sense of the class war. To be impartial and non-committal on the issues of that conflict is to accept the present control of education by the exploiting class. The plea for such false partiality must not tie the hands of informed educational research workers. Their deliberate alignment with the workers' movement does not necessarily distort their findings and render them unscientific. On the contrary, this alignment will eventually result in placing the finest fruits of research at the free disposal of the whole human race.

"*The proletarian movement and the teachers. Freedom for the masses 'a conquest not a gift.'* The educational program demanded by our present social and economic situation cannot be limited to isolated phases in the life of the individual or of the community of individuals. It must embrace every phase. It cannot mean mere education within the present political and legal framework. It must mean a complete transformation of the entire social systems; and especially of the economic arrangements upon which that system is based. It cannot be limited to a few local committees. It must be a nation-wide program, developing as an integral part of a worldwide program of precisely the same character. It cannot be limited to academic discussion in the schools and colleges. It must be a program of direct action by the masses on their own behalf. It cannot be an outcome of a theoretical harmonizing of differences between the masses and their present rulers while the latter still retain power to enforce an actual decision favorable to themselves. It pre-supposes a decisive transfer of power to the masses." (In this one paragraph, couched in the now too familiar complicated verbiage common to Marxian writers, Dr. Langford is calling upon the elite corps of Communist teachers to do everything in their power under Party discipline to effect a complete transformation of our entire way of life, to integrate their activities with the world Communist movement, and to use their positions of professional prestige and influence to wreck and completely destroy our form of government and to erect a Communist government in its place.)

"The teachers have an important part to play in this emancipation both in and out of school."

"The self-interest of the teachers unites them with all workers. Not a few members of the teaching profession may be alarmed at the proposal that teachers should identify themselves with labor in this movement. Even to some who accept the principle that teachers must act in accordance with the self-interest the proposal may sound highly humanitarian, not to say quixotic.

"Such would-be realists among the teachers have much in common with the industrial psychologist who recently invited the members of his profession to adapt their professional skill to the requirements and purposes of business as the surest road to advancement.

"The self-interest on which the proletarian program is based should not be confused with servility or opportunism. So long as we have a social order in which profits, not human beings, are the supreme good, the teachers generally, as well as the children who depend upon the labor of both, must continue to accept the jackal's share of the good things of life.

"When teachers today throw in their lot with business they are not merely betraying the children; they are betraying themselves. The self-interest of informed members of the teaching profession is the interest of all workers, *the interest of the coming masters of society*, whose accession to *power* can be hastened or delayed but not indefinitely postponed. (Committee's italics.)

"Teachers can work on any one of many issues. Effective social action by thoughtful teachers need not presuppose their acceptance of the proletarian program in its entirety. They can join with other teachers or laymen on working on any one of a dozen problems, each of which is of vital concern for teachers and for education. They can work for adequate social insurance for all workers, for equal educational and vocational opportunity, regardless of race or sex or economic status, for adequate care and protection of mothers and children, for freedom of speech, for a right to organize, for the prevention of war and fascism, for the better understanding and defense of the proletarian movement.

"The need for a broad united front. Teachers who take an active part in the attack on any one of these problems soon realize that the problems are inseparable from each other and from the revolutionary program as a whole. The same process shows them the urgent need for a *united front* of all workers and their allies against the concerted forces of obscurantism and reaction. It shows them the need for combining their efforts with those of all groups which are fighting this battle.

"Among these groups must be included the Communist Party. The proposals of the Party are consistent with the dialectical approach to the problems confronting the teachers. The Party will eventually be recognized as the indispensable vanguard of the workers and their supporters in their struggle for emancipation from the rule of capitalism and building of socialism. (Committee's italics.)

"A word should be said here in refutation of a prevalent notion that the Communists are trying to gain political power for and by themselves by a sudden insurrection. To accept this idea is to ignore the mass basis of the revolutionary program of the workers. It is to ignore the objective social factors and the psychological factors which give rise to that movement and assure its eventual success—factors apart from which any attempts to bring about the transfer of power to the workers would be sure to fail.

"Until events have conspired to show the necessity for such a transfer, and until large masses of the workers have accepted this necessity, all the Communists in the Third International could not bring it about. But when that moment arrives—when the American workers in city and country, educated largely through their own mistakes and through the smashing of their illusions—themselves begin to move—then all the forces of reaction will not stop them."

Dorothy Canfield Fisher

It was pointed out elsewhere in this section of the report concerned with Dr. Langford's enormously significant book, that one of the individuals who was most active in paving the way for its publication was Dr. Dorothy Canfield Fisher. Her record of activity with Communist-dominated groups, together with the affiliations of the other individuals mentioned by Dr. Langford as having assisted him in his undertaking, are herewith set forth. Mrs. Fisher has been affiliated with the following Communist-dominated organizations:

I. *American Committee to Save Refugees.* Other individuals who were active in this organization included: Lillian Hellman, Dr. Edward K. Barsky, Jerome Chodorov, Kyle Crichton, Muriel Draper, Professor Henry Pratt Fairchild, Ann Gillmor, Dashiell Hammett, Rockwell Kent, Dr. John A. Kingsbury, Corliss Lamont, George Marshall, Ruth McKenny, Philip Merivale, Professor Walter Rautenstrauch, George Seldes, Herman Shumlin, Professor Henry E. Sigerist.

II. *American Friends of Spanish Democracy.* Other individuals connected with this organization included: Corliss Lamont, Bruce Bliven, Professor Henry Pratt Fairchild, Freda Kirchwey, Professor Robert Morss Lovett, Vito Marcantonio, Professor H. A. Overstreet, Mary Van Kleek, Dr. Thomas Addis, Professor Henry E. Sigerist, George Seldes.

III. *American Congress for Peace and Democracy.* Other individuals connected with this organization included: Professor Harry F. Ward, Professor Robert Morss Lovett, Lewis Alan Berne, Professor Franz Boas, Howard Costigan, Abram Flaxer, Professor Willystine Goodsell, Donald Henderson, Rockwell Kent, Professor Kirtley F. Mather, Lewis Merrill, Samuel Ornitz, Mervyn Rathborne, Donald Ogden Stewart, A. F. Whitney.

172   UN-AMERICAN ACTIVITIES IN CALIFORNIA

IV. *American League for Peace and Democracy.* Other individuals connected with this organization included: Lewis Alan Berne, Howard Costigan, Professor Henry Pratt Fairchild, Abram Flaxer, Professor Willystine Goodsell, Clarence Hathaway, Donald Henderson, Rockwell Kent, Professor Kirtley F. Mather, Samuel Ornitz, Mervyn Rathborne, Donald Ogden Stewart, Frank Tuttle, Max Yergan, A. F. Whitney.

V. *American Society for Cultural Relations with Russia.* Other individuals connected with this organization included: Professor Franz Boas, Sidney Buchman, Jerome Chodorov, Marc Connelly, Norman Corwin, Mrs. Walter Gelhorn, Lillian Hellman, Robert W. Kenny, Professor Robert J. Kerner, Freda Kirchwey, Professor Max Lerner, Professor Robert Morss Lovett, Professor Robert S. Lynd, Lewis Milestone, Herman Shumlin, Gale Sondergaard, Frank Tuttle, Albert Rhys Williams.

VI. *U. S.-Soviet Friendship Congress.* Other individuals connected with this organization included: Zlato Balakovic, Lillian Hellman, Professor Kirtley F. Mather, Paul Robeson, Professor Henry E. Sigerist, R. J. Thomas, A. F. Whitney, Professor Max Yergan.

VII. *Congress of Youth.* Other individuals connected with this organization included: George Soule, Professor Max Yergan, Professor Robert Morss Lovett, Reid Robinson, A. F. Whitney, Rev. Stephen H. Fritchman.

VIII. *Coordinating Committee to Lift the Embargo.* Other individuals connected with this organization included: Lewis Alan Berne, Ben Gold, Donald Henderson, Lewis Merrill, Mervyn Rathborne, Marcel Scherer, A. F. Whitney, Arthur Garfield Hayes, Robert W. Kenny, Lee Pressman, Maurice Sugar, Paul Robeson, Professor Franklin Fearing, Professor Ralph H. Gundlach, Lillian Hellman, Dashiell Hammet, Langston Hughes, Rockwell Kent, Freda Kirchwey, Dr. Thomas Addis, Dr. Edward K. Barsky, Mary Van Kleek, William Gropper, Professor Max Yergan.

IX. *Films for Democracy.* Other individuals connected with this organization included: Professor Franz Boas, Rexford G. Tugwell, Dudley Nichols, Marc Connelly, Lillian Hellman, Dashiell Hammet, Lee Pressman, A. J. Isserman, Professor Robert K. Speer, Freda Kirchwey, Professor Robert Morss Lovett.

X. *Joint Anti-Fascist Refugee Committee.* Other individuals connected with this organization included: Zlato Balakovic, Max Bedacht, Professor Henry Pratt Fairchild, Howard Fast, Abram Flaxer, William Gropper, Lillian Hellman, Ring Lardner, Jr., John Howard Lawson, Vito Marcantonio, Carey McWilliams, Philip Merivale, Arthur Upham Pope, Professor Walter Rautenstrauch, George Seldes, Herman Shumlin, Gale Sondergaard, Donald Ogden Stuart, Professor Dirk J. Struick, Dalton Trumbo, Professor Max Yergan.

XI. *League of Women Shoppers.* Other individuals connected with this organization included: Freda Kirchwey, Tess Slessinger, Mary Van Kleek, Lillian Hellman, Professor Helen M. Lynd, Gale Sondergaard, Ella Winter, Katherine Bauer, Muriel Draper, Mrs. Howard Costigan.

XII. *Reichstag Fire Trial Anniversary Committee.* Other individuals connected with this organization included: Dr. Thomas Addis, Zlato Balakovic, Max Bedacht, Earl Browder, Germaine Bulcke, Philip Connelly, Guy Endore, Phillip Evergood, Professor Henry Pratt Fairchild, Frederick Vanderbilt Field, Abram Flaxer, Leo Gallagher, Ben

Gold, William Gropper, Lillian Hellman, Donald Henderson, Langston, Hughes, Sam Jaffe, Rockwell Kent, Ring Lardner, Jr., Professor Kirtley F. Mather, Arthur Upham Pope, Mervyn Rathborne, Professor Walter Rautenstrauch, Ferdinand Smith, Donald Ogden Stuart, Dalton Trumbo, Louis Weinstock, Dr. Max Yergan.

XIII. *Schappes Defense Letter.* Other signers of this letter in defense of a Communist teacher included: Dr. Thomas Addis, Professor Raymond T. Birge, Benjamin J. Davis, Jr., Rev. Stephen H. Fritchman, Langston Hughes, Rockwell Kent, Freda Kirchwey, John Howard Lawson, Albert Maltz, Vito Marcantonio, Professor F. O. Matthiessen, Professor H. A. Overstreet, Paul Robeson, Donald Ogden Stuart, Professor Dirk K. Struick, Professor F. W. Weymouth.

XIV. *Writers and Artists Committee for Medical Aid to Spain.* Other individuals connected with this organization included: Kyle Crichton, Granville Hicks, Langston Hughes, Rockwell Kent, Donald Ogden Stuart.

XV. *American Roundtable on India.* Other persons affiliated with this organization included: Rev. Stephen H. Fritchman, Lillian Hellman, Arthur Upham Pope, Lee Pressman.

V. J. Jerome

Dr. Langford, in acknowledging his indebtedness to the individuals who assisted him in writing this blueprint for Communist attack through the field of education, paid particular attention to V. J. Jerome. Mr. Jerome, whose true name is Isaac Romaine, is a veteran Communist Party functionary. It was Jerome who came to Hollywood several years ago from New York for the purpose of organizing the first Communist fronts in the motion picture industry, having taken over those duties from Stanley Lawrence; and he lost no time in coordinating the Communists in the motion picture industry with the functionaries in the downtown section of the Los Angeles County Communist Party. Jerome, noted for his skill as a propagandist and his adroitness in organizing mass cultural movements, has for many years been a member of the Central Committee of the Communist Party of the United States, co-editor of its monthly ideological publication, and chairman of its Cultural Commission. On January 21, 1953, Jerome, now 55 years of age, still functioning as chairman of the Cultural Commission, was found guilty of conspiring to advocate the unlawful overthrow of the Government of the United States, in a jury trial before United States District Judge Edward Dimock in New York. Jerome, like other Communist Party functionaries, was busily attending to high level party matters of policy and his participation in front organizations would therefore have produced more harm than good to the cause. In the case of prominent people in cultural and professional circles, the question is quite different; their names in the front activities lend a semblance of prestige and dignity to the front groups, and attract scores of other people, many of whom are non-Communists and carefully kept in ignorance of the real objectives and practices of the Party. Jerome, however, did participate in two front organizations as follows:

I. *Celebration of Fifteen Years of Biro Bidjan, Soviet Union Colony.* Other individuals who were connected with this organization included: Ben Gold, Louis Weinstock, Max Bedacht, Alexander Bittleman, Joseph

R. Brodsky, Morris Carnovsky, Dr. Bella V. Dodd, William Gropper, Rockwell Kent, Carol Weiss King, Vito Marcantonio. Weinstock, Hungarian-born member of the Communist Party's National Review Commission, which is charged with the duty of taking disciplinary action against disaffected members, was also convicted with Jerome in the trial above-mentioned, as was Alexander Bittleman, a Russian-born member of the party's Central Executive Committee.

II. *Statement by American "Progressives" Defending Moscow Purge Trials.* Other individuals connected with this movement were: Louis F. Budenz, Morris Carnovsky, Professor Haakon M. Chevalier, Kyle Crichton, Lester Cole, Guy Endor, Elizabeth Gurley Flynn, Harrison George, Dashiell Hammett, Clarence Hathaway, Lillian Hellman, Granville Hicks, Langston Hughes, John Howard Lawson, Corliss Lamont, Albert Maltz, A. B. Magil, Bruce Minton, M. J. Olgin, Samuel Ornitz, Professor Holland Roberts, Professor Morris Schappes, George Seldes, Professor Henry E. Sigerist, Professor Bernhard J. Stern, Anna Louise Strong. Elizabeth Gurley Flynn, charter member of the Communist Party of the United States and for years in charge of its activities in the women's field, was also convicted in the trial above-mentioned.

Caroline Whitney

Caroline Whitney, to whom Langford expressed gratitude for assistance, was affiliated with the following Communist dominated organizations:

I. *American Youth Congress.* Other individuals connected with this organization included: Bruce Bliven, Professor Robert Morss Lovett, Reid Robinson, Mary Van Kleek, James Waterman Wise, Professor Robert K. Speer, James Carey, Jack McMichael, William Kerner, Dr. Bella V. Dodd, Gil Green, Celeste Strack, Rockwell Kent, Earl Browder, Harper W. Poulson, A. F. Whitney, Rev. Stephen H. Fritchman, David Hedley.

II. *Consumers National Federation.* Others connected with this organization included: Bruce Bliven, Dr. Bella V. Dodd, Professor Henry Pratt Fairchild, Mrs. Walter Gelhorn, Israel Amter, Rose Nelson, Max Perlow, Mervyn Rathborne, Grace Hutchins.

III. *Milk Consumers Protective League.* Others connected with this organization included: Rose Nelson, Dr. George Barsky, Arthur Kallett, Rose Schneiderman, Susan Jenkins.

Grace Hutchins

Grace Hutchins, who also received an acknowledgment from Dr. Langford for helping him with his book, was connected with the following Communist-dominated organizations:

I. *American League Against War and Fascism.* A contributor to the September, 1936 issue of *The Fight Against War and Fascism,* issued by the above-mentioned organization. Others connected with this magazine were: Professor Robert Morss Lovett, Earl Browder and James Lerner.

II. *Consumers National Federation,* above-mentioned.

III. *Farmers Educational and Cooperative Union of America.* Others who assisted in the Communist infiltration of this organization are Robert W. Dunn and Anna Rochester. These individuals, together with

Grace Hutchins, have been identified as Communist Party members before the Congressional Committee on Un-American Activities.

IV. *Friends of the Soviet Union.* Others connected with this organization included: Earl Browder, James W. Ford, William Z. Foster, Clarence Hathaway, Donald Henderson, Granville Hicks, Roy Hudson, Langston Hughes, Mary Van Kleek, Corliss Lamont, Professor Robert Morss Lovett, J. B. Matthews, Robert Minor, Jack Stachel, Albert Rhys Williams, M. J. Olgin, Alexander Trachtenberg, Robert W. Dunn, Louis F. Budenz, Joseph R. Brodsky, W. E. B. DuBois, Arthur Garfield Hayes. Mr. Trachtenberg was also convicted in the New York case above-mentioned.

V. *International Labor Defense.* Other individuals connected with this organization included: Henri Barbusse, Whitaker Chambers, Robert W. Dunn, Robert Minor, Frank Spector, Harry Bridges, Marcel Scherer, Elizabeth Gurley Flynn, Dr. Bella V. Dodd, Howard Costigan, Professor Kirtley F. Mather, Vito Marcantonio, Leo Gallagher, John Howard Lawson, George R. Anderson, Carol Weiss King, Max Bedacht, James W. Ford, William Z. Foster, Samuel Ornitz, Elaine Black, Clarence Hathaway, LaRue McCormick, Harrison George, Ben Gitlow, Paul Crouch, Earl R. Browder.

VI. *John Reed Clubs.* Others connected with this organization included: Robert W. Dunn, Michael Gold, William Gropper, Arthur Garfield Hayes, A. B. Magil.

VII. *League of Women Shoppers,* above-mentioned.

VIII. *Prisoners Relief Fund.* Other individuals connected with this organization included: Robert W. Dunn, Elizabeth Gurley Flynn, Professor Bernhard J. Stern, Maurice Sugar, Anita Whitney.

IX. *Tallentire Jubilee Committee.* Other individuals connected with this organization included: Joseph R. Brodsky, Max Bedacht, Robert W. Dunn, William F. Dunne, James W. Ford, Elizabeth Gurley Flynn, William Z. Foster, Michael Gold, William Gropper, Rockwell Kent, Ruth McKenny, Anna Louise Strong, Bruce Minton, Alexander Trachtenberg.

Margaret Morris

Margaret Morris, who also helped Dr. Langford, has been connected with the following Communist front organizations:

I. *National Student League,* which maintained a school at 114 West 14th Street in New York City, at which Margaret Morris was a teacher. Other individuals listed with this organization included: Michael Gold, E. P. Green.

II. *Schappes Defense Committee Open Letter,* above-mentioned.

V. T. Thayer

V. T. Thayer, who also collaborated on material mentioned in the Langford opus, was a member of the following Communist-dominated organizations:

I. *American Committee for Democracy and Intellectual Freedom.* Other individuals connected with this organization included: Paul Robeson, Professor Zachariah Chaffee, Jr., Lillian Hellman, Professor Henry Pratt Fairchild, Professor Sophronisba P. Breckinridge, Professor Edward C. Tolman, Professor George P. Adams, Professor Robert S. Lynd,

Professor Kirtley F. Mather, Professor H. A. Overstreet, Freda Kirchwey, Dashiell Hammett, Donald Ogden Stuart, Herman Shumlin, Rockwell Kent, Morris Carnovsky, Professor Max Yergan, Mary Van Kleek, Professor Willystine Goodsell, James B. Carey, George Seldes.

II. *American Committee to Answer Attack on Public Education.* Other individuals connected with this organization included: Professor Franz Boas, Professor Walter Rautenstrauch, Lewis Alan Berne, Professor Henry Pratt Fairchild, Professor Willystine Goodsell, Carol Weiss King, Professor Robert S. Lynd, Herman Shumlin, Professor Max Yergan, Professor H. A. Overstreet, Professor Robert J. Speer, Professor J. Robert Oppenheimer, Professor Edward C. Coleman.

III. *American Youth Congress.* Others connected with this organization included: Bruce Bliven, Professor Morss Lovett, Reid Robinson, Mary Van Kleek, James Waterman Wise.

William H. Kilpatrick

One of the Communist front joiners, whose influence very obviously dominated the Langford book, and who stands high in the esteem of its author, is Professor William H. Kilpatrick, who is referred to 73 times in Langford's text and who receives numerous flattering references for having helped in the entire crusade for reorienting the minds of American school children. Professor Kilpatrick has officially been listed by governmental agencies as having been affiliated with the following Communist front organizations:

I. *American Committee for Anti-Nazi Literature.* Others connected with this organization included: Professor Thomas A. Bisson, Professor Franz Boas, Rockwell Kent, Freda Kirchwey, Professor Frederick L. Schuman, James Waterman Wise.

II. *American Committee for Protection of the Foreign Born.* Other individuals connected with this organization included: Lewis Alan Berne, Professor Franz Boas, Donald Henderson, Carey McWilliams, Rockwell Kent, Professor Robert Morss Lovett, Vito Marcantonio, Professor Walter Rautenstrauch, Reid Robinson, Donald Ogden Stuart, Dr. Thomas Addis, Arthur Upham Pope, George Seldes, Herman Shumlin, Professor Max Yergan, Professor Bernhard J. Stern, Frederick Vanderbilt Field, Carol Weiss King, Howard Costigan, Muriel Draper, Abram Flaxer, Professor Edward C. Tolman, Frank Tuttle, Professor J. Raymond Walsh.

III. *Committee for a Boycott Against Japanese Aggression.* Other individuals connected with this organization included: John L. Childs, Paul Robeson, Dashiell Hammett, Professor Robert Morss Lovett, Professor Max Yergan, Professor Henry Pratt Fairchild, Professor Robert S. Lynd, Ben Gold, Professor Henry E. Sigerist, Lewis Alan Berne, Freda Kirchwey, Morris Carnovsky, Professor Walter Rautenstrauch.

IV. *Associated Film Audiences.* Others connected with this organization included: Professor Franz Boas, Professor Rexford B. Tugwell, Dudley Nichols, Marc Connelly, Lillian Hellman, Dashiell Hammett, Lee Pressman.

V. *Greater New York Emergency Conference on Inalienable Rights.* Other individuals connected with this organization included: James B. Carey, Professor Henry Pratt Fairchild, Freda Kirchwey, Vito Marcantonio, Professor Robert K. Speer, James Waterman Wise, Professor Max

Yergan, Professor Sophronisba P. Breckinridge, Professor Walter Rautenstrauch, Professor Harlow Shapley, Dr. Bella V. Dodd.

VI. *National Emergency Conference.* Other individuals connected with this organization included: Dr. Thomas Addis, Lewis Alan Berne, Professor Franz Boas, Professor Sophronisba P. Breckinridge, Professor Henry Pratt Fairchild, Professor Walter Gelhorn, Professor Ralph H. Gundlach, Carol Weiss King, Freda Kirchwey, Professor Alain Locke, Professor Robert Morss Lovett, Professor Robert S. Lynd, Carey McWilliams, Mervyn Rathborne, George Seldes, Professor Harlow Shapley, Professor Robert J. Speer, Donald Ogden Stuart, Professor Kirk J. Struick, Maurice Sugar, Professor Edward C. Tolman, Dr. J. Raymond Walsh.

VII. *National Emergency Conference for Democratic Rights,* mentioned above.

There can be no question whatever about this master plan to warp our children's minds to Communism; and this process of capturing the mind of great masses of impressionable youth is a basic ingredient of every totalitarian regime. Sounds of horror and revulsion were heard from the American intellectuals at Hitler's efforts to thus indoctrinate the youth of Germany, and it is high time that these same gentry learn that it is quite as proper, although somewhat late, to exhibit the same sort of revulsion toward the efforts of the international Communist appartus to indoctrinate the minds of American school children and college students. We have seen by the documentary references mentioned above in this portion of the report that the concept of carefully planning the infiltration of our educational system had its origin in the Kremlin shortly after the revolution of 1917, that a whole section of the Communist International or Comintern was devoted to that specific purpose, and that the Communist Party of the United States has doggedly inensified its efforts in that direction since the creation of the Communist Party in this Country in Sepember, 1919. In the book just described, by Dr. Langford, we see the detailed techniques by which the Communists seek to accomplish this long-range objective.

PUBLIC SPEAKING AND FREEDOM OF SPEECH

Every university publishes an official catalog of courses as a guide to students who, by reading the descriptive material in connection with each course, can select the line of individual study they wish to pursue. In fact, the average student has no other way of determining which courses he shall take than by referring to these official catalogs in which the various courses offered by the university are described in general terms.

In the catalog of a California university a course in speech was described as consisting of class discussion on a critical analysis of the writings of great English and American authors, as a foundation for training in oral rhetoric—a study of literary style in public speaking.

Another course in the department of speech at the same university was described in the catalog as concerned with teaching the principles of oral argument and logic by class discussion of social problems.

Both courses were taught by the same instructor.

An undergraduate student at this university, having read the descriptions above set forth, decided that he would like to take each of the courses to improve his public speaking, and enrolled in the latter course first. His initial impression of the instructor was favorable, but he soon discovered that a great deal of the dogmatic opinion expressed in class was becoming extremely biased and slanted. The instructor's views appeared consistently pro-Soviet, pro-Communist and constantly deriding American institutions. The instructor advocated Communist professors in every university for the purpose of showing the students the Communist point of view, because, as he expressed it, "Communism is such an important force in the world today." The student, who, for obvious reasons, must remain anonymous, wrote to the committee as follows:

"I dropped the course before the semester ended. One of my reasons for doing so was that I found Professor X's formula for proving evidence too intricate and difficult. I also decided that the time I had spent in the class was largely wasted because Professor X's viewpoint was biased instead of being objective. I had originally enrolled in the course because [of] the general catalog listing speech courses * * *"

The student then declared that he soon found the catalog description of their course to be "a fraud and a deception," since, as he saw it, a course described as teaching the principles of oral argument and logic based on class discussions of social problems, "should, above all, be taught by an instructor with an objective approach to the problems he is dealing with. But to my estimation Professor X never made the slightest attempt to be objective. In fact, he seemed primarily interested in using the classroom as a forum to promote his own viewpoint."

The student left the university but returned shortly thereafter and enrolled in the first course described in the catalog under the same instructor. The student wrote: "I want to make it clear that I did not enroll in Professor X's class for the purpose of 'spying' on him. Taking his course merely fitted in with my previous plans. I wanted to take all three of my courses in the forenoon so I could leave for home at 12 o'clock. This would leave the entire afternoon available for recreation or study.

"However, I was curious to know if Professor X would be echoing the Communist Party line of 1951 in the same fashion as he echoed the Communist Party line of 1948. I decided that instead of becoming angry and challenging statements and arguing with him, I would attempt to write down everything he said in the classroom. In this way I could be more objective in determining if he followed the 'pattern' of the current Communist Party line."

It should be stated parenthetically here that the student in question contacted the committee on his own volition, after he had taken both of the courses in question, and that neither this student, nor any other student, was ever employed by the committee, with or without remuneration, for the purpose of acting as a campus spy or reporting to the committee on the activities of his instructors in class.

The average student would naturally be attracted to a public speaking course described as a study of the writings of representative English and American authors for the purpose of improving his vocabulary and learning something about the use of rich and expressive English. Years ago this same public speaking course was described in the catalog in terms almost identical with those employed at the time the student in question decided to take it. In those days, however, it was taught by another instructor.

At that time great stress was placed upon the writing of Robert Louis Stevenson and particular attention was devoted to explaining in class how Stevenson could use extremely simple words for the purpose of lending deft touches of color and description to his writing. For example, from the *Silverado Squatters,* in describing his trip up the mountains, Stevenson wrote:

"A rough smack of resin was in the air, and a crystal mountain purity. It came pouring over these green slopes by the oceanful."

And from the same source, in describing his reaction on passing a wheat field over which the wind was blowing, Stevenson said:

"The wind blew a gale from the north; the trees roared; the corn and the deep grass in the valley fled in whitening surges; the dust towered into the air along the road and dispersed like the smoke of battle."

Then from his essay, *The Old Pacific Capitol,* a description of Monterey, Stevenson described the waves as he observed them on his solitary walk along the ocean front. He wrote:

"The waves come in slowly, vast and green, curve their translucent necks, and burst with a surprising uproar that runs, waxing and waning, up and down the long key-board of the beach. The form of these great ruins mounts in an instant to the ridge of the sand glacis, swiftly fleets back again, and is met and buried by the next breaker."

In the same essay he describes the Monterey fogs as follows:

"From the hilltop above Monterey the scene is often noble, although it is always sad. The upper air is still bright with sunlight; a glow still rests upon the Gabelano peak; but the fogs are in possession of the lower levels; they crawl in scarves among the sandhills; they float, a little higher, in clouds of a gigantic size and often of a wild configuration; to the south, where they have struck the seaward shoulder of the mountains of Santa Lucia, they double back and spire up skyward like smoke. Where their shadow touches, color dies out of the world. The air grows chill and deadly as they advance. The trade-wind freshens, the trees begin to sigh, and all the windmills in Monterey are whirling and creaking and filling their cisterns with the brackish water of the sands. It takes but a little while till the invasion is complete. The sea, in its lighter order, has submerged the earth. Monterey is curtained in for the night, in thick, wet, salt, and frigid clouds, so to remain till day returns; and before the sun's rays they slowly disperse and retreat in broken squadrons to the bosom of the sea. And yet often when the fog is thickest and most chill, a few steps out of town and up the slope; the night will be dry and warm and full of inland perfume."

In this public speaking course as it was taught years ago, these same excerpts from the writings of Robert Louis Stevenson were studied by the class and explained by the instructor for the purpose of showing how a careful use of words can give a rich and flexible vocabulary to the student and thus provide him with the ingredients of graceful and expressive speech.

Reorientation

Now, let us see what happened to this course in the passing of the years. Instead of studying the works of "representative English and American authors," the course, when taken by our anonymous student, concentrated almost entirely upon the writings of John Stuart Mill, the Scotch philosopher and apostle of freedom. And instead of studying all of Mill's works, almost the entire attention of the class was concentrated on his essay called, *Liberty,* written in 1859. Its central theme is a contention that neither a government nor a people has the right to coercibly control expression of opinion; that "the power itself is illegitimate."

In discussing social systems, Mill said: "While we repudiate with the greatest energy that tyranny of society over the individual which most socialistic systems are supposed to involve, we yet look forward to the time when society will no longer be divided into the idle and the industrious; when the rule that they who do not work shall not eat, will be applied not to paupers only, but impartially to all."

In addition to the essay of John Stuart Mill on liberty, the class also studied the 1797 indictment against Thomas Williams for publishing Thomas Paine's *Age of Reason,* in the court of George III, and Thomas Erskine's famous speech for the defense. Next came Erskine's speech in defense of Paine. Then came a piece of Alexander Meiklejohn—"Teachers and Controversial Questions," wherein this noted apologist for Communist teachers cheerfully advocated swinging wide the academic doors to disciplined members of an international conspiracy dedicated to the subversion of our institutions, distortion of our way of life and the overthrow of our government by fair means or foul. Having finished the Meiklejohn article, the class next launched into a study of *Abrams* v. *U. S.* wherein the Supreme Court of the United States upheld the conviction of five men—Russian-born—for conspiring to advocate the unlawful subversion of the government.

The next case to be studied was *Gitlow* v. *New York.* Next was the case of *Near* v. *Minnesota,* in which a statute was declared unconstitutional in that it would not allow a newspaper to make accusations of inefficiency against public officers without proving the charges—even of criminal malfeasance. Then came Justice Black's opinion in *Martin* v. *City of Struthers, Ohio,* wherein a member of a religious organization called

Jehovah's Witnesses was arrested and convicted for ringing doorbells. The case was reversed, Justice Black saying, "* * * Door-to-door distribution of circulars is essential to the poorly financed causes of little people." Next came a study of the case of *Prince* v. *Massachusetts,* wherein a statute forbidding children under 12 to sell newspapers was upheld, despite the fact that a juvenile Jehovah's Witness was involved. Next came a study of the case of *Harry Bridges* v. *California.* This involved an analysis of the decision by Justice Black wherein the question involved was the publishing by newspapers of comments concerning pending litigation in California.

There were other cases, all involving the right of freedom of speech, civil liberties, freedom of circulating documents, and similar political activities, with heavy and emphatic stress being laid on the rights of the defendants. Bearing in mind that the overwhelming majority of the class time was devoted to a study of John Stuart Mill's *Essay on Liberty,* and the rest of the time to a study of legal cases and opinions, the question obviously is, what had all this stuff to do with public speaking? Some of the basic material might possibly have been used in a class in political science or a class in law, or even a class in philosophy—but it is extremely difficult to ascertain what a study of all of this sort of material has to do with the course as advertised in the university catalog to be an "intensive study of essays chosen from the writings of representative English and American authors."

The student submitted his verbatim notes of the professor's remarks in class to the committee, and here are a few excerpts which may be read in the light of the instruction laid down by Professor Langford in his textbook.

"Should subversive opinions be expressed? The other day the Supreme Court upheld a decision limiting the freedom of expression by sending 10 Communists to jail. They ruled under the Smith Act. If I say let's overthrow the government by force and violence should this idea be suppressed? Are you of the opinion that no opinion should be oppressed by the government? Even if the effect would be to overthrow the government? Are you acquainted with the First Amendment to the Bill of Rights? There seem to be some restrictions. The Bill of Rights says there shall be none, but the Supreme Court says some. Who do you think is right, the Supreme Court or the founding fathers? Do you think people should be prohibited from saying they want to overthrow the government?"

Instructor, to a student: "Why do you want to be coy and say that to restrict the freedom of speech by the Supreme Court is not to restrict it; I asked you to defend your opinion that to restrict speech is not to abandon it."

Instructor: "Remember the Supreme Court recently sentenced the Communists for advocating certain views."

Student: "We have to assume some risk."

Instructor: "Those who want to suppress the press want to overthrow the government. The Supreme Court, for an example, suppressed the freedom of speech."

Student: "We are not in a position to know why the Supreme Court reached its decision. The Supreme Court decision was given by a group of learned men; well-qualified to render a fair decision."

Instructor: "Are we to be governed by a group of elite lawyers? Are we regressing? How many of you think we are making progress? The Supreme Court believes advocating overthrow of the government should be suppressed. Do you think this is progress? Is it progress for the court to say certain opinions should be suppressed? Do you think it is progress when our system periodically breaks down and causes unemployment? The national debt now amounts to astronomical proportions. Is it five hundred billion? It is so high that we do not even know the exact figure. We have inflation. Do you call this progress? We can now kill 200,000,000 people with the atomic bomb. The human race is on the verge of self-suicide. Our present policy is to rapidly build up our power to stop the Russians. Eminent generals say that we should drop bombs on China. Then the Russians will get jittery. Now, unless you think universal destruction is progress you had better define your terms."

Instructor: "* * * But where are people who claim some people are infallible * * * what is the position of the Catholic Church in regard to morals? It is a dogma when the Pope speaks ex-cathedra, he cannot make mistakes, that answers your question as to who thinks he is infallible. Whoever represents the voice of God, Jesus, for instance, is infallible. Perhaps He didn't think He was infallible but what about His followers? Some of the followers of General MacArthur think so. Some Members of Congress refer to MacArthur as the Voice of God."

Instructor: "The National Education Association convention in San Francisco says that the point has been reached where teachers are afraid if they try to explain a part of the world. The Communist view is that capitalism holds the seeds of its own destruction, the Communists merely have to help it along. How about the viewers-with-alarm that say we are moving toward socialism through high taxation? Isn't free enterprise being more or less unwillingly transformed? This isn't the question of what people want or don't want. Unfortunately, Marxist dogma is being proved right. Look at Iran with its nationalization; we are just a little behind. Without increasing controls modern society could not endure. So in this part the Marxists have a point."

Instructor: "You don't think a person does not think it is dangerous to have unpopular views? For example, let us suppose you want a job with the government. A young man from the FBI will come around and ask you such questions as, 'Do you like Russian music? Or do you believe in racial equality?' Don't you think this will make people afraid and force them to play safe? Every once in a while a committee charges this university with being a hotbed of Communists. Don't you know where a man will lose his job because of his opinions? In totalitarian countries we find people are watched for having so-called 'dangerous thoughts.'

Student: "It seems that this is very true in the United States. We don't have room in our minds for unconventional thoughts."

The following interchange of opinion between the instructor and a student is particularly revealing.

Instructor: "Do you think thoughts should be suppressed?"

Student: "In totalitarian countries all independent opinion is suppressed. In this country we allow freedom of independent opinion. But don't think that we should be allowed to criticize the government."

Instructor: "What do you mean by not criticizing the government?"

Student: "I mean the Communists. They should not be allowed to criticize the government unless they try to improve the government."

Instructor: "How can they improve the government without freedom of discussion? Then you say that Mill is wrong. Why can't we benefit by the improvements the Communists suggest? We cannot know if the Communists are wrong if we prevent them from discussing their views."

Student: "What about the methods the Communists use in Russia?"

Instructor: "Every nation exaggerates its benefits. The Russians, of course, present themselves in glowing terms."

Student: "What about Russia and China?"

Instructor: "We have never been there so how do we know?"

Student: "There have been people who have been there and wrote books. They can't all be wrong."

Instructor: "Undoubtedly. (Instructor discusses Mill's views.) What about a similar modern situation?"

Student: "By depriving the Communists of their freedom we deprive ourselves of freedom of discussion."

Instructor: "What is the sense in calling America the land of the free and home of the brave if people are afraid to express their opinions?"

Student: "The American people are slowly having it pounded into their heads that the Communists are a bad influence."

Student: "The so-called Communists are gangsters."

Instructor: "I don't think that this is the case. They are more like soldiers in the war dedicated to an ideal. You never hear of them making any money. They have to go to jail. They are a fanatical people who believe in their cause. They may be wrong, I think they are."

Student: "Some of the traitors got large sums of money."

Instructor: "I think this is the opposite of the case. I believe that they got very little money."

In a class discussion concerning whether or not members of the Communist Party should be permitted to teach in institutions of higher learning this discussion occurred.

Instructor: "That's what Mill says—the National Education Association says you must teach the principles of Communism."

Student: "The NEA says that Communists should not be allowed to teach."

Instructor: "What would Mill say? Mill would say the NEA contradicts itself. I think he (Mill) feels the truth will emerge when men of opposing views are both allowed to teach. Everywhere we find attacks on Communists of which there are practically none, then we find attacks on pinks, etc., what do you think?"

Student: "Education should be objective."

Instructor: "You mean educators should have no views of their own? Unfortunately there are no facts in controversial issues, you would need two teachers. Do you think Mill is wrong?"

Student: "No."

Instructor: "Mill's principle would say we need agnostics to teach in the religious University of San Francisco and theologians to teach at this university."

Student: "I see where the University of San Francisco course in explaining Communism is sending students to report on the speeches of Communists."

Instructor: "I'd hate to think what would happen if we did the same thing here. It would be a good idea to attend Communist meetings, not to refute, but to find out if there was any truth in what they said."

Student: "The trouble is that if you had two people of opposite views teach, the student would believe in the man who was able to present his case in the most able way."

Instructor: "In a speech course we condition the students against eloquence. I think we might get an able Marxist and an able capitalist, both equally gifted and both interested in honestly trying to give the truth, but the very idea is foolishness, isn't it? We're as bad as the Russians who don't give the anti-Communists a chance to teach."

Student: "How many of us could speak with feeling about Democracy or Communism? Public apathy is our first fault."

Instructor: "Or the First Amendment? The Sons of the American Revolution are against the social welfare state, this is contrary to the Constitution, I may be wrong, any questions?"

Student: (Referring to the talk given at the beginning of the class by the instructor): "The speaker says the Communist Party is small in size."

Instructor: "You don't think this is a sign of weakness?"

Student: "The Communist Party is small in size because so few people accept their ideas."

Instructor: "The Communists have failed to gain a foothold in the United States. * * *"

Student: "The soldiers in Korea don't know what they are fighting for."

Instructor: "In the second world war men fought overseas because they got an invitation from the President. Our attitude toward the colored race is not democratic, we only give lip service to democracy."

In discussing some of the fundamental aspects of religion and Christianity, the class discussion is a reflection of the materialistic line of thinking advocated in the Langford text. Here are some excerpts from the class discussion:

Student: "One way to strengthen a doctrine is to attack it."

Instructor: "But Mill does not mean suppression. What is essential is that we be forced to re-examine an opposing doctrine (instructor reads from Mill's *Essay on Liberty*). Well, it is quite clear that practically everybody takes at least stock in obeying the Christian principles, except for mumbo-jumbo once a week to make us feel good. Over a period of centuries the church has dwindled for making the mistake of founding itself on error, what difference does it make when the world was founded? But has science discredited the Golden Rule? Has science undermined those precepts? Christ had no geology to impart to his followers. Well, has science undermined morality? Science is concerned with the laws of nature; religion is concerned with what souls can be saved. There need be no conflict between religion and science."

Student: "When the scientist try to drop bombs they are not always successful."

Instructor: "No more successful than is prayer? How many of you believe the meek are blessed? Practically none of you raised your hands. What are the blessed? Does Christ bless the meek? This is a recipe for getting into heaven." (A student reads from a Bible she has brought to class.)

Instructor: "There is no doubt it requires a great deal of interpretation. Why should the poor in spirit be blessed? How many of you would agree that a man is better off without money? Many passages in the Bible extol the proletariat. How many of you believe the Christian recipe is the right one? But you live in a society where Christianity is the official belief. Well, what should we say, is Mill right?"

Student: "In ways I believe in Blessed are the——"

Instructor: "Did Christ mean it or not?"

Student: "Not literally."

Instructor: "This is dangerous—you can interpret metaphysics in any sense. Christ clearly indicates there are obstacles to get into heaven."

Student: "Some people are actually swindlers and get caught, but others don't."

Instructor: "The Bible says every man is his brother's keeper, will people feed their neighbors when they starve?"

Student: "Most people will."

Instructor: "But these high taxes are unequally placed on the people and they can't."

Student: "Christ says we should give all we have and then some."

Instructor: "He also says if a man steal your coat give him your cloak; you would probably put him in jail, wouldn't you?"

Student: "Can't part of the Bible be sound?"

Instructor: "What part is sound?"

Student: "What about 'Thou shalt not kill?'"

Instructor: "How could we support the war? In short, do you think Mill is right? Actually Christ is a meaningless creed to us."

At another point in the course the discussion reverted to the trial of the 11 members of the National Committee of the Communist Party of the United States before Judge Medina at Foley Square, New York. It will be remembered that several attorneys for the defendants were cited for contempt by the judge at the conclusion of the trial after they had subjected him to an unprecedented and ceaseless harangue. They appealed their contempt sentences, the appeals were turned down by the United States Supreme Court, and they served their terms. Note the none too subtle twist given to this aspect of the case during a class discussion.

Student: "During the trial of the 11 Communists their lawyers made improper and insulting remarks to impede justice."

Instructor: "How does it follow that the Communist lawyers were impeding justice? Lawyers are allowed to do things that help their case. They might have been trying to get a new trial. Do you believe in free speech if it doesn't go too far? If it doesn't damage our beliefs? We consider a speech violent or ill-tempered if we disagree with it."

From the foregoing we can compare the way this course is given at the present time and the way it was given several years ago. Formerly the course followed its description in the catalog, was devoted to the studying of the works of English and American authors who were masters of prose for the purpose of enriching the students' vocabulary and improving their facility of expression. There were no political discussions, no efforts to slant the instruction into political or religious channels, no undue emphasis placed on the materialistic side of life. Under the impact of Marxian leaders such as Dr. Langford, the course was obviously reoriented. The materialistic side of life was heavily emphasized; instead of studying the writings of the masters of English prose, heavy emphasis is laid upon the morbid elements of Mill's *Essay on Liberty* and on a long series of legal decisions highlighting the attack on civil liberties and freedom of expression. In this course, reoriented as it has been, we see the propaganda that plays the now familiar and gloomy theme: the American way of life is not so good. The Communists are not so bad. Religion is nothing but superstition. The Federal Bureau of Investigation is ridiculed. What on earth has all this stuff to do with public speaking? Under the thin pretext of presenting controversial issues concerning freedom of speech, the students are slipped a slimy mess of propaganda that obviously serves a cardinal (red, that is), objective: (1) Communists are being deprived of their right of free speech in America. (2) Communists are not so bad after all. (3) Communist Party members should be allowed to teach in our institutions of higher learning.

In praising the Communists, damning the Supreme Court for convicting them, sneering at the Smith Act, ridiculing the FBI, calling religion nothing more than a series of superstitious beliefs, and churning up all of this other turgid material in a class supposed to be devoted to the teaching of the art of speech, the instructor only has recourse to a shop-worn excuse. Such instructors usually claim that they deliberately swing the class discussion into controversial channels for the purpose of stimulating class interest. In this instance, however, the instructor is impaled on the horns of a dilemma. Either the student was the victim of a fraudulent statement in the university catalog, or the instructor reoriented his course away from the catalog's description.

TEACHERS' PROPAGANDA KITS, 1953 MODEL

About two months prior to the publication of this report teachers throughout the United States, both in the primary schools and in the institutions of higher learning, were flooded with bundles of propaganda material issued by an independent union, The United Electrical, Radio and Machine Workers of America. This organization, expelled from the CIO because it was found to be Communist-dominated, has its headquarters at 11 East 51st Street in the City of New York. Its general president is Alfred J. Fitzgerald, its general secretary-treasurer is Julius Emspak, and its director of organization is James J. Matles. The union has a membership of approximately 350,000 members. The letter which accompanied these so-called "Teachers' Kits," was signed by Mr. Emspak and addressed to, "Dear Friend." The letter was as follows:

"We are sending you our 1953 edition of the Teachers' Kit which contains various materials available to you through the educational department of our union. We feel that these materials may be used as possible aids in bringing the union point of view to teachers and students.

"During recent years we have had many requests from teachers for basic materials concerning our union. The material we enclose has been chosen because we believe it best answers some of the many questions asked by teachers and pupils alike. What position does the union take on prices, taxes, civil liberties and women in industry? What is the attitude of the union to the Government economic policies? Are the statistics presented by the Government on cost-of-living accurate?

"Our members—consisting of more than 300,000 men and women throughout the Nation—have a keen interest in our schools and are aware of mutual problems confronting both teachers and factory workers. It is well known, for example, that many teachers in the Nation receive less in compensation than the least skilled workers in our plants, with consequent bad effects in the entire educational system.

"We feel that the material we are enclosing and the discussions that may grow from its use are of great importance in explaining to your students the important role of organized labor. Undoubtedly much material reaches you from various organizations and the U. E. feels that teachers and students alike will benefit by reading material about a labor union by a labor union.

"We hope you will call this Teachers' Kit to the attention of your colleagues and friends in the school and community organizations in which you participate. Please feel free to write us if you have any special requests or suggestions.

"Sincerely yours,

(Signed)   "JULIUS EMSPAK
"General Secretary-Treasurer."

This Teachers' Kit, included in a package with the foregoing letter, the following items:

(1) Excerpts from resolutions passed at the 17th national convention of the union, urging its members to "check anti-labor trend in public education," and stating that kits are being sent to "as many teachers as we can reach."

(2) A broadside offering teachers the use of four 16 mm. motion picture films free of charge. The films are entitled, *Industries Disinherited; The Great Swindle; Our Union;* and, *Deadline for Action.* A blank is provided, giving spaces for the name of the teacher and the address of the school to which the films are to be sent.

(3) A 1953 calendar, being a hang-up type of calendar with a propaganda picture above each successive calendar page. Examples of the propaganda material contained in this item include a cartoon of a young couple standing timidly before a marriage license window, and recoiling from the clerk who is demanding: "Are you now or have you ever been a member of the Communist Party?" Another cartoon shows a speaker about to take the rostrum at a Fourth of July celebration, and being cautioned, "Don't be afraid to mention the Declaration of Independence—just don't quote it." Another cartoon shows two men engaged in decorating a church for Christmas services. One man is standing on a ladder hanging up a large sign which reads: "Peace on Earth." The other man warns him, "Better say that's a quote from the Bible or it might be mistaken for Communist propaganda."

(4) A booklet entitled, *One Step Leads to Another.* The front cover of this item shows a workman reading a newspaper, and being watched by a shark with its mouth open. The successive six pages are arranged like a cartoon strip. Each page depicts the apathetic workman reading his morning papers. The headlines state successively: "Order Reds Jailed; Aliens Deported; Mob Lynchings Reported; Plan Attacks Jews, Catholics; Sentence Top Labor Leaders." In each instance the workman is disinterested. Then the booklet declares: "It happened." The workman is next shown locked in a jail cell. He peers through the bars complaining, "Hey—all I did was to ask for a raise!" The uniformed guard turns in the corridor to glare at him, snarling: "Communist!"

(5) Another item comprises a 20-page booklet for the kiddies called "Chug-chug," the story of a toy train. Here is the class struggle concept disguised under a thick sugar-coating for juvenile consumption. Briefly, it tells the story, profusely illustrated, of a poor worker's family—mother and two little kiddies, Donnie and his sister, Susan.

On page 1, these two embryonic Marxists are shown peering lovingly at little Chug-chug, an electric train running on a circular track in a toy store. It peers back just as lovingly at the children through the toy shop window. Obviously, Donnie, Susan and Chug-chug were simply made for each other. The kids then do the natural thing. They ask Chug-chug to come home with them, but on the next page the toy train replies sadly, "I cannot come, I cost too much."

Well, Donnie and Susan take their problem to Pop, who just happens to be employed at starvation wages in a nonunion factory. He patiently explains to the kiddies that he has to pay rent, buy food and clothes, and he just doesn't have enough money left over to buy Chug-chug. But these are persistent kids who do not give up easily. They keep pestering Daddy for Chug-chug, until he and his co-workers manage to unionize the factory. At once the wages are raised, the deal is made at the toy shop, the kids get Chug-chug, and everyone lives happily ever after.

The class-struggle theme, which readers of this report who have also read the section containing excerpts from the Communist Manifesto should now thoroughly understand, is unobtrusively slipped in when, on page 15, Donnie asks: "But if everybody joins the union, who is there left on the other side?" and Susan chimes in, "Yes, who is on the other side?" Daddy then explains, "On the union side are working people, and on the other side are the bosses and bankers."

On the same page, above this dialectic conversation, is a cartoon showing three members of "The other side." They are depicted as bloated members of the bourgeoisie attired in evening clothes, wearing silk hats, smoking cigars, and lounging happily with their kind of Chug-chug, a pile of money bags.

Another item in the Teachers' Kit is a 23-page booklet entitled, "Who Does the Work?" which also constitutes propaganda fodder for America's Donnies and Susans, only in this booklet they are called Johnny and Nancy.

The first picture in this item shows Pop leaving for work, whereupon these curious youngsters ask, "Mommie, why do people work?" Mother then takes over for the ensuing 19 pages, assisted by as many cartoons depicting the proletarian workers as toiling (none too happily) at a variety of jobs. Then, on page 16, Johnny asks, "Does everybody work?" Here is where mother really gets in her lick. "No," she declares, "there are some people who don't work for a living. Some people live from the work of others and do nothing useful." Mother is assisted in making herself crystal clear on this matter by the accompanying cartoons of four members of the bourgeoisie—the familiar rich, bloated exploiters of the downtrodden, toiling masses. On page 18, the first pair are shown in a sumptuous office, fully equipped with a stock market ticker, a carved desk, a seltzer bottle and glasses and a profit chart that indicates how easily one could make a fortune by doing nothing. One of these plump gentlemen is seated with his feet on the desk, reading the Wall Street Journal. The others stand nearby, smoking cigars and gazing happily at the profit chart on the wall. On the next page another pair of the idle bourgeoisie are shown lounging on their private beach under the palms. Their corpulent forms are stuffed into bathing trunks, and the setting includes the customary props: cigars, liquor and stock market reports.

(6) The next item is a folder which attacks the Smith Act under the terms of which scores of Communist leaders and members of the National Committee of the Communist Party of the United States

have been convicted. The act is called the "thought control bill," and the 350,000 members of the union are urged to work for its repeal.

(7) The next item is called the *"U. E. Steward,"* Volume 6, No. 1, January, 1953. This 22-page booklet is the regular monthly publication of the union. This particular issue, included in the Teachers' Kit, urges repeal of the McCarran Immigration Act, discusses a California meeting with representatives of the United Mine, Mill and Smelter Workers (also expelled from the CIO because found to be Communist-controlled) and urges aid for Messrs. Matles and Emspak, who are said to have run afoul of the vested interests because of their alleged red activities.

(8) The next item in the Teachers' Kit is called, *"Frame-up!"* In it the entire judicial process of our country is attacked—nine cases being termed deliberately framed and instigated by big business for the purpose of exploiting the works. Here, again, is played the familiar somber air of the Marxian class-struggle. In connection with the Harry Bridges case this folder says: "Harry Bridges. He organized the longshoremen and fought for their welfare. After charges against him had not been proved in three previous frame-ups, he was framed again in 1950 and sentenced to five to seven years in prison."

These examples of current Communist propaganda flooding our educational institutions again prompts the committee to point out that whereas excerpts from the Communist Manifesto, and quoted material from other official Communist publications do not make for particularly easy or spicy reading, nevertheless, a familiarity with such documentary data provides one with the equipment necessary for the detection of subtle Party propaganda. Thus, in the first children's booklet dealing with the desire of Donnie and Susan for the toy train, we find an example of the class-struggle concept which forms a basic part of the Communist Manifesto; in the second juvenile propaganda booklet dealing with Johnny and Nancy, we find the class-struggle developed, and accompanied by the Marxian concept of surplus value also set forth in the Communist Manifesto. It cannot be emphasized too much that until one is familiar with the ideology, historical development, international aspects and current organization of the Communist apparatus, he is simply not adequately equipped to understand current propaganda and Party activities. The committee feels that such basic information must first be made available to the Legislature and the people in understandable form, and then illustrated with practical, current examples of how the American Communist Party uses these basic doctrines of Marx in sugar-coated form for the purposes of propagandizing and recruiting new members.

It should hardly be necessary to add that a union of electrical, radio and machine workers, completely Communist-dominated at the top, whose 350,000 members are strategically placed in sensitive positions throughout the country, is a menace to the American way of life.

In April, May and June of last year, several former members of the Communist Party who were also officers of the United Electrical, Radio and Machine Workers of America, appeared as witnesses before the United States Senate Subcommittee on Internal Security. They all testified that to their positive knowledge the union was completely Communist-controlled at the top, and their testimony was contrasted with the now familiar pattern followed by other union members who refused to answer any questions concerning their Communist affiliations and activities on the ground that their answers would tend to subject them to a criminal prosecution.

INTERNATIONAL PARTY LINE FOR YOUTH

While in the United States such Communist-dominated unions as the United Electrical, Radio and Machine Workers of America and the United Public Workers of America with its teachers' union subsidiaries, are propagandizing concerning the class-struggle and the alleged invasion of the fields of academic freedom and civil liberties for teachers, the international organizations are simultaneously carrying on an intensive propaganda crusade for peace.

There is nothing new about this so-called peace propaganda on the part of the Communist apparatus. During the period of the non-aggression pact between the Soviet Union and Germany, the Party line was based on the same old peace theme. American Communists fomented an epidemic of strikes in our defense industries, and at the same time Communist teachers and professors were lending their names and their prestige to a whole new series of front organizations advocating resistence to conscription, the ROTC, military preparedness and any defense measures on the ground that the government was trying to regiment and militarize American youth. Of course, this propaganda is simply part and parcel of the patient, long-range blueprint of the Soviet Union for world domination in the name of international Communism. The whole tenor of these peace propaganda crusades can be summed up when we understand that the Communists believe it is perfectly moral and proper for the Soviet Union to maintain an enormous standing army and work feverishly to catch up with us in the atomic weapons race, to Communize one country after another and exploit the populations thereof and compel them to produce materials for the Soviet war machine, but that it is somehow evil and immoral for other countries to take adequate measures to insure their own protection in the face of such an international threat. When the Soviet Union was invaded on June 22, 1941, the propaganda did an abrupt switch, the epidemic of strikes in American defense plants was ended, and the Communists assisted us with everything at their disposal to produce the sinews of war for the purpose of enabling the Soviet Union to adequately defend itself against German aggression. When the war was over there was an immediate resumption of the old militant cry for peace, the old accusations that the United States and Great Britain were warmongers; and that international Party line propaganda has been accelerated and continued until the present time.

Plainly, it is of the utmost importance to the Soviet Union that large numbers of American youth, especially in our institutions of higher learning, should be organized, disciplined and alerted to carry on this propaganda campaign with the active assistance of undercover Communist faculty members.

In August, 1951, the Executive Bureau of the World Federation of Teachers Unions convened in Vienna, passed a series of resolutions, and sent copies of its decisions to every Communist-dominated teachers' organization in the world.

The committee has available the *International Bulletin of Education*, published by the World Federation of Teachers Unions, a subsidiary of the World Federation of Trade Unions, for April, 1951. This bulletin is published at the headquarters of the World Federation of Trade Unions, 94 Boulevarde Auguste-Blanqui, Paris 13, France. On page 1, under the heading of "Appeal to Educational Workers of All Countries to Strengthen the Fight for Peace," are taken the following excerpts:

"Teachers, professors, educational workers: American imperialism, whose hands are stained with the blood of the women, the old men, and the children of Korea, is seeking to spread the flames of war to the entire world, and to hurl humanity into the furnace of a new world war.

"Teachers, professors, educational workers: the disastrous results of the armaments race, the new attacks on your fundamental rights, the new cuts in budgets for public education and health already weigh heavily upon you.

"Expose the attempts of various governments to use the schools in their preparations for war. Fight against the setting up in the schools of parliamentary youth organizations, and against educating the children in the spirit of hatred towards people, of racial discrimination, and of war.

"Get all democratic groups to voice vehement protests against the use of the radio, the press, the cinema, and other means of mass propaganda for the purpose of preparing the youth for a war. Bring up your children in a spirit of understanding and friendship toward peoples, make of them true partisans of peace."

Excerpts from the resolutions of the executive bureau of this organization following its fifth international conference at Vienna in August of 1951, are as follows:

"(3) To continue to expose, without let-up, the reactionary leaders of teachers' organizations in America and in Great Britain who are trying with all their might to set up a new, splitting 'world federation' of the teaching profession with the aim of fighting the international movement of teachers, of tying the schools to the war machine, and of subordinating the interests of the teachers to the interests of the imperialists and to the preparation of a new world war.

"(4) To strengthen its ties and increase its cooperation with democratic organizations—on an international, national and local level in the interests of the struggle for peace, for the betterment of the economic conditions of the workers and against the militarization of education towards this end; to direct the F. I. S. E. (French initials for the World Federation of Teachers) to strengthen and develop its cooperation with the International Women's Federation, the World Federation of Democratic Youth, and the International Union of Students."

"(7) The national teachers' organizations are called upon to conduct actively the work of committees for the defense of peace in the schools and other educational institutions, and to transform them into real centers of a struggle on the part of the teaching staffs for putting into effect the resolutions of the 2nd World Congress of the Partisans of Peace.

"(8) To recommend to the organizations of teachers in France, Italy, Belgium, Great Britain and the United States of America to develop in cooperation with the committees for the defense of peace in the schools and other educational institutions, demonstrations and protests of the masses of workers against the increased war budgets, against military propaganda in the schools, against the setting up of parliamentary youth organizations, and for the increase of budgets for public education, for the improvement of the social and economic conditions of teachers; to unite in this fight the organizations of young people, of students, of women, of trade unions, as well as the parents of the students.

"(9) To conduct a tireless struggle for the democratic education of children and of youth; to expose the policy of the countries which tend to militarize the schools; to create among large masses of the population hostility towards teachers and professors who propagandize for a new war; to organize mass movements for the purpose of dismissing such teachers from their positions in the schools and other educational institutions."

The committee is not aware that any teacher or university instructor in California has expressed himself in favor of a new world war, but it should be pointed out here that in case such an opinion is expressed outside of the classroom by a teacher who makes no effort to communicate his convictions to his students, who takes no direct or subversive action to destroy his own government for the purpose of putting his ideas into practice, that how he thinks should, under our system of government, is his own affair. The same thing, of course, applies to teachers and faculty members who are sincere in their belief that Marxism is a good thing. So long as they do not use such convictions for the purpose of indoctrinating the students with whom they come in contact, or for concealing their affiliations with an organization dedicated to the subversion of our form of government, then, they, too, are entitled to believe as they choose.

However, the Communist World Federation of Teachers Unions would immediately throw out a teacher or professor who propagandizes for a new world war, and at the same time emit howls of anguish when official agencies presume to uproot teachers and professors who propagandize for the subversion of our government and the furtherance of international Communist domination. These inconsistencies, of course, are quite common to Communist propaganda.

On page 6 of the bulletin is a list of the members of the Executive Bureau of the World Federation of Teachers Unions. An examination of this list alone gives eloquent proof of the Communist character of the organization. The members represent France, the U. S. S. R., Bulgaria, Italy, the German Democratic Republic, Romania, Poland, Czechoslovakia and Austria. This thoroughly Communized bureau sent greetings to its Chinese comrade teachers saying:

"Dear Comrades: At its February meeting in Sofia, the Executive Bureau of the World Federation of Teachers Unions heard with greatest interest the report of Comrade Fan Minh on the heroic struggle of the Chinese people for the defense of peace against the American imperialists.

"The Executive Bureau expresses its hearty congratulations on the results which you have gained in the struggle for peace. Your success is also our success, for the struggle for peace is indivisible, and its defense is the task of all progressive humanity."

Pages 37-45 of the bulletin contain an analysis of conditions in American schools, entitled: "Big Business in American Schools." It hails the subversive efforts of the Communist-dominated teachers unions in this Country. It attacks the appointment of retired military leaders to boards of university regents and trustees, citing as outstanding examples of what it terms "militarizing of American campuses," the appointment of Admiral Chester Nimitz as a regent of the University of California, and the appointment of General Dwight Eisenhower as president of Columbia University.

The National Education Association of the United States is abused for presuming to urge the dismissal of Communist teachers; but, on the other hand, an entire page and a half is devoted to singing the praises of the left-wing teachers unions, along with complimentary statements about the American opponents of the loyalty oaths for teachers and other public employees.

"There is resistance," says the bulletin. "* * * There are teachers and professors who are actively fighting against political inquisitions, loyalty oaths, and other measures destructive of academic freedom. Such are the eight teachers in New York, who have been dismissed for refusing to answer questions about their political affiliations. Such are the 26 professors at the University of California in Berkeley, and the 13 in the State College in San Francisco who were dismissed for their refusal to sign anti-Communist oaths.

"A particularly significant example is that of the activity which is developing on the 'loyalty oaths' in the San Francisco State College and throughout California and all the United States.

"The students of the San Francisco State College took the initiative and are still leading this magnificent movement. At this time a large committee for the repeal of the Levering Law (a law in California which under the pretext of 'civil defense' imposed a 'loyalty oath' upon 1,300,000 public service workers) is being organized in support of a non-signing professor, and among the broad masses of the population. The 'Committee of Students for Academic Freedom' has become by far the most representative and active organization of students that ever existed in any university in the Country. It organized street meetings and public meetings to protest against the loyalty oath."

DEVELOPMENT OF STUDENT COMMUNIST ORGANIZATION IN THE UNITED STATES

A few months ago Communist book stores in California announced at all underground Party organizations the publication of a book which was hailed throughout Communist circles in this country as a brilliant contribution to Communist literature. It was written by William Z. Foster, Chairman of the Communist Party of the United States, and is entitled *History of the Communist Party of the United States,* International Publishers, Inc., New York, 1952. This volume is intended to do for the American Communist movement what a similar book did for the Communist Parties of the world. That volume was published under the auspices of the Politburo of the Communist Party of the Soviet Union, and is entitled *A History of the Communist Party of the Soviet Union.* It was translated into 28 different languages, and millions of copies were printed and circulated in every country where the Communist movement existed. Foster's book performs precisely the same function for the Communist Party of this Country. The pattern of world Communism, techniques to be used by Communist organizations in the several countries, plans for the subversion of colonial possessions, and the entire blueprint for world domination is set forth in the official *History of the Communist Party of the Soviet Union.* The Foster book, dealing with the history of the Communist Party of the United States, also contains the same sort of blueprint for Communist activities in this Country, much of the material being couched in the peculiar Aesopian language heretofore mentioned.

In discussing the development of American Communism, Foster takes particular pains to point out that the youth was a source of tremendous strength for the gathering Communist forces, showing how the Young Communist League developed from other youth organizations and burst into full bloom in 1924. As was described in the committee's 1951 report, the various youth organizations under the Marxian banner in this Country were the Young Communist League, American Youth for Democracy, and now the current Marxian organization known as the Labor Youth League. Despite the changes in name, the organization itself has remained fundamentally constant, being simply a part of the international Communist apparatus, as is the Communist Party of the United States. There are reams of documentation to establish the fact that the present Communist youth organization is simply a continuation of its predecessors under another name. For documentation of the fact that it is connected with an international Communist movement, one only has to refer to an official document known as the *Program of the Young Communist International,* published by the Young Communist League of America, 43 East 125th Street, New York City, and printed in England by the Dorrit Press, Ltd., 68-70 Lant Street, London, S. E. 1. This document, now a collector's item, but as timely and as authoritative now as when it was originally published, proclaims on page 17 that: "The Young Communist International is a section of the Communist International working upon the basis of the program and statutes of the Communist International. On this basis the Young Communist International has drawn up its own program, which lays down its own specific tasks within the struggle of the Communist International for Communism."

From this basic document we also see that the use of young Communists the world over to propagandize for peace, Kremlin style, is nothing new. Thus from page 45, we quote:

"The Communists decisively repudiate the slogan of 'the defense of the fatherland'—when this is used in respect of the capitalist state—as signifying and endorsement of imperialist war. On the contrary, it is in the interest of the working class of every country which is waging an imperialist war, to stand for the defeat of its own bourgeoisie, in order the more rapidly to overthrow it and thus be able to end the imperialist war. The Communists therefore propagate revolutionary defeatism in imperialist wars.

"The Communists, however, decisively declare themselves for the defense of a revolutionary socialist fatherland against imperialism. The Union of Socialist Soviet Republics is the socialist fatherland of the toilers of the whole world. The Communists likewise recognize the revolutionary right and duty of national defense against imperialism for the rebellious oppressed people of the colonies and semi-colonies. In a struggle between the imperialist powers and the Socialist Soviet Republics, or a war against a national revolutionary movement of the oppressed peoples, the working class must fight for the victory of the revolutionary side, and work not only for the fraternization but for the going over of the troops of the imperialist powers to the side of the revolution."

And on page 47 we find this, as applicable today as it was the moment it was written:

"The Young Communist League combats both compulsory and voluntary forms of bourgeois military training of the youth, not in the spirit of pacificism, but from the standpoint of the class struggle. Hence it sets up against bourgeois military training its own voluntary military training of the working class through its own proletarian organizations.

"Where military training of the youth is compulsory the Young Communist League adopts a similar attitude towards it as to the army itself, of which such training is a component part. This applies to entry into these organizations as well as disintegrating work within them. The Young Communist League tells the young workers called up for service in these organizations to join them and to carry on educational and disintegrative work there. The Young Communist League organizes this work. In the voluntary training organizations the Young Communist League, apart from the struggle against them which it carries on from the outside, also organizes enlightenment and disintegrative work from within. It is inadmissible to renounce internal disintegrative work in military training organizations for the youth, i.e., to prevent educational and organizational work among the young workers in these organizations."

And from pages 60-61 we find the young Communists directed to propagandize in the fields of religion and recreational activity, as follows:

"The Young Communist League pays special attention to the struggle against the church and religion by means of untiring educational work. 'Religion is the opium of the people.' Religion is one of the most important themes for exerting influence on the youth in the interest of the existing capitalist social order. It is particularly harmful among the working youth in rural districts and colonies.

The Young Communist League popularizes among the working youth the philosophy of dialectual materialism.

"As a supplement to its political, cultural and educational work, the Young Communist League also seeks as far as possible to satisfy the need for entertainment and recreation on the part of the working youth. It by no means, however, copies the bourgeois and social democratic forms of entertainment and recreation, but seeks for new methods of genuine proletarian sociability and entertainment which, in the last analysis, also serves to develop class-consciousness and Communist training. Proletarian festivals, political satires, dramatic circles, choirs, youth homes, camps, outings, rambles, etc., are used by the Young Communist League for this purpose.

"The educational work of the Young Communist League is carried on in a systematically organized manner. In the first place the Young Communist League carries out mass educational work, which in the main consists of the propaganda of Communist principles in various forms among the broad masses of young toilers. Furthermore, the Young Communist League conducts systematic work to educate its members in the basic questions of political science, and, in addition, carries on the higher training of the league cadres by a number of special measures, courses and schools."

An example of one of the special schools which is functioning in the State of California is the California Labor School, with its headquarters in the City of San Francisco and an active branch in the City of Los Angeles. It formerly also operated a branch in the City of Palo Alto.

Note the similarity of the language used in the program of the Young Communist International, quoted herewith, and that used by Dr. Langford in his textbook from which the committee has heretofore quoted. Thus, from page 74 of the program of the Young Communist International, we find the following language:

"The bourgeoisie does not rest content with exploiting an enormous number of children; it enslaves them intellectually too. Schools and all state educational institutions are used by them as instruments of bourgeois class education. As a supplement to this school education, there are the religious, reactionary, and so-called 'neutral' children's organizations which contain considerable numbers of working class children, are supported by the bourgeoisie and exert an enormous influence. Social democratic children's organizations work in perfect harmony with them. The church, the press, the cinema, etc., are also used as a means to inbue the children with a capitalist ideology. The working class sets against the class education of bourgeoisie its own revolutionary class education of the proletarian children."

"In order to assist this revolutionary class education of the growing generation, to organize its struggle against exploitation and mental slavery, to train new fighters from its midst who will struggle in the ranks of the Communist movement for the social revolution and the construction of Communism, the Young Communist League organizes, under the leadership of the Communist Party, Communist children's leagues.

"There can be no Communist education and training unless the proletarian children are drawn into the struggle and work of their class.

"The basis of the entire educational work of the Communist children's league is the systematic drawing in of the children into the proletarian class struggle, in a form understandable to the children, and adapted to the interests of various ages, as well as, where possible, their attraction in certain forms into the revolutionary activity of the Young Communist League and the Communist Party."

Years ago the Communist Party did maintain separate groups of teen-age children in an organization which it called the Young Pioneers. Several years ago the Young Pioneers was disbanded and the juveniles of America were recruited through commissions of the Communist Party itself and highly specialized units of the Young Communist League or other youth organizations which succeeded it, such as American Youth for Democracy and, at the present time, the Labor Youth League. When the authors of the document from which we have been quoting mention a "systematic growing in of the children into the proletarian class struggle, in a form understandable to the children," they might well have been referring to the two items included in the United Electrical, Radio and Machine Workers "Teachers' Kit" intended for the capturing of the juvenile mind and impressing it with the concept of the Marxian class struggle.

Many uninformed people will undoubtedly read these pages and then wonder why a mere handful of Communist students in this country can, after all, cause very much danger. The committee wishes to point out that in 1939 there were 22,000 members of the Young Communist League and that the members of that organization had already managed to infiltrate and capture a much larger organization. Late in 1933, Viola Ilma conceived the idea of uniting all American youth groups into one huge organization. At this time the Communist Party was operating on college campuses through a potent front organization called the National Student League. When the first American Youth Congress was held in 1934 at the insistence of Miss Ilma, delegates were sent not only from the National Student League but from a horde of other Communist front organizations, many of which were formed for that purpose. These young Communist delegates immediately insinuated themselves into the key positions, gradually undermined all opposition, and by 1939, the American Youth Congress with nearly 5,000,000 members was utterly controlled by the Communist Party of the United States through its youth organizations and their front groups. Gilbert Green, then national chairman of the Young Communist League, was a member of the executive board of the American Youth Congress, thereby providing a good example of how one man in the right place, with a few strategically located comrades, could actually manipulate a much larger organization to suit his own whims. Even Foster says in his recent book. "Communist influence was powerful in the American Youth Congress," (History of the Communist Party of the United States, op. cit., pages 310-311).

WHO IS HYSTERICAL?

An important ingredient in present Communist propaganda consists in an effort to convince the American people that anyone engaged in the investigation of Communist infiltration in the educational field is hysterical and a menace to academic freedom and civil liberties. If we paid much attention to the Communist propagandists who specialize in this particular subject, we would regard teachers and professors as pitiable individuals cowering in an atmosphere of terror; afraid to express themselves freely on any controversial subjects without running afoul of these hysterical persons who would immediately set up a loud clamor to have them hurled from the schools into outer darkness and damned forever as agents of the Kremlin.

In looking over the accumulated files of this committee regarding university professors and teachers over the past 14 years, and considering the number of front organizations to which they have contributed their time, their influence and their prestige, as well as their money, the committee is utterly unable to detect among them any element of fear or any stifling of freedom of expression. As a matter of fact, the committee has become rather inured during the 14 years of its existence to having teachers and professors defy the committee, castigate its members, sneer at the State Legislature and refuse to answer all questions about Communists or front organization affiliations on the ground that their answers might tend to incriminate them. We do not consider this any evidence that freedom of expression is being stifled.

During the several months that the committee has been working with the universities and colleges in California to prevent Communist infiltration and to rid the campuses of persons with documentable records of Communist affiliation, it has detected not even a slight evidence of apprehension on the part of the overwhelming majority of teachers and faculty members who have no records of such affiliations. On the contrary, the committee has found a sincere effort on the part of university administrators to cooperate in achieving a desirable practical result, and nothing but relief on the part of the non-Communist faculty members that at long-last some practical, serious, concentrated and cooperative effort is being made to get the job done in a manner that will not interfere with academic freedom, in the true sense of that term.

It is no longer necessary to approach the campus program with a blowing of trumpets and beating of drums, which only served to irritate college administrators and bring the institution concerned into public disrepute. As has been already stated, however, during the era when very few people troubled themselves about paying much attention to the Communist problem, it *was* necessary to hold frequent and public hearings for the purpose of breaking through this lethargic attitude and persuading some of the college administrators to cooperate with the committee instead of throwing up road blocks in its path. Now, however, that all of the colleges and universities in California, together with the 11 state colleges, are cooperating with the committee we hear a constant clamor about hysterical witch hunts, campus gestapos, red-baiting, and a stifling of a freedom of expression.

Two of the foremost experts of the United States on the subject of Communist infiltration in the educational field are Dr. J. B. Mathews, formerly head of the research department for the Congressional Committee on Un-American Activities, and Eugene Lyons, former editor of the *American Mercury* magazine, former Moscow correspondent, and writer of numerous books of the best-selling variety objectively dealing with all phases of the Communist menace.

Mr. Lyons wrote a piece for the February, 1953, issue of the *American Mercury* magazine, and in it he says:

"For a community of the gagged, educators seem to be strangely vociferous in support of Stalinist causes. A study of addiction to Red false-fronts made by Dr. J. B. Mathews shows its incidence to be highest among educators, who make up over 25 percent of those who join Communist-controlled activities and step into Communist booby traps. Evidently they are terror stricken—that they may be mistaken for conservatives. Professor Ludwig Lewisohn of Brandeis University came close to the realities when he wrote: 'The only scholar, the only type of student, who is still forced into a defensive position on American campuses today is the conservative teacher or student, the religious teacher or student.' There is a grim joker in the hysteria over hysteria. It is the attempt to correlate Communist conspiracy with free speech, independent thought, dissenting opinion, academic freedom. That's the psychological gimmick: to extend these noble values to cover spying, theft of official secrets, plotting, lying under oath, and covert corruption of young minds.

"Undoubtedly many of the fomenters of the hysteria over hysteria are truly concerned with freedom. These are the parrots, the dupes, the dopes. Their confusion stems from the premise that Communists 'despite everything,' are a species of social crusaders.

"But so far as conscious comrades and fellow-travelers are concerned, the goals of their strategy are fairly obvious. In the measure that they succeed, they adroitly transfer the onus from the accused to the accusers. They intimidate those who would expose Stalin's crowd. At the same time they promote the fairy tale, so helpful to their operations, that effective resistance to Red skulduggery is impossible within the limits of the Bill of Rights. Which is nonsense. The founding fathers could hardly have intended to leave their republic powerless to hunt out those dedicated to its destruction.

"Some years ago the smear-word for too-earnest anti-Communists was 'Red baiter.' It actually deterred many an American from interfering with the Kremlin rackets. Timorous souls hid or watered down their hatred of Communism for fear of that label.

"Today 'hysteria' and 'McCarthyism' serve the same deterrent purpose, precisely as the manipulators of those specious tags planned it. And again, too, many enemies of Stalinism with a milquetoast streak dilute their anti-Communism with pious assurances that *they*, God forbid, are not hysterical or McCarthyite.

"The hysteria bogey must be demolished to clear the road to more effective struggle with the Communist menace, which is the central task of this period. The danger today is not hysteria but complacency."

(*American Mercury Magazine,* February, 1953, pages 23-33.)

COMMUNISM AND ACADEMIC FREEDOM

In 1948, several members of this committee, together with the committee's counsel were invited to go to the City of Seattle, Washington, where a newly created legislative committee was investigating Communist penetration of the faculty at the University of Washington.

When the Washington State committee was formed the California committee sent its official documents, the resolutions creating the committee, and other pertinent material for the purpose of assisting the Washington legislature, and thereafter held several conferences with members of the newly created body.

In the summer of 1948, the guests from California listened with intense interest while public hearings in Seattle developed facts concerning the extent of Communist infiltration of the University of Washington. The entire procedure, from beginning to end, was conducted in a cooperative spirit between the administrators of the University of Washington and the members of the Washington State legislative committee. As a result of the public hearings and disclosures three faculty were dismissed: Joseph Butterworth, Herbert Phillips, and Ralph Gundlach.

In 1948 and 1949, the President of the University of Washington was Dr. Raymond B. Allen, who is now the Provost of the University of California at Los Angeles. So far as the committee is aware, Dr. Allen is the first educator in the United States to go through an experience such as this, to take a practical hard-headed and objective view of the problem and forthrightly recommend the dismissal of those members of the faculty who, according to the indisputable evidence, were found to be connected with the Communist Party. This was accomplished with full regard to the protection of civil liberties, academic freedom and freedom of expression, but the controversy stirred up such a furor in the Pacific Northwest that the Regents of the University of Washington were moved to publish a book comprising 125 pages, which they called, *Communism and Academic Freedom, the Record of the Tenure Cases at the University of Washington.*

In this book Dr. Allen made several statements which the committee feels worthy of repetition here, particularly in view of the fact that he is now the head of the University of California at Los Angeles, and that the state university and all of its eight campuses, are cooperating fully with this committee in the effort to eliminate subversives from the faculty and prevent the infiltration of others to replace them.

In the introduction to this book, discussing the fundamental question of whether members of a conspiratorial and secret organization such as the Communist Party should be permitted to teach in a university, Dr. Allen wrote:

"The question of whether members of the Communist Party should be allowed to teach on the faculty of an American university has been debated for many years. The problem certainly is not peculiar to the University of Washington. It is one that has caused difficulty in many institutions, seriously affecting both the internal and external relations of colleges and universities throughout America. The problem is an extremely delicate one, for it involves fundamental questions of academic freedom, and it is one which must be faced without the benefit of conclusive judicial findings on the nature of the Communist Party. The problem is one which, in my view, has been too long neglected by universities everywhere and which, even when it has been examined, has been touched only on its periphery and never before faced head-on nor subjected to definitive study with full academic procedures and safeguards.''

''As has been pointed out, the question raised by these tenure cases are the University of Washington's alone. It is not surprising, however, that first detailed attention should be given them in the northwest. Throughout the history of this area liberal thought and freedom of action have been highly prized. But it is commonly accepted, I believe, except by those devoted to Communism itself, that Communism is parasitic on real liberalism, that Communism thrives best where there is a background of honest liberalism, and that Communism, generally speaking, has taken advantage of tolerance of liberal thought and action to further its ends. It is not strange, then, that problems of Communism and education have been more acute in the Pacific Northwest, perhaps, than in other parts of the United States. Thus the university's problems, while in no sense different from those which might have arisen elsewhere, came into being against a background of the liberal thought and action of the Pacific Northwest.''

Elsewhere in the introduction Dr. Allen states that:

''It should be said also that in the open committee hearings no effort was made by committee members to elicit testimony on the political or social views of faculty members other than those who, for some concrete reason, were believed to be, or to have been, members of the Communist Party. It is to the credit of the committee that it limited its inquiry to those situations where there was an actual question of Communist Party membership.

On pages 90-91 of the report, Dr. Allen stated:

''I would point out that the teacher and the scholar have special obligations with respect to the sincerity of their convictions which involve questions of intellectual honesty and integrity. Men in academic life—teachers, scholars, and scientists—are engaged in a vocation which is concerned with the finding of truth and its dissemination, with the pursuit of truth wherever it may lead. Is it possible for an individual, however sincere, to embrace both this unhampered pursuit of truth and, at the same time, the doctrines and dogmas of a political party which admits of no criticism, of its fundamental principles and programs? Put in another way, a teacher may be ever so sincere in his belief in Communism, but can he, at the same time, be a sincere seeker after truth, which is the first obligation and duty of the teacher? My answer to these questions is, 'He cannot.' Therefore, I believe these men, by reason of their admitted membership in the Communist Party described in the above findings, to be incompetent, intellectually dishonest, and derelict in their duty to find and teach the truth.

''There is, in other words, a higher duty imposed upon members of the academic community than upon other men. For centuries universities have survived in the western world, not without difficulties and serious attacks from both without and within, primarily because of their impartiality, objectivity, and determination to seek truth and not be propagandists in partisan political, economic, and other debates. The University of Washington could not exist if every member of its faculty were to engage in clandestine political activity and to take sides secretly on every partisan political and economic issue that comes before the people. Clandestine activity such as Butterworth's and Phillips' in the Communist Party means that they have forsaken their duty to protect the university's integrity and to pursue an objective quest of truth in favor of a propagandistic mission entirely unrelated to real educational and scholarly effort. In my opinion every member of the faculty must discharge this higher duty if a university is to maintain its proper function, identity, and integrity. The integrity of an institution begins and ends with the integrity of the people that comprise it and give it meaning and life.

"The fact that the Communist Party, U. S. A., has not been declared an illegal conspiracy by the courts is not relevant to the issue of university employment of active members of the Communist Party. A much closer analogy would be that of a judge attempting to conceal a financial interest in a firm that was involved in litigation or receivership in his court. It is not against the law for any American citizen to own stock in a company. It would be occasion for removal from office, however, if it were discovered that a judge had prejudiced his decision by the ownership of stock in a company in such a case. An important function of the university is to teach citizenship. For this teaching to be in the hands of faculty men who secretly belong to an organization advocating the complete overthrow of the American system should be no more tolerated than the unethical and immoral behavior of the judge. (Honest, aboveboard criticism of the capitalistic system, which no one contends is perfect, is quite another matter and goes on every day both inside our universities and in the business world.)

"In defense of Joseph Butterworth and Herbert J. Phillips it is plain that it was never specifically stated to the faculty that membership in the Communist Party was not sanctioned by the administration. It is further suggested that, since it was probably fairly well known that there were Communists on the faculty, this was tacit acceptance of the fact and that, therefore, approval could be inferred. Speaking for myself only, as head of the institution for more than two years, I can recall specific instances when, responding to public attacks made on the university for harboring members of the Communist Party, I said publicly that in my opinion and to the best of my knowledge there were no Communists on the faculty. Still under these compromising circumstances, Butterworth and Phillips, by their present admission then members of the Communist Party, failed to come forward to either disabuse the public of the untruth the president had expressed or to come to the president himself and admit the fact. Certainly in these particular circumstances and, I am told, in similar situations in the past, it should have been plainly apparent to any member of the faculty that membership in the Communist Party was frowned upon by many people of the state and certainly by the administration of the university. It cannot now be alleged that, simply because a hard and fast rule was not laid down, these men did not know that they were carrying on activities which were in high disfavor in the university community. If they did not think such membership was in disfavor, why did they keep their membership secret?''

In commenting upon a minority report submitted by two professors who served on an academic committee appointed for the purpose of making recommendations concerning the action to be taken against the faculty members who were charged with being members of the Communist Party, Dr. Allen had this to say:

''In this statement, there is a lengthy discussion of incompetence in terms of intellectual capacity and balance. Robinson and Sholley (the writers of the minority opinion) declare:

'Surely we may not outlaw all professors who hold beliefs contrary to whatever may be the current conceptions, superstitions, and emotions of the general populace; we must not close the academic doors to a modern Galileo or Darwin.'

''If my memory of the activities of these truly great men serves me correctly, they did not find it necessary to join a secret organization to propagandize for their ideas and discoveries. In fact they carried them openly and vigorously to the market place of academic and public opinion and there fought for them and won. Robinson and Sholley declare:

'Our profession is ornamented by men who hold religious beliefs which contravene the findings of physical science,'

to which it may be replied that these people openly and proudly profess their beliefs. The same can be said of the illustration citing George Bernard Shaw and asking if, because he proclaimed most vigorously the strong opinion that vaccination is a menace to mankind, he is incompetent to teach grammer? Of course he is not incompetent to teach, but here again G.B.S. holds his views on vaccination openly, and everybody who has followed his writings and his beliefs knows about them. This is quite different from joining a secret organization to propagandize against vaccination. What I am saying is that, in the American tradition, people have a right to know the real views of their public servants and that these views should be held openly, in the tradition of the American town meeting. It seems to me we have come a long way from this rich tradition of our founding fathers if we must tolerate secret membership in a clandestine political organization by men to whom the community looks for leadership and objective thought in our universities. Is this the standard of conduct and ethics which the public expects from its public servants? I think not.

Discussing the case of Professor Ralph Gundlach, Dr. Allen had this to say:

''I had said earlier at another faculty meeting that members of the Communist Party were not welcome at the University of Washington. I put it even more badly, saying that, if we had any members of the party on the faculty 'they would be smoked out.' Unfortunately the committee has misinterpreted my testimony. The point is not too material, however, because Gundlach alleges that he is not now, nor has he ever been, a member of the Party.

"It is most important, I believe, to determine if Gundlach is a member of the Party or, what is equally important, a 'front' for the Party. When I asked him the direct question, 'Are you a member of the Communist Party?' Gundlach told me, 'No one can prove that I am, and I cannot prove that I am not.'

"The testimony in this hearing establishes that the present 'party line' is that cards are *not* issued to members. The official record of membership is kept 'underground' to the end that no one will be able to find a written record of membership either of those who are active members or of those for whom openly held membership would not serve the interest of the Party. In the final analysis proof of membership by direct evidence is impossible, and only an 'admission' of membership would be conclusive.

"Three admitted former Communist Party members testified that Gundlach was a member of the party, and they had attended 'closed' meetings with him. All testified not out of desire to do so, but under a compelling sense of loyalty and interest in the welfare of this university.

"The report states: 'The evidence does establish beyond doubt that the respondent Gundlach is, at least, a sympathizer with, and an active supporter of, substantially all the policies of the Communist Party, U. S. A. If he is not presently a member of the Communist Party, his membership is either a deliberate effort to avoid the adverse consequences which he might fear would accompany Party membership or is caused by relatively minor personal ideological differences with the Communist Party. * * * Thus, the only positive and direct testimony on the subject (Gundlach's Party nonmembership) comes from the respondent himself. However, we have not been satisfied with the testimony of respondent taken as a whole. We feel that he has been evasive on many matters, and we cannot accept at face value his self-serving testimony on the point of party nonmembership. Under these circumstances, we make no definite finding. Particularly we believe that, if respondent was not and is not a Party member, he could readily and voluntarily have adduced much better supporting proof.'

"Indeed, Gundlach joined, sponsored, and took active part in many 'front' organizations, all of them listed as subversive by the Attorney General of the United States. He devoted more time to these 'fronts' than did all the other respondents combined. Gundlach was as consistent with the changing 'Party line' as the line was inconsistent with itself.

"If Gundlach is not a Party member it would have been easy for him to answer 'no' when I asked him. His reply was that 'No one can prove that I am a member, and I cannot prove that I am not' supports the assumption that he is a member. I pointed this out to him at the time of the interview. His refusal to answer supports my contention that, taking him at his word before the committee that he is not a member (and for this purpose only ignoring the contrary testimony of the witnesses Costigan, Smith, and Armstrong that he was a member), he has at the very least been one of that special group of Party workers who deliberately do not become Party members so that they may better serve the purposes of the Party. Entirely aside from whether he pays dues and carries a card, Gundlach has done more for the Party than any other respondent.

"Whether he is formerly a member or not, Gundlach, in my opinion, is no less guilty of 'incompetence' and 'neglect of duty' and perhaps more guilty of 'intellectual dishonesty' than either Butterworth or Phillips."

In concluding his remarks, Dr. Allen summarized his position as follows:

"I agree with the committee's findings of fact concerning the Communist Party, U. S. A. Having established the nature and characteristics of the Party as inimicable to the future welfare of the institutions of freedom of the United States, it follows that secret membership in such a Party by Butterworth and Phillips disqualifies them for membership in the faculty of the University of Washington within the causes for dismissal listed in the administrative code—specifically on the grounds of incompetency, dishonesty and neglect of duty.

"In the case of Gundlach I agree with the majority recommendation that he be dismissed for reasons detailed in Section 3 of this report."

"In conclusion I wish to emphasize what I have said elsewhere: 'Freedom is essential to sound education. That academic freedom must be maintained at any university of the name is beyond question. But academic freedom consists of something more than merely an absence of restraint placed upon the teacher by the institution that employs him. It demands as well an absence of restraint placed on him by his political affiliations, by dogmas that stand in the way of a free search for truth, or by rigid adherence to a "Party line" that sacrifices dignity, honor and integrity to the accomplishment of political ends. Men, and especially the teacher and the scholar, must be free to think and discover and believe, else there will be no new thought, no discovery, and no progress. But these freedoms are barren if their fruits are to be hidden away and denied. Men must be free, of course, but they must also be free, and willing, to stand up and profess what they believe so that all may hear. This is an important, if not the most important part of our American heritage of freedom. It is this American heritage of freedom that must be cherished and sustained by our systems and institutions of education if they are to survive'."

SERIOUSNESS OF COMMUNIST INFILTRATION

We have already indicated that there is no such thing as a dormant, inactive member of the Communist Party. This, of course, is true whether he is a member of a labor union, a front organization or a university faculty. His activities are directed from above, carried out with military

precision, and fitted into a vast pattern of closely meshed, well-synchron-
ized Party activity that has been planned with all of the care and strategy
of a military campaign. We fully realize that the following example,
although hypothetical, will be regarded by most readers as utterly fantastic. Let us hasten to state, therefore, that every basic ingredient of
the following situation has been carefully drawn from well documented
sources and that the situation is not nearly so fantastic as it may appear.

Suppose we were members of the education commission of the Communist Party of California. We determine to concentrate our efforts toward the infiltration of a large and influential university. The entire
disclipined, secret Party apparatus is at our disposal: its propaganda
machinery, its front organizations. We decide to operate through a tiny
campus unit that has been in existence for years. We have already established valuable contacts in several enormously wealthy foundations—
an Alger Hiss in the Carnegie Foundation, a Louise Branston through
whom influence can be exerted in the Rosenberg Foundation, a former
teacher in a Communist school buried deep in the heart of the Ford
Foundation. We select an outstanding scholar—a man under Party discipline, but entirely unsuspected, we get him a substantial grant from
one of the foundations, we build up his academic prestige, and we manage
to place him on a campus.

In the meanwhile our fronts, composed largely of professional people
—fellow travelers, dupes and Party members—go to work in the area
immediately adjacent to the university campus. Our ultimate objective.
is to place our man in a position from which he can kick open the academic portals to other Party members. This may require years, but we
have been taught the cardinal virtue of Marxian patience. At the same
time our young Communist members at the university set about to capture and control the student paper. This is relatively easy, since they
have the advantage of expert adult guidance and the added advantage
of a well-formulated strategy. They have no scruples about smearing and
undermining the opposition, which is unorganized, undisciplined and
therefore impotent.

Our small campus unit is activated, its members are given specific assignments, and the entire smoothly-geared apparatus is operated to
accomplish a single objective: the placing of our undercover man in the
desired position of influence. If, in due time, he is made an assistant dean
of the college of liberal arts and sciences, the job is almost done. Now we
have only to undermine the dean.

This can be accomplished in a variety of ways, the dean can be surrounded by Party people in his own office; he can be smeared and subjected to a vicious whispering rumor attack; he can be lured into a front
organization and accused of being a Party member; his students can be
turned against him; he can be offered an exceedingly attractive and
flattering position, taken out of the university, "kicked upstairs" and
then fired. In our work, remember, the end justifies the means. We are
working for the world Communist revolution. Nothing must be suffered
to interfere.

Once our man is on the campus, all Party members must scrupulously
avoid him—and even criticize him occasionally as being too conservative.
Thus he is carefully protected, built up, groomed for the all-important
strategic position. At the same time, of course, there are other details

that require attention. We know that our off-campus apparatus can provide scholarships, create academic prestige, and send a hand-picked supply of applicants to seek faculty jobs at the university.

Experience has taught us, however, that we need a parallel apparatus inside the institution as well. Our undercover Party member, now the new dean of the college of liberal arts and sciences, must have concentrated in his hands an effective appointive power so our personnel can be readily slipped into the university. Most universities have academic committees that must pass on all applicants for faculty positions. We must change this. Our man may not be able to arbitrarily appoint full professors, or assistant or associate professors single handed without the consent of an academic committee. But we will try to arrange matters so he can appoint his own advisory committee. Of course, he will appoint men he can handle; ambitious men from his own college of liberal arts and sciences. After all, he is the dean.

Finally the spade work is done; the competition has been eliminated and our man is in the position to carry out our objectives. Shall we allow him to work alone? No, we learned long ago that all persons in such important positions must never be permitted such latitude. Earl Browder's wife was a Soviet judge, once a power in the international espionage school in Moscow; Marcel Shearer, the industrial scientist who also graduated from the espionage school and headed a spy ring in the United States, was married to another trusted party functionary, Lena Chernenko; and when, in California, Philip Connelly turned to alcohol as a means of brief escapism, he was teamed up with Dorothy Healy, a hard-bitten functionary who joined the Young Communist League when she was 14 years of age. No, we will provide our new dean with a new secretary, and perhaps a clerk and a switchboard operator for good measure.

Now we are ready to function. Is the university engaged in secret scientific research for the armed forces? We have two excellent research men from the east. They are reliable Communists with no record of front affiliations, they were never allowed to take Party publications, and neither of them ever was issued a Party card. They are "sleepers," drawn from a reservoir of comrades carefully developed for this very purpose. They are given the necessary academic prestige, provided with the necessary recommendations, apply to our dean and are approved without a hitch. How would the government go about determining the loyalty of such people?

We must, of course, take care not to over-do this work. Success will be measured in the quality and security of our personnel, not in its quantity.

Do we need men to re-orient a popular course in political science? In economics? In speech? Very well, Dr. Langford and his collaborators have shown how simple it is to effect such re-orientation, and we will provide the personnel and the direction.

Eventually we perfect our dual apparatus, the off-campus apparatus to provide personnel; the on-campus apparatus to put our men in the proper places and protect them from exposure. All of this has required several years of hard, coordinated, patient labor. But we have had one enormously vital weapon handed to us: the incredible apathy of the American public and its utter illiteracy concerning the practical aspects of power Communism. Naturally, we have encouraged this naive and indifferent attitude by our front groups and our propaganda.

Gradually the campus atmosphere changes. As key courses are "reoriented," as "reactionary" professors are replaced from our reservoir of "progressive" and "liberal" personnel, as our student nucleus solidifies its control of the university paper, and as our personnel is filtered into the recorder's office and into other strategic administrative positions, the academic atmosphere becomes vastly "liberalized."

Candidates for doctorates who are "progressives" have an easier time than their more conservative colleagues. Those who presume to speak out against the new order are subjected to a vicious attack from all sides and branded as hopeless reactionaries. And in the process of effecting this change, it is always easy to enlist the vociferous support of a flock of non-Communist idealists who can be manipulated by flattery into lending lip service to our entire enterprise.

To those readers who are skeptical after having perused the above hypothetical situation, we respectfully direct attention to pages 201-218 of the committee's third report, issued in 1947, as a thoroughly documented example of the planning, patience and eventual success with which the Communist Party handles a long-range plan of infiltrating its personnel into key campus positions.

THE CALIFORNIA PLAN

During the spring and early summer of 1952, when the committee was discussing the entire subject of educational infiltration with the college and university presidents in California, it was decided that the committee would provide the expert assistance and the documentation, when required, together with its power to subpena witnesses and question them under oath, and that the colleges and universities would, on the other hand, make full use of the committee's facilities and keep it advised concerning campus problems. The plan is working, and working far better than any of us anticipated. Much remains to be done and the committee hastens to add that it does not intend to relinquish its prerogative, indeed, its duty, to use is powers in all cases and in connection with any educational institution where the necessity arises.

As we have heretofore stated, during the 10 months that this cooperative plan has been in existence, more than a hundred persons with documentable records of Communist activities and affiliations have been removed from the educational institutions of California. We are quite aware of the fact that in accomplishing this result without fanfare and publicity, the committee will be charged in some quarters with keeping the facts from the public. Fourteen years of practical experience in this field has indicated, however, that it is far better (where conditions permit) to go about this business of counter-Communist activity with as little fanfare as possible, and that this is especially true where schools and universities are concerned.

In exposing Communist front activities and in certain other phases of the work, public exposure is not only desirable but highly necessary. In the matter of preventing infiltration of our colleges and schools, on the other hand, it is far more practical to accomplish the purpose in such a manner that the Communist Party is not given an opportunity to whip up front organizations and turn on propaganda and create martyrs—in other words, to conduct the investigations and achieve the results in such a manner that the committee does not provide the Communist Party with ammunition in the very process of combating its efforts at academic infiltration. When hearings are involved, full public exposure is not only inevitable, but desirable.

For several years the committee has been concerned with the business of working to eliminate Communists from universities, only to see them obtain other teaching positions a few months later at some other institution. Under the present plan adequate measures are being perfected to prevent such an occurrence. This can in no sense be construed as an unholy alliance between the committee and the universities to establish and maintain a black list. A man may have a constitutional right to be a member of the Communist Party, but he has no right to continue that secret membership and work as a teacher, a professor or a public servant at the same time. Universities have not only the right but, as we view it, the duty to protect themselves against Communist infiltration, and it is downright silly to oust a Communist from one institution only to allow him a haven of protection in another.

It is one thing to take effective measures to deny employment to persons with clear records of Communist affiliation; it is quite another and far more difficult matter to get rid of them after they have been hired and entrenched in their positions. In the present phase of Communist activity the emphasis must be placed on prevention although, of course, the matter of eliminating the entrenched Party members can by no means be neglected.

Educators need expert assistance in determining whether an admitted ex-Communist has actually broken away from Party discipline or is merely seeking to divert suspicion; whether a man who is connected with front organizations is a Party member, a susceptible liberal, or a Marxian dilettante; whether a newly-formed organization is Communist-controlled and masquerading behind a respectable facade or was sincerely created for a laudable purpose. This is where expert guidance and a balanced attitude are essential.

Through such cooperation as now exists between the California schools and universities and the committee, it is far easier to learn the facts and gauge the extent of the infiltration and take necessary practical and legislative steps to effectively combat the problem. The committee is now preparing a survey of each separate institution, which, when completed with the assistance of the institutions concerned, will do much to shed light on a situation that has for years been clouded by a lack of cooperation and liaison between the institutions on the one hand and the committee on the other.

Several months ago the committee was requested by the Los Angeles City Board of Education to conduct an analysis of its employees, both academic and administrative. More than 26,000 persons comprised the full complement of the board's emplyees and the committee had neither the office staff nor the funds to complete such an ambitious undertaking. Funds were accordingly furnished by the Board of Education, two experienced clerks were employed and, by the time this report is published, the job will have been completed. It should be added that the funds were used only for necessary and itemized expenses incurred in the survey, and were expended by a public accountant who was in no way connected with the committee.

An analysis of this survey will immediately disclose the extent of infiltration among the employees of the Los Angeles City Board of Education by persons with documentable records of Communist and Communist front affiliations. The Board of Education can then study the records and take such practical action as may be indicated.

Interest was focused on the Los Angeles City School System as an indirect result of the Housing Authority investigation and hearings in that city conducted by the committee in September and October of 1952, at which it was revealed that Jean Benson Wilkinson, the wife of Frank Wilkinson, was a teacher in the Los Angeles School System and at the same time affiliated with the left-wing Los Angeles Federation of Teachers. Further investigation indicated that Mrs. Wilkinson was a member of the Communist Party with her husband and certain other persons who were active in a master plan to infiltrate the entire Los Angeles City School System with both academic and administrative personnel. The Board of Education at once communicated with representatives of the committee and unanimously voted to ask for the personnel analysis above-mentioned.

By way of summary it should be pointed out that there is no heavy infiltration of Communist teachers in the schools and universities of this State. But, as one might naturally expect when for more than 30 years the Communist Party has concentrated on infiltrating our educational institutions and has been suffered to operate during that time with relative freedom and virtually no resistance, the infiltration attempt has succeeded only too well. True, the numbers of Communist Party members and fellow travelers are small, but even one campus Communist is one too many—and if he managed to indoctrinate one student who becomes an Alger Hiss, a Klaus Fuchs, or a Julius Rosenberg, then we must share in the responsibility for having allowed him to remain in a position that afforded him an opportunity to thus spread his poison propaganda in such a fertile field.

But, as we have shown, Communists are never dormant. We simply do not find one lone party member in an educational institution. He must have Party contacts both on and off the campus and indulge in an activity that is constantly expanding. There is far more danger in underestimating the extent of this infiltration than in overestimating it; it has been treated too lightly for too long. The issue must be met, and the committee believes it can most effectively be met by close cooperation with the educational administrators. In California this has been accomplished.

Since last June, other legislative committees, mostly of the United States Congress, have announced their intent to investigate this subject. On November 29, 1952, Chairman Velde stated that the House Committee on Un-American Activities would investigate Communist influences in education. On the same day Senator Pat McCarran announced that his Senate Subcommittee on Internal Security would follow the same course. On December 29, 1952, Senator Joseph McCarthy declared that his committee would, "investigate the Nation's colleges in a search for subversive influences." On February 20, 1953, Representative Jackson called on the California Association of School Administrators to aid the House Committee in its investigations. This stimulated interest in the subject has brought a wide variety of responses from educators. The extreme left has raised the charge of hysteria and witch-hunting; the extreme right has demanded full-dress public hearings with all the trappings of television and radio coverage; the vastly more numerous group of educators who comprise the middle ground, have pledged cooperation, but expressed some concern that the sudden attack from all quarters at once may develop into more of an exhibition than investigation.

THE GADAR PARTY

During World War II this committee was requested to make an investigation of an organization of Indians in California known as the Gadar Party. After the Japanese residents had been excluded from the western defense command area and relocated in centers established for that purpose as a precaution against espionage activities, it was discovered that the Gadar Party, organized in India for the purpose of emancipating that country from British control, had been heavily infiltrated by active members of the Communist movement, some of whom had been graduated from the Lenin School for espionage agents in Moscow. Authorities were apprehensive lest the Communist element in this organization, fanatically dedicated to an anti-British, and therefore an anti-American policy during World War II, was potentially dangerous to the American war effort. Accordingly, a report was confidentially made to the proper authorities after several months of investigation.

Following the commencement of active hostilities in Korea there was a renewed interest manifested in the activities of the Gadar Party, and the committee has, on its own initiative, conducted an extensive survey which it deems proper to include in this report for the purpose of showing the extent of Communist infiltration in the organization and the scope of its activities. This is done for the purpose of making public for the first time a complete history and analysis of the movement to show how a racial minority group in California can be used as a cover for espionage and subversive political activities by the international Communist movement, and, in all fairness, to indicate that the organization was successful in stamping out such activities.

Furthermore, the facts contained in the ensuing account of the international activities of this group provides an example that illustrates the fact that Communist activities must never be regarded as purely localized matters, but since the movement itself is essentially international in scope, all local activities must be regarded against a background of the world master plan, the current international Communist Party line.

ORIGIN OF THE GADAR PARTY

The Gadar Party was organized at Lahore, Punjab, India, in 1907 as part of a movement to emancipate India from British control and to establish a free united states of India, with a democratic form of government. The word *Gadar* is derived from the Arabic and means traitor. At one time it was commonly used as an epithet to designate any Indian who resisted British authority. Har Dayal, the founder of the Gadar Party, deliberately applied the term to his followers as a gesture of open contempt and defiance against what they considered to be the ruthless British imperialist domination of their country.

Har Dayal was educated at the University of Punjab, and after an exceptionally brilliant academic career received his M.A. degree and a scholarship which enabled him to complete his studies at Oxford University in England. It was after he finished his education abroad that he returned to India and resolved to devote the balance of his life to the rapidly growing movement to free his country from British domination.

Shortly after the Gadar Party was organized Dayal was sought by the British authorities, but managed to elude them and made his way to France. He traveled throughout Europe, came to the United States, was an instructor at Stanford University and in 1913 served as editor of the *Hindustani Gadar News,* an organ of the California Gadar Party. In 1914 he was arrested on a deportation warrant by U. S. Immigration officers, but left the country voluntarily and remained in Europe until the end of World War I. Thereafter he returned to the United States and died of a heart attack in New York City in 1942.

From its inception in 1907 the Gadar Party attracted Indians throughout the world. The organization which started as a rebellious political movement ultimately assumed the character of a semi-religious crusade, and its members became highly indoctrinated with a sense of fanatic loyalty to each other and to the Gadar Party.

A striking example of this fanaticism is found in a trial held in the United States District Court of San Francisco in 1918, and which involved the activities of the California Gadar Party in connection with the first world war. A Gadar member named Ram Chandra had succeeded Har Dayal as editor of the *Hindustani Gadar News,* but soon was operating the paper for his personal financial gain instead of for the organization. He sold a news service to American papers, and was regarded as a traitor by members of the party. When he and 30 other defendants were arrested on charges of violating the Neutrality Act, it was believed that he might betray his associates, and reveal the secret activities of the group. The United States Marshal in San Francisco, realizing the political tension generated by this case, and fearful that some physical injury might be inflicted on potential witnesses, had all spectators searched as they entered the courtroom. A Gadar assassin, however, had concealed a revolver in his turban, and when the Ram Chandra was about to testify concerning the subversive activities of the organization, rose in the audience, took deliberate aim and shot the witness as he sat there on the stand. The assassin stood calmly with the gun in his hand until he, in turn, was shot by the United States Marshal.

Members of the Gadar Party have frankly stated on numerous occasions that they would cooperate with any nation or any organization working to further the effort to free India from British rule. Hence, during the first world war the Party was suspected of being pro-German. During World War II, it was suspected of being pro-Japanese and pro-German. Since 1945, it has been suspected of being pro-Russian.

SUBHAS CHANDRA BOSE

The All India National Congress and the Gadar Party, although entirely separate organizations, have worked closely together for a common purpose, the leaders of one group often being affiliated with the other. Prominent among the leaders of the congress was Subhas Chandra Bose (not to be confused with Ras Bari Bose). He, like Har Dayal, was educated in England, and was thereafter appointed deputy commissioner for the British government in Bengal. He soon became deeply interested in the movement to free India, however, and resigned from his highly lucrative position to devote full time to the cause. Immediately after his resignation he was arrested and imprisoned, but escaped and went to Switzerland. From there he went to Italy, where he became intimately acquainted with Benito Mussolini.

After the outbreak of the second world war, Bose returned to India where he was promptly arrested and imprisoned, and once more managed to escape. This time he went direct to Italy, thence to Germany and finally to Tokio. As of January 8, 1944, Bose was reported by the *Domei News Agency* as having transferred his activities from Singapore to Burma, where he set up his Japanese-controlled "Provincial Government for Free India," as "another important step in the preparation for the launching of destructive forces" to loosen the British grip on India.

It is important to bear in mind the profound and widespread influence of Subas Chandra Bose on Indians throughout the world, and their abiding devotion to the cause commonly espoused by the Gadar Party and the All India National Congress. Bose had repeatedly told his followers through written material and through the facilities of the Axis-controlled radio that India would never emancipate herself without the assistance of foreign nations. He convinced them that help could not be expected from the allied powers, and assured them of the aid and cooperation of the Berlin-Tokio Axis. This concept is the real key to any logical conclusion to be drawn from this report. Bose planted the idea that those who sought to free India must have foreign aid. After World War II it was only natural that the Soviet Union emerged as the only real power to which the Gadar Party and its followers could turn. This was, of course, bolstered by the Soviet propaganda machine concerning the emancipation of all Asia, and even more by the revolution in China. In 1943, Bose broadcast from Singapore: "Now that India's neighbor, Burma, has achieved its freedom, nothing on earth can keep the Indians enslaved any longer." (*Time*, August 16, 1943, page 26.)

THE GADAR PARTY IN CALIFORNIA

Har Dayal started the Gadar Party in California in November, 1913, but it had no formal organization until it was incorporated on January 22, 1917, the first directors being G. B. Lal, now science editor for the Hearst papers, H. Chandra and H. Sharman. Between 1913 and 1917, the party had no regular membership and no constitution, but was simply a loose association of Indians who issued propaganda material and raised funds to build the party into a larger, more effective organization.

On March 31, 1916, the Gadar Party purchased lots 1 and 2 in block 1069, situated on the west side of Wood Street in the City of San Francisco, about 400 feet north of Geary Boulevard and adjacent to the Laurel Hills Cemetery. On this property, since known as No. 5 Wood Street, a three-story building was erected consisting of a garage, a room for printing presses, a large meeting room and library on the second floor, and eight sleeping accommodations on the third floor. This property has been the state headquarters for the Gadar Party from its inception.

On June 6, 1928, a corporate charter was issued to the Hindustan Gadar Party. The purposes of the organization were expressed in this charter as follows:

"To encourage the establishment of a system of government in India which shall be free from all foreign control, and which shall have as its aim the greatest good for the greatest number, and which shall guarantee freedom of thought, speech, press and organization, and ensure the minimum necessities of life to all;

"To publish a periodical review of political, economic, social and intellectual conditions in India by voluntary contributions, and without sale."

Directors of the corporation in 1928 were: Lakar Singh, Isleton, California; Charn Singh, Merced, California, and Tarjan Singh, Palmeda, California.

It may be estimated with a fair degree of accuracy that there were never more than 1,500 members of the California Gadar Party at any one time out of an Indian population in this state of approximately 6,000. However, Gadar Party members refer to "inside" and "outside" members of the organization. By inside members they allude to those who participate in the affairs of the party and have the right to vote for its officers. By outside members they mean any Indian who has financially helped the organization, and they, combined with the inside members, would clearly bring the total of all Indians affiliated with the party to considerably more than 1,500.

Each of the Gadar Parties throughout the world was purely autonomous—there being no organizational connection between them. The contacts between these groups in the United States were informal and indirect. And in India, for obvious reasons, the Gadar Party members were compelled to work individually and underground.

The California party adopted a formal constitution which was placed into operation in 1928. Its essential provisions defined the membership as comprising five classes, as follows: (1) Honorary members—"Any person who is in sympathy with the principles of the Hindustan Gadar Party and is over 21 years of age." (2) Associate members—an honorary member who also pays $5 annual dues. (3) Active members—any person who "is a Hindustanee by birth," over 21, and who agrees to obey the constitution, by-laws and statutes of the party and who pays $25 annual dues. (4) Special members, being anyone who, in addition to fulfilling the qualifications for an active member, pays $100 annual dues. (5) Life members—any person qualified as a special member who "pledges in addition his time and income, after meeting the minimum needs for a moderate living."

Provision was made to establish state committees of nine members each, except for Marysville where the large Indian population justified a committee of 11. The term "state" is apparently used here in the Indian sense of area or region. Committee members were to be elected by secret ballot for a six-year term. Each "state" committee managed the area under its particular jurisdiction, and each elected two of its members to what was known as the Central Panchayat.

The Panchayat comprised 19 members, 11 to be elected by the five state committees—three by Marysville and two by each of the others.

Three commissioners (life members or functionaries) were ex officio members of the Panchayat, and they appointed five others.

The Panchayat was an extremely powerful body—but the influence of the three commissioners and their five appointees was usually sufficient to dominate it. This group of 11 men made by-laws, rules and regulations; it could amend the constitution; it appointed the three-man commission for life terms; it could supersede any state committee, and its members served for six-year terms. The three commissioners actually ran the Gadar Party—and one of them usually did most of the work. It selected its own officers, president, secretary and treasurer, who served the Panchayat in those capacities. The commission was also empowered to "appoint its agents abroad and to issue credentials to such agents."

For a short time following the adoption of this constitution in 1928, its provisions were, to some extent, followed. But as time went on the entire direction of the party fell upon one man, whose activities will later be discussed in detail.

Immigration Status of Gadar Party Members in California

From the Immigration and Naturalization Service it was learned that under the Immigration Act of 1917 the only Indians admitted to the United States were visitors and students whose stay was supposed to be temporary. However, the act contained a limitation of five years after which no deportation proceedings could be instituted. Many students and visitors therefore were allowed to enter the state, vanished among their countrymen for five years, and were then free to remain as long as they pleased.

In 1924 the law was changed to remove the five-year statute of limitations against deportation proceedings, so any Indian who entered subsequently to 1924 could be sent back at any time. Under these conditions it would appear that the Indian population would steadily decrease. But while there has been some change in that direction, it was not so pronounced as might be expected, since many entered the state illegally and when the older residents returned to India for visits their younger relatives frequently assumed their identity and entered the state unnoticed. Thus the Immigration Service cites the example of one Dalip Singh, "who entered the United States in 1907 and returned to India in 1925, taking all his old papers with him. These papers he gave to his nephew, who assumed his identity. When he had smuggled into the United States and was questioned by immigration officers he produced the papers of his uncle. Sometimes this resulted in a man 20 years old claiming to be 40, and the burden was on the government to prove he was not the person he claimed to be."

The Immigration report continued: "It was found necessary to combat this deception in nearly every case when the Indian was arrested by having an investigation conducted by the British authorities in the man's native village in India. It was not long before the Indians were able to overcome this obstacle. This was done by immediately writing to their home village when they were arrested, bail being placed by the Gadar Party. The story was then arranged for in their home village. In many cases the only officer in that village is a native, and probably a kinsman of the person under investigation. In time these investigations in India began to give negative results.''

Several Indians who came into California illegally have become wealthy, and aroused the envy of many of their countrymen. They have been subjected to attempts at blackmail, and coerced through threats to inform the immigration authorities that unless the victim paid for his continued residence his illegal immigration status would be disclosed. As will be seen, ths practice gave rise to small but potent ''thuggee'' groups that murdered potential informers for a price. There has been a tendency to attribute this long record of unsolved murders in Cali-. fornia to the Gadar Party on the part of law enforcement officers, but, as far as can be determined from all existing evidence, this blanket charge is without foundation.

On April 25, 1944, a check of the records in the Sacramento office of the State Department of Criminal Indentification and Investigation revealed the following open homicide cases, all involving Indians, most of whom were Gadar Party members:

1925.   Juala Singh murdered. Body found in brush near Walnut Grove on October 29, 1926.

1927.   Bhala Singh, disappeared. Made numerous loans to friends and associates. Was kept under the influence of liquor for two weeks, then taken to a hospital. Was never seen again after his friends removed him from the hospital.

1927.   Amar Singh, disappeared. Went out to start irrigating pumps on his ranch near Biggs, California, at 3 a.m. in July of 1927, and was never seen thereafter.

1928.   H. R. Mehra, murdered. Shot and body thrown in a river. Discovered on May 29, 1928. Reported to have assisted in the murder of another Indian, and was insisting on payment of the money promised him for his part of the job.

1929.   Naranjan Singh, Fresno. Originally reported as a suicide, but it was later learned that three days before his death decedent drew $5,000 from the bank for the purpose of financing a trip to India.

1929.   Kishan Singh, murdered. Body discovered in a pond near the Santa Fe depot in Stockton.

1929.   Sher Singh, kidnapped near Butte City and never seen since. All of his close acquaintances returned to India immediately after the kidnapping and disappearance.

1929.   Dasunda Singh, murdered. Choked to death on a ranch near Marysville.

1930.   Amar Singh. A blind Indian, originally reported to have committed suicide near Yuba City. Subsequent investigation disclosed, however, that decedent had a large sum of money, which was claimed and taken by a friend.

1930.   Buja Singh, alias Daku Singh, murdered. Choked to death near Walnut Grove in August, 1930.

1930.   Bola Singh, murdered. Shot by Bosant Singh near Walnut Grove. Murderer arrested in Victoria, B. C., and committed suicide in jail.

1931. Nagani Ram Dhami, murdered. Decedent had acted as an interpreter for the U. S. Government. He was shot on a street in Sacramento by Marian Singh on February 9, 1931.

1931. Sant R. Pande, murdered. Decedent was a student at the University of California. His headless body was discovered in Cache Slough on March 3, 1931.

1943. Omar Singh, Broderick, California, disappeared. Gave information about the Gadar Party to a government agency on September 15, 1943 and has never been seen since.

From a reliable informant who has been a member of the Gadar Party in California almost since its inception, it was learned that the Gadar Party never actually ordered the murder of anyone. The informant pointed out, however, that small groups of members in California have murdered several Indians for a variety of reasons—political, for monetary gain, and to prevent the government from obtaining critical information. This statement has been verified by similar declarations by three other independent informants. One statement, taken in writing, read, in part, as follows:

"On Tuesday I went to Chico to the rice fields where they had called a meeting for the purpose of collecting $10,000—$25 from each man; they said the money was for the purpose of destroying their enemies and all those who worked against the party or for the state or federal government."

An excerpt from another written statement, taken from a separate and independent informant, read as follows:

"The next night we went to Kishan Singh's house and 14 members were sitting in the vineyard. Just they were sitting on the ground with the wine * * * I believe everybody drank wine that night, and they discussed the matter and collect the money and they gave——the job to bring Sher Singh and give the job to—— for the killing. They collect the money, about $2,000 in cash, from every person and hand over to——and they promised to pay him the rest of the money soon."

This informant continued with minute details of the attempted murder, together with the names of those present and the amounts contributed by each. Among those present on this occasion were Naranjan Singh, Joga Singh, Arjan Singh, Nidhan Singh, Bhan Singh, Kishan Singh, Sunder Singh, Kehar Singh, and sixteen others.

The Sikhs in California

Since most of the Indians in this state are Sikhs, and 85 percent of the total Gadar Party membership was comprised of Sikhs, it is important to know something of their history, religion and temperament. This is especially true in view of the fact that the Gadar Party was originated in the Punjab where the Sikhs also originated about 1500 A.D.

The Sikhs were not a nationality, but rather a religious sect bound together by additional ties of military discipline. In two wars against British troops the Sikh forces were defeated, and their home state, the Punjab, was annexed by the British as a part of their Indian domain.

Thereafter the Sikhs proved steadfastly loyal to the British Army and were used extensively throughout English possessions in Asia as soldiers and military officers by the English forces.

With the opening of the Twentieth Century there was a plague of widespread famine in India and an epidemic of mass revolt against British rule. The colonial authorities at once took drastic counter measures, and the repressive steps increased to such an extent that all India seethed with hatred of the English. It was at this time that Har Dayal launched the Gadar Party, to which he rallied Sikhs and other Indians throughout the world to help rid the country of British rule.

There is a Sikh temple in Stockton where religious services are regularly conducted, and to which the worshippers come from all over the State on religious days of special significance. Almost exclusively engaged in farming, the Sikh has, with the exception of the homicidal inclinations displayed during the period from 1930 to 1945, been a well-behaved, productive and reliable resident.

Activities of the Gadar Party

When Har Dayal inaugurated the Gadar Party in California in 1913, it operated loosely, as has been seen, issuing some propaganda material but devoting most of its efforts toward building its membership and raising funds. After 1916, however, its operation was quite different. Printing presses were set up at the Wood Street headquarters, virtually all California Indians were affiliated with the movement in one way or another, and certain revolutionary activities were undertaken on a rather ambitious scale.

While underground Gadar work caused a revolt in the Malay States, troop mutinies at Rangoon, Singapore, Cawnpore and Hong Kong in 1915 and 1916, these efforts were assisted by funds and leaders sent from the Gadar Party in California. Some of the latter were, in fact, arrested while plotting an attack against the government arsenal at Lahore. In 1918, the California Gadar Party raised a large sum for the purchase of two ships, the *Maverick* and the *Annie Larsen*. These vessels were to transport men, arms and ammunition to India for use against the British. The plot was discovered, arrests were made, and among the 30 defendants who were found guilty were the German consul and vice consul in San Francisco. It was during this trial that Ram Chandra was killed in the courtroom by Ram Singh, as heretofore described.

According to immigration reports, the Gadar Party purchased an airplane and trained some of the members as pilots; bombs were manufactured, and on one occasion when a member of the California Gadar Party returned to India the officers there found a supply of explosives concealed in the false bottom of his trunk.

During the first world war many Gadar Party members traveled from California to Berlin. Some of them returned to San Francisco and urged active cooperation with the German war effort—not because the Gadar Party was essentially pro-German, but rather because Germany was emphatically anti-British. With the defeat of Germany the Gadar Party resumed its independent activities, continuing with the circulation of the paper, the raising of money for use in India and a loose liaison with other units and individual members in foreign countries was established.

During World War II, as has been stated, the contacts with Germany were resumed, but on a limited scale. Japan and China were Asiatic nations with whom India had much in common. The Japanese propaganda for the unification of Asia in a "coprosperity sphere" exerted a tremendous appeal—and the activities of Subhas Chandra Bose were exceedingly effective. With the defeat of the Axis powers only one great nation remained through which the Gadar Party hoped to accomplish its purpose—the Soviet Union.

Communist Infiltration of Gadar Party

The Gadar Party was a natural target for Communist infiltration. Here was a conspiratorial, highly disciplined group that was fanatically dedicated to rid India of imperialist domination. Its members were scattered throughout Canada, the United States, Africa, Asia and South America. The party was well financed and operated in secrecy. Clearly, it fitted in perfectly with Russia's post-war plans for the Communizing of Asia.

Almost from the time of its inception in California the Gadar Party membership included some highly indoctrinated Communists, but there has never been any discernible connection of any kind between the Communist apparatus in this state and members of the Gadar Party who are also known to be Communists. Occasionally an Indian Communist would appear at a front meeting, in the Communist schools, or would receive favorable attention from the Communist press in California, but these occurrences are exceedingly rare. Bipan Chandra, mentioned in the 1951 report of this committee, is an illustration of a highly placed Communist Party member who had no connection with the Gadar Party.

This pattern appeared at utter variance with usual Communist practice. In cases where the Communist was known to be a member of the Gadar Party, he would remain completely aloof from all contact with the California Communist apparatus; in cases where the Communist was not a member of the Gadar Party, his connections with the orthodox Communist apparatus were easily established. Recent investigation has apparently provided a logical explanation to this puzzling question, as will hereafter be explained.

Gadar members insist that while some of their associates in the party became highly indoctrinated Communists, they were converted in Russia or Europe; not while they were in California. With a few exceptions, this contention seems to be fully substantiated by all available evidence. After an extensive survey, an excellent report was developed by the San Francisco Police Department which stated, in part: "Thus far no information could be obtained to definitely link the Gadar Party in any way with the Communist Party."

Gadar Communist Agents

Teja Singh Azad was probably the most fiery, indoctrinated and active Communist of all. Teja, who sometimes used the name Teja Singh Giani, was born about 1901 at Aloona, Gadaspur, India, the son of Desa Singh. His real name is believed to be Samundar Singh. In 1925 Teja, who as a young man had participated in uprisings against the British, was sent by the Indian Gadar Party to attend a military school in Constantinople. It was intended that eventually he should return to train and lead a Sikh republican army of the Punjab.

Teja went to Constantinople and became a Turkish citizen, received his commission as a reserve officer in the Turkish army, and then went to Berlin for a conference with Isher Singh, who had been active in Gadar activities in California, and who was then one of the Gadar Party's most influential foreign agents. Teja had become a member of the Indian Gadar Executive Committee several years before.

From Berlin Teja went to France, and on November 27, 1929, sailed from Havre for New York on the *Isle de France*. He then went to Detroit for a conference with prominent Gadar leaders, proceeded thence to San Francisco and established himself at the Gadar Party headquarters, No. 5 Wood Street, on December 14, 1929. In the meantime Isher Singh had entered Mexico, and Teja secretly met him at a prearranged rendez- vous on the Texas-Mexican border, whereupon Isher returned to Europe.

During January and February, 1930, Teja was extremely active in San Francisco. He formed the Hindustan-American Trading Company as a cover for political activities—principally the shipping of critical materials to the Gadar underground in India. He traveled throughout the state, delivering impassioned lectures to various Gadar groups. Drawing upon his Turkish training, Teja instructed his associates in the latest techniques for the manufacture of bombs and explosives, and told them how to make poisons and blow up buildings. He persuaded the Gadar Party to buy an airplane; he installed a new printing press at No. 5 Wood Street, and continued his lectures and his propaganda activities until October, 1931.

On January 27, 1932, Teja, at the urgent request of immigration officials, departed from San Francisco on the *S.S. Rakuyo Maru*. He landed at Panama on February 12th, where he indoctrinated the Gadar Party members there with new enthusiasm, founded another cover organization—the Hindu Trading Company—collected $5,660 and then departed for a tour of duty in South America. There he continued his organizing, collected $50,000 more and returned to Europe in July, 1932.

The point in relating Teja's activities in such detail during this remote period lies in the fact that this shrewd and capable Gadar Party member, impatient with the progress being made by that organization, turned to Communism and thenceforth operated as a highly placed member of both parties simultaneously. It should be added that one of Teja's disciples was arrested in San Francisco, and among his effects were found detailed formulae and lecture notes on the making of explosives.

Nidhan Singh first came to California in 1913. Two years later he was working on the *Gadar News* in San Francisco. In 1918, he was one of the 30 defendants convicted in the espionage trial heretofore mentioned. It is highly important to note, for reasons that will be fully developed later, that while he was free on bond, Nidhan was making contact with Agnes Smedley, the Soviet agent who was to play such an enormously vital role in the Chinese Communist revolution and in softening the way for Communist revolutionary movements throughout the entire area of the Far East.

After serving his sentence, Nidhan devoted most of his time to Gadar activities, and was elected president of the California organization in 1930. He was an ardent admirer of Teja, worked closely with him and was put in contact with Sikhs in Russia, India and Afghanistan for the primary purpose of sending more Indians to Moscow for specialized training as revolutionary activists.

In June, 1931, Nidhan was arrested by immigration authorities and charged with being an undesirable anarchist. Almost immediately pressure in his behalf was exerted by the Communist-controlled Berlin League Against Imperialism and its American counterpart, the International Labor Defense. The case was finally dismissed, and two years later Nidhan went to Moscow for training at the Lenin School. He is now a Communist member in the Punjab Assembly, having been elected to that highly important position during the general election of 1951-52.

Achar Singh China came from Afghanistan to California in 1927 or 1928 and, like the other members of this minority group of Gadar Party members, went to Moscow for Communist training in 1932. After completing his course there, he returned to San Francisco via Berlin in July, 1934. He tried to recruit the Gadar members at No. 5 Wood Street to Communism, and, like the others, toured the state making inflammatory Communist propaganda speeches. He continued this activity during most of 1935, during which time he is known to have been in touch with Gurmukh Singh in India, another Gadar who had also become converted to Communism. Achar then went to France in December, 1935, for a conference with a French Comintern agent. He is now believed, on reliable information, to be an active leader in the underground Communist Party in India.

Other members of the Gadar Party who also went to Moscow for espionage training and who vanished into the Indian Communist underground were, directly or through intermediaries, influenced by Teja. Thus Hermander Singh Sadhi, a former editor of the Gadar paper in San Francisco, went to the U. S. S. R. in 1922. Joga Singh, who ran the Wood Street headquarters with Naranjan Singh, in 1929, later graduated from the Moscow academy. In 1932, six more were recruited for Russian training: L. Singh Hundal, who had studied at the University of Washington before coming to California; Chanan Singh, a former University of California student; Harbans Singh, once head of the Gadar group in Stockton; Jaswat Singh; Achar Singh China, abovementioned; Prithi Singh Azad, who also graduated from the notorious Lenin School, and Bhagat Singh.

As late as June, 1947, Kuldip Singh, who helped with the printing presses at No. 5 Wood Street as an assistant to Keshar Singh, was surreptitiously teaching night classes at the Communist California Labor School in San Francisco—and at the same time assiduously circulated Communist propaganda material among his Gadar Party contacts.

Other Indians who, while connected in one way or another with the Communist organization, are not known to be party members, include such figures as Munsh Singh. While secretary of the Gadar Party he was also contributing articles to the Communist *Daily People's World* in San Francisco.

INDIA AND WORLD COMMUNISM

In 1853, Karl Marx wrote a series of eight articles on India for the *New York Daily Tribune*. These articles, together with a study of the correspondence between Marx and Frederich Engels, shows that the founders of Communism considered India the key to the conquest of all

Asia. These views were recently collected in a booklet, *Karl Marx—Articles on India,* printed by Jayant Bhatt, New Age Printing Press, 190-B, Khetwadi Main Road, Bombay, India, and distributed by the People's Publishing House in that city. This little booklet is highly significant for two reasons. It was originally issued in 1940, and after the successful Red revolution in China, was re-issued in 1951 and made available to Communists not only in India but throughout the world. Secondly, it has a running commentary by Rajani Palme Dutt, Communist member of British Parliament and expert on India.

In the complicated affairs of international Communism—especially since the last war, and more particularly since the war in Korea—there has been a sharp division of Communist organizations into an underground apparatus and a semi-legal organization.

Orders are directly sent to the underground by Kremlin agents. The vast above-ground organization—the actual Party members, fellow-travelers and Marxists, are kept abreast of the swiftly changing scene by the writings of such men as Jacques Duclos of France, Pieck and Eisler of Germany, and Rajani Palme Dutt of England. Thus when Dutt digs up the early Marxian material on India and the collection is republished in 1951 and then appears on the shelves of Communist book shops throughout the world, it simply means that an alert is being sounded; the signals are being called and a way is being prepared to soften up India for the kill. The committee's copy of this important publication was obtained recently at the International Book Store, 1408 Market Street, San Francisco, California.

On the heels of Dutt's booklet came a flood of propaganda pieces—most of them slanted to show that Marx had charted the path for Lenin to follow in bringing about the Russian revolution of 1917; that Lenin charted the path for Stalin to follow in establishing strong Communist bases throughout the world; that Stalin charted the path for Mao Tsetung to follow in bringing about the Chinese revolution; that Mao Tsetung has now charted the way for an Indian Communist revolution as a final step toward the Communizing of Asia.

In the booklet mentioned above Dutt says that a full study of Marx's writings "would show how continually he had in the forefront of attention the distinctive problems of Asiatic economy, *especially in India and China* (committee's italics), the effects of the impact of European economy upon it, and the conclusions to be drawn for the future of world development as well as for the emancipation of the Indian and Chinese people. This close attention is instanced by some 50 references to India in *Capital* and the considerably larger number of references in the Marx-Engels correspondence."

THE COMMUNIST PARTY OF INDIA

No report concerning the activities of the Gadar Party in California, and the extent of its Communist infiltration, can be made intelligible unless the background of the Communist Party of India is also understood, at least fully enough to show that while China was the number one target for the Communizing of Asia, India, most assuredly, is target number two. We have now considered the nest from which the most prominent Communist agents in India were hatched, and the circumstances attending their indoctrination. It now remains to describe current

Communist Party conditions in India for the purpose of relating that situation to the international Communist strategy and the activities of not only the Gadar Party in California, but of the orthodox Communist Party apparatus in this state to further the Communizing of India by a campaign of propaganda and recruiting that is now being intensified.

Following the Marxian concept, an attempt was made in 1922 to plant a Communist organization in India, but these plans were met by the British with considerable success. The Party was outlawed and its leaders were imprisoned. Manabenda Nath Roy, one of the earliest Kremlin agents, clashed with Stalin in 1929 and was swept from power. He had been one of the founders of the All-India Trade Union Congress in 1920 and, as a Communist functionary, was well aware of the extent to which it was infiltrated. He therefore opposed it, and in 1940 was elected president of the Indian Federation of Labor.

In 1924, the Indian Communists were instructed to bore their way into all phases of local government, pursue disrupting tactics and prepare the way for a series of general strikes. At the same time the Communist propagandists were viciously attacking Mahatma Gandhi as a patriarchal despot.

By 1927, the membership of the Communist Party of India had grown so rapidly that the leaders were compelled to warn rank-and-file comrades that ''An Indian who calls himself a Communist must be a Communist like the others in the rest of the world.'' This Kremlin alarm was caused by a fear that if the party organizations in China and India were allowed to grow too fast they might develop too independently and evolve their own peculiar brand of Marxism. The iron control of Moscow must be maintained at all costs, and these vast, seething masses of Asiatic peoples had demonstrated their capacity to slowly absorb their would-be conquerors.

Divide and Conquer

It is extremely important to bear constantly in mind that in Russia, in China, in the Iron Curtain countries, the Communist technique for conquest has been precisely the same: (1) infiltration, (2) disruption, (3) coalition, (4) conquest. India presented an ideal field for the employment of this technique—and this is how it was operated. From 1922 to 1924, the Party concentrated on infiltration. From 1924 to date, on disruption. The process of forming a common Communist front from the radical wings of the dissident political elements is now under way.

The infiltration was accomplished chiefly through the All-Indian Trade Union Congress, through which an interminable series of strikes was launched. These disruptive tactics continued, while as early as 1942 the Communists (not the British) told the Hindus and Moslems through the Central Committee of the Communist Party of India: ''To the Hindu masses we must explain that what is just in the Pakistan demand, namely, the right to autonomous state existence, including the right of separation, must be conceded. * * * Similarly, we must get the congress-minded people to recognize the urgency of the congress conceding the right of self-determination of the Moslem nationalities and thus hasten the achievement of congress-league unity.'' This apparent plug for unity was actually a political wedge driven deeply between the Moslems and the Hindus—according to the old principle of ''divide and conquer.''

The hostility between Moslem and Hindu dates back to the middle ages—and it is hardly likely that the Communists, who thrive and flourish on such conflicts, would do anything but secretly pile fuel on the fire. One has only to consider the technique by which the Soviet Union has Communized the Balkan countries and China to realize that the same infallible system would inevitably be used in India. It has now passed into stage two. Next will come the effort to form radical elements in both factions and bring them together in a Communist-dominated coalition.

According to the well-known Communist writer, A. M. Dyakov, the importance of India on the time table of world revolution was recognized by Lenin, who told the third Congress of the Comintern in 1920 that the rumbles of revolution were sounding in many colonial countries and that "British rule is at the head of these countries, and their revolution is maturing in proportion to the growth of the industrial and railway proletariat, on the one hand, and to the increase and the brutal terrorism of the British—who are more frequently resorting to massacres, public floggings, etc., on the other."

In 1925, Stalin established the strategy for the Indian Communists by directing them to enter and break up the princely states and the wealthy classes. (*Marxism in the National and Colonial Question*, J. V. Stalin, 1927, page 217.) This concept was re-emphasized by Georgi Dimitrov in 1935 when he issued a Comintern directive for the establishment of united and popular fronts in all non-Communist countries. Since that time the Indian Communist Party has sent its agents into the All-India Trade Union Congress, the Indian National Congress, the Moslem League, and other organizations to start small put powerful Communist Party fractions.

By 1941, this concentrated strength in the National Congress was shown by the change toward the war. In the words of Dyakov: "In the period of the second world war the struggle against the British rule in India did not cease until the attack of Hitler Germany on the U. S. S. R., the alignment of forces in India was essentially no different from the prewar one. It was not merely a question of the National Congress refusing to render active assistance to the war efforts of Britain, but what was much more important was that until June, 1941, an antiwar mass movement was going on in India, in which workers and partisans, students and peasants participated actively. This movement was expressed in the form of strikes, in various conferences of protest against drawing India into the war and also in strike actions against the rise in prices, etc." (*New Stage in India's Liberation Struggle*, A. M. Dyakov, New Age Printing Press, Bombay, 1950.)

Emancipation of India, 1947

In 1946 the demonstrations were stepped up. Airmen and naval personnel revolted; 300,000 workers went on strike in Bombay; students incited riots and spread Communist propaganda. In March of that year Prime Minister Atlee suggested independent status for India as part of the British Commonwealth of Nations, with the Dominion split into Hindu and Moslem provinces. The Moslem League agreed in August. While the high-level political conferences were in progress, the Communists insisted on complete Indian freedom, pointing up its line with a series of strikes and riots and a heavy propaganda barrage. During the first six months there were 1,115 strikes involving a half a million workers. Says Dyakov: "The first official expression of the deal between the British ruling circles and Indian bourgeoisie and landowners was Atlee's declaration in the House of Commons on February 20, 1947, about Britian's 'withdrawal' from India in June, 1948, and the transfer of power to the Indians." (New Stage in India's Liberation Struggle, op. cit.)

The Communist Party of India, as did the Gadar Party, naturally hailed this emancipation of India as a signal victory. But the Kremlin had other ideas. From the viewpoint of the Soviet Union, the country must be kept in a state of ferment, and it was essential to keep up the old attack against "British imperialism." So, as Dyakov was forced to admit, the Indian Communist leaders were made to swallow their words of approval and "re-evaluate" the situation. He says: "* * * In June 1947, the Communist Party of India also was not able to give a corrective valuation of the Mountbatten plan and characterized it not as an imperialist maneuver but as a certain step forward. It did not immediately understand the treachery of the leadership of the National Congress and counterposed its right to its left wing as though the latter were the progressive one." (New Stage in India's Liberation Struggle, op. cit.)

By December, 1947, however, the Kremlin directives had been received, the "re-evaluation" occurred, and "the Communisty Party of India gave a correct estimate of the Mountbatten plan as a new imperialist maneuver and characterized the Nehru Government as a whole as a government of the Indian big bourgeoisie, which had entered into an agreement with British imperialism and formed an alliance with the Indian princes and landlords."

This business of a Communist Party being unceremoniously yanked back into line by Moscow is, of course, nothing new. The American Party experienced a dose of the same bitter medicine of *mea culpa* in 1945 when Earl Browder was expelled. This subject has been described in detail earlier in this report.

The Indian Party knew very well that India had, indeed, emancipated herself, as did all other informed Indians—including leaders of the Gadar Party. But Moscow's long-range designs toward the subjugation of Asia required extensive propaganda ammunition, which could hardly be found if the Indian Communists were allowed to admit that India was at last free.

Speaking of the Communist Party of India's development, Dyakov declared: "* * * The Communist Party of India, which in 1942 comprised a total of two thousand members, increased its membership to 16,-000 in 1943 and toward the beginning of 1948, to 90,000." Frequently such statistics, when cited by known members of the Communist Party are extremely misleading. In this case, however, the estimates given by Mr. Dyakov are fairly well substantiated by many non-Communist experts.

In linking the Indian situation to the Kremlin's program to subvert other Asiatic countries, Dyakov concludes: "The new stage in the people's liberation struggle in India is an expression of the sharpening of the crisis of the colonial system of imperialism after the second world war. The distinctive features of this new stage in India are, to a considerable extent, analagous to the distinctive features of the new stage and development of the liberation in other colonial and semicolonial countries. In China, Burma, Indonesia, Indo-China and the Philippines, as well as in India, not only the feudalists but even the big bourgeoisie have at this new stage gone over even more openly to the camp of imperialism."

And he concludes thus: "The world-historic victory of the Chinese people, and the formation of the People's Republic of China, the uprising in Burma and Malaya, the struggles of the peoples of Viet-nam and Indonesia, the strengthening of the anti-imperialist camp headed by the Soviet Union are causing alarm among the native and foreign exploiters of the Indian popular masses and are strengthening the determination of the fighters for a people's democracy in India." (*New Stage in India's Liberation Struggle,* op. cit.)

Rajani Palme Dutt, whose comments about Marx's views on India have already been mentioned, wrote another propaganda booklet called, *The Situation in India,* which was issued at the Khetwadi Main Road Press, Bombay, in 1950. On pages 6 and 7 he sums up the role of Indian in the implacable Communist plan for world domination by quoting Lenin:

"Already in 1923, 27 years ago, Lenin wrote of the decisive majority of mankind, represented by Russia, China, India and the colonial people and the guarantee of the victory of world socialism: 'In the last analysis, the upshot of the struggle will be determined by-the fact that Russia, India, China, etc., account for the overwhelming majority of the population of the globe. And it is precisely this majority that during the past few years has been drawn into the struggle for emancipation with extraordinary rapidity, so that in this respect there cannot be the slightest shadow of doubt what the final outcome of the world struggle will be. In this sense, the complete victory of socialism is fully and absolutely assured'."

"Last year," continues Dutt, "on the thirty-second anniversary referring to this prediction of Lenin, we were able to celebrate the completion of the victory of the Chinese People's Republic under the leadership of the Chinese Communist Party.

"Today the alignment of India, even under the government which was set up by imperialism to serve as its satellite and protegé, can no longer be counted on by the Anglo-American block, and has taken, under the overwhelming pressure of popular anti-imperialist feeling, the first hesitant steps toward association with China and the Soviet Union in opposition to the latest decisions of the Anglo-American block on Korea and on the Acheson plan for wrecking the United Nations.

"New currents are stirring in India. The mighty example of the victory of the Chinese Republic is exercising its profound effect on all the colonial and semicolonial countries of Asia in the imperialist orbit, and not least on India. The war of aggression of western imperialism against the Korean people has aroused the outspoken anger and indignation of the widest sections of opinion in India."

These confident words of prophecy by Lenin were written about a year before he died—and at a time when the ponderous social and political world forces were quite different than they are in 1953. There were no purges of the old bolsheviks under Lenin—no insatiable thirst for personal power at any price. There was a Cheka, or Soviet secret police which

Lenin used as a bloody instrument of terror to crush the counter-revolutionary forces, but it was not used to perpetuate him in power as an absolute dictator.

Neither was there any regime by terror in satellite nations—no mass rumblings of counter-revolution. Today the Lenin prophecy about the peoples of Asia being a solid, invincible force to communize the world is demonstrably untrue. Red China is just commencing to have troubles from within, and there are large numbers of Chinese on Formosa who can hardly be termed pro-Communist. As the Balkan countries have a Tito, and as China has a Chiang, so will India have a staunch anti-Communist whose followers will far outnumber the agents of the Kremlin. For fact cannot be changed by propaganda—and without being apologetic about British imperialism, until India gets a taste of the Moscow variety, it hasn't seen anything yet.

With India bounded on the north by countries that are wholly Sovietized, like China and Tibet, and semi-Communized countries like Iran and Afghanistan, and with the U. S. S. R. itself abutting on Kashmir—the situation at the present time is indeed critical. But that question, as well as the counter-measures that are being taken, belongs in a later section. Here we are chiefly concerned only with the Communist Party of India as an organizational entity, the activities of which we must understand in order to appreciate the dangers inherent in a group of Indian internationalists operating through such a medium in California as the Gadar Party.

For many years the Party headquarters in India was at Bombay. So were the Party bookstores, the Party press and the Party propaganda machinery. Subordinate units are located at Madras, Travancore-Cochin, Bengal, Pakistan, Bihar, Punjab, Travancore, Uttar Pradesh, Amritsar and Nepal.

Communist bookstores in India are situated as follows:

In Bengal, the National Book Agency, Ltd., 12 Bakim Chatterjee Street, Calcutta 12. In Bihar, the People's Book House, opposite B. N. College, Bankipore, Patna. In Bombay, the Current Book House, Lotus Buildings, Hornby Road, Bombay 1; People's Publishing House, 190 B Khetwadi Main Road, Bombay 4; People's Book House, 278-9 Narayan Peth, Laxmi Road, Poona. In Madras, New Century Book House, 199 Mount Road, Madras 2. In Punjab, Quami Kitab Ghar, Rainak Bazaar, Jullundur City. In Travancore, B Silvilinganathan, Bhuthapandy, Nagercoil. In Uttar Pradesh, Adhunic Bastak Bhander, 7 Albert Road, Allahabad; Delhi Book Centre, 269 Irwin Road, New Delhi; Progs (Book Corner), 122 Municipal Market, Con. Circus, New Delhi; People's Book House, 7 Bishweswarnath Road, Lucknow.

From these stores the propaganda literature gushes forth in an ever increasing torrent—but the main stream divides and redivides until the small, steady rivulets reach the railroad station bookstands, the trade union offices, the front organizations, the student groups, and finally the tiniest party cells—as is the Communist system the world over.

The names of the leading Gadar members who were active in California and who, becoming impatient, went to Moscow for training, have already been given. Some of these activists were trained at the Lenin School, some at the Frunze Military Academy, others at the Far Eastern University and the special Oriental School at Baku.

It will help us to understand something about the Oriental patience and capacity for complicated, long-range planning on the part of those master strategists of the Kremlin if we know that as early as 1921 an entire section of the Red Army General Staff College on Vosdivzhenka Street in Moscow was established under General Snessarev to study the problem of infiltrating and communizing India, Tibet, Iran and Afghanistan. This was considered as an extremely long-range undertaking, in view of the powerful British control in those areas. But the Comintern wanted the precious oil of Iran and the control of the strategic Indian Ocean. A Pan-Hindu Revolutionary Committee was established in the Comintern and functioned in deep secrecy for several years—even conducting its own special military intelligence school. The president of this committee was Tivel, the former secretary of Zinoviev, which is an indication of the important character of the project.

Among the Americans who played important roles in preparing the way for Communist domination in India were, Alexander Bittleman, Jack Johnstone, Frederick Vanderbilt Field and Phillip Jaffe.

Communist Agents in India

From Tibet, Burma, the Malay States, Indio-China, Red China, Iran and Afghanistan, Communist agents have easy access to all parts of India, spreading the web, sowing the seeds of revolution. They, these roving agents, are working with the older functionaries, who include the following:

G. M. Adhikari, editor of the Indian Communist Party's official paper, *People's Age,* since 1943. He holds a science doctorate from Berlin University, has been a member of the Communist Party of India since about 1925 and is the author of several propaganda pieces.

Muzaffar Ahmed, one of the founders of the Communist Party of India, is most active in Bengal.

A. S. R. Chari, an industrialist, contributing pieces to the *People's Age* and also to the Communist London *Daily Worker.* He is a former member of the Communist Party of India Central Committee.

Shripat Amrit Dange, president of the All-India Trade Union Congress in 1949, and a member of the executive committee of the World Federation of Trade Unions. He is also a member of the Bombay Legislative Committee and of the Politburo of the Communist Party of India. Dange was born in Bombay in 1900, and during his student days became editor of a weekly newspaper devoted to the propagation of Marxism during the mid-twenties. He has served as assistant secretary of the All-India Trade Union Congress, is one of the founders of the Communist Party of India, has been frequently imprisoned and in 1945 led the All-India Trade Union Congress delegation to attend the World Trade Union Congress. He attended meetings of the Executive Committee of the World Federation of Trade Unions at Moscow in 1946 and in Paris in 1947. In the summer of the latter year, he visited both in the Soviet Union and Yugoslavia.

Sardar Sohan Singh Josh, is a Communist Party leader in the Punjab where he was formerly editor of a Communist weekly paper. During the latter part of 1952 he was reliably reported to have been elected as a Communist member to the Punjab State Assembly.

Som Nath Lahiri, the only Communist member of the Indian Constituent Assembly. He is a graduate of Calcutta University, edited a Bengali daily paper, and was formerly counselor of the Bangal Corporation.

S. S. Mirajkar, vice president of the All-India Trade Union Congress, chairman of the Bombay Provincial Committee of the same congress, a member of the Bombay Municipal Corporation. He was born in Bombay province about 1900 and has been an active member of the Communist Party since about 1923, and served as an adviser to the 27th International Labor Conference in Paris in October, 1945, and was a delegate to the 29th session of the same conference at Montreal in September, 1946.

Bankivu Mukherji, a member of the Communist Party of India since about 1940 and a delegate to its first congress, which was convened in 1943. Mukherji has served as president of the All-India Kisan Sabha in 1944-1945, and is a former member of the Bengal Provincial Assembly.

B. T. Ranadive, an activist and member of the Politburo of the Communist Party of India, prominent at its first party congress in 1943, a contributor to *People's Age,* and a member of the All-India Trade Union Congress in 1946.

Teja Singh Swatantar, who is the same person as the notorious Teja Singh Azad, heretofore mentioned. Since the Gadar Party is here specifically and prominently involved, his biographical sketch, taken from official sources, is quoted in full:

"Born about 1895, Punjab. Sikh. Former member of the group in the Gadar Party which merged with the Communist Party. Attended Khalsa College, Amritsar. Received military training in Turkey and has visited the United States, South America and the U. S. S. R. Elected a Member of the Punjab Legislative Assembly in 1937. Active in organizing the peasants of the Punjab. Vice President of the All-India Kisan Sabha. Swatantar was Secretary of the Punjab Communist Party before the independence of Pakistan."

Since Rajani Palme Dutt is an expert on the Communist Party of India, here is his record, also taken from official sources:

"Vice Chairman, Executive Committee, British Communist Party. Born 1896, Cambridge, England; father was a doctor practicing at Cambridge, prominent Bengali family; mother, Swedish. Married. Attended Perse School, Cambridge; Baliol College (Scholar), Oxford, B.A. First Class Hom., classics, history, philosophy; sent down from Oxford for socialist activities, allowed to return to take degree. Secretary, International Section, Red Labor Research Dept., 1919-1922; charter member, British Communist Party, 1920; Editor, *Labor Monthly,* which he founded in 1921 (banned during World War I); Chairman, Communist Party Reorganization Commission, 1922; member, Communist Party Executive Committee since 1922; Editor, *Workers' Weekly,* 1922-1924; a member, Executive Committee, Communist International, 1935; Editor, *Daily Worker,* 1936-1938; contested Sparkbrooke, Division of Birmingham as Communist Party candidate, 1945, endorsed by G. B. Shaw; now member Political Committee and Chairman, International Committee of the British Communist Party. Published numerous books including *The Two Internationals,* 1920; *The Labor International Handbook,* (edited, 1921);

Modern India, 1926; *Fascism and Social Revolution,* 1934; *India Today,*
1940. Has visited U. S. S. R. on numerous occasions. Lived in
Sweden and Belgium because of poor health for a number of years
prior to World War II. Active worker for Indian independence;
spent four months in India for the London *Daily Worker.* Became
general secretary of the British Communist Party in Pollitt's place
during early period of Nazi-Soviet alliance. Doctrinnaire Marxist
intellectual. Chairman, British Empire Communist Party Conference, London, February, 1947; French Communist Party Congress,
Strassbourg, June, 1947.''

SOVIET POLICY ON INDIA

One great obstacle in the path of the Kremlin effort to Communize ·
India has been the British control of that country. Prior to the last war
British power was much too strong. Now that Great Britain has been
weakened, her withdrawal from India has largely removed the last great
barrier in Russia's determined scheme to seize that country.

This conclusion is amply corroborated by an evaluation of the sort of
propaganda material that has been issued on an ever increasing, indeed
unprecedented, international scale since 1947. This propaganda content
may be seen from even a superficial examination of the Cominform bulletin from Budapest; the publications of the World Federation of Trade
Unions; the special publications issued by the Communist Party of
China as guides for the Indian comrades; the articles, booklets, pamphlets and leaflets distributed by propaganda units throughout the
world and especially in California.

During the secret negotiations between the U. S. S. R. and Nazi
Germany in 1940, Russia's designs on India were disclosed. Most of the
negotiations were conducted between Molotov and von Ribbentrop. On
November 12, 1940, Molotov arrived in Berlin and shortly thereafter a
draft treaty was concluded; there was, however, a secret protocol which,
according to David Dalin in his book, *Soviet Russia and the Far East,* Yale
University Press, New Haven, 1949, was to "fix the spheres of influence
of each of the four powers. * * * The sphere of the Soviet Union was
described as follows: 'The Soviet Union declares that its territorial
aspirations center south of the national territory of the Soviet Union in
the direction of the Indian Ocean.' ''

Now that Great Britain has granted independence and dominion
status to India, and with the division of that country into two armed,
antagonistic groups, conditions are ripe for revolutionary activity.
Hence the Kremlin's Chinese agents were ordered to invade Tibet while
the UN forces were pinned down in Korea. We protested and backed up
our objection with force when Korea was invaded, but we sat weakly by
as the Chinese Communists invaded Tibet and subjugated her by force.
Afghanistan has also been heavily infiltrated, and many of the former
Gadar Party members who were Moscow-trained have been active there
and in Iran.

Soviet-Indian Missions

While the U. S. S. R. has been surrounding India on the northeast and
west, she has simultaneously been sending missions into the country and
inviting large delegations of Indians to China and Russia. Originally,

these Soviet delegations were linked to the All-India Trade Union Congress, but since 1949, they have assumed a cultural tone.

Thus, in the summer of 1952, Nikolai Tikhanov headed a Soviet delegation to participate in the First Indo-Soviet Cultural Congress at Bombay. At this meeting a constitution was drafted for the "all-round promotion of closer cultural relations between the Indian and Soviet peoples." Dr. A. V. Baliga, famous Indian surgeon, was elected chairman of the organization's national council of 64 members after the congress had been opened by the temporary chairman, Professor Deshmukh, former mayor of Bombay.

One of the principal addresses was delivered by Harindranath Chattopadhayaya, "who is well known in the Soviet Union as a poet, actor and public leader." An excerpt from his speech shows why he is regarded so favorably by the Kremlin.

> "I have been in the Soviet Union, a country that is molding a new type of man. We were shown everything we wanted to see. The whole pattern of life in the Soviet Union is shaped to promote man's good, and friendship between the Indian and Soviet peoples, but our friendship can no more be prevented than the tides of the sea can be stopped."

The account of the affair, taken from *New Times,* No. 28, July 9, 1952, Soviet propaganda organ, describes the experiences of the Soviet delegation during a tour.

> "As representatives of Soviet culture we were given the friendliest reception everywhere we went. Particularly memorable was the welcome we received in Amritsar. Our cars could hardly make their way through the streets, which were thronged with people eager to greet the representatives of the land of socialism. Shouts of 'Long live Indo-Soviet friendship! Long live Stalin!' could be heard everywhere."

"* * * A message of good will to the Soviet people from the people of the Punjab" was adopted when the Soviet group visited in that region.

In describing the trip to Amritsar, Capitol of East Punjab, the *New Times* article revealed the utter hypocrisy of the Communist Party line toward India. Earlier in this section of the report it was shown how the partition of India into Hindu and Moslem groups was enthusiastically advocated and supported by the Communists. Now, hear this:

> "We were surprised to find it (Amritsar) full of ruins, as though pitched battles had been fought there. This, we were told, was the result of Hindu-Moslem massacres provoked by the British after the partition of India. Indian progressives, its artists among them, are doing much to expose the intrigues of the British and American imperialists who are artificially inciting discord between India and Pakistan."

At Madras, the Soviet writer says, another rousing welcome was accorded his delegation. Similar enthusiasm for Iron Curtain life was met at Bombay, Delhi and other towns. In fact, according to the *New Times* writers. "Everywhere we were keenly aware of the irresistible urge towards knowledge, progress and culture; we saw how eager the Indians were to give expression to their creative power, how strong their desire for peaceful, constructive labor, for the preservation of peace.

> "To millions of Indians the Soviet Union is the symbol of a better future. Many people we spoke to said with emotion, "Russia has shown us the way. The Soviet Union is the country where the future has become the present'."

It strains credulity to imagine many Indians stepping forward to the visiting Soviet agents of Communist culture, and uttering this neat, well-rounded phrase: "Russia has shown us the way. The Soviet Union is the country where the future has become the present." If the late Lincoln Steffens had stepped up and said, describing his trip to the U. S. S. R., "I have seen the future and it works," it would seem natural. He *did* make that statement in England not long after the revolution. But Steffens was thereafter an ardent pro-Communist, and as a professional journalist such phrases were his business. The phrases, in fact, are curiously similar.

During the winter of 1951-1952, an Indian international film festival was attended by representatives of the Soviet motion picture industry. (New Times, No. 30, July 23, 1952, page 25.) This delegation included Leonid Varlamov, A. Sologubov, G. Monglovskaya, and I. Sokolinkov. They made use of their visit by turning out a documentary film on a journey from Bombay to Madras and thence to Delhi and Calcutta, with frequent side trips to pick up shots of rural squalor.

Among the Indians who were mentioned as most cooperative with the visiting Communists were: Professor Mukerjee; Chandraleksha Patel, the dancer; Ghosh, the film director; and "Harindranath Chattopadhayaya, whom we had met during his visit to the Soviet Union," and who played a leading role in the cultural congress above-mentioned. The New Times account of this affair stated:

> "Again and again, in our talks with India's film people, we felt what a burden their far from equal 'cooperation' with Hollywood was to them and how glad they would be to get rid of it. The American film companies have India's national film industry bound hand and foot. For example, the use of technicolor is now barred to the Indian film maker. The screen is swamped with Hollywood films although many of them are definitely disliked by the audiences. Indian films and actors, on the other hand, are exceedingly popular. The shots we made in Delhi of an original parade of Indian film actors, which attracted many thousands, are evidence of this.

> "Everywhere we went we found a deep regard for the Soviet people, and there were unforgettable scenes in some of the villages. The people would learn in advance, in some miraculous way (sic), of the coming of the Soviet delegation and thousands of them, carrying portraits of Lenin and Stalin, would turn out to give us a joyous welcome. Our cars would be surrounded by a solid wall of villagers pressing upon us modest gifts of coconuts and lemons.

> "The film actors on our delegation, Vera Maretskaya, Alexander Borisov and Pavel Kadochnikov, were greeted like old and close friends. In Calcutta we saw portraits of Stanislavsky, Memirovich-Danchenko and Vakhtangov, the famous Soviet stage directors; in Madras actors discussed with us the work of Einstein, Gerasimov,

Romm, and Alexandrov in the cinema. In Bombay we saw the live sale books about the Soviet Union have.

" 'There is nothing surprising about this,' Chandralekhapatel told us. 'Life in Russia, the country where all working people are free and happy, interests all honest people in India—all who believe in India's happy future'."

If the motion pictures made in America and exhibited in India are of the same variety as those shown in other foreign countries, the Philippines, for example, it is little wonder that they are relatively unappealing to the average Indian. Most of them depict an America populated by gangsters, drunks, semiliterate millionaires, juvenile delinquents, western outlaws, cheap politicians and women of easy virtue. The Soviet Union, quick to take advantage of this condition, has carefully sent pictures that depict the emancipation of the Russian peasants; pictures with a high propaganda content based on the class-struggle theme. These Russian pictures are semidocumentary. Industrial and agricultural developments, cultural and scientific progress—however distorted for propaganda purposes—are heavily emphasized, while the written propaganda stresses the glorious emancipation of the Chinese people and the foul designs toward India of the decadent American and English imperialists.

Strikes, Riots and Murder

Labor strikes have always been, and will continue to be the chief weapon in the Kremlin arsenal for use in non-Communist countries. "Every strike," said Lenin, "is a tiny revolution," and on the American scene we have observed ample evidence of how the strike can be manipulated by shrewd Communist specialists to widen the breach between the workers and the management, to accelerate the class struggle, to bring new recruits into the party from the ranks of labor. In California there was the infamous San Francisco general strike of 1934; the North American Aircraft strike in 1941; the motion picture studio strike in 1945—all used by the Communist Party for its own subversive purposes.

Since the war the Communists have been fomenting a series of strikes to whip up dissatisfaction with the new government of India—and, of course, in cold disregard of the consequent disruption of the national economy and suffering by the people.

Thus early in February, 1947, a dispatch from Bombay to the Communist newspaper in San Francisco described a general strike in the Cawnpore industrial region by 100,000 Communist-led workers, and the government simultaneously exposed a plot to sabotage Indian railroads.

In June, 1949, a Communist-inspired strike resulted in fighting with police at the Bengal Potteries Factory, and 13 days thereafter, mass attacks against police headquarters were launched near Sarampore.

When looting and other crimes reached epidemic proportions at Hyderabad, the Communists bitterly attacked the Indian government for failing to send troops to restore order; when the troops arrived, the Communists switched completely and launched a vicious propaganda crusade against a fascist regime which sought to enforce its will on the people by armed force.

The Indian Ministry of Information recently issued a booklet entitled, *Communist Violence in India*. It cites documented examples of murder, sabotage, kidnapping, robbery and the fomenting of a long series of violent strikes and disorders. These predatory raids were made by Communist guerrilla forces and were staged for three primary purposes: (1) field training in the guerrilla tactics so successfully used by the Chinese Reds; (2) to terrorize anti-Communist elements; (3) to seize loot, arms and ammunition.

In a series of Communist Party documents seized by Indian government authorities, all doubt is removed concerning the use of violence, the guerrilla tactics, the terrorism and the precise conformity to the pattern for revolution as prescribed by Mao Tse-tung in the propaganda material heretofore described and issued by the Chinese Communist Party. One such booklet, called *Course for the Cadres of the Shock Brigade*, instructs these party activists as follows:

"The guerrilla activities mean the *raiding* of the police station; ambushing police parties to anihilate and collect arms from them; *sabotaging* the enemy's communication lines, cutting of telephone and telegraph lines for isolating the enemy; *attacking* the enemy with great surprise from his rear, flank and unguarded or weak spots to delay and wear him out and to beat and destroy him, and lastly establishing independent operating bases in various parts of the country." (Committee's italics.)

On February 28, 1949, the Prime Minister, Jarwaharlal Nehru, stated to the Constituent Assembly:

"The Communist Party of India has, during the past year, adopted an attitude not only of open hostility to the government but one which can be described as bordering on open revolt. This policy has been given effect intensively in certain limited areas of India and has resulted in violence, indulging in murder, arson and looting, as well as acts of sabotage. The house is well aware of the Communist revolts that have taken place in countries bordering on India. It was presumably in furtherance of the same policy that attempts were made in India to incite people to active revolt.

"The Communist Party of India has recently concentrated on the issue of a general strike on the railways as well as other essential services of paramount importance to the community. It has looked upon these strikes not from the trade union or economic point of view, meant to better the lot of the workers, but as a weapon designed to create a chaotic state in the country, which, it is thought, would help the party to gain its other objectives, whatever they might be. It is deliberately seeking to create famine conditions by paralyzing the railway system, so that foodstuffs should not be transported, the object being to create a general background of chaos, a breakdown of the administration and mass uprising. A large number of Communist Party members have gone underground and the government have a mass of evidence in their possession to indicate that organized attempts are being made to conduct campaigns of sabotage, more especially on the railway system. The permanent way was to damage, locomotives interferred with, and general sabotage of vital installations, telephones, telegraph and power stations were aimed at. Honorable members will remember the destruction of the Calcutta Telephone Exchange some time ago.''

Mr. Nehru, in the concluding portion of his remarks, demonstrated that Communist tactics are basically the same in India as elsewhere in the world—and that they must be dealt with firmly and courageously. He said:

"* * * The Communist Party of India * * * appears to be bent on flouting the opinion of the majority of workers and has pursued a technique of terrorizing those who do not agree with its policy. While interfering with the freedom of action of others, it demands full freedom for itself to carry out its own anti-social and disruptive activities. If any action is taken by the government to check these activities, protests are raised on the ground that civil liberties are being interferred with. As a part of this technique, organizations for the ostensible object of protecting civil liberties are started, their real object being to encourage these antisocial activities. The government are anxious that the civil liberties of the people should be fully maintained. But it is not the government's conception of civil liberty to permit methods of coercion and terrorism to be practiced against the general community.

"In furtherance of this policy, the government have arrested a number of the members of the Communist Party of India and have taken such other precautionary measures as they deem necessary. They have advised provincial governments to do likewise so as to insure that vital installations are protected against sabotage. They have no doubt that in doing so they have the full support of the country and of this House, which is wedded to democratic procedure and is entirely opposed to methods of violence.''

When, in 1942, the Communists suddenly achieved an open status, they found themselves in a rather embarrassing position: by being devoted to Russia they were forced into an allegiance to Britain—the very thing the Congress Party detested—and which, of course, led to a breach. Here was the Indian Communist Party that had been emitting torrents of abusive propaganda against the hated British imperialists and urging complete Indian independence, suddenly becoming allied with the U. S. S. R.—and Britain. When the war ended in 1945, most of the world's Communist Parties were regarded at least as collaborators —but the Indian comrades were darkly viewed by their own countrymen as traitors.

Lamely, the Indian Communists again commenced to damn their erstwhile ally, Great Britain, and hailed the Nehru regime, but the mass political memory in India was not caught short; the Communists, even at best, were then and still are evaluated as utterly unreliable. They were unceremoniously chucked out of the Congress Party.

There then came a remarkable occurrence; one that removes any vestige of lingering doubt concerning the complete hypocrisy of all Communist parties. In 1947, India won her freedom, and Nehru headed a new government. The time for treading easily had passed; now it was expedient for the Indian Communists to unleash an era of open, active, defiant revolution. This, indeed, was almost exactly paralleled in America where Browder, the capitalist collaborator, was expelled and replaced by Foster, the militant Marxist.

In India Joshi had been leading the party softly from 1936 to 1947. Now, however, it was time to change the party line; so, at the Indian Communist Party's second congress, out went Joshi and in went Rana-dive, the advocate of direct and militant action. Once again Nehru became a villain, and the Party propaganda began to extol the heroic "people's" liberation movements in China, Indonesia, Burma and Ma-laya. But this carefully planned regime of violence and terror frittered out. Late in 1949, Moscow launched a new "peace crusade," based on the Stockholm peace appeal. The militant Ranadive was not the proper leader for this sort of thing, so out he went and in came Rao with orders to concentrate on underground subversion with an accompaniment of terroristic tactics where they would do the most good.

CHINESE PATTERN FOR INDIAN REVOLUTION

It is necessary to understand that as the Russian Revolution of 1917 provided a master plan of strategy to be studied and followed by the Communist parties of the world, so the experiences of the Chinese Com-munists provide a pattern for the colonial and semicolonial Communist parties throughout Asia. The textbook, *History of the Communist Party of the Soviet Union,* is the international Communist authority on tactics and strategy for revolution. The writings of the Chinese Red leaders pro-vide the blueprint for revolution in Asia—and particularly India.

The following booklets, all obtained from Communist bookstores in California, prove their value to Indian Communists in unmistakable terms, and all of them were also sold in the Indian Communist bookshops. They are:

(1) *Strategic Problems of China's Revolutionary War,* by Mao Tse-tung, May, 1951. First Indian edition printed by Jayant Bhatt at the New Age Printing Press, 190-B Khetwadi Main Road, Bombay 4, and pub-lished by the People's Publishing House at the same address.

(2) *Aspects of China's Anti-Japanese,* by Mao Tse-tung, People's Pub-lishing House, Bombay.

(3) *China's New Democracy,* by Mao Tse-tung, 1951. People's Publish-ing House, Bombay.

(4) *On the Party,* by Liu Shao-chi. People's Publishing House, Bombay, 1951.

(5) *Lessons of the Chinese Revolution,* by Mao Tse-tung and Liu Shao-chi. People's Publishing House, Bombay, 1950.

(6) *Chinese Revolution and the Communist Party of China,* by Mao Tse-tung. People's Publishing House, Bombay, 1950.

(7) *Stalin on China,* People's Publishing House, Bombay, 1951.

All of this literature stresses the Russo-China bloc, the organization and discipline of the Communist Party of China, the strategy and tactics of revolutionary warfare, the freedom and democracy of its Communist regime, the decadent and imperialist nature of the Anglo-American capitalists. It is also significant that this propaganda material, written in Moscow and China, reprinted in India, distributed through the propaganda channels in that country, is now being distributed in the

Communist bookstores throughout the United States. This, of course, can only mean that the American Communist Party is being alerted for the purpose of playing its assigned role in the global strategy pointed toward the eventual Communizing of all Asia. Here are some excerpts from the foregoing sources that are now being studied by the Communists of India and the United States.

From *Lessons of the Chinese Revolution,* by Mao Tse-tung and Liu Shao-chi, People's Publishing House, Bombay, 1950:

"This experience of China's revolutionary victory is very important for the people of the countries which are still under the rule of imperialism and their domestic reactionaries. That is to say, the characteristic of armed struggle which appeared in the course of China's revolution can, under certain historical conditions, become the common characteristic of all revolutions of other colonial and semicolonial countries. This has been explained in the *Outline for the Colonial and Semi-Colonial Revolutionary Movement* issued by the Sixth Congress of the Communist International in August, 1928.

"* * * It becomes absolutely clear that the characteristic of an armed people opposing armed counter-revolution does not pertain to China's revolution alone. Under the present conditions, it can and should become the common characteristic of the liberation struggle waged by many colonial and semicolonial peoples."

The Cominform Bulletin of January 27, 1950, is cited as follows:

An editorial published on January 27, 1953, in *For a Lasting Peace for a People's Democracy,* organ of the information bureau of the Communist and workers' parties, commented that, "The path taken by the Chinese people, as Comrade Liu Shao-chi noted, 'should be the path taken by the people of many colonial and semicolonial countries in their struggle for natural independence and people's democracy.' The editorial further pointed out:

" 'As the example of China, Viet-nam, Malaya and other countries shows, armed struggle is now becoming the main form of the national liberation movement in many colonial and independent countries.'

"It went on to stress the significance of China's revolutionary experience for India. After the publication of this editorial, Ranadive, General Secretary of the Communist Party of India, issued a statement expressing 'full acceptance of the conclusions drawn by this editorial.' He added:

" 'Under the leadership of Comrade Mao Tse-tung the Chinese Communist Party has successfully applied the teachings of Lenin and Stalin in the course of the victorious liberation struggle of the Chinese people. The lessons of this victorious liberation struggle of the Chinese people will serve as an infallible compass for the Indian Communist Party and working class, which are responsible for the task of leading the national liberation struggle'."

From *China's New Democracy,* by Mao Tse-tung, Bombay, 1950, People's Publishing House. On the inside front cover of this item, appears the following:

''*Lessons of the Chinese Revolution,* by Mao Tse-tung and Liu Shao-chi. This booklet contains three important documents: (1) *Introducing the Communist,* by Mao Tse-tung; (2) *On the Party's Mass Line,* by Liu Shao-chi; (3) *An Armed People Oppose Armed Counter-Revolution,* by Editor, *People's Daily,* Peking.

''All the three documents deal with the question: what is the correct path of national liberation for the peoples of colonial and semicolonial countries?

''The valuable experience of China, which has successfully overthrown the imperialist-feudal yoke, is obviously indispensable for the people of India, whose problems and tasks are to a great extent similar to that of the Chinese people.''

THE GADAR PARTY IN CALIFORNIA—1945-1953

All members of the Gadar Party in California, as elsewhere, were pledged to do anything necessary to bring about the freedom of India from British domination. As we have seen, this led to anti-British cooperation with Germany during World War I and to anti-British cooperation with the Axis powers in World War II. Since 1945, it also led to active cooperation with the Soviet Union, which had for its major objective an intensive anti-British, anti-American campaign during the postwar period to undermine the prestige of those powers among the peoples of Asia. Russian propaganda linked Great Britain and the United States together as imperialist warmongers intent on ruthlessly exploiting Asia for their own financial gain. Added to this highly successful campaign was the fact that the Kremlin had shown the Chinese Communists how to stage a successful revolution—and urged the Indian people to use the tactics of the Chinese Reds in an all-out effort to produce the same result in India.

This appeal was extremely effective with the Gadar Party. Huge sums of money were raised and sent to Gadar underground agents in India—most of whom were also Soviet agents. This dual allegiance was well known to the leaders of the Gadar Party in California, who have frankly admitted that since Russia was working to free India it was only natural that these two movements, the world Communist organization and the Gadar Party, should, to some extent, join forces. The two movements were strikingly similar in many respects. Each was a secret, conspiratorial movement with international affiliations; each was comprised of a disciplined, highly trained membership fanatically dedicated to the achievement of the same objective—but for very different reasons. In addition, the Gadar Party and the Communist Party each had a powerful underground organization of activists scattered throughout India. Communist agents were far more numerous, of course, and had been carefully placed in strategic positions in Tibet, Iran, Malaya, Indonesia, Burma, Afghanistan and other critical areas. Furthermore, the Communists controlled an enormous propaganda machine that was of incalculable use to the whole joint undertaking.

We have already explained, in tracing the rise of world Communism, how news of the Russian Revolution of 1917 electrified the radical wing of the American Socialist Party and convinced its leaders that only through the practical application of Marxist principles: discipline, force, militant strikes and violent revolution, could its objective be attained. The radical wing of the Russian Social-Democratic Party had used Marxism as its guide, and Lenin added his own concept of a disciplined elite group of fanatic activists and his own concept of Communist strategy. The winning of the revolution in Russia convinced American radicals that here, at last, was the tried and tested recipe for success, and the way was thereby opened for the creation of the Communist Party of the United States.

The Communist revolution in China electrified radical elements throughout Asia precisely as the Communist revolution in Russia had electrified American radical elements. Its effect was most successful, however, on the people of India and especially on the radical element in the Gadar Party.

Lenin School Graduates

In California, several prominent members of the Gadar Party, impatient and restive at the delay in attaining any practical success in the drive to emancipate India, turned to Communism and urged the entire membership to do likewise. Led by the fiery Teja, several members left for Moscow to take the four-year course at the Lenin School, which since 1926 has been operated as a university at which selected party members are trained in the fine arts of sabotage and espionage.

This academy of treason has produced some noted graduates. From the United States: Steve Nelson, Marcel Scherer, Loretta Starvus Stack, Rudy Lambert, Eugene Dennis, Harold Ware, Ben Gold, James Ford, George Siskind, Clarence Hathaway, Mrs. Earl Browder. From England: Rajani Palme Dutt, Harry Pollitt, William Gallacher, Arthur Horner, Emile Burns, William Rust. From China: Mao Tse-tung, Liu Shao-chi, Chu En-lai. From Korea: Kim Il Sung. From India, by way of California, Teja and his followers. Graduates of this huge Red school are the real leaders of the world Communist movement, chosen because of their special talents for subversion, and intensively trained in Communist politics and ideology before they are given the special courses in train wrecking, street fighting, guerrilla tactics, underground organization, disruption of transportation and communication systems, contamination of food and water supplies, and the extremely refined and delicate art of espionage.

This was the academy, then, to which Teja and his group were sent for special training. Some of them later returned to California to secure additional recruits from the ranks of the Gadar Party, but the majority were sent to provide leadership for the Communist underground in India. As will be seen, however, the vast majority of Gadar Party members in California viewed these Communists agents with considerable suspicion. The older members in particular were apprehensive that if they permitted large numbers of their colleagues to operate under the iron discipline of the international Communist apparatus they might succeed in throwing off British control only to find India firmly lodged in the iron clutches of the Kremlin—thus exchanging one form of domination for a far more ruthless and complete domination by a totalitarian dictatorship.

So the Gadar leaders in San Francisco agreed to supply Teja with funds but firmly refused to turn control of their organization over to the Communists. They believed that Teja's group of underground Kremlin agents (who still maintained their Gadar membership) had developed excellent facilities for disseminating anti-British propaganda, as indeed was true. The fact that these dual agents were also using funds from Gadar members in California to spread anti-American propaganda was immaterial and completely subordinate to the main objective. The sole purpose of the Gadar Party was to achieve the freedom of India, and during this era it was quite aware that the Soviet Union had the same purpose. Very well, they would collaborate—but not to the extent of submitting to Communist control of the Gadar Party itself.

While the funds were being sent to Teja it was necessary to maintain a liaison between the Gadar officials in San Francisco and the Communist underground in India. From time to time secret meetings were arranged —surrounded with all the necessary ingredients—precautions against detection, elaborate preparations to provide a safe means for the transfer of the funds. In some instances counter-intelligence work emerges from its prosaic and often painstaking routine of research, checking, following of leads and sheer tedium and assumes elements of intrigue and secrecy that far exceed the fiction writer's concept of such subjects. This was true of certain aspects of the links between the Gadar Party and the Communist underground in India. It was also true of certain aspects of the FAECT espionage operation in Berkeley, and especially true in connection with certain phases of the murder of Everitt Hudson. All of these subjects were discussed in the previous reports of this committee. It is plain, however, that the more interesting and colorful elements in such cases usually are obtained through sources that cannot, for a variety of good reasons, be revealed. Consequently, they cannot be included in a public report, although, it may be said parenthetically, they certainly provide intriguing material for discussion among those who work together on such cases.

In 1946, the Indian Communists decided to send their ace propagandist to California in the person of one Fazal Ilahi Qurban, who had been directing underground activities in the Punjab. He delivered speeches in San Francisco, Sacramento, Stockton and Fresno, advocating closer cooperation with the Soviet Union, urging Gadar members to join the Communist Party, asking for more funds. His propaganda technique was good, but not good enough to sway the Gadar officials, who were becoming concerned at the intensified efforts to communize their entire movement.

Qurban declared that the Indian Congress was much too weak to bring about the unification of India; he insisted that the Communist-dominated All-India Trade Union Congress was the proper instrument through which to work together with the heavily infiltrated Moslem League, and that these two organizations provided the only media through which the country could be unified—naturally with Communist assistance. He gained a few converts, but only a few; and when he departed the situation remained much the same. The Gadar Party would continue to send funds; it would maintain its liaison with the Communist agents in India, but there the collaboration ended.

Then, in 1947, India won her freedom and became part of the British Commonwealth of Nations. Nehru headed the new government and the wave of Communist strikes, riots, sabotage and disruption was once more unleashed. The Party line had to be changed a bit, too. This was not emancipation, said the Communists. This was only a ruse engineered by the Anglo-American imperialists. They had divided the country into Hindu India and Moslem Pakistan. American money would be used to enslave the Indian people more ruthlessly than ever. Then came demands for more money from Teja and his Soviet agents to the Wood Street headquarters of the Gadar Party in San Francisco. The demands were accompanied by letters explaining the new party line and declaring that the fight to free India from the grip of the Anglo-American imperialists must be prosecuted with renewed vigor.

. This frantic effort to continue Gadar support was, of course, to be expected. After all, the Gadar Party had been operating on a far-flung basis since 1907—10 years before the revolution in Russia, almost 20 years before there was a Lenin Academy for espionage specialists. The Gadar members were highly respected by the masses of India, while the force and violence tactics of the Indian Communists, the contradictory course of their party line and their obvious control by a totalitarian power had all combined to weaken their prestige. Gadar members had been executed, imprisoned and driven underground during the long battle against British control. Gadar agents had been strongly entrenched in carefully prepared positions before Teja had even started his freshman year at the Lenin School. Wealthy Gadar Party farmers in California had provided huge sums for the Indian Communists, to whom it was extremely important that this situation be continued.

Liquidation

The old wooden structure at No. 5 Wood Street became a scene of acrimonious debate. Communist agents, in person and by letter, insisted that the relationship be continued, that India was far from free, that more and larger sums be raised. The older Gadar officials contended that their work was ended; their objective at last realized, and proposed that the Gadar Party be liquidated. They pointed out that, after all, dominion status placed India in the same political position as Canada; that India had formed her own government, and had her own diplomatic representatives. The fact of the matter, they declared, was that India *had* been emancipated, and fact was much more convincing than propaganda.

In addition to these convictions, the wiser and older members of the Gadar Party had grown weary of the long struggle and had few illusions concerning the Soviet Union's long-range scheme for a Communist revolution in India, Chinese style; and they had taken a long and sober look at what had happened behind the Iron Curtain. They wanted India free, but permanently, not temporarily.

Shortly after India had been formally established as a dominion and had appointed her diplomatic representatives, 30 influential Gadar Party members met at the Wood Street headquarters and unanimously voted to disband the organization.

When this news reached the Communist underground contacts in India violent letters of protest were received from Teja and two of his agents.

Gurmukh Singh and Nidahm Singh. These gentlemen were informed that the decision would stand. Messages of protest and a variety of pressure tactics persisted until 1951, when a carefully drafted announcement was published in the *Phulwari,* an Indian newspaper of general circulation at Jullundar, stating that the Gadar Party had disbanded and had no connection whatever with any other political organization. The statement was also carried by several other Indian papers of general circulation, copies of which are in the possession of this committee, together with the English translation of the article.

In December, 1947, another resolution was passed to the effect that the Gadar Party should offer to donate its Wood Street premises to the new Indian Government together with a sum of $10,000 which had been raised by popular subscription to renovate and modernize the building. The offer was made to Prime Minister Jawharlal Nehru and the Indian Ambassador to the United States.

The older Indians in California wished the Indian Government to preserve the building as a memorial and to use it as a cultural center, while younger Indians suggested selling it and sending the proceeds to some school, library, or similar institution in India. The Gadar Party complied with the wishes of its older members, since they were the persons who had raised the funds with which the premises were acquired in 1917 and had guided the destinies of the Gadar Party in California since its inception.

On July 25, 1949, S. K. Kirpalani, Indian Consul-General in San Francisco, notified the former Gadar Party leaders that their offer had been accepted and that the building would be kept, either as a residence for government representatives or as a cultural center. In July, 1952, the formal conveyance of transfer was completed.

CONCLUSION

While the Gadar Party was being disbanded, the Indian Communists were meeting with stiff opposition from Nehru's government. In the elections of 1951-1952, they met with little success, although from those parts of the country where their strength was most concentrated they managed to elect formidable slates of candidates. It is from the underground apparatus, however, rather than the relatively small fragment of the exposed portion of the party, that the most trouble can be expected. The Soviet Union is far from infallible in its subversive strategy, and the most powerful weapon against it consists in spreading accurate information about its now-familiar tactics as widely as possible among the people.

Meanwhile, the Soviet Union is hammering home the idea that Asia must be solidified to resist the imperial designs of Great Britain and the United States—and this campaign is meeting with considerable success.

India's first general election following her independence was commenced in the autumn of 1951 and completed in May, 1952. Communist candidates received about 5 percent of the total vote, which gave them 27 representatives in Parliament and 180 in the State Assembly. The next general election will not be held until 1956, and in the interim the Communist underground will be vastly strengthened and prodded into increased activity. This prediction is amply corroborated by the vastly increased propaganda material now being culled from far-flung international sources and distributed to Party members everywhere. The stacks of this material—all carrying the same line—are increasing every day in the Communist bookstores of California.

What is the relation of all this to current Communist activities in California? The significance is of enormous practical importance. From this material we learn that the Communizing of India stands in a position of highest priority on the Communist agendum of world conquest, a matter that certainly *should* be of prime significance to all of us. We also know that from the Indian population of California important Communist agents were recruited and are now working with fanatic dedication and renewed vigor to sow the seeds of revolution in India. We also must realize that these agents still have valuable contacts in this state, and now that the Gadar Party has disbanded, are already working to fill that vacuum by setting up a new organization through which to raise funds and recruit new agents. This situation must, therefore, be closely watched and publicly exposed before it can solidify.

Perhaps the most important conclusion to be drawn from this section of the report on the Gadar Party is that one can never hope to cope with a local problem until one is thoroughly familiar with its international implications. For Communism is not local; it is a global conspiracy, and every local activity is fitted neatly into the master plan. It is relative simple for any investigator worthy of the name to assemble information concerning Communist activities, but it is quite another matter to intelligently evaluate that information, draw the proper conclusions from the assembled facts and determine on an adequate and practical plan of counter action. And this is true no matter what phase of Communist activity one may be investigating.

Are we concerned with educational infiltration in California? Very well, we must then know something about the background of Abram Flaxer in New York and the United Public Workers of America, of which he is president. We must also know about Dr. Langford's instructions to Communist teachers about the reorientation of their courses along Marxian lines. We must know about the World Federation of Trade Unions and the International Federation of Teachers Unions.

Are we concerned with trade union infiltration? We must then turn to the Profintern, to the Party's Trade Union Commission in the United States and once again to the World Federation of Trade Unions.

Are we concerned with Communist youth activities? We cannot possibly deal with this problem unless we know that the Labor Youth League was preceded by the American Youth for Democracy, and that it was in turn preceded by the Young Communist League—and that all were simply parts of the Young Communist International, a section of the Comintern.

Clearly, then, one cannot adequately prepare to meet a situation such as threatened attempts to recruit party agents and raise funds from the Indian population of California unless one is familiar with conditions in India and with the history of Gadar Party activities in this State.

As matters now stand, the Gadar Party has been disbanded. It collects no dues, it holds no meetings, it sends no funds to India, it issues no propaganda, it has given its old Wood Street headquarters to the anti-Communist Indian Government. Its leaders have steadfastly resisted the demands of Teja and his followers, and their anti-Communist attitude has been established beyond doubt.

The fact remains, however, that the Indian Communists will not quit trying to raise financial support and recruit potential agents from our Indian population. Experience has demonstrated that Lenin School graduates do not give up so easily.

FRONT ORGANIZATIONS

In its 1951 report, this committee devoted considerable attention to the major front organizations which were operating most extensively in California during the years 1949 to and including 1951. They are as follows: The National Lawyers Guild; the Civil Rights Congress; the National Congress of Arts, Sciences and Professions; Scientific and Cultural Conference for World Peace; American Continental Congress for World Peace; Committee for Peaceful Alternatives to the Atlantic Pact; American Peace Crusade; Emergency Conference on World Peace and China; Committee for a Democratic Far Eastern Policy; American Committee in Aid of Chinese Industrial Cooperatives; Bill of Rights Conference; National Committee to Defend the Twelve Communist Leaders; International Workers Order; Congress of American Women; National Council of Soviet-American Friendship; Joint Anti-Fascist Refugee Committee; School of Jewish Studies, and Union of Progressive Veterans.

The most effective weapon that can be used to combat the activities of these camouflaged Communist fronts is public exposure. While too much publicity is not, at this phase of counter-Communist activity, desirable in the handling of educational infiltration, it is of enormous benefit in dealing with the fronts. Throughout all the years of its existence this committee has uniformly followed the consistent practice of giving this subject the most widespread publicity, and in 1948, devoted an entire report to the subject of front organizations.

We have heretofore pointed out that in addition to the major front groups that occupy the attention of all official agencies investigating the problem and which have been in existence for a number of years, there are also innumerable smaller front organizations that are created almost overnight to spread propaganda, attract recruits and to raise funds for Party purposes. These organizations come and go, but they are inevitably operated by the same trusted handful of Communist experts. For the purpose of conducting a field study of the activities of these groups, the committee presents herewith some of the material from its files concerning the operation of these fronts, most of them relatively small in number and short-lived, but some of them being merely local subdivisions of parent national organizations.

SAN FRANCISCO HEARING ON FRONT ORGANIZATIONS
SEPTEMBER 11 AND 12, 1951

For the purpose of pursuing its practice of publicly exposing the activities and identifying the officers of the major front organizations operating in the San Francisco Bay region in 1951, the committee held a two-day public hearing at the San Francisco City Hall on September 11th and 12th of that year. The organizations investigated were: (1) Committee for a Democratic Far Eastern Policy, 935 Market Street, San Francisco, Room 307. (2) California Labor School, 321 Divisadero Street, San Francisco. (3) American-Russian Institute, 101 Post Street,

San Francisco. (4) East Bay Arts, Sciences and Professions Council, 1740 University Avenue, Berkeley. (5) East Bay Civil Rights Congress, 1740 University Avenue, Berkeley.

As will be readily seen from the excerpts of the transcript of this hearing, hereinafter quoted, most of the witnesses were exceedingly hostile toward the committee, were accompanied by attorneys who themselves had long records of affiliation with Communist front organizations, and followed the well-known Party directive by refusing to answer all questions concerning the front organizations to which they were affiliated on the grounds that if they gave truthful answers to such questions they would subject themselves to possible criminal prosecution.

The hostile witnesses, so-called because of their obvious refusal to answer pertinent questions propounded by the committee, were: Dr. William Berke, Eloise Brown, Torben Deirup, Ernestine Gatewood, Alice Hamburg, Rose Isaak, Edith Jenkins, Judith Kerner, Holland Roberts, Decca Treuhaft and Bette Sue Wallace. Witnesses who appeared pursuant to subpena and cooperated with the committee were: Norman Miller, Aaron Sargent, Thomas E. Stanton, Jr., and Earl S. Wilson.

Alice Hamburg

The first witness to be examined was Mrs. Alice Hamburg, who was accompanied by her attorney, Joseph Landisman. In response to preliminary questions, Mrs. Hamburg testified that she had resided at 682 San Luis Road in Berkeley for approximately three years and prior to that time had resided at Los Banos where her husband, Samuel, was engaged in farming activities. The Hamburgs, she said, came to California in 1924 from South Dakota. She had also resided at 547 Spruce Street in Berkeley. She stated that she was executive secretary of the East Bay Council of the Arts, Sciences and Professions, and that its office was located at 3015 Shattuck Avenue in the City of Berkeley. Despite her attempts at evasion, which are obvious from the transcript, she gave the committee considerable information of prime importance. Note, from the excerpt below, how she said that she "supposed there would be a recording secretary," connected with the organization, and later admitted that she, herself, acted in that capacity.

"Q. (By Mr. Combs): And do they maintain, as far as you know, any office personnel, secretarial help, or anything of that sort?

"A. As far as I know they do not.

"Q. No secretarial help at all?

"A. You—do you mean paid help?

"Q. No, I mean—I didn't say paid help; secretarial help, paid or unpaid.

"A. Well, every organization has a secretary; I mean all the organizations I have ever been acquainted with, like the PTA's.

"Q. Does this one?

"A. Yes, it has.

"Q. Does it; one or more persons?

"A. Secretary—now, let's see. I suppose there would be a recording secretary, for instance.

"Q. Do you know what duties the recording secretary performs?

"A. Well, taking notes, I imagine, of the meetings.

"Q. Keeping a list of the members?

"A. I don't believe so.

"Q. Is any list of members kept?

"A. Well, I think so. I think that as far as I know it operates as an open and above-board organization, and I really don't know any reason why the list of members should not be kept.

"Q. Well, I don't either. I am just trying to find out if there is a list kept.

"A. Yes.

"Q. And where is the list kept? 3015 Shattuck Avenue?

"A. I imagine so. I really haven't any access to it, so I don't know.

"Q. Do you have any connection with the organization yourself?

"A. Yes, I have. I am the recording secretary."

Mrs. Hamburg explained that she had been engaged in the capacity of recording secretary, attended meetings of the organization's executive committee and generally attended to the secretarial affairs of the organization for about a year and a half. She said that the members of the executive committee comprised six or eight persons but her memory became faulty when she was questioned concerning their identities, although she did state that the executive director of the organization was Mr. Henry Rubin, who resided in Berkeley and was also an ex officio member of the executive committee. When pressed further she also stated that Sandra Cooper did some secretarial work for the organization, was a member of the executive committee, and that so were Barbara Sicular, Dr. Martin Abel and Mrs. Jean Ryden. Treasurer of the organization, she explained, was Mr. Louis Gottlieb.

The East Bay Council of Arts, Sciences and Professions, Mrs. Hamburg declared, held cultural and educational meetings from time to time and sponsored speakers from various places in the Bay region and elsewhere to address the guests and members of the organization. Having laid this foundation, the committee then proceeded to question Mrs. Hamburg concerning the various meetings and functions in which she had participated.

"Q. (By Mr. Combs) : Now, were any functions for the East Bay Arts, Sciences and Professions Council held at your home, Mrs. Hamburg?

"A. I have had a meeting at my house at which we had a speaker; I don't know whether you'd say it was officially sponsored by the ASP, but a number of people who were interested in having a meeting thought it might be nice to have it in a home.

"Q. When was that?

"A. I can't tell you the exact date, but it was some time during the month of July—let's see, it was during the summer, and I can't tell you the exact date.

"Q. This year?

"A. Yes, this year, this summer.

"Q. Who was the speaker?

"A. The speaker was John Howard Lawson.

"Q. Mr. Lawson was then residing in Southern California, was he not?

"A. I don't know very much about Mr. Lawson, but I believe he does.

"Q. How were the arrangements made for Mr. Lawson to speak at your house?

"A. That I can't tell you, I'm sorry. You would just have to get the information from Mr. Rubin, because I was simply asked if I could have a meeting at my house and I said yes. I was very much interested in hearing Mr. Lawson speak. I had never heard him before, so we had the meeting, but I had nothing to do with the arrangements.

"Q. I see. You had meetings in your home addressed by Mr. Paul Robeson?

"A. I'm sorry, but I have not, no. I never have. I have had meetings sponsored by the American Friends Service Committee and the PTA.

"Q. Have you attended meetings in Alameda County at which Mr. Robeson did speak?

"A. In Alameda County, meetings?

"Q. Yes.

"A. I don't recall. I don't know what would be so bad about it. I think Mr. Robeson is a very good singer. I have heard him in concert. I don't believe I have ever heard him speak.

"Q. Never heard him speak?

"A. Well, you know a singer does announce the names, titles of songs, and does say something, you know.

"Q. Yes, Mr. Robeson quite frequently says something.

"A. Yes, but I enjoy his voice primarily, singing, very much.

"Q. Now, are you acquainted with David Jenkins?

"A. David Jenkins? He has been pointed out to me various times.

"Q. Do you know him? Have you met him?

"A. Oh, I think I met him a long time ago. I haven't seen very much of him recently.

"Q. Now, have you ever had any functions in your home in Berkeley for the benefit of the California Labor School?

"A. A long time ago——

"Q. At 547 Spruce Street?

"A. Well, you people have very fine records.

"Q. Thank you.

"A. In 1944, I believe it was, we had an affair at my house.

"Q. December 17th, wasn't it?

"A. You are much better than I am.

"Q. Wasn't that about right, late in 1944?

"A. I really don't remember the date.

"Q. It was an afternoon cocktail party, wasn't it?

"A. I don't think it was a cocktail party. As I remember, I think it was a sort of get-together. I didn't have anything to do with refreshments, other people did. I think it was rather a nice afternoon, as I recollect.

"Q. What was the nature of the refreshments, if you recall? Cocktails?

"A. Well, I was not in charge of the refreshments, and I don't remember, I am sorry.

"Q. All right. Now, among those who sponsored the meeting—and this may refresh your memory somewhat—were Professor and Mrs. Leo Rogan of the University of California who reside on Keith Avenue in Berkeley——

"A. I don't recall that at all.

"Q. Do you know Professor Rogan?

"A. Well, I hope to meet him some day.

"Q. Do you know him?

"A. He's dead, unfortunately.

"Q. Did you know——

"A. Not very well.

"Q. You did know him, didn't you?

"A. Well, I was an economics major at the university. I never was fortunate enough to have a course——

"Q. You still haven't answered the question.

"A. Did I know him?

"Q. Yes.

"A. I knew just about everybody in the economics department over there. I knew who he was.

"Q. Did you know him?

"A. What do you mean by knowing him?

"Q. Have you ever met him?

"A. I don't believe I met him. I'm sorry, I think I had a passing acquaintance with everybody in the economics department——

"Q. Now, you say you had the acquaintance of everybody in the economics department. He was in it, so you knew him?

"A. If that's what you mean, if I knew——

"Q. Did you know Professor and Mrs. Edward G. Rowell?

"A. Did I know them? Yes, I have known Mrs. Rowell for some little time.

"Q. They sponsored this benefit for the California Labor School that was given at your home in Berkeley, did they not?

"A. Yes. You really have much more information about that than I can remember.

"Q. Now, do you know Mr. Sidney Roger?

"A. Yes, I have heard Sidney speak.

"Q. You say you know Mr. Roger?

"A. Yes, yes.

"Q. How long have you known him, about?

"A. I think I met him in 1944, about, probably, but I don't see him very often.

"Q. Was he at this party?

"A. I believe he was.

"Q. He is sitting right behind you, isn't he? Isn't that him right there (pointing).

"A. Oh, yes, I didn't know he was there.

"Q. You recognize him?

"A. Yes."

Pursuing this line of questioning, Mrs. Hamburg was brought back once more to her testimony concerning Paul Robeson.

"Q. (By Mr. Combs) : Now, in the following year, 1945, Mrs.
Hamburg, a reception was given for Paul Robeson at 605 Wood-
mont Avenue, Berkeley, for the benefit of the California Labor
School. Did you attend that function?

"A. Well, I was there part of the time. I wasn't able to attend
the whole meeting.

"Q. Who lived there then?

"A. I don't know. I think it was the Chevalier home.

"Q. Haakon Chevalier?

"A. Yes, I think so. I wasn't there much of the meeting. I missed
Mr. Robeson's singing unfortunately."

And having elicited this information, the witness was asked about yet
another meeting of the same general type.

"Q. (By Mr. Combs) : Now, Mrs. Hamburg, you attended another reception honoring Paul Robeson at 2860 Shasta Road,
Berkeley?

"A. Really, I have forgotten.

"Q. At the residence of Mrs. Helen Freeland Gibbs?

"A. I suppose—you have the information.

"Q. And did he speak or sing, or both, on that occasion?

"A. Well——

"Q. Do you recall?

"A. Well, it was very hot that evening——

"Q. You have an excellent memory if you remember the tem-
perature.

"A. I remember I had to go out of the room, and I actually
couldn't hear him. I was very sorry.

"Q. Well, you don't know whether he sang, spoke, or both?

"A. No, I don't, but I think he sang.

"Q. You don't think he spoke?

"A. I don't know. Singing is louder. I was outside.

"Q. Mr. Roger was there on that occasion, wasn't he?

"A. I don't remember.

"Q. Did you know Nathan Yanish or Yannish?

"A. Did I know him?

"Q. Yes.

"A. Well, I have met him.

"Q. Do you know where he is now?

"A. I haven't the slightest idea.

"Q. Barbara Sicular, you remember her being present on that
occasion?

"A. No, I don't.

"Q. Theodore Gorbacheff?

"A. I don't know.

"Q. Mrs. Brodeur?

"A. I don't know her.

"Q. Goodman Brudney?

"A. No, I don't know.

"Q. Mrs. Hamburg, do you remember a function which was given
on June 1st, 2d and 3d of this year at the Rockridge Women's Club?

"A. Yes.

"Q. 5582 Keith Avenue near College?

"A. Yes, I referred to that when I mentioned tickets, the sale of tickets.

"Q. That's the one you sold the tickets for?

"A. Yes, that was a festival and arts show.

"Q. You attended it, didn't you?

"A. Yes.

"Q. How was the sale of tickets? Was the show pretty well patronized?

"A. Fairly well.

"Q. What did they sell for, how much per ticket?

"A. Some $1.20 and some 60 cents apiece.

"Q. How many people present, just a rough approximation?

"A. You mean one affair?

"Q. The entire affair.

"A. Well, I would say eight to nine hundred people. There were three days. There were different affairs, different activities.

"Q. Now, Earl Robinson participated in the entertainment?

"A. Yes.

"Q. And the Mimi Kagan dancers?

"A. Yes.

"Q. And the California Labor School Chorus?

"A. Yes.

"Q. And Mr. Paul Jarrico was there, too?

"A. Yes.

"Q. Did you know him previously?

"A. No.

"Q. Did you know his wife, Sylvia?

"A. No.

"Q. Do you know anything about Mr. Jarrico's profession?

"A. No, I think he is connected with the movie industry.

"Q. In writing, acting, or what?

"A. I don't know, I am sorry.

"Q. Now, these functions were given for the benefit of the California Labor School, given for the benefit of the California Labor School in Oakland or San Francisco, if you know?

"A. In Oakland, as I recall.

"Q. And that was located on Broadway?

"A. Yes. I don't recall the address.

"Q. Have you ever been up there?

"A. I was up there once, I believe.

"Q. Now, Mrs. Hamburg, who was the head of the California Labor School at Oakland at the time these functions were given? Was that Mr. Hursel Alexander?

"A. I don't think so.

"Q. Do you know?

"A. I think Gordon Williams.

"Q. You mentioned him previously in your testimony?

"A. Yes, you asked me about him. I said I had met in 1944.

"Q. All right. I believe that's all. Witness excused."

Readers of this portion of the report are respectfully directed to the names of the individuals concerning whom this and the other witnesses were questioned. As the documented information unfolds concerning front activities in Alameda County it will be noted that the names of these individuals appear over and over again with almost monotonous repetition as the leading participants in this important phase of the Communist Party's activity in the East Bay area.

Torben Deirup

The next witness to appear before the committee at the San Francisco hearing was Mr. Torben Deirup, 1629 Josephine Street, Berkeley, accompanied by his attorney, Mr. Richard Gladstein. Deirup had formerly resided at 1317 Cornell Street in Berkeley, had lived at 1034 Ninth Street in Albany and is a native Californian, having been born at Chico.

The witness testified that his wife's name was Anne Weymouth Deirup, the daughter of Professor Frank Weymouth, formerly on the faculty at Stanford University and now teaching in Los Angeles. The relationship between the two families was further solidified by the marriage of Professor Weymouth to Torben Deirup's mother.

During 1945 and 1946, Mr. Deirup served in the United States Army and the committee was interested in ascertaining the accuracy of its information concerning his attendance at the California Labor School under the GI Bill of Rights. That portion of the transcript reads as follows:

"Q. (By Mr. Combs): Now, after you were discharged from the army, did you go to school under the GI Bill?

"A. No.

"Q. You didn't?

"A. No.

"Q. Didn't you attend the California Labor School?

"A. Oh, I'm sorry. I—I—I think on that question I will have to take advantage of my privilege to refuse to answer the question on the ground it might incriminate me.

"Q. Have you discussed it with Mr. Gladstein?

"A. (Consulting with counsel): I will not answer any questions in regard to the California Labor School.

"Q. For what reason?

"A. On the grounds it might tend to incriminate me.

"Q. All right. Now, according to the information the committee has, Mr. Deirup, you not only attended the California Labor School under the GI Bill of Rights, but after you had taken instruction there, you taught a class in the school in 1950. The name of your class was 'Science and Society,' is that correct?

"A. I refuse to answer for the same reasons."

Since issuing its 1951 report the committee received abundant evidence of the fact that the Communist newspaper, *Daily People's World,* was no longer being distributed to undercover members of the Communist Party but was delivered by courier in bundles to certain trusted individuals and by them distributed to the persons who were eventually to receive the individual copies. The committee was also informed that Mr. Deirup was one of the persons in Berkeley to whom bundles of this newspaper were regularly delivered for such distribution. Accordingly he was questioned as follows:

"Q. Is it not a fact, Mr. Deirup, that you receive a bundle of *Daily People's Worlds* that is delivered to your residence at 1629 Josephine Street in Berkeley every day, a bundle containing four copies of the paper?

"A. I will refuse to answer that question.

"Q. On what grounds?

"A. On the ground that it might tend to incriminate me."

This witness also proved to be far less cooperative than his predecessor on the witneess stand, Mrs. Hamburg, because when asked by the committee whether or not he was a member of the East Bay Council of the Arts, Sciences and Professions Council he also declined to answer that question on the ground that he might incriminate himself. He had pursued the same tactics when questioned about his affiliation with the Civil Rights Congress, the Young Communist League, American Youth for Democracy, and certain specific meetings the committee was reliably informed that he had attended.

"Q. Now, did you ever hear of an organization known as the Young Communist League?

"A. I refuse to answer that question.

"Q. Whether or not you ever heard of it?

"A. On the grounds it might tend to incriminate me.

"Q. Is it not a fact that you were a member of that organization as of the twenty-ninth day of May, 1943?

"A. I will refuse to answer that question for the same grounds.

"Q. Is it not a further fact that on the twenty-ninth day of May, 1943, you drove your automobile, which in that year bore license number 9X2180 to a closed meeting of the Young Communist League at the Sons of Herman Hall, 12th and West Streets in Oakland, and that while there and in attendance at that meeting you conferred, among other people, with Lloyd Lehman and Wilhelmina Loughrey?

"A. I refuse to answer the question.

"Q. On what grounds?

"A. On the ground that it might tend to incriminate me.

"Q. Is it not a fact that on the twenty-second day of August of 1943 you drove the same automobile to a party for the benefit of the *Daily People's World* at Paris Park in the City of Albany, and while there you conferred with the following people: Herbert Kalman, Herbert Naboisek, and Ruth Brudney?

"A. I refuse to answer the question on the ground it might tend to incriminate me.

"Q. Is it not a fact, Mr. Deirup, that on the tenth day of October, 1943, you drove in the same automobile to the residence of Jacqueline Griffin, 272 Coventry Road, Berkeley, California, where you attended a function for the purpose of raising funds for the *Daily People's World*?

"A. I refuse to answer the question on the ground that it might tend to incriminate me.

"Q. All right. Is it not a fact that on the fifteenth day of December, 1943, you drove in that same car to a closed meeting of the trade union section of the Communist Party of Alameda County at Party headquarters in the City of Oakland, and at that time and place the other people who were present were Bernadette Doyle, Steve Nelson, Herbert Kalman, Jack Manley, Ruth Brudney and Carl Shirek?

"A. I refuse to answer the question.

"Q. On what grounds?

"A. On the grounds it might tend to incriminate me.

"Q. Is it not a fact, Mr. Deirup, that on the twenty-first day of November, 1943, in the same automobile you drove to the Oakland Auditorium Theater at 12th and Fallon Streets in the City of Oakland, and there attended a celebration of the tenth anniversary of the recognition of the Soviet Union by this country, an affair sponsored by the Council for American-Soviet Relations? The affair started at 8 p.m. in the evening and Anna Louise Strong was the principal speaker. Others spoke briefly. Earl Robinson, Frank Manley, Frank Parsons, Professor Ralph H. Gundlach, Nathan Yanish, Anthony Jurasek, Wilhelmina Loughrey——

"A. I refuse to answer the question on the same grounds.

"Mr. Combs: Mr. Chairman, insofar as the records of this committee are thoroughly documented concerning some of the individuals whose names I have read, I believe it would be proper for us to comment on those names concerning which there is proof in the record adduced at previous hearings, so some of these people can be more readily identified.

"Frank Parsons has been before the committee and admitted his Communist Party membership. Nathan Yanish was formerly connected with the *Daily People's World* and arrested recently for Communist activities. Wilhelmina Loughrey has been before the committee and has identified herself as a member of the Party and the owner of premises at Orinda where, according to the testimony of Paul Crouch last year, he lectured at a school of the Communist Party. Mrs. Loughrey also has admitted that she was in charge of the Twentieth Century Bookshop, the place where Communist literature is disseminated in Berkeley near Sather Gate; and Professor Ralph H. Gundlach was a teacher at the University of Washington, who, in 1948, with Professor Herbert H. Phillips, was discharged for Communist activities. Mr. Robinson, of course, is in all of our reports.

"Q. Mr. Deirup, the next question is this: Is it not a fact that on the thirtieth day of January, 1944, you drove the same car to a meeting which was held at Danish Hall, 164 11th Street in Oakland, to a function which was given by the Communist Party of Alameda County for its members and its friends, and among those present with whom you conferred were Ruth McGovney, Goodman Brudney and Rose Segure?

"A. I refuse to answer on the grounds it might tend to incriminate me.

"Mr. Combs: Now, for the record, Mr. Chairman, Ruth McGovney appeared before this committee at a hearing in Oakland in December, 1947 and testified frankly that she had been a member of the Communist Party, was no longer affiliated with it, and testified at some length concerning her activities and experiences. Goodman

Brudney was arrested for contempt in Stockton, 1940, in connection with the investigation of the State Relief Administration, convicted of contempt and served a term in jail. Rose Segure was identified as a Communist Party member by her superior, Paul Crouch, who was organizer for the Communist Party of Alameda County at a time when he testified she was a member.

"Q. Now, Mr. Deirup, is it not a fact that on the twelfth day of August, 1944, you drove your same car to the residence of Herbert Kalman, 1019 67th Street in Oakland, and attended a function there with others for the purpose of raising funds for the *Daily People's World*?

"A. I refuse to answer the question on the ground it might tend to incriminate me.

"Q. And is it not a fact that on the 15th day of October, 1944, you drove the same car to the Oakland Auditorium mass meeting given to commemorate the 25th anniversary of the Communist Party of the United States? In order to refresh your memory, the principal speaker on that occasion was Mr. Robert Minor, who was then Vice President of the Communist Political Association of the United States, and others who were observed attending the meeting and with whom you conferred were Clarence Tobey, Sylvain Schnaittacher, Frank Parsons, who has been heretofore mentioned, Nathan Yanish, heretofore mentioned, Morris Smolan, David Cadel, Justice Vanderlaan, Richard Singleterry, Ruby Heide, Frank Jurasek, previously mentioned, Ruth Brudney, heretofore mentioned, Carl Shirek, heretofore mentioned, John Delgado, Rose Segure, heretofore mentioned, and Morris Marshak. Do you recall those people being present on that occasion?

"A. I refuse to answer the question on the grounds it might tend to incriminate me.

"Q. Now, in 1945, Mr. Deirup, you had another car, didn't you, other than the one I mentioned? When did you get the car that you now drive?

"A. I don't know.

"Q. You can approximate it, can't you?

"A. My memory is terrible.

"Q. I see it is.

"A. I actually don't know.

"Q. Don't you really?

"A. Oh, I imagine I got it two or three years ago. I imagine it would have been after that.

"Q. And did you in 1945, own an automobile bearing license number 9V9208?

"A. I wouldn't have the faintest idea.

"Q. You wouldn't know. Well, the record so shows. I looked it up.

"A. I have no doubt, but——

"Q. All right. Is it or is it not a fact that on May 20, 1945, you drove an automobile bearing that number to a forum meeting at the Ebell Hall, 1440 Harrison Street, Oakland, the meeting being sponsored by the Communist Political Association of Alameda County?

"A. Refuse to answer the question on the ground it might tend to incriminate me.

"Q. Now, from January 9, 1950, to and including the eighteenth of March of that year, is it or isn't it a fact that you were the co-ordinator of the Friday night forums on world news which were held at the California Labor School in Oakland, and that you there lectured on 'Science and Society'?

"A. I refuse to answer the question for the previous reason.

"Q. On the ground that it may tend to incriminate you?

"A. That's right.

"Q. Now, on June 30th, last year, you held a benefit party for the *People's World* in your own home, 1629 Josephine Street?

"A. I refuse to answer that question on the ground it might tend to incriminate me.

"Q. And that on September 3d, of last year, you also held a benefit party for the *People's World* in your home at 1629 Josephine Street?

"A. Refuse to answer the question on the ground it might tend to incriminate me.

"Q. What is your wife's name, Mr. Deirup?

"A. Anne.

"Q. I now show you what purports to be a photostatic copy, Mr. Deirup, of an invitation to the launching of the American Youth for Democracy, Y. W. C. A. Building, 1515 Webster Street in Oakland on Sunday, December 19, 1943, from 1.30 to 5.30 p.m. Did you ever hear of American Youth for Democracy?

"A. Yeah.

"Q. You have?

"A. Uh-huh.

"Q. Were you ever affiliated with it?

"A. Refuse to answer the question on the ground it might tend to incriminate me.

"Q. When did you first become acquainted with American Youth for Democracy?

"A. I haven't any idea.

"Q. You know the period of time during which it existed, don't you, roughly?

"A. It was some time ago.

"Q. Isn't it a fact that the Communist youth organization in the United States was originally the Young Communist League? It went out of business and was replaced by American Youth for Democracy, it in turn went out of business and was replaced by the Labor Youth League which now exists, is that not a fact?

"A. I don't know.

"Q. You don't know?

"A. Well, I will refuse to answer the question, I think, on the ground it might tend to incriminate me."

At this point the witness was shown a document, in photostatic form, the original having been theretofore introduced and thoroughly identi-fied and authenticated at a hearing which was held in Oakland in 1946. The document contained considerable data concerning American Youth for Democracy, together with the names of numerous individuals concerning whom this witness and also Alice Hamburg had been questioned. It also contained the name of the witness' wife, and read, in part, as follows:

"The names of the East Bay Arrangements Committee are on page 4 and are as follows: Sandra Martin, State Vice President, CIO, National Council member; Mayer Frieden, National Council member; Tom Chambers, shop steward, UERMMWA, Local 1412, CIO; George Gray, business agent, United Steel Workers of America, Local 1798, CIO; Ross Lunche, patrolman, National Maritime Union; Justin Vanderlaan, chief shop steward, IFTEAD No. 89, AFL; Jean Bryant, secretary, Shell Local, FAECT; Anne Deirup; Dash McMichael, student, Pacific School of Religion; George Williams, instructor, Starr King School for the Ministry; Vicki Landish, senior representative, Welfare Council, University of California; Charlotte Flanner, President, University of California AYD Club; Jacqueline Norman, Vice President, University of California AYD Club; Ethel Hanck; Donna Bushnell, secretary, North Berkeley AYD Club; Mitzi Cooper, South Berkeley AYD Club; Jake Price, South Berkeley AYD Club; Donna Church, committee; Herb Sacks, Alameda AYD Committee; Jack Bushnell, circulation manager, AYD *Spotlight;* Jack Fortson, Richmond AYD Committee; Jerry Hill, Sausalito AYD Committee.

"Sponsors for Northern California American Youth for Democracy included: Professor Thomas Addis, formerly a professor at Stanford University; Professor Arthur G. Brodeur; Mr. Bartley Crum, Mrs. Ruby Heide, Mr. George Irvine, Professor Alexander Kaun, Mr. Richard Lynden, Mr. Steve Murdock, Mr. Mervyn Rathborne"—Mr. Chairman, in connection with Mr. Rathborne, I think it might be well to point out that when Mr. Rathborne testified before this committee several year ago, he, among other witnesses that we had during that period, testified under oath that he had never been a member of the Communist Party. At the trial of Harry Bridges in San Francisco, Mr. Rathborne was a government witness and testified that he *had* been a Communist Party member for many years.

"Mr. Gladstein: Mr. Combs, doesn't that just prove he lied on both occasions?

"Mr. Combs: It certainly proves he lied on the first occasion, Mr. Gladstein, and also shows what kind of a person they had as a sponsor for AYD in Northern California.

"Q. Mr. Deirup, have you ever been a member of the Communist Party?

"A. I refuse to answer that question on the ground it might tend to incriminate me.

"Q. Have you ever been a member of the Young Communist League?

"A. I refuse to answer that for the same reason.

"Q. Have you ever been a member of the Communist Political Association?

"A. I refuse to answer that also.

"Q. Of American Youth for Democracy?
"A. I refuse to answer that——
"Q. All on the same grounds?
"A. On the ground it might tend to incriminate me.
"Q. Or the Labor Youth League?
"A. I refuse to answer that for the same reasons.
"Q. That's all."

Decca Treuhaft

The next witness to appear before the committee was Mrs. Decca Treuhaft, the wife of Robert Treuhaft, Oakland attorney and counsel for the Civil Rights Congress and other Communist front organizations. She was accompanied by her attorney, Francis McTernan, Jr., the brother of John McTernan, of Los Angeles, who has appeared before this committee on innumerable occasions as counsel for hostile witnesses and Communist front groups.

Mrs. Treuhaft testified that she resided at 730 59th Street in Oakland, and had lived there about a year, and had previously resided at 675 Jean Street in that city. By way of foundation, she was questioned concerning her activities and testified that in 1943, she worked for the Office of Price Administration and was also affiliated with the United Federal Workers of America, which has been prominently mentioned in this report in connection with the section on educational infiltration. She was secretary for Local 221 of that union in San Francisco.

Mrs. Treuhaft, whose maiden name was Jessica Mitford was previously married to Esmond Romilly, who served as a volunteer in the International Brigade when he was 17 years of age and went to Spain to fight for the army of the People's Republic during the Spanish Revolution.

Having volunteered this biographical data to the committee, Mrs. Treuhaft lapsed into a steadfast condition of noncooperation, relying upon the Fifth Amendment to the Constitution of the United States in refusing to answer questions about her Communist front and Communist Party affiliations on the ground that the answers might tend to incriminate her. Such responses were given by the witness when she was asked whether or not she was financial director of the California Labor School in Oakland in 1944; whether or not she was acquainted with the directors of the institution at that time: Ruby Heide, Professor Leo Rogan, Professor A. M. Kidd, Bernard Young, David Jenkins, Holland Roberts, Gordon Williams, Thomas Addis and Professor Edward L. Holme; all listed on the official documents of the California Labor School and mentioned prominently in the *Daily People's World* as having served as directors for this Marxist institution listed as subversive and Communist-dominated by the United States Department of Justice and by the California committee on numerous occasions.

Mrs. Treuhaft's specialty, according to records of the committee, was in operating the Civil Rights Congress in Alameda County. The main office of that organization in 1950 was situated at 1740 University Avenue, and we need only to cite an extremely brief portion of this witness' testimony for the purpose of indicating the type of questions she refused to answer on the ground that if she did so she would be incriminating herself.

"Q. (By Mr. Combs) : Now, in 1950, is it not a fact that the Civil Rights Congress had an office in Berkeley at 1740 University Avenue and that you were at that time designated as the Field Representative of the Berkeley chapter of the Civil Rights Congress?

"A. Decline to answer the question for the same reasons.

"Q. And that Lloyd Lehman, identified by himself when he appeared as a witness before the committee as Chairman of the Communist Party of Alameda County, worked in the office with you from time to time; the office I mentioned, 1740 University Avenue?

"A. I decline to answer for the same reason.

"Q. And that since 1950, or since May of that year, you have been the Director of the Civil Rights Congress, that is, the East Bay Civil Rights Congress, a position which you have continuously held ever since May 31st, 1950, and which you now hold?

"A. I again decline to answer for the same reason.

"Q. Now, is it not true that the Civil Rights Congress maintained a commercial checking account in the Main Branch of the American Trust Company, which is located at Center and Shattuck Avenues in the City of Berkeley, and that such account is still maintained in that branch?

"A. I refuse to answer for the same reason.

"Q. That the account opened on March 7th, 1950, and at that time you signed the application for the account as secretary, Cleophus Brown, who has heretofore been a witness before the committee, was listed as a secretary, and Kathleen Vickerson, listed as office secretary, and that any of the two of you were authorized to draw checks?

"A. I decline to answer for the same reason.

"Chairman Burns: Mr. Combs, inasmuch as those facts are evidence so far as documents or records are concerned, I think the chair should instruct the witness to answer this question regardless of the reason given on self-incrimination. I will so instruct the witness to answer the question, either yes or no.

"Q. (Mr. Combs) : Put it this way. I will reframe it. It will be a little easier for you. Did you or did you not sign the application card for the opening of that commercial account?

"A. I refuse to answer on the grounds it might tend to incriminate me."

Later in the hearing the committee produced a teller from the bank with the ledger sheets and other pertinent documentary data, together with signature card, all of which were photostated and introduced as exhibits at the hearing, and which convinced the committee beyond any question of a doubt concerning Mrs. Treuhaft's activities with the Civil Rights Congress.

By the time her testimony was nearing its conclusion Mrs. Treuhaft had established such a fixed and persistent pattern of refusing to answer all questions on grounds of self-incrimination that her responses became mechanical and automatic. Consequently, after invoking the constitutional protection and refusing to answer several critical questions, she made an amusing and ridiculous response when she was suddenly questioned about her affiliation with an obviously innocuous organization, as follows:

"Q. (By Mr. Combs): Now, do you recall attending a closed meeting of the Communist Party on January 28th of this year, 1951, a meeting which opened at 10 o'clock in the morning and closed at 5 o'clock in the evening, at 2002 San Pablo Avenue, El Cerrito?

"A. I must decline to answer that question on the ground to answer it might tend to incriminate me.

"Q. Do you deny you attended such a meeting?

"A. I must again decline to answer the question.

"Q. Do you recall on April 8, 1951, attending a meeting which was given for Hursel Alexander at 3009 Grove Street, Berkeley, California?

"A. I must decline to answer that question for the same reason.

"Q. Are you acquainted with Mr. Hursel Alexander?

"A. I must decline to answer that question for the same reason.

"Q. Are you aware of the fact he represented himself in Sacramento as a legislative agent for the Communist Party of California?

"A. I decline to answer that question for the same reason.

"Q. Do you recall calling upon the Berkeley Police Department a few months ago on an occasion on which you were accompanied by Mrs. Alice Hamburg, who testified this morning, and made a protest to the Chief of Police at the Berkeley Police Department over the alleged mistreatment of a man in Berkeley?

"A. I must decline to answer that question for the same reason.

"Q. Are you acquainted with Mrs. Alice Hamburg?

"A. I must decline to answer that question also.

"Q. *Are you a member of the Berkeley Tennis Club, Mrs. Treuhaft?*

"A. I must decline to answer that question——

"Q. (Laughing): I don't think you will find that cited as a subversive group, the Berkeley Tennis Club.

"A. How do I know what your committee decided?

"Q. I believe that's all."

Eloise Steele Brown

Eloise Steele Brown, the next witness, testified that she lived at 1020 59th Street in Oakland and had resided at that address about two years, theretofore having lived at 1907 Berkeley Way in the City of Berkeley. She graduated from the University of California at Berkeley in 1943, having majored in social welfare, and had done social work in the Bay area region. Mrs. Brown had been employed as a director of teen age activities for the Y.W.C.A. at 2134 Austin Way, Berkeley. At the time she appeared before the committee she was a full-time employee at the Salvation Army's maternity hospital which is located at 2974 Garden Street in the City of Oakland.

The witness testified that she knew of the California Labor School, the Civil Rights Congress and the East Bay Council of the Arts, Sciences and Professions. When asked, however, about her affiliation with these organizations she followed the familiar pattern of refusing to answer on the ground that if she did so she might tend to subject herself to a criminal prosecution. Mr. Francis McTernan, Jr., also appeared as counsel for Mrs. Brown. This witness, like the others, was questioned concerning a series of meetings, some of which were alleged to have been held in her own home, and was given the time and place of each meeting and the persons believed to be present, but in each and every instance she refused to answer the questions for the same reason.

"Q. (By Mr. Combs): Is it not a fact that on January 24th of this year you attended a closed meeting of the Communist Party of Alameda County at the residence of Mrs. Lela Thompson, 367 Lester Street, Oakland, California?

"A. Decline to answer on the ground answering might tend to incriminate me.

"Q. Are you acquainted with Herbert Stanley Kalman?

"A. Decline to answer on the same grounds.

"Q. Is it not a fact that you attended a meeting to raise money for the *Daily People's World* at the residence of Mr. Kalman?

"A. Decline on the same grounds.

"Q. Last time being July 29th, last year—same answer?

"A. Yes.

"Q. Same reason?

"A. That's right."

Rose Isaak

The next witness was Mrs. Rose Isaak, 522 41st Street, San Francisco, California, and previously a resident at 1641 Seventh Avenue in the same city. Mrs. Isaak was represented by Richard Gladstein, and after admitting the fact that she was before the committee, had lived at the addresses heretofore mentioned, and had once been employed in a San Francisco bookstore, adopted the same attitude as the witnesses who had preceded her on the stand. As a matter of fact, Mrs. Isaak was served with a subpena while she was actually in the premises of the American-Russian Institute, 101 Post Street in San Francisco. The committee was quite aware that in probing the activities and nature of the American-Russian Institute in San Francisco it was getting into sensitive ground. Not only is this organization one of the most potent of all Communist front organizations, it has also been used as a cover for exceedingly delicate activities on the part of visiting comrades who come to the Bay area from time to time from all over the United States. At the time Mrs. Isaak was questioned concerning her relationship with this organization, the committee had in its possession her own signature on a bank signature card in connection with the account maintained by the organization, and also an article in the Communist newspaper describing her as Executive Secretary for the American-Russian Institute.

This documentation, later introduced as exhibits, was not known to Mrs. Isaak at the time of her examination, and in that light some of her responses are worth noting, although there is no sense in burdening this report with long verbatim excerpts from the transcript of this particular hearing once the pattern of defiance has been recognized. Of course, the committee drew its own inevitable conclusions when witnesses refused to answer questions concerning their subversive affiliations and activities on the ground of self-incrimination.

"Q. (By Mr. Combs) : It's a fact, isn't it, you are the executive secretary in San Francisco for the American-Russian Institute, 101 Post Street?

"A. I refuse, same reason.

"Q. You refuse for the same reason. Let me refresh your memory just a little bit. When were you served with a subpena?

"A. Let me see—this Monday—I think it was Friday.

"Q. Served Friday?

"A. That's right.

"Q. Where were you when you were served?

"A. Refuse to answer on the same grounds.

"Q. I can tell you where you were because I was there, right outside the door. There is a sort of swinging door in your place, isn't there?

"A. (Conferring with counsel) : I decline to answer——

"Q. You decline to answer. Well, it was at 101 Post Street, I will assure you of that, because I was there when you were subpenaed. Let me read to you. I think this will bring it out probably as well if not better than your testimony, a description of your activities in connection with the American-Russian Institute, which was published in the *Daily People's World* on the seventh day of October, 1944. This article was written by Mrs. Edises, and that is a caricature of you in connection with the article, Mrs. Isaak, and I am quoting from the article. This is about the American-Russian Institute: 'The institute is master-minded by probably the singlest-tracked person in San Francisco. I give you Rose Isaak. The American-Russian Institute was formed by a group of San Francisco educators in 1932, nine months before the Soviet Union was recognized by this government. Rose, who was at the time head of the book department at Paul Elders was in at the inception of the organization. Since she became executive secretary, the institute has grown to be a major cultural force in San Francisco and is the indispensible source for material in all things Russian. Through its Speakers Bureau, the institute has been able to comply with requests from schools, clubs, study groups, parent-teacher associations and other organizations —in 1944 the institute branched out on a more ambitious radio program with a series of seven broadcasts over station KGO in San Francisco.' Do you know where Mrs. Edises got the material she used for the publication of that article?

"A. (Consulting with counsel) : I decline to answer that because it might tend——

"Q. You decline to answer on the ground your answer might tend to incriminate you?

"A. That's right.

"Q. Did you confer with Mrs. Edises before the article was written?

"A. (Consulting with counsel) : I decline on the same grounds.

"Q. You decline for the same reasons?

"A. Yes.

"Q. Do you know Mrs. Edises?

"A. (Consulting with counsel) : I decline to answer."

The committee established that the San Francisco chapter of the American-Russian Institute maintained a banking account at the Grant Avenue Branch of the American Trust Company, and that Dr. Holland Roberts, as director, and the witness, as executive secretary, not only opened the account but were authorized to draw checks, their signatures being affixed to a card provided by the bank for that purpose. Canceled checks produced by the committee disclosed that Mrs. Isaak drew a check in the sum of thirty dollars ($30) once every month and sent the check to the National Council of American-Soviet Friendship in New York City, such a check having been drawn by her on the twenty-fifth day of July, 1951, bearing number 4431 and a similar check in the same amount and payable to the same organization having been drawn on the first day of August, 1951, this check being numbered 4439. Check number 4430, drawn on July 25, 1951, was for the sum of nine dollars and fifty-six cents ($9.56) payable to the International Book Store in San Francisco. This propaganda outlet for the Communist Party has been thoroughly established as such by the testimony of numerous witnesses who have heretofore appeared and testified before the committee. It is, of course, quite natural that the material used to stock the library of the American-Russian Institute in San Francisco should be secured from the Communist Party store in the same city.

Frequently when a witness's attention has been diverted from a particularly critical question to other and more prosaic matters, such as bank accounts, checks, signature cards and matters of office routine and bookkeeping, an abrupt return to the main subject can produce the desired result. Thus, after Mrs. Isaak had been questioned on such matters at considerable length, she was brought back to the question of her presence at 101 Post Street when she was served with the subpena:

"Q. Mrs. Isaak, you remember the last question I asked you when you were conferring with Mr. Gladstein, your attorney; I asked you whether or not when the process server came up to your office at 101 Post Street to serve you with the subpena, you first told him your name was not Rose Isaak?

"A. There was some conversation which I don't remember, and I told him I was Rose Isaak, and he served me a subpena.

"Q. Now, you say you had some conversation you don't remember?

"A. I don't remember in detail any conversation, but he served me the subpena, and he couldn't——

"Q. Pardon?

"A. And he couldn't have served me unless I told him I was Rose Isaak.

"Q. Let's explore that a little bit. He first came in and then he left after the first conversation with you?

"A. I don't remember.

"Q. You don't remember that?

"A. No.

"Q. Your recollection is he just had one conversation with you and then he handed you the subpena?

"A. That's my recollection.

"Q. Don't you remember that he came in there and talked to you and then he left and got positive identification of you and then came back and had another conversation with you, and then served you with the subpena?

"A. If he did that, that must have been for just a little—for just a minute. He didn't leave. I mean, he didn't go away for any length of time, or anything of that sort.

"Q. He didn't go away for any length of time, but he left your office, didn't he?

"A. He went out the door. I don't remember."

Thus, the witness who had refused flatly to even admit her presence at 101 Post Street at the time she was served with a subpena, and refused to admit that she was the Executive Secretary of the American-Russian Institute at that address even after listening to the article in the *Daily People's World,* did, in effect, make such an admission after her attention had been diverted to other matters.

Edith Jenkins

Edith Jenkins was the next witness to appear before the committee. She testified that she resided at 465 Belvedere Street in San Francisco, theretofore resided at 47 Woodland Avenue in that city, and had been married to David Jenkins for almost 10 years. This witness was called for the purpose of questioning her concerning her activities with the Committee for a Democratic Far Eastern Policy. When asked whether she had ever been in the organization's office, Room 307 at 935 Market Street, San Francisco, she refused to answer the question on the ground that she might incriminate herself, and invoked the same reason for refusing to answer any questions about the California Labor School, of which her husband served as director for a number of years. David Jenkins' Communist affiliations were established when he appeared as a witness before the committee in 1946 and was shown a photostatic copy of a record from the Board of Elections of the City of New York Borough Office Number 188, dated June 16, 1944, which showed that he was there listed as a Communist Party member. (Third Report, Un-American Activities in California, page 99.)

In connection with the testimony of Mrs. Jenkins, the committee introduced documentary evidence consisting of publications of the Committee for a Democratic Far Eastern Policy together with other material to establish the fact that the organization was subversive in character and controlled by the Communist Party.

Ernestine Gatewood

Ernestine Gatewood was called before the committee for questioning in connection with her activities as Registrar of the California Labor School. Miss Gatewood formerly resided in the City of San Diego, 2980 Ocean View Boulevard. She was closely associated in that city with Evelyn Akerstein and other well-known members of the San Diego Communist Party. Her San Francisco address was 2211 Geary Street, the witness having come from San Diego to San Francisco early in 1949. She, also, declined to answer questions concerning the California Labor School on the ground that her answer might subject her to a criminal prosecution, being frequently guided in that regard by her counsel, the ubiquitous Mr. Gladstein. The committee was especially interested in linking the witness to Dr. Holland Roberts, who replaced

David Jenkins as Director of the California Labor School, having been reliably informed that Miss Gatewood commenced her duties as Registrar of the red schoolhouse on Divisidero Street in 1949 at a salary of $47.20 a week and was working as registrar as late as August 20, 1951.

Bette Sue Wallace

Bette Sue Wallace, accompanied by her attorney, Francis McTernan, Jr., declined to answer questions concerning her alleged connection with the Committee for a Democratic Far Eastern Policy, and adopted the same line when questioned concerning her attendance at the California Labor School, her subscription to the Communist newspaper and similar questions. In her case, as with some of the others, the information was secured through documentary evidence, including a signature card obtained from a bank in San Francisco showing that the witness was authorized to sign checks on behalf of the San Francisco chapter of the Committee for a Democratic Far Eastern Policy. Miss Wallace testified that she previously lived at 415A Vallejo Street and that her present address was 1347 Kearny Street.

Judith Kerner

Judith Kerner, the wife of William Kerner, Director of the Committee for a Far Eastern Policy, testified that she lived at 2114 Baker Street in San Francisco having lived all her life in that city, and that prior to her marriage she was a professional dancer known as Judith Job, and had received much favorable mention in the Communist newspaper which alluded to her as Judith Job even after her marriage to Mr. Kerner. This witness, like those who preceded her, continued the same montonous pattern of answering questions that were not concerned with Communism more or less freely, but flying for cover to the Constitution of the United States when interrogated concerning her affiliations with the California Labor School, the Arts, Sciences and Professions Council, the Chinese Cultural Cabaret, the Committee for a Democratic Far Eastern Policy, the Chinese Workers Mutual Aid Association and the Mimi Kagan dance group. According to the committee's information, which it considers exceedingly reliable, all of these groups were thoroughly Communized and Mrs. Kerner was connected with each and every one of them.

Dr. William Berke

The next witness to appear before the committee was Dr. William R. Berke, formerly Berkowitz, a dentist whose office is located at 516 Sutter Street in San Francisco and who resides at 500 Noriega Street in that city. His attorney was Mr. Gladstein, who assisted him in determining which questions to answer and which questions to avoid answering on the ground that truthful responses might subject him to a criminal prosecution.

Thus, he refused to state whether he ever supported Herbert Nugent, a candidate for supervisor of the City and County of San Francisco on the Communist Party ticket, and two years later sponsored Oleta O'Connor Yates as a Communist candidate for the same position. Mrs. Yates was, at the time, chairman of the Communist Party in San Francisco, and only in February, 1953, convicted by a federal jury in Los Angeles County for conspiring to teach and advocate the overthrow of the United

States Government by force and violence. Dr. Berke also ducked questions concerning his membership on the faculty of the California Labor School, and in that connection his testimony is worth quoting:

"Q. (By Mr. Combs): Now, is it not also true that you have taught courses and lectured at the California Labor School in this city?

"A. I shall decline for the same reasons.

"Q. On the ground it may tend to incriminate you?

"A. Yes.

"Q. Would you complete the answer, please, each time, so there will be no mistake in the record.

"A. I am sure I——

"Q. That in 1948, in April of that year, you gave a study course at the California Labor School on Soviet Policy and Life?

"A. I shall decline on the ground that it may tend to incriminate me.

"Q. And that the documentation—and this is what I am saying because I have it before me—the issue of the *Labor Herald* for that year 1948, that in 1949 you were a coordinator according to the circular issued by the Labor School, a coordinator of five weekly lectures on Fact and Might of the Soviet Union, those classes commencing January 11, 1949?

"A. I shall decline to answer that also on the grounds that it may tend to incriminate me.

"Q. That you were also connected and have been for several years with the American-Russian Institute, San Francisco Chapter, 101 Post Street in this city?

"A. I decline to answer that on the ground that it may tend to incriminate me.

"Q. And that at the present time you are the Chairman of the American-Russian Institute Peace Committee, and have signed papers soliciting money from the sale of peace stamps?

"A. I decline to answer that question on the ground it may tend to incriminate me."

At this point the witness was questioned concerning other matters for awhile and then brought back to the red schoolhouse on Divisadero Street with the following results:

"Q. Well, now, on August 18, 1950, you were an instructor at the California Labor School in a course called the *Soviet People?*

"A. I shall decline to answer that also on the ground it might tend to incriminate me.

"Q. Have you ever been to the Soviet Union?

"A. (Conferring with counsel): No, I have never been to the Soviet Union.

"Q. Are you a student of the Soviet Union and its government, people and culture?

"A. I should like to think that I am, yes.

"Q. You have no hesitation in answering that question?

"A. No, it happens to be true.

"Q. Well, now, let me follow it with this question then: In connection with your studies of the Soviet Union, did you study the history of that country prior to October, 1917, or has your study confined itself to the activities of the people and the culture of the country since that date?

"A. Well, I can best answer that by saying that anyone who studies historical background, whether it be of our country, which I have done also, I like to think, or of the Soviet Union, that it does exceed——

"Q. Precedes October, 1917?

"A. Precedes October, 1917, yes.

"Q. Have you studied the doctrines of Marxism?

"A. (Conferring with counsel): I might answer that question that anyone who concerns himself or herself with studies about sociological backgrounds in governments would of necessity have to study the type or form of government which may be present in any given era. Now, in that case, I would say that much as in the schools for Slavic studies which are held in many of our major universities, I have studied Marxist doctrines, yes.

"Q. Well, assuming that the articles in the *Daily People's World* are accurate and that you did teach at the California Labor School— now, just a minute, Mr. Gladstein, just a minute; this is a hypothetical question.

"Mr. Gladstein: I know. I wanted to give you a hypothetical answer.

"Q. In order to teach a course any place on the history of the Soviet Union you would of necessity have to know something about Marxism.

"A. I think so.

"Q. If you did teach there you would have to.

"A. *I tried awfully hard.*" (Committee's italics.)

Dr. Holland Roberts

The last witness to appear before the committee during this San Francisco hearing,.and certainly the most important one in the category of hostile witnesses, was Dr. Holland Roberts. This was not his first appearance, as he had been examined in Oakland in 1946 on the same occasion that David Jenkins appeared and was questioned concerning his Communist Party affiliations. At that time Jenkins was Director of the California Labor School and Dr. Holland Roberts was its educational director. Since 1946, however, Jenkins has drifted out of the Communist Party's open apparatus to a large extent, while Dr. Holland Roberts became increasingly active in all phases of Party work. He replaced. Jenkins as Director of the California Labor School, he ran the American-Russian Institute with the help of Rose Isaak, he was selected to make a trip to the Soviet Union on a "peace" mission, and his contacts with visiting functionaries from all over the United States and in some instances from abroad, have become matters of common knowledge.to all official investigative agencies.

In the estimation of this committee, Dr. Holland Roberts is one of the most highly placed, active, capable and devoted servants of the Communist cause in all of Northern California. In view of his important status, at least in the opinion of this committee, it was deemed fitting to go into his biographical history to a considerable degree. He, like the other witnesses, relied heavily on the shop-worn device of crawling underneath the Fifth Amendment to the Constitution when questioned about activities that if carried to their ultimate conclusion would effectively destroy that entire document, amendments, Bill of Rights, and all.

The witness' attorney was Mr. Gladstein. It should be stated, however, that in the person of Dr. Roberts the committee was dealing with a much more important sort of witness than any of those who preceded him. Furthermore, Dr. Roberts was exceedingly careful to avoid answering any question that might lead to a revelation of his activities, whether open or underground. He would not even identify his own photograph, nor his own signature on the bank account card for the American-Russian Institute. In refusing to answer these questions, Dr. Roberts, as well as the other recalcitrant witnesses, were, in the committee's view, susceptible to contempt proceedings. While the committee has by no means abandoned its prerogative of citing witnesses for contempt, it has learned by experience that numerous contempt convictions only subject the witnesses to punishment for the commission of a misdemeanor; they emerge as proletarian martyrs so far as the Communist Part is concerned, the trials are an expense to the taxpayer and a burden to the committee which has to forego its other activities and attend the various hearings and assist in the preparation of the cases. If any sound and practical purpose were to be achieved by prosecuting every recalcitrant witness for contempt, the committee would, of course, pursue that course. It has successfully prosecuted more than a hundred witnesses for contempt during the fourteen years of its existence, and it has not yet lost a case.

Laymen are not aware of the fact that in dealing with highly-developed Communist Party members one is dealing with individuals who are fanatics; the 10 Hollywood witnesses who went to jail rather than answer pertinent questions put by the Congressional Committee on Un-American Activities, the persons who refused to testify before federal grand juries concerning Party activities, and the sad-eyed Rosenbergs who patiently explained to their kiddies the operation of the electric chair, are examples of highly-developed Communist fanatics whose entire lives are dedicated to furthering the world Communist revolution. Consequently, although convinced that contempt had repeatedly been committed during this San Francisco hearing—and especially by Dr. Holland Roberts, the committee decided against prosecuting the witnesses for contempt. In every case where the witness refused to answer pertinent questions, the committee was able to introduce documentary evidence to establish the material facts; in addition, the committee drew its own conclusions from the testimony of witnesses who, when questioned about their Communist affiliation and front activities, refused to answer on the ground that if they responded truthfully they would subject themselves to criminal prosecution. In such cases the committee has no other alternative except to draw the logical conclusion and that is, of course, the committee's prerogative.

During the preliminary and basic portion of his interrogation, Dr. Roberts testified that he was born in Springfield, Nebraska, moved to Illinois when he was quite young, worked his way through the University of Chicago, enlisted in the United States Army and served for two years, one of which was spent in the army of occupation at Coblentz. Thereafter, he was ordered to Brest at a time when the Russian troops were beginning to revolt against being forced to subdue the bolsheviks at Archangel. This, it will be remembered from that portion of the report which deals with the history of the Russian revolution, was the early stage of the revolt which was characterized by the refusal of large groups of Russian soldiers to fire upon the Communist forces and during which large masses of the Czar's troops became disaffected and joined revolutionary units.

The committee had considerable evidence to the effect that the witness was greatly impressed by the incipient revolution that he witnessed while stationed at Brest, but when asked about this, Dr. Roberts refused to answer on the grounds that his answer might tend to incriminate him.

In 1919, he and his wife moved to Quincy, Illinois, where he taught science in the local high school. In 1920, he was Principal of Arlington Heights High School near Chicago, remained there for five years and then accepted a position teaching English at the Chicago Normal College. In 1931 and 1932, he did graduate work at Columbia University, taught at Lincoln School Teachers College there and began to specialize in the field of education. The committee was informed that while teaching at Harrison Senior High School in New York he inherited some money which he used for the purpose of making a trip to the Soviet Union. Although the witness was quite frank in answering the other questions, he declined to discuss his trip to the Soviet Union or the inheritance of the funds he is alleged to have used for that purpose on grounds that his answer might tend to incriminate him. An example of his evasiveness in this matter is disclosed by the following excerpt from his testimony:

"Q. (By Mr. Combs) : And when you went to the Soviet Union you and your family were part of the group led by the Anglo-American Institute, a group comprising American teachers and students, and with that group you spent about eight weeks in Moscow?

"A. I must decline as before for the same reason.

"Q. That your interest in the Soviet Union continued when you returned to this country to become an English instructor at Stanford University School of Education in California?

"A. I think if you separate those two, I can answer one of them. But if you are going to put them together, I am afraid that technique won't work at this time.

"Q. Well, I tried, Mr. Roberts.

"A. I watched you very carefully this morning, and I thought you were very clever.

"Q. Let's split the question and get at least half of it in the record. You did return to the United States after your trip abroad?

"A. My attorney advises me that I hadn't said I hadn't said I was abroad.

"Q. Well, I guess you didn't but at any rate you did teach at Stanford University and in the School of Education, didn't you?

"A. Oh yes, I did.

"Q. When did you commence your affiliation with Stanford?

"A. 1934, the fall of 1934.

"Q. Thank you. Now, Dr. Roberts, you continued your work at Stanford until the end of 1943, until the 1944 term, did you not?

"A. Through either the spring or the summer of 1944. At this moment, I think it was through the summer. I am rather certain it was."

The witness, continuing with the preliminary portion of his testimony, stated that his present residential address was 3891 La Donna Avenue in Palo Alto where he had resided since 1939, prior to that time having lived at 1035 Parkinson Avenue in the same city. His employment was not continued by Stanford University, and he thereafter pursued the work on an increasing scale which resulted in his full time employment at the Communist California Labor School in San Francisco and his directorship of the American-Russian Institute, together with other similar activities.

The witness was shown a monthly newsletter published by the American-Russian Institute for Cultural Relations with the Soviet Union, 101 Post Street, San Francisco, California, called the "U. S. S. R. Fact Sheet," Vol. 5, No. 2, dated May, 1951. It contained a photograph of Holland Roberts above the following legend, "Lenin Graduate Students with Holland Roberts of the U. S. Delegation Autographing." The Lenin graduate students, of course, referred to the graduates of the Lenin Academy for espionage activities heretofore mentioned in connection with that section of this report dealing with the Gadar Party, but the witness declined, on grounds of self-incrimination, to identify his own photograph or to admit that he was in fact in the Soviet Union in 1951.

Dr. Roberts stated that he was president of the California Federation of Teachers in 1936 or 1937, and still maintained his membership in the organization. He refused, on grounds of self-incrimination, to admit that he was, in 1939, a sponsor for the Friends of the Abraham Lincoln Brigade, comprising Communists and fellow-travelers who went to fight in the Spanish Revolution; he declined, for the same reason, to admit sponsorship of the Civil Rights Congress of Northern California with Louise Bransten; lecturing at the Tom Mooney Labor School (the predecessor of the California Labor School) in 1942; acting as chairman of the 36th Soviet Birthday Celebration at the Scottish Rite Auditorium in San Francisco under the auspices of the Russian-American Society; acting as a member of the Board of Directors of the Tom Mooney Labor School as of January 7, 1944; that he taught a course at the California Labor School in the fall of 1944; that in the same year he was listed as a state sponsor for American Youth for Democracy; that in March of 1945, he addressed a banquet for delegates to the Intercollegiate Conference sponsored by American Youth for Democracy at the Hotel Shattuck in Berkeley; that on May 8, 1945, he was photographed with Vyacheslav Molotov and Harry Bridges at a reception given by the American-Russian Institute for Mr. Molotov in San Francisco; that in September, 1945, he was elected vice president of the Committee on Education of the National Council of American-Soviet Friendship; that on May 16, 1946, he was one of the principal speakers at an inauguration dinner of the American-Russian Institute in Los Angeles at which Constantine Siminov, a Soviet official, was the honored guest; that in July, 1946, he was a principal speaker at the Political Action School at Asilomar, California; that he was ever acquainted with Victor R. Jewitt, mentioned as a Communist in the reports of the California Senate Committee on Education.

In connection with his visit to the Soviet Union in 1950, Dr. Roberts, when shown an eight-page leaflet entitled, *Americans in the U. S. S. R.,* for November and December of 1950, refused to identify his own photograph, alleged to have been taken in the Soviet Union on the occasion of his visit. This refusal to identify his own photograph bordered on the ridiculous, because anyone possessed of common sense of the garden variety could tell at a glance that the likeness was perfect. Indeed, Mr. Aaron Sargent, attorney for the Sons of the American Revolution, who happened to be seated in the audience as a spectator, came to the stand as a volunteer witness and removed any doubt about the photograph being, in fact, an excellent and unmistakable likeness of the witness.

Dr. Roberts' customary aplomb was visibly shaken to some extent when he was shown a document in the nature of a confidential communication from the National Council of American-Soviet Friendship, Incorporated, 114 East 32d Street, New York 16, New York, dated April 9, 1951, addressed, "Dear National Council Member," and signed, "Richard Morford, Executive Director." Dr. Roberts was, at the same time shown the following documents which were sent with the Morford communication: "National Council of American-Soviet Friendship, Inc., Memorandum to: Leadership in the National Field. From: Richard Morford, Executive Director; Date; Wednesday, April 11, 1951," and signed by him. "National Council of American-Soviet Friendship on the Occasion of its Annual Meeting—April 5, 1951;" "Supplement, National Field Memorandum Concerning Objectives Listed in the Statement of the National Council of American-Soviet Friendship, April 5, 1951." "Agenda, Conference on Policy and Program, April 5, 1951, Professor Henry Pratt Fairchild, presiding." "Annual Report by the Director to Members of the National Council, submitted at the Annual Meeting of the National Council of American-Soviet Friendship, April 5, 1951." "Report to the Membership, Board and Officers of the National Council of American-Soviet Friendship at the Annual Membership Meeting, April 5, 1951," setting forth the membership of the organization. "National Council of American-Soviet Friendship, Inc., December 31, 1950," setting forth the financial condition of the organization.

Dr. Roberts' attention was called to that portion of the communication from Richard Morford which read: "Your careful examination of the annual report of the director is asked. Two other reports were submitted to the annual meeting and I enclose these. *It is necessary again to caution that these reports are for your private information only. You will understand the reason.*" (Committee's italics.) Dr. Roberts' response to this line of questioning was:

"A. Well, that is much too direct an approach here.
"Q. I meant it to be.
"A. I decline to answer on the ground it might tend to incriminate me."

This line of questioning was designed to establish the fact that the San Francisco Chapter of the American-Russian Institute, 101 Post Street, and headed by Dr. Roberts, was in fact simply a subordinate division of the National Council of American-Soviet Friendship in New York. To that end the evidence was summarized as follows:

"Mr. Combs: Now, Mr. Chairman, I don't think it is necessary to read all these names, the directors of the organization, into the record, but from an examination of the records themselves—and I am sure Dr. Roberts can bear me out, if he will, he did make a pretty thorough examination of these many things, the American-Russian Institute is affiliated with the National Council of American-Soviet Friendship. It is quite obvious from an analysis of these documents and from the bank accounts of the Institute in San Francisco that they regularly sent checks in the sum of $30.00, signed by Holland Roberts as Director and Rose Isaak as Secretary, to the National Council of American-Soviet Friendship as dues. That appeared in our records already through the actual checks themselves. You don't care to comment on that, Dr. Roberts?

"A. No, no, thank you."

Regarding his visit to the Soviet Union during the latter part of 1950, the record is as follows:

"Q. (By Mr. Combs): Dr. Roberts, I want to ask you some questions about your trip to the Soviet Union in the latter part of 1950, by way of New York, Paris, London and Warsaw, which has been fully reported, as you are well aware. Now, I want to finish just as briefly as I possibly can, so if you are not going to answer the questions, if you and your counsel don't mind a compound question on this one subject only—I will ask this entire question and then you can answer just once or not as you prefer. Is that satisfactory?

"Mr. Gladstein: (Nodding affirmatively.)

"Q. All right. Is it not a fact that late last year, you, as a member of a delegation of thirty-three Americans to the Second Annual World Congress for Peace flew in a chartered plane from New York City to Paris and thence to London; that the congress was originally planned to be held in Sheffield, England, but that you and the other delegates were not allowed to remain in England because on landing in that country you were taken to Scotland Yard by British immigration authorities and other officials and there questioned at length, and after six hours you returned to Paris; that you described all of this in a speech which you gave at the California Labor School on Friday evening, December 22nd, 1950, the occasion having been attended by several other people, and that Edith Jenkins was mistress of ceremonies on that occasion; that you described your trip, and you added that there were more progressives in San Francisco than Great Britain, and better organized in public positions, and I am quoting verbatim from a talk you made on that occasion; that after two days in Paris the 33 of you delegates left for the Peace Conference at Warsaw, Poland; that you traveled by train to Brussels and thence by plane to Prague, and thence to Warsaw. From Paris on the expenses were paid by various European peace and progressive organizations, your budget having been limited by reason of the fact, which you explained on this occasion, by your original intention to have the meeting in Sheffield, England. Eighty-one nations were represented at the Warsaw Peace Conference, out of which came the following proposals: (1) Prohibition of all atomic weapons and all modern weapons of mass destruction. (2) Condemnation of armed intervention in the internal affairs of other nations. (3) Reduction and control of armaments. (4) U. N. negotiations to end Korean war with Red Russia participating. (5) Prohibition of all war propaganda. (6) Establishment of a world council for peace.

"That you were Chairman of the Warsaw Conference Propaganda Commission; that the above points that I have just enumerated were adopted at the conference; that one O. John Rogge voted contrary and was immediately accused of being a stooge of Tito of Yugoslavia on the floor of the congress; that the United States was accused of being the aggressor in Korea and Red China was said to be thoroughly justified in the invasion and conquest of Tibet; that out of the six-day conference in Warsaw, dominated by the Russians, there came a permanent world peace council, functioning through a bureau headed by Frederic Joliot-Curie of France, former head of the French atomic effort, and that the organization, that is, the council also has a secretariat, and according to the report in the *World News and Views,* one of the documents I have asked you to identify, the speeches of Fayayev and Ehrenburg from Russia, Joliot-Curie and Cot from France and Pietro Nenni from Italy were the highlights of the conference; that Pierre Cot, a former member of the French Cabinet said—and I quote from the article, the publication I asked you to identify;

" 'To our friends from the U. S. S. R. and the new democracies, the Korean affair was clear from the beginning an aggression by the U. S. A. against a small heroic people who wanted only their liberty. Personally, I unreservedly agree with this analysis, but you must realize that many of our fellow countrymen at first hesitated and that their hesitation did not necessarily prove them to be agents of American imperialism.'

"That at the conference in Warsaw you attended there were about two thousand delegates and a thousand clerks, stenos and observers; that after the Warsaw meeting was over you were invited with—I have forgotten how many now, let's see, 19—19 others, Americans, to go on to the Soviet Union; that you were elected chairman of that commission, that you did go to the Soviet Union and you remained in the Soviet Union for 10 days. During that time you were invited by the Soviet Peace Society, in fact a plane was furnished by the Russians, and you landed at Moscow at night, your tour was confined to Moscow, Leningrad and Stalingrad. That you personally inspected the Stalin palace at Moscow and other housing projects there, and at the other places I have also mentioned. The two photographs I showed you and which you refused to identify were taken of you autographing the documents for students while in the Soviet Union as a representative of the 19 people I have mentioned; and in your description of these experiences, on the day I have mentioned, Edith Jenkins and William Kerner also spoke of their experiences. You stated that at the Stalingrad Tractor Factory, which you visited, that you were impressed by the numerous signs for peace and saw no evidences of any warlike tendencies on the part of anyone connected with the factory, and that you were particularly impressed with the fact that they were turning out tractors instead of tanks, and I wish to—(that is the end to the complex question, except this specific question)—is it not true that at the very time you went through that factory you had a discussion with a man by the name of Alexander Stepanov, who described himself to you as the head of the tank department of that factory? Now, that is the complex question. Will you—if it is not true, tell us where the error lies?

"A. Mr. Combs, Senator Burns, and Members of the Committee, you cannot possibly appreciate how regretful I am that I cannot go into this matter with you. I must decline to answer the question.

"Q. On what grounds?

"A. On the ground it might tend to incriminate me.

"Q. That is all."

Conclusions

What conclusions can be logically drawn from this hearing? It is crystal clear that among the major Communist front organizations operating in the Bay area we must include those which were the subject of this hearing. The committee placed on the witness stand a succession of individuals who were connected with these various operations, accompanied by their attorneys, and in all instances, with the possible exception of Mrs. Hamburg, the witnesses responded freely when questioned about their places of origin, their educational background and their places of residence, and they steadfastly followed the same precise pattern in refusing to answer any questions touching upon their Communist affiliations or their front organization activities. It must, therefore, be concluded that each and all of these front organizations are engaged in secret, conspiratorial activities as parts of the Communist machine; that the liaison between them is established by the fact that David Jenkins and others mentioned in connection with this hearing, traveled throughout the Bay region to one function after another, and by the fact that the California Labor School and the San Francisco American-Russian Institute are both operated under the expert supervision of Dr. Holland Roberts, who was selected to head an American delegation to the Soviet Union and whose full time is devoted to furthering the Communist cause; that, as will be seen from the next subdivision of this same general topic dealing with front organizations, each and every one of these front organizations, together with a host of minor fronts, have been accelerating their operational activities since the date of the committee's San Francisco hearing in September of 1951 until the present time.

The San Francisco hearings were open to the press and fully reported in the metropolitan newspapers in the Bay area. This having been done, and these organizations having been branded as Communist-controlled, the public has thus been fully alerted to the true character of this phase of the Communist Party's Bay area activities.

COMMUNIST FRONT ACTIVITIES IN THE EAST BAY AREA, 1951-1953

An example of the sort of Communist front activity that continuously operates in the more populous urban areas of the State is to be found in Alameda County from the latter part of 1951 until January of 1953. It will be noted that in addition to the major fronts, the Arts, Sciences and Professions Council; the American-Russian Institute; the California Labor School; the International Workers Order; the Civil Rights Congress; the Committee for a Democratic Far Eastern Policy—there are numerous smaller front groups created to serve a particular purpose and quickly liquidated when the purpose has been accomplished. Most important of all, it will be seen that many of the individuals mentioned by the witnesses in the San Francisco hearing participated in all of these activities, but that on some occasions such well-known party functionaries as John Howard Lawson, the motion picture writer, came up from southern California to provide expert direction and advice.

On June 7, 1952, an organization called the *Trade Union Committee for Repeal of the Smith Act* staged a motorcade through the streets of Oakland, propagandizing for the repeal of the federal legislation under which top-flight members of the Communist Party's official family were convicted and sentenced to prison terms for conspiring to teach and advocate the unlawful overthrow of the United States Government. Active in this affair were: Theodore M. Kalman, Leo Kanowitz, Martin Harwayne, Louis E. Gottlieb, William Lowe, Helen Lima and James E. Kalman.

On July 12, 1952, a rally was held for the purpose of raising money for the Communist newspaper, the *Daily People's World*, at 2016 Seventh Street in Oakland, at 8.30 p.m. Approximately one hundred and fifty people attended this affair, including: Wilhelmina Loughrey, Lloyd W. Lehman, Mayer Frieden, Lloyd K. Vandever, Norris Lafferty, Evelyn Frieden, Helen Lima, and Saul Wachter.

On July 26, 1952, another motorcade was staged by a new front organization operating in the East Bay area and known as the *California Emergency Defense Committee*. This organization was created for the purpose of raising funds for the benefit of those members of the Communist Party's functionaries who were arrested under the provisions of the Smith Act. Participating in this affair were: John Howard Lawson, Theodore M. Kalman, Evelyn Frieden, William Lowe, Saul Wachter, and others from localities as far distant as Riverside, Lakeport, Chico and San Fernando.

On August 4, 1952, Gertrude Kalman made the necessary arrangements for a meeting of the East Bay Youth Cultural Center, held at Lake Merritt boat house for the purpose of hearing an address by Professor Morris U. Schappes. In 1934, Professor Schappes appeared before a New York State Legislative Committee on Un-American Activities and admitted, under oath, that he was not only a member of the Communist Party but also had been appointed to its Educational Commission and had delivered the annual report for the commission at the 10th Convention of the Communist Party of the State of New York in 1938. At the time he testified before the committee, Professor Schappes was on the teaching staff of the College of the City of New York, having been a faculty member at that institution for 13 years. In 1936, he was not recommended for reappointment, and several Communist front organizations immediately launched an all-out effort to obtain his reappointment.

A Schappes Defense Committee was created in the summer of 1941 and attracted sponsors from virtually every major college and university in the United States. The effort to reinstate Professor Schappes was unsuccessful and since that time he has been touring the Country lecturing before Communist front organizations and other Marxist groups—including the East Bay Youth Cultural Center, above-mentioned.

On August 22, 1952, the Labor Youth League staged a beach party to raise funds for the benefit of the *Daily People's World* and also to solidify their organization. It will be remembered that this organization is simply a continuation of the Young Communist League, operated to attract the younger Marxists and pave the way for their formal induction into the Community Party itself after they have been brought along to a point of political maturity.

Several years ago the committee subpened Mr. John Howard Lawson and interrogated him at considerable length concerning his Communist affiliations and activities. At that time Mr. Lawson was a man who appeared to be at least 50 years of age; certainly he was not far away from his fiftieth birthday, and yet he participated in this Labor Youth League beach party in August, 1952. The young Marxians gathered at the home of Martin D. Newman, 2115½ Ninth Street, Berkeley, California. Those who assisted Mr. Lawson in conducting this affair included Leo Kanowitz and Jacques B. Templin.

On August 23, 1952, the East Bay Committee to Save the Rosenbergs convened in the home of Jack N. Kositsky, 1219 Walnut Street, Berkeley. As the name of this organization indicates, it was created for the purpose of mobilizing sympathy in behalf of Julius and Ethel Rosenberg, convicted atomic spies under sentence of death, and to agitate for the commutation of their sentence. Active in this affair were: Philip Eden, Robert Greenberg, Zelda Chevalier and Marcus Billings.

On August 30, 1952, a benefit affair for the purpose of raising funds for the *Daily People's World* was held in the home of Mayer Frieden, 1034 28th Street, Oakland. This affair, attended by 23 persons, was also held in honor of Mickey Lima's birthday. Lima has long been known as an active functionary of the Communist Party in the Bay area.

On September 13 and 14, 1952, an unusually large and important affair, called *The People's World Bazaar,* was held at 1970 Chestnut Street, in the City of Berkeley; approximately 126 persons attended this two-day convention, which quite obviously was not entirely devoted to the raising of funds for the Communist paper. This conclusion is arrived at by noting that the persons who attended came from such widely separated localities in California as Livermore, Twainharte, Los Angeles, Sonoma, San Fernando, Stockton, Vallejo, Hollywood, San Diego and Sacramento. One of the delegates to this affair came from New York City. Among the better-known participants were: Mayer Frieden, John Howard Lawson, William Beltram, Paul Chown, Travis Lafferty, Lloyd

K. Vandever, Martin Harwayne, Roy R. Noftz, Torben Deirup, W. R. DeLappe, Theodore Kalman, Pele Murdock (formerly Mrs. Bertram Edises), Genola Burks, Louis E. Gottlieb, Saul Wachter, Wayne Hultgren, John Karwoski, Wilhelmina Loughrey, Nat Yanish and Lloyd Lehman.

It will be remembered that Torben Deirup appeared as a witness before the committee at its San Francisco hearing concerning front organizations in September, 1951. John Howard Lawson has already been mentioned, and has been identified by several former members of the Communist Party as the individual in the motion picture industry who was most active in heading the Communist infiltration in organizations in Hollywood. Paul Chown has been identified as a Communist Party member by sworn testimony, as has been Wayne Hultgren, Nat Yanish, Lloyd Lehman and Wilhelmina Loughrey.

On October 2, 1952, the American Committee for Protection of the Foreign Born sent its national executive secretary, Abner Green, to Oakland for the purpose of stirring up interest and raising funds in behalf of Communists who had become enmeshed in legal difficulties with the United States Immigration and Naturalization Service, and faced deportation to the lands whence they came. This meeting was held at 1819 10th Street in the City of Oakland, and the chairman for the evening was Mr. Henry Saunders, an attorney associated with the Oakland firm of Edises and Treuhaft, specialists in the handling of legal matters for left-wing labor unions and Communist front organizations, and in providing advice and direction for Communist Party members.

On October 18, 1952, the Bay area annual festival was held for the International Workers Order lodges of Northern California. This affair was also held at 1819 10th Street in the City of Oakland, and proclaimed that it was convened in honor of the seventieth birthday of the national president of the International Workers Order, Mr. Rockwell Kent, the artist (not to be confused with Norman Rockwell). One hundred and seven persons were in attendance at this meeting. The Communist character of the affair is at once disclosed by virtue of the fact that among those who were featured as speakers were William Schneiderman, for years the head of the Communist Party of California, and heretofore identified as the head of District 13 of the Communist Party of the United States, comprising California, Arizona and the Territory of Hawaii. Mr. Alvah Bessie, motion picture writer whose record has heretofore been mentioned in reports of this committee, was also a speaker. The communities represented by those who attended this annual festival for one of the most potent and dangerous Communist-dominated organizations in the United States, were: Oakland, Berkeley, San Francisco, Los Angeles, El Cerrito, Ventura, Sacramento, San Carlos, Petaluma, Albany, Palo Alto, Richmond, Fresno, Concord, Pleasanton, Santa Rose, San Lorenzo, Orinda, San Mateo, San Rafael, Boulder Creek, Atherton, Montague, Emeryville, Castro Valley, Penngrove, Vallejo, Lolito, Mountain View, Sebastapol, San Diego, San Bernardino and Alhambra.

On November 19, 1952, the East Bay Council, Arts, Sciences and Professions sponsored a meeting which was held in LeConte school auditorium in the City of Berkeley, where Professor Dirk J. Struick addressed an audience on the subject of "Science and Academic Freedom." Mr. Sidney Roger, heretofore mentioned, acted as chairman of the evening and among the 45 persons present were: Alice Hamburg, Barbara Sicular and Louis Gottlieb, all of whom were identified by Mrs. Hamburg as having been active in the affairs of the Arts, Sciences and Professions Council in the Bay region. Like Professor Schappes, Struick has long been identified with Communist-dominated organizations. Here is his record:

(1) *American Committee for Democracy and Intellectual Freedom.* Others who were connected with this organization included: Prof. Franz Boas, Prof. Robert S. Lynd, Prof. Robert K. Speer, Prof. Edward C. Tolman, Paul Robeson, Lillian Hellman, Prof. Henry Pratt Fairchild, Prof. S. P. Breckenridge, Prof. Kirtley F. Mather, Prof. H. A. Overstreet, Dashiell Hammett, Rockwell Kent, Hugh de Lacy, Freda Kirchwey, Mary Van Kleek, Prof. Willystine Goodsell, George Seldes, Prof. Walter Rautenstrauch, Lewis Alan Berne, Robert W. Kenny, Prof. Robert Morss Lovett.

(2) *American Committee to Save Refugees.* Others who were connected with this organization included: Prof. Franz Boas, Prof. Robert K. Speer, Prof. Edward C. Tolman, Lillian Hellman, Prof. Henry Pratt Fairchild, Prof. Frank W. Weymouth, Dashiell Hammett, Prof. Haakon Chevalier, John Howard Lawson, Rockwell Kent, Prof. H. A. Overstreet, George Seldes, Prof. Henry E. Siegerist.

(3) *American Youth for Democracy.* Others who were connected with this organization included: John Howard Lawson, Prof. Kirtley F. Mather, Robert W. Kenney, Philip M. Connelly, Mayer Frieden, Sandra Martin, Ruby Heide, Steve Murdock, Dr. Holland Roberts.

(4) *Artists Front to Win the War.* Others who were connected with this organization included: Rockwell Kent, Lillian Hellman, Paul Robeson, Alva H. Bessie, Paul Jarrico, John Howard Lawson, George Seldes, Prof. Henry Pratt Fairchild, Prof. Morris U. Schappes.

(5) *Harry Bridges Defense Committee.* Others who were connected with this organization included: Hugh de Lacy, Prof. Ralph H. Gundlach, Dashiell Hammett, Lillian Hellman, Paul Jarrico, Prof. Robert Morss Lovett, Prof. Walter Rautenstrauch, Paul Robeson, George Seldes, Prof. Frank W. Weymouth, Philip M. Connelly, Hugh de Lacy.

(6) *Committee to Defend America by Keeping Out of War.* Others who were connected with this organization included: Prof. Franz Boas, Lewis Alan Berne, Philip M. Connelly, Abram Flaxer, Rockwell Kent, Prof. Robert Morss Lovett, Harper Poulson, George Seldes, Prof. Walter Rautenstrauch.

(7) *Statement Defending the Communist Party.* Others who also signed this document included: Prof. Franz Boas, Prof. Henry Pratt Fairchild, Frederick Vanderbilt Field, Prof. Norman E. Himes, Dashiell Hammett, William Kerner, Rockwell Kent, Harper Poulson, Prof. Walter Rautenstrauch, Paul Robeson.

(8) *Council for Pan American Democracy.* Others who were connected with this organization included: Prof. Franz Boas, Rockwell Kent, Prof. J. Raymond Walsh.

(9) *Jefferson School of Social Science.* Others who were connected with this Communist school included: Dr. Bella V. Dodd, Prof. Bernhard J. Stern, Prof. Walter Rautenstrauch, Frederick Vanderbilt Field, Prof. Alain Locke, Prof. Morris U. Schappes.

(10) *Joint Anti-Fascist Refugee Committee.* Others who were connected with this organization included: Prof. Henry Pratt Fairchild, Abram Flaxer, Lillian Hellman, John Howard Lawson, Carey McWilliams, Prof. Walter Rautenstrauch, George Seldes, Paul Robeson.

(11) *American-Russian Institute.* Others who were connected with this organization included: Dr. Holland Roberts, Rose Isaak, Prof. Robert S. Lynd, Prof. Henry E. Sigerist, Prof. Henry Pratt Fairchild, Frederick Vanderbilt Field, Abram Flaxer, Rockwell Kent, Prof. F. O. Matthiessen, Mary Van Kleek.

(12) *National Emergency Conference.* Others who were connected with this organization included: Lewis Alan Berne, Prof. Franz Boas, Prof. S. P. Breckinridge, Prof. Henry Pratt Fairchild, Prof. Ralph H. Gundlach, Prof. William H. Kilpatrick, Freda Kirchwey, Prof. Alain Locke, Prof. Robert Morss Lovett, Prof. Robert S. Lynd, Carey McWilliams, George Seldes, Prof. Robert K. Speer, Prof. Edward C. Tolman, Prof. J. Raymond Walsh.

(13) *National Federation for Constitutional Liberties.* Others who were connected with this organization included: Prof. Robert K. Speer, Prof. Edward C. Tolman, Carey McWilliams, Dr. Bella V. Dodd, Dashiell Hammett, Prof. Alain Locke, Prof. Robert Morss Lovett, Prof. Robert S. Lynd, Prof. F. O. Matthiessen, Prof. Walter Rautenstrauch, George Seldes, Prof. Franz Boas, Hugh de Lacy, Prof. Bernhard J. Stern, Paul Robeson, Alva H. Bessie, Prof. S. P. Breckinridge, Paul Jarrico, Freda Kirchwey, Prof. Henry Pratt Fairchild, Abram Flaxer, Prof. Willystine Goodsell, Prof. Ralph H. Gundlach, Prof. Kirtley F. Mather, Prof. H. A. Overstreet, Prof. Frank W. Weymouth.

(14) *Letter Defending Communist Leaders.* Other signers of this document included: Prof. Franz Boas, Dashiell Hammett, Rockwell Kent, Prof. Robert Morss Lovett, Prof. Kirtley F. Mather, Prof. Walter Rautenstrauch.

(15) *Open Letter for Closer Cooperation with the Soviet Union.* Other signers of this document included: Prof. Haakon Chevalier, Prof. Henry Pratt Fairchild, Prof. Willystine Goodsell, Dashiell Hammett, Prof. Norman E. Himes, Rockwell Kent, John Howard Lawson, Prof. Robert Morss Lovett, Prof. F. O. Matthiessen, Prof. Walter Rautenstrauch, George Seldes, Prof. Bernhard J. Stern, Mary Van Kleek, Prof. J. Raymond Walsh.

(16) *Reichstag Fire Trial Anniversary Committee.* Others who were connected with this organization included: Abram Flaxer, Lillian Hellman, Rockwell Kent, Prof. Kirtley F. Mather, Prof. Walter Rautenstrauch.

(17) *William Schneiderman-Sam Darcy Defense Committees.* Others who were connected with these organizations included: Carey McWilliams, Prof. Walter Rautenstrauch, Prof. S. P. Breckenridge, Prof. Norman E. Himes, Rockwell Kent, Prof. F. O. Matthiessen, Prof. Bernhard J. Stern.

(18) *Veterans of the Abraham Lincoln Brigade.* Others who were connected with this organization included: Paul Robeson, Dashiell Hammett, George Seldes, Prof. Bernhard J. Stern, Prof. Henry Pratt Fairchild, Lillian Hellman, Prof. Ralph H. Gundlach, Prof. F. O. Matthiessen, Prof. Robert S. Lynd, Prof. Walter Rautenstraugh, Prof. Franz

Boas, Prof. Robert Morss Lovett, Prof. Kirtley F. Mather, Prof. Edward C. Tolman.

On November 21, 1952, a meeting of the East Bay *People's World* Forum was held in the home of William Beltram, 3708 Laguna Avenue, to discuss ways and means to assist Julius and Ethel Rosenberg, convicted atom spies.

On November 25, 1952, a group of 34 persons, including William Beltram, Wayne Hultgren and Martin Harwayne, met in the Northbrae Methodist Church, 1953 Hopkins Street, Berkeley, to listen to an address by Dr. Jerome Davis. This affair was sponsored by the Peace Committee of Alameda and Contra Costa Counties.

On November 8, 1952, the Oakland branch of the Civil Rights Congress sponsored a party in honor of its chairman, Mrs. Callie Frost. This meeting was held at the home of Martin Harwayne, 3655 West Street, Oakland.

On December 7, 1952, the Oakland branch of the Civil Rights Congress met at the home of Robert E. Treuhaft, 730 59th Street, Oakland, to "hear how the doctors and lawyers in Los Angeles exposed the un-American committee."

On December 9, 1952, the California Emergency Defense Committee met at the International Longshoremens and Warehousemens Union hall, 160 Grand Avenue, Oakland, to hear speeches by William Schneiderman, William Lowe, and Simon Gerson. Both Lowe and Gerson are well known in Communist Party circles, the former being a functionary in Alameda County and the latter having taught in the Communist school in New York. Among the 63 persons who attended this affair were: Mayer Frieden, Mickey Lima, Jean Tobey Lowe, Roy Noftz, Genola Burks, Saul Wachter, Nat Yanish, Francis Harwayne, Herbert Kalman, Gene Kalman, Bernice Kalman, Eloise Steele Brown, Pele Murdock (formerly Mrs. Bertram Edises), and Evelyn Frieden.

On December 11, 1952, there was a meeting of the East Bay Division of the Committee to Save the Rosenbergs at 700 21st Street, Oakland, pursuant to a call issued by the chairman, Mrs. Genola Burks.

On December 13, 1952, the Peace Committee of Alameda and Contra Costa Counties met at the home of Nat Yanish to organize propaganda urging an immediate peace in Korea.

On December 31, 1952, the East Bay Arts, Sciences and Professions Council held a New Year's Eve party in the home of Mrs. Alice Hamburg, 682 San Luis Road, Berkeley. Forty-one persons attended this affair, including Sidney Roger, Charles Drasnin, Lenore Mary Sherwood, John Karwoski and Irene Rosenberg.

On January 2, 1953, the Committee to Secure Justice for the Rosenbergs met in the Willard Junior High School, Berkeley. This gathering, attended by 215 persons, included Lloyd Lehman, Alice Hamburg, Sanford Koretsky, Barbara Sicular, Dr. Ephraim Kahn, Saul Wachter, Charles Drasnin, Nori Lafferty, Lee Coe, Theodore Kalman, Lenore Mary Sherwood, Edward Olkowski, William Beltram, Leo Kanowitz, Marcus Billings, John Karwoski, Lloyd K. Vandever, Martin Harwayne, Philip Eden, Roy Loftz, Herbert Kalman, Nat Yanish, Robert Luthy, Julian Petrofsky and Mayer Frieden.

On January 3, 1953, the Committee to Defend the Rosenbergs, having been turned down by the Berkeley City Council when the organization sought to maintain a table or desk at the southeast corner of Telegraph Avenue and Allston Way in that city for the purpose of distributing propaganda on behalf of the convicted espionage agents, flooded the council with the customary pressure letters, including those from the following sources: Dr. Legrande Coleman, M.D., in his capacity as Chairman of the East Bay Arts, Sciences and Professions Council; from Sidney Roger; from David Rappaport, representing the Students Civil Liberties Union, and from Dr. Ephraim Kahn, William Lowe, Robert Luthy, Annette Greenberg, and many others.

Thus from the foregoing it will be seen how front organization activities have been operated in Alameda County during the past two years. The committee has, of course, made no effort to give a list of all of the activities during that time, since space will not permit. This East Bay area is typical of similar activities in San Francisco and in Southern California and the committee has set forth the names of some of the individuals who participated for the purpose of demonstrating how these specialists are kept busy running these organizations in their ceaseless round of activities.

ERRONEOUS FRONT LISTINGS

Communist front organizations not only masquerade behind a respectable facade, endeavoring in all cases to conceal the real control and objectives of the organizations by claiming to have some humanitarian purpose, but they have also made use of the names of loyal individuals without authority. From time to time the committee has received letters of protest from persons who have been listed as officers of various front organizations and who, in fact, have had no connection whatever with these movements, their names having been used without authority and for the deliberate purpose of using non-Communist individuals as window dressing to divert suspicion. In such cases the committee is always eager and willing to do everything in its power to correct this despicable practice.

Since the issuance of the 1951 report, the committee has received four letters from individuals who fit into this general category. The committee has made an investigation in each instance for the purpose of ascertaining the true facts, and is appreciative of the opportunity to make the proper corrections herewith.

On May 30, 1951, the committee received a letter from Mrs. Francis Albrier, 1621 Oregon Street, Berkeley. The writer said: "I am one of the citizens who was led to believe that this organization's (the California Legislative Conference) activities were solely for good government and legislation—whose activities were honorable." Mrs. Albrier stated that she attended a meeting of the California Legislative Conference in Fresno and was scheduled to serve on an FEPC panel, but left before the meeting was over. Thereafter she discovered that her name was listed without her consent as a member of the Executive Board of the California Legislative Conference, as a representative of the California Association of Colored Women. Mrs. Albrier informed the committee that she immediately severed all connection with the organization, the California Legislative Conference, upon learning of its Communist control.

On September 13, 1951, the committee received a letter from Mr. Edward Burbridge, Editor of the *Los Angeles Herald-American,* 1107½ East Vernon Avenue, Los Angeles. On March 10, 1947, the Communist newspaper, the *Daily People's World,* in reporting a meeting of the Los Angeles Youth Council, listed Mr. Burbridge as a sponsor of that affair, but erroneously listed his name as "Eddie Burrige," of the *California Eagle.* The committee referred to this function in its 1951 report in connection with the activities of Vicki Landish Fromkin.

Mr. Burbridge states that he did attend the meeting, had no idea of its Communist flavor, and had never authorized the use of his name as a sponsor. On September 18, 1951, the chairman of the committee, Senator Hugh M. Burns, replied to Mr. Burbridge, pointing out that the inaccuracy in the *People's World* article had been duly noted and that the committee would gladly make the correction in its next report, particularly noting Mr. Burbridge's emphatic statement that he was completely opposed to all forms of Communist activity. Mr. Burbridge said: "My name has never been mentioned in connection with any Communist organization and never will be, because I refuse all invitations to meetings sent me by organizations I suspect of being Communistic." On October 27, 1951, Mr. Burbridge acknowledged Senator Burns' letter, courteously thanked him for his interest in rectifying the error, wished the committee continued success and reiterated his anti-Communist position. The committee is happy to have been afforded an opportunity to set the record straight.

On January 12, 1952, a letter was received from Prof. Ethel J. Apenfels, of the New York University School of Education. Prof. Apenfels called attention to the fact that in the committee's 1949 report she was mentioned as having acted as a sponsor for the Cultural and Scientific Conference for World Peace, which was held in New York City in March of that year. Prof. Apenfels' name had been taken from an official list issued by the conference itself, and which was also carried by the New York Times in March of 1949. Prof. Apenfels stated positively that she did not in any way participate in or attend the meeting and enclosed a letter from a member of the California State Senate assuring her that the committee would cooperate in every possible way to correct the error. She said: "Senator —— wrote that you have already spent a great deal of your own time getting the names and reputations of other individuals cleared. It is indeed encouraging that I can write to you knowing that you will look at the facts in my case."

The committee does not issue "clearances," but is eager to cooperate in such matters, as has already been stated, and is glad to state that it has found no evidence that Prof. Apenfels had any connection with the conference, although her name was listed and used by this Communist-dominated movement without her knowledge or consent.

On April 23, 1952, the committee received a letter from Mr. Frank Lovejoy, the motion picture actor, which, being brief, is herewith quoted in full:

"I have had recent occasion to discover that the Los Angeles District of the California Federation of Womens Clubs, has assumed, since the publication of your Fourth Report, in 1948, of Communist front organizations, that I have been a member of the Progressive Citizens of America.

"Understandably, I am greatly concerned over this assumption because it is not based on fact and if it is a general assumption, it presents a picture entirely contradictory to my frequent appearances in opposition to Communism. It is also a contradiction to the kind commendations I have received from the Army, Marine Corps, Treasury Department and other governmental agencies for professional services which I was happy to render, though they were indeed modest, to help further the precepts of our government.

"In fairness to the committee, I feel this assumption should never have been drawn from your report as it referred to those whose names appeared in the advertisement in the November 3, 1947, issue of the *Hollywood Reporter* as 'members of the acting profession' and not as members of the Progressive Citizens of America. It was in the former category, as an individual and a member of the acting profession, that I signed the petition.

"I wish the record to be unmistakable clear, and I am sure that is your wish. On November 3, 1947, I was not a member of the Progressive Citizens of America. Prior to that date I had never been a member of that organization nor have I been a member of that organization subsequent to that date.

"I assure you that Mrs. Lovejoy, known professionally as Joan Banks, who also signed the petition, and whose name appears in the same section of the report, was not, is not and has never been a member of Progressive Citizens of America.

"I will assume that information herein contained will be given distribution equal in scope to that accorded your reports.

"Yours very truly,

"Frank Lovejoy"

In reply to Mr. Lovejoy's letter of April 23, Senator Burns wrote the following response on May 12, 1952:

"Dear Mr. Lovejoy: Thank you very much for your letter of April 23, calling attention to the fact that your name was mentioned in our 1948 report in connection with the Progressive Citizens of America.

"In checking this we find the report stated the advertisement referred to was 'contributed by the actors' division of the Progressive Citizens of America,' and carried the signatures of both you and your wife, Joan Banks.

"We greatly appreciate your advising us of your feelings against Communism and stating you have never been a member of the Progressive Citizens of America. We will be happy to print your letter in the next edition of our report, which will be completed in March of 1953.

"Again thanking you, and trusting this meets with your complete satisfaction, I am,

"Sincerely yours,

HUGH M. BURNS, Committee Chairman"

INDEX

288   UN-AMERICAN ACTIVITIES IN CALIFORNIA

M

N

O

www.ingramcontent.com/pod-product-compliance
Lightning Source LLC
Chambersburg PA
CBHW071407050326
40689CB00010B/1784